99 Days to Panama

An Exploration of Central America by Motorhome

DR. JOHN & HARRIET HALKYARD

Brindle Press
Houston, Texas USA
www.BrindlePress.com

First Printing 2005

Visit our Web site at www.BrindlePress.com for ordering books and for updates to the information contained in this book.

Halkyard, Dr. John and Harriet.
99 Days to Panama: An Exploration of Central America by Motorhome, How A Couple and Their Dog Discovered this New World in Their RV/Dr. John and Harriet Halkyard. —1st Edition

Includes bibliographic references and index.
ISBN 0-9749080-3-7
1. Travel Essay.
2. Travel Guide.
3. Camping.
4. Central America.

Library of Congress Control Number: 2004098624

Cover and text design © 2005 TLC Graphics, www.TLCGraphics.com
    Design by Monica Thomas
Photo calibrations and map illustrations by Kathleen Cudahy
Photos by John and Harriet Halkyard except where indicated otherwise

PREFACE

We wrote this book to demonstrate how easy it is to visit Central America. We want to encourage motorhomers to explore this fascinating part of the world. Hopefully those who take vicarious pleasure in our adventures will be encouraged to visit these friendly people someday. Whether you fly into selected destinations, or drive all the way, we know you too will return with interesting stories.

ABOUT THE AUTHORS

JOHN HALKYARD was born in Syracuse, New York, attended Purdue University and received his doctorate in Ocean Engineering from MIT. He has helped develop some of the most advanced deepwater offshore oil and gas production systems in use today. HARRIET was born in England and traveled throughout Europe before moving to Australia, where she taught at the National Institute of Dramatic Art, in New South Wales. She then settled in San Diego where she established a Destination Management Company and worked in tourism for 20 years. Harriet and John currently reside in Houston, Texas.

ACKNOWLEDGMENTS

We would like to thank our daughters, Tanya and Natalie, for letting us go; Gail Gutmann for handling our business while we were away, Joan Rotaru for proofing and encouraging; Kathleen Cudahy for making our pictures printable, as well as Carol Kulish, Bill Cone, Catherine Woodward, Bert Shelton, Kathe Kirkbride and Colleen Regan for their input. Thanks also go to Tim Barger, author of *Out in The Blue,* for his advice and encouragement to self-publish. Ed Horton helped John have the independence to take time off for adventure. Harriet would like to thank her parents for inspiring her to travel to unexplored places and for showing her that anything is possible.

Most of all, we would like to thank the residents of Central America whose hospitality made this trip what it was.

Table of Contents

OUR JOURNEY

CHAPTER 1
Into Mexico

The Owl and the Pussy-Cat went to sea
In a beautiful pea-green boat.
They took some honey, and plenty of money,
Wrapped up in a five-pound note

THE OWL AND THE PUSSY-CAT
Edward Lear

THE MAYA BELIEVE LIFE
COMES FROM MAIZE

I WAS SITTING IN THE LITTLE THAI restaurant waving my arms at the ceiling. "The trees were enormous. They reached the sky and then some. It was like being swallowed by vegetation and we were completely and utterly lost."

Kathleen's attentive eyes were wide. "Weren't you worried you might break down or something?"

"Nah! We had everything we needed: enough food and water for a week. Eventually some ingenious and helpful local would come along and either insert a twisted paperclip into the engine and thus fix it, or fetch help.

"Looking into the undergrowth it was like the corner of a plant shop," I continued, "You know, where they've crammed all the pots together to make the plants look bigger and fuller. Only these plants *were* big and full, and had lizards and spiders and all sorts of insects eating them and making their homes in them. Some leaves were so long that Eve would have only needed one. Others were so small that they would have hardly covered the head of a pin."

I pulled out some pictures and showed her one of our little motorhome overwhelmed by jungle on a gray damp dirt road, "Look."

"Wow! That's incredible! You really ought to write a book."

■■■

About a year earlier we had bought a little motorhome, with a fantasy about driving to Panama when John retired. We took a quick drive to California and back to Houston, and made a couple of weekend excursions, but we were inexperienced motorhomers.

After Christmas, I made repeated visits to the consulates to make sure we had the correct documents for a British and a U.S. citizen, for the motorhome and especially for Brindle, our mongrel dog. We had done virtually no planning as to where we would go and what route we would take. There were friends to visit in El Salvador and Guatemala, and we wanted to do at least two weeks of total Spanish immersion to work on the language. We also wanted to transit the Panama Canal. Ultimately we wanted to have a fun trip and return safely with the dog. We weren't even sure that we could take the dog all the way; we had heard that some countries wouldn't let dogs in. If that was true we would just change our route.

John quit work on Friday and we had a farewell party over the weekend. Our inexperience was illustrated on Sunday evening when John backed the motor-home into our brick flower box and knocked the handle off the waste water or "dump" system.

DAY 1
Tuesday, January 14, Heading South

Our first stop was the RV store. Fortunately, they had the replacement part for the waste water system and we were out of there in less than an hour. We emptied our waste tanks, filled the propane tank and at last we were off. We had no schedule but we wanted to be back for our daughter's graduation four months away.

Our first overnight stop was the Wal-Mart parking lot in Raymondville, Texas. I realized that we were not prepared for the cold weather here or in the mountains to the south. Since we were going to the tropics, I had not packed much in the way of warm clothes or bedding and it soon became clear that two light blankets would not be enough, so we purchased a comforter. One of my main concerns from the beginning was storage. I now wondered, 'what am I going to do with a comforter when it gets hot?'

At last we were together without outside distractions. I had a map of Central America fixed to the table and covered with plastic. We ate dinner shifting our plates from one country to another as we outlined our route over the long list of places we wanted to visit. We had anticipated this for so long and were excited that our adventure was about to begin. We didn't know what to expect but looked forward to the journey.

DAY 2
Wednesday, January 15, Into Mexico

The guidebooks recommend crossing borders at daybreak, but this was not to be our style. Throughout the trip we usually crossed borders at mid-day, while most everyone was at lunch. Luckily on this day it all went very smoothly. We got the "green light", literally, so we did not warrant an inspection from customs as we entered into Mexico. Most of the traffic entering here doesn't stop at all because Matamoros is part of a *free zone.* You don't need documentation to enter if you're only staying a couple of days in the border zone, but don't forget your papers to re-enter the U.S.

Since we were going into the heart of Mexico we did need to go through some formalities. We had to drive in a full circle around the building to reach the area where we could park and obtain the vehicle permit. All in all, it only took us ninety minutes and $57 to cross this border. (All money is in U.S. dollars, unless otherwise indicated.) Even though we had signs in the windows announcing the *Perro Peligroso* (dangerous dog), she wasn't mentioned so we didn't need to show her papers, but we made sure to have them with us.

Immediately after crossing the bridge we saw a large supermarket chain store, Soriana. We needed to buy some Scotch whiskey for a friend in Guatemala. John almost turned into the parking lot when I noticed steel arches over the entrance that would have decapitated the motorhome. There are numerous eighteen wheelers all along the roads in this area and this setup is designed to keep them out. A security guard directed us to park in a no parking zone on the street in front. I stayed in the vehicle while John went inside. It was a huge, modern market with a liquor store next to the meat counter. John got a nice deal on a Chivas Regal. We later learned that many parking lots and especially private homes in

Latin America have low barriers over their entrances to keep large vehicles out. This prevents thieves from driving a truck into the driveway and cleaning out the house.

It seemed appropriate, to us, in a funny sort of way, that one of the first things we saw in Mexico was an elephant on a flatbed truck. The circus was in town!

For the first hundred miles south of the border we drove through rich, flat farmland. There were massive fields that stretched as far as the eye could see; they looked as though they had just been sown with a spring crop. This was highly cultivated flat land.

There are two ways to travel south from Matamoros. One is through Ciudad Victoria where, according to our Mexican camping book, there is a nice trailer park. It provides a convenient first stop in Mexico and it is the route most people take. The other way is to stay closer to the coast on Route 180, which diverges from the Victoria route 120 miles south of the border. We took the coastal route planning to stay on the beach at La Pesca.

There is a gas station, Chinese restaurant, and huge truck parking area at the route 180 turnoff that would have been perfect for a dry camp, but it was relatively early so we pressed on. We climbed up through pastureland and upon arriving in the higher altitude we found ourselves in rolling hills of chaparral and sage. There were herds of goats and cattle grazing on the sides of the road tended by boys or old men. One herd must have had over 200 goats and was being moved by two *vaqueros* on horseback. The cowboys were wearing straw summer Stetson hats and their saddles had leather straps dangling like the fringe of a skirt.

The road surface was horrific. Often it looked good and we'd get up to 50-55 miles an hour and then we would encounter some grim potholes. Then there were the sunken patches, which caused the motorhome to rock and leap like a bronco. The result of such road hazards was that things broke. The most notable was the rotating plate from inside the microwave, which leaped to the floor.

This microwave was a last minute replacement before leaving home. Two days before we left, John tried to make some popcorn in the built-in microwave that came with the RV, but it didn't work. There wasn't time to get it fixed, so John marched into the house and removed the one from our kitchen and placed it in the motorhome. It did not exactly fit the space, but we could get it into the hole, and to prevent it from bouncing around we packed it in with the deflated soccer balls we were carrying as gifts. We had not fastened the microwave in properly, thinking it would stay put. Mistake! As it bounced up and down the glass plate inside hit the door, opened it, and crashed to the floor. This was a really rough road. John figures the accelerations in the back were greater than 1.5g. Things jumped out from behind a three inch "fenced" shelf to get to the floor.

Also, to deliberately slow the traffic there are the notorious *topes* (toe-pays). This is the Mexican version of a speed bump. Every RV travel book on Mexico we have seen comments on these. They are RV killers. Sometimes we had to come to a virtual stop to climb over them, while other traffic took the opportunity to dart past us. Other times there might be a string of up to a dozen *topes* at the beginning of a town. Not all of them are signposted. Sometimes, just to trick you, there are signs and **no** *topes*. Occasionally you will see vendors lined up by the *topes* to sell local produce. They know that traffic will be at a near standstill so they will be hard to ignore.

We realized that we just couldn't rush through anywhere. We slowed down, and tried to shake the high-speed life we had been living out of us, as if it were sand from our shoes.

The shadows were getting long and we had no idea where we were going to stay for the night. La Pesca was thirty miles off the main highway and now out of the picture. It was pleasant country but there was absolutely nothing there. We were on a hilltop in the wilderness of Tamaulípas. The nearest place on the map was Soto La Marina, half an hour away, but we had no guarantee that there would be anywhere there to park for the night.

There was a restaurant on a hilltop, and a woman standing outside a little store that was part of the enterprise. We bought something from the store and she said we could park at the back of the establishment for the night. We could see for miles in all directions over the tall golden grass that looked like velvet as the wind stroked past. The grass gave way to short chaparral fading into gray green before a flat horizon of brilliant blue. I turned in a circle. Apart from the restaurant all I could see in any direction was chaparral meeting sky at the curvature of the earth.

The sky was clear and the stars were extra brilliant. They dropped in a curtain to the horizon. There were no lights in any direction and the stars looked like they had been polished by the wind. It was cold. We were glad we had our new comforter.

RIGHT: First Night Camping in Mexico

Day 3
Thursday, January 16, Tamualípas to Tuxpán

As we drove south we came down in elevation and the scenery became more green and lush, dotted with great cattle ranches. I have never seen so many cattle and such sleek animals. They were mostly Brahma with enormous humps on their shoulders. There was big money in the area judging by the quality of the fencing and the corrals. As we approached the coast there was more cultivation of crops, at first in large fields and then in smaller plots close to homes.

We stopped at a roadside stall and bought about 30 terrific tangerines for a dollar. The fruit was tied together like a necklace. I ate four immediately, spitting pits out of the window as we went. We also got some oranges so we could enjoy fresh juice in the morning. My plastic juicer was one of the things that hit the floor and had broken, so squeezing them became a small challenge.

The Tropic of Cancer was signposted and we passed it with enthusiastic high fives. We were in the Tropics!

The previous night we had started out a little too late to find a place to stop and we didn't want to be in the same position. Tonight we were aiming for a trailer park in Poza Rica, but we were in Tuxpán forty miles away and it was getting late.

Rather than press on, we changed our plans and headed for the beach on the other side of Tuxpán. Following the signs to *La Playa,* and various instructions from locals, at last we glimpsed the beach between a string of shanty homes and palms. It was getting dark and we couldn't be too fussy. We pulled off the road and stopped at a stall selling beer and chips and asked for advice. The owner said we could stay right where we were parked. It was a little close to the road and not a very good location, but it would have to do.

A car stopped next to the motorhome, and a girl came over trying to speak English with us. She had been partying somewhere up the beach and was on her way home. She invited us to follow her to her home, where she said it would be safe to park. It was now dark, and we decided not to follow this stranger to some unknown location nearly an hour away. We thanked our new friend for her offer.

We had a couple of bottles of beer that we bought from our host. My, they went down easy! Six ounce bottles stack up really fast when you are thirsty. Brindle had a great time with the local dogs; they played in the sand then sat under the table as we enjoyed our drinks.

We then strolled the fifty yards to the beach. It was glorious. And there was a large parking area under the palms where there was plenty of room to pull up the bus. This was the place! Normally it would be crowded on a Saturday night in the summer, but now there was no one. We drove down the hard-packed sand road and parked with the palm fronds sweeping the dust off the roof and the waves breaking just 100 yards away. Then it started to rain and the palms beat on the roof as the wind came up. It was decidedly cold overnight.

DAY 4
Friday, January 17,
Tuxpán Beach to the Emerald Coast

At first light we let Brindle out and she ran up and down the beach and found more dogs with whom to discuss the important matters of the day. It was a cold gray morning with wind whipping the waves. It was refreshing and fun and made the beginning of the trip all the more exciting. For the second time we had been extraordinarily lucky in finding a great campsite.

Heading back through the town of Tuxpán we turned south on route 180 again towards Veracruz. Today we took it much slower. It had taken us three days of driving to understand that these were not U.S. highways and we were not in a

rush. We were on vacation. We didn't need to break anything else.

We passed through the busy commercial town of Poza Rica and, following the signs, found the ruins of El Tajín. Although the establishment was well prepared for visitors with a large parking lot and a gift shop, there was little information on the site and none in English.

Totonac people who reached their zenith between 900–1150 A.D. had once inhabited the site. The name *El Tajín* means hurricane, which might be a story in itself. The pyramids were interesting, really spectacular, and carefully restored. They certainly rival many of the archaeological sites in the Yucatan and Guatemala. Not all the lines were straight and some stairs had sweeping bends and curves and rolling sloping walls. It was unclear whether these wavy walls were the original design or the effects of time. The structures were not very high. We wished there had been some literature available on the people who had lived there.

It was a popular tourist attraction and there were several groups of locals visiting. A lady came up and gave me a friendly hug and asked if her family might take her photo with me. She was very short compared to me and we all laughed at the contrast.

Some Totonac performers, called *Voladores,* gave a demonstration of an impressive religious stunt. Four men climbed a 75-foot post, carefully wrapping a rope around it as they went up. They tied the other end around their waists. A fifth man climbed up and was playing a drum and a whistle on the very top. The musician sat and suddenly the

four men dropped off the top and spun slowly to the ground in a spiral as the ropes unwound to the music. It was quite spectacular. They wore traditional costumes of full white blouses with embroidered sashes that streamed in the breeze. The Totonac originated this

impressive religious act of faith that spread to many other peoples of Central America. I have also seen pictures of similar religious performances from Africa, which makes for interesting conjecture.

In the parking lot there were some twenty RVs of various makes and sizes. This was our first encounter with a caravan. A caravan is a group of motorhomes traveling together. This one was roaming for 45 days around Mexico on a tour package.

We met up with two professional caravans during our trip. They are a great idea for people who want to see an area first-hand, but also want the security and planning that an organized group can

LEFT: Making friends at the Tajín Ruins, Mexico
RIGHT: Voladores beginning their spiral descent

provide. Although each night is scheduled they do not usually have to travel in convoy. There are tours arranged at interesting locations, coaches set up to transfer individuals into town if the camp is too far out, and there are group meals so they can get to know each other. The wagonmaster runs it and can always call the office in the U.S. for guidance. Most important, there is a second economies. Contact information for caravans is included in the reference section of this book.

A hundred yards before the entrance to Tajín, a blindfolded donkey walking in circles caught my eye. As a child one of my favorite books was a story of a donkey that drew water from a well by walking in circles. I had to see what was going on. It was a brick factory.

staff vehicle, or caboose, which has a mechanic and a bilingual guide on board. On this caravan all the rigs were required to have CB radios. The rule is that the caboose never passes the last vehicle, so if someone breaks down he will be there to do any repair that he can or call for help. Joining a caravan costs about a hundred dollars a day, which does not include food or gas. It is like a cruise where you do the cooking and the driving. While caravan traveling is not for us, there is definitely a market for it. We were happy to see more people exploring this part of the world and adding their tourist dollars to the local

We got out for a closer look. The donkey's blindfold only covered one eye so he would not be startled by the man in the middle who was shoveling clay and pouring water from a bucket into a chimney-like structure. Perhaps the blindfold also prevented the donkey from getting giddy. The donkey walked in circles turning a screw inside the chimney. This action mixed the clay-dirt and water and extruded the mud out of the back into a pile. A woman then scooped the mud up with her bare arms and loaded it into wheelbarrows. Young men took the wheelbarrows to another area of the brickyard and then scooped three handfuls of clay into a brick mold. They leveled the mold with a practiced sweep of a board and turned the formed brick out onto the ground. The bricks took a day to dry enough to be stacked to cure in long rows. Later they would be fired. One of the workers emptying the kiln proudly rapped a brick so I could hear its clear tone, as if he were a crystal salesman making his finest glass ring. The donkeys were pulling hard, leaning out against their braces, and would occasionally stop only to be urged on again with a click of the tongue or a whistle. It was quite an enterprise with three donkeys keeping the workers supplied with mud to be made into bricks.

We had seen numerous working animals: cowboys on horseback, and horses, donkeys and oxen pulling carts. The donkeys appeared to be the most down-trodden, with loads that seemed far too great for the little beasts.

After El Tajín we made our way to the town of Papantla, eight miles south of the ruins. Papantla is the center of one of the world's largest vanilla-producing zones. We never saw a vanilla plant. We were looking for a tree or a shrub, but later research revealed it is actually a vine. It is the only orchid that produces edible fruit. We probably saw plenty, but didn't recognize the thick vines with succulent leaves climbing up the palm trees as vanilla.

We almost got lost and stuck in the very narrow streets of Papantla. Our wing mirrors stuck out precariously. We nearly broke them off more than once

against trucks passing in the opposite direction. There is a set screw which, when removed, should permit the wing mirrors to swing in. Unfortunately these were so corroded that when John tried to remove them, the screws broke off with the mirror still locked in the out position. We decided to park and search for the *mercado* (market) on foot. Our 22-foot Class C motorhome is about as big as a medium sized truck. I would not want to navigate anything larger through these towns.

There were local men in the traditional white shirt and pantaloons of the Totonac going about their business. Women wore lacy white skirts and shawls over embroidered blouses. We found a little street market and bought some pork and vegetables for supper, and then we were given directions to the main market. We ended up climbing to the cathedral overlooking the *zócalo,* or town square. It was busy and fun with balloons for sale and all sorts of people milling about.

In front of the cathedral I was surprised to see so many animals. There were dogs and birds of all sorts, from chickens to parrots, and unknown critters in shoeboxes

LEFT: Donkeys working at a brick works near El Tajín Ruins, Papantla, Mexico
RIGHT: Waiting for the Benediction of the animals in Papantla, Mexico

with breathing holes punched into the lids. Handlers ranged from housewives to children and old men. We learned there was to be a benediction of the animals at three o'clock. We would have liked to stay, but it was already three-thirty and there was no sign of any action from the church. Besides, Brindle was waiting back

that he was neither. He was a music teacher and could teach ten different instruments from harp to guitar. He sang us refrains from various European countries, *Frere Jacques* in French, plus German, English and other songs. He wanted to tell his students where we were from. From a battered old briefcase

at the bus. It made me smile to watch one girl chase her escaped chicken around the fountain. She then posed for me with her prized bird.

We needed to find a place to camp before dark and we still hadn't found the *mercado* we were looking for, where they sold the *ropa típica,* or traditional clothes.

We were making our way back down the hill when an old man came up to us. Talking excitedly in Spanish he proclaimed that he was Totonac and asked us where we were from. He sang us snippets of songs from around the world to show his knowledge of foreign cultures. We were not sure if he was drunk or crazy to begin with, but it turned out

that he clutched in front of his belly he produced two photographs. He handed one to each of us showing very different views of the Tajín ruins we had just visited. He claimed the sepia print, showing one of the pyramids interwoven with plants, still part of the jungle, was taken in 1804. He wrote 1950 on the back of the other one that showed part of Tajín that had been partially restored at that time. To our amazement he insisted that we keep the prints. We took a picture of him promising we would send him a copy.

He was more interested in receiving postcards of where we were from that he could share with his students. We got his address and mailed cards and his photo as soon as we returned home. We also enclosed some music scores for him. What a smile we won today.

We left Papantla and headed for the Emerald Coast. This place is packed with trailer parks. We noticed the same 23-vehicle caravan from El Tajín parked at the Hotel Playa Paraiso, but we kept

another dog, or at least wants to play like a dog. She approached, tail wagging, getting down on her front legs and pouncing up, trying to encourage the sheep to play. That was a mistake. Bidoingggg! The sheep reacted as sheep do and head-butted Brindle. Poor dog! She was startled and confused for a

going. A few miles farther we camped in trailer park Quinta Alicia all by ourselves. This whole area along the beach must have been a coconut farm at one time as all the campsites are under rows of coconut palms.

A short walk along the two-lane highway next to our campsite we encountered a sheep tied up along the road. This was not an unusual sight, but a new experience for Brindle. She thinks that everything with four legs is

moment but not injured. This was the first of many close encounters and unusual experiences Brindle would have with various animals. She shook her head and trotted off.

LEFT: Photograph of Tajín Ruins taken in 1804 (Courtesy Ricardo Porres)
ABOVE: Tajín Ruins in 1950 (Courtesy Ricardo Porres)
RIGHT: Ricardo Porres and John in Papantla

I had read somewhere that falling coconuts kill more people than are killed by sharks. This indicated to me that I was safer in the water than out, and that we should not park under coconut trees. Nevertheless, we slept well to the rustling of palms and waves breaking. We were under the comforter again though. Winter still had its hold on the Gulf Coast.

Day 5
Saturday, January 18,
Emerald Coast to Veracruz

We could not drive any faster so the only way to speed up was not to take breaks. This is not so easy when you keep seeing interesting things. The first

stop was at a field of small papaya trees. It is strange to see fruit growing straight out of the trunk of the tree. The trees can grow to about twenty feet, and I've seen the fruit as big as two feet long in the markets. John is not into plants, but by the end of the trip he could at least recognize the difference between papaya and mango trees. Beyond these papayas was a banana plantation.

We reached Veracruz in the afternoon and parked on the harbor. Strolling along the cold waterfront we passed stands with venders selling T-shirts and seed necklaces. It was an interesting con-

trast between the touristy stalls and the heavy industry across the harbor. On the other side of the gray waters we saw the McDermott Derrick Barge 101, which is an enormous floating crane, capable of lifting three thousand tons. The dog was not permitted on the pier so we tied her up and walked down the pier to see the interesting tributes to those who had helped construct the port facilities. These included a handsome statue of a diver, apparently one of the British who were instrumental in building the harbor.

It was a gray, chile walk but we dawdled because this was the first place where John's cell phone worked, so we took the opportunity to check in with our daughters.

Our first misadventure was in Veracruz. We were struggling through town looking for the camp-site when John decided to change lanes in order to turn left along the waterfront. This would have been fine had there not been a policeman behind us and had John not crossed a solid white line in making his maneuver. The motorcycle cop told John to follow him and led us the wrong way down a one way street! Then he invited John out of the bus and they discussed the matter. I was very well behaved and stayed where I was seated: a very difficult thing for me to do. John returned for his wallet and told me about the fine. The policeman handed him a rag and told John to put the money in it and return it. Honestly! It was pure *mordida* or pay-off. Either we pay him a hundred dollars or we go with him to the police station.

LEFT: Young papaya trees
RIGHT: Tribute to those who helped to build the Port of Veracruz. The large derrick barge beyond is used for offshore construction.

I thought we should have negotiated this down, but John is a pushover and also felt the pressure to find the campsite before dark. We have learned since then that you *can* negotiate these bribes and even play dumb, but this was our first encounter of this kind. John listed it as a toll on his expense record! Veracruz and Tampico are notoriously unfriendly to RVers. They are good towns to bypass if you are driving an RV. It really upset me to think we had been ripped off like that.

We found the campsite without any more trouble. It was a wide strip of grass between a side road and the water, sitting right on a beach in one of the better parts of town. Waiting for us was the same caravan of motorhomes we had encountered at the Tajín archeological site, and had seen camped on the Emerald Coast the night before. This time we had the opportunity to talk with the wagonmaster. This group was from Adventure Caravans.

Some of the caravaners were having a group dinner at the restaurant across the road from the campsite. Others were taking advantage of the locals who would wash the vehicles for ten dollars per coach. We hired one, and the motorhome has never looked so clean since. Power hookups were extended to each one of the caravan participants, but we would have had to pay extra to plug in. We opted to go without city power.

As long as we were making good mileage, thus charging the batteries, we only needed city power to use the microwave or air-conditioning. The refrigerator could run on either propane or electricity. In a pinch we could use our own gasoline-powered generator. We were really self contained.

Day 6
Sunday, January 19, Lake Catemaco

We were taking our trip one day at a time. We had no schedule or itinerary planned other than to eventually reach Panama and transit the Canal. John was reading the guidebooks and directed us to the next night's stop. But if we didn't get to an actual trailer park we figured we could park almost anywhere. I would

start driving and John would specify the route and eventually reveal a plan for the day. I was just enjoying the drive.

Today we were aiming for Villahermosa, and from there we could see a road on the map heading south towards Tuxtla Gutierrez. We could have taken the toll road but opted for Route 180, the slow coastal road.

Although this was Sunday morning, oxen plowing the fields greeted us. There also were all sorts of produce

The countryside was like the moors of England except that instead of bracken and heather there was short palms and cactus. Then the scrub was cleared for areas of sugar cane and we also passed apple trees in blossom.

The dog seemed to be having a fine time. Originally she was nervous as the bus rattled and rolled along. She would try to climb up on our laps as we drove or curled right between us. Now she was becoming more relaxed and sat up on

stands and shops open throughout the villages. There is a pretty stretch with Laguna Alvarado on one side and the Gulf of Mexico on the other. The town of Alvarado had all sorts of street vendors waiting to pounce on all the vehicles as they slowed for the *topes*. One young man came up to us carrying a cluster of little straw-wrapped bundles. John asked what they were, to which he replied *cangrejos*. John was driving so I grabbed the dictionary: crabs.

the couch were she could see out. She was meeting plenty of new friends. We walked through Santiago Tuxtla to see the largest stone Olmec head, which is now located in the central square. It was there all right but looked a little out of place with a roof to protect it from the elements and a little fence to protect it from people like us. The Olmecs were

ABOVE: Examining the Olmec head in Santiago Tuxtla, Mexico

the predecessors of the Maya. Their huge animal and human stone carvings were only uncovered in 1925. Most of the carvings were relocated to the *Parque Nacional de La Venta* in Villahermosa in the 1950s, but the largest head found its way here to this *zócalo:* the Santiago Tuxtla central park.

We needed bananas, garlic and a couple of other things and found the *mercado* at the side of the square. I was about to take Brindle back to the motorhome when we saw other dogs wandering freely about. We thought we would see how it went with Brindle on a short leash in the market. We immediately came across all sorts of dogs throughout the building. A man carrying a great side of beef hoisted it over one dog that didn't even look up. We did our shopping and went back to the bus to find our bikes still strapped on the front of the motorhome. I kept thinking that one day they would be gone in spite of the two cable locks.

We found a place to stay for the night by the water in Lake Catemaco: La Ceiba Restaurant and Trailer Park. This high mountain lake is a hidden charm. Boats were lined up along the shore waiting to take visitors on lake tours to see bird life, and the monkeys that occupy one of the islands. We arrived early enough to explore the town on foot. There were big old trees along the shore with chairs, and attractive rest areas where locals and tourists alike could enjoy the view out of the sun. There was an attractive church and to our delight several internet cafes on the main street. Imagine an open shop front with no glass window, but a row of computers facing out. It was a busy town full of activity, but not crowded. We would happily return for a longer visit.

The motorhome was situated with a view across the lake. We always tried to orient the motorhome with a good outlook from the dinette window. Behind us in the campsite under a great fig tree, was a man from the U.S. who had moved there with his trailer home and decided to stay. He was building a shade over his home and cement block walls around it to protect it from the elements. It wasn't going anywhere.

Shortly after we got settled three motorhomes from Germany pulled up. They moved on again after talking to the management only to return in half an hour to park next to us. I guess they decided that La Ceiba was the best camp in town. Apart from the two caravans, we encountered more motorhomes from Europe or Canada than we did from the States. Could it be that Americans (United States Americans that is) are less adventurous than the Canadians or Europeans?

Day 7
Monday, January 20 Lake Catemaco, Veracruz to La Venta, Oaxaca

It was a clear, cool morning at Lake Catemaco and we decided to take a walk on the malecón (jetty) and see to our internet work before we headed south. First we had our traditional breakfast: yogurt for me and Raisin Bran for John. We were only a week out and we were already beginning to feel that we might not have enough time to see everything.

The Isthmus of Tehuantepec is the shortest distance from Atlantic to Pacific in Mexico. The road was a very slow, winding, two-lane highway through the mountains, and had a very bad surface. The potholes were badly repaired and subsidence to the right and then to the left made the bus rock like a boat that had hit the perfect wave! We frequently found ourselves driving on the wrong side of the road to avoid particular obstacles. Fortunately, there was not much traffic. There were numerous buses of every shape, color, quality and size, but not many private cars in this part of the country. Each little two door car had five passengers squeezed in even if it didn't have taxi painted all over it.

Then there are the 18 and 20 and 22 wheel big rigs. Then there are the enormous trucks! They seem bigger than those seen in the U.S., and they crawl up and barrel down these two lane mountainous roads. The trucks don't usually hold us up much, as our little motorhome has a lot of pick up and go, so we can usually overtake them on the uphill stretches. The truck drivers indicate when it is safe to overtake by putting on their left turn signal. You do have to do a little mind reading to be sure that he isn't about to turn left, but the system seems to work.

It is only about 136 miles across the Isthmus, but it took us over four hours to cross it. At last the undergrowth had the feeling of the tropics: green and dense with very large leaves. Once over the Continental Divide we descended toward the Pacific. We turned east onto the Pan-American Highway at a little crossroads called Ventosa, which appropriately enough means, windy. There is a meteorological phenomena associated with the Isthmus which results in incredible winds here all the time. It must have been gusting to 50 mph. Even though the road surface on the highway was perfectly good, all the traffic, except for the occasional little car, was crawling along at 35 mph. We were fighting to keep our high profile motorhome on the highway.

Yachting friends we met in Panama, explained that this Isthmus is notorious with the sailing crowd as well. The wind blows across the Isthmus and out to sea a long way. David told us that he thought he was being clever by sailing far out to sea from the Gulf of Tehuantepec, but that was a mistake. The winds blowing offshore with a good fetch generate huge waves making for a very uncomfortable ride. Apparently the experienced sailors pass this area close to land, where the wind hasn't had enough distance to impart much energy to the seas. This makes it a windy but calm passage.

Well, there we were on this windswept and desolate flatland and the sun was getting weak. Once again we were in search of a place to stay. There was no protection from the wind even if we could pull off the road. We saw a sign for the town of La Venta, (The Sale). I'm always a soft touch for a sale and we laughed as it sounded like El Viento (wind). We had only gone about 12 miles from the turnoff at Ventosa, but we were ready to stop. It had been a tiring drive. We turned right off the highway onto the dirt road to town looking for a place out of the pummeling wind.

Talk about a desolate place. Rectangular block-houses with the occasional adobe wall lined the street. There were dirt patches between some of them. Others shared a wall. There was virtually nothing green as I presume nothing could take root in the incredible wind. Even the few trees there looked as if they had their leaves stripped off. In most towns and villages there are all sorts of ornamental plants outside, even at the poorest of homes. Here there was nothing. There wasn't even any litter as the wind had taken that to other places. It reminded us of the ghost towns you find in the western U.S. Their only reason for existing in the first place was some incredible mineral find, which was eventually depleted, so all the people left. There was no one about here now either.

We passed the main part of town seeing nothing of interest except a small store and a windswept town square with a few shops on the side. There were still no residents visible. We kept driving; thinking there must be something at the far end of town. All we needed was someplace off the road and out of the wind to park for the night. South of town was as desolate as the drive in, with a road leading into windswept nothing. We turned around and headed back for the center of town. Our first stop was behind a rather large warehouse looking building next to the town square. There was a basketball court but no one could ever play basketball in this wind. We felt isolated and vulnerable. We decided to head for the little store we had seen on the way in where we hoped there would at least be a sign of life.

We pulled up in the lee of the little *refresquería,* to one side of the door, slightly protected from the wind. There was a three-brick high bulwark to step over to enter the shop, and it was dark. The windows had been covered to keep out the searing sun. Once our eyes had accustomed to the gloom, we saw an old man seated in a chair with his back to the door and a red bandanna around his head. A young lady in a flowered dress welcomed us from behind the counter that was piled high with displays of snacks and goodies. We asked if we could park for the night out in front. There was lots of nodding of heads, *"No problema, seguro"* (no problem, it's safe). We always liked to hear seguro when we asked permission to park. We bought a load of junk food and as she had no beer, she offered us a bottle of alcoholic fruit drink. *Refresquerías* usually just sell refreshments like sodas and chips, unlike the *pulperías* that are more like mini grocery stores. We returned to the bus a few steps outside her front door.

Before consuming the drinks we took a little walk with the dog across the street and around the square. There was indeed some life in this town, but it was huddled down inside some very small and secluded shops next to one corner of the square. All the time we had to work to keep the wind from blowing us away and to struggle to keep the sand out of our mouths and eyes. Even Brindle couldn't wait to get inside out of the wind.

When I went to return the bottles, the lady in the shop introduced me to her mother, Dolores, the proprietor. Dolores insisted that we move our motorhome into her backyard, which had more protection from the wind. We accepted and drove around the back, forgetting the height of our vehicle. A high wall with a gate that was about three inches wider than our motorhome enclosed her backyard. As John maneuvered slowly through the gate, a set of overhead cables scraped over the air-conditioning. I yelled and John stopped before we ripped one out from the wall. I climbed on the roof and held the cable up as we passed under. We drove in far enough so the gate could just close behind us.

It seemed that in this small walled yard we should have been afforded some protection from the wind, but we were still rocked and buffeted. John assured me that the wind would die down after sunset. Then we thought it would let up at sunrise. Not! We were sandwiched very close between two houses, and grateful for the protection we did have. It did not matter. The wind did not disturb our sleep. It was fun sleeping with the wind howling and the bus rocking all night.

The sky was clear and the stars were brilliant.

Day 8
Tuesday, Jan. 21, La Venta
Oaxaca to Ocozocoaulta, Chiapas

In the morning I went back to the shop to thank Dolores for her hospitality. I gave her the surviving sprig of pink carnations that had been gracing our table since Houston, and invited her to see our *casa móbil*. She was very interested but she said her legs were not good and she asked about steps. Nevertheless, she hobbled around the back, pulled herself up into the motorhome and plopped down on the couch, embracing the motorhome and all that was in it with warm smiles. She was enthralled. She wanted to know all about the vehicle, how much it cost, could she get one in Mexico. Then there were the standard questions of how many children we had

and what they were doing. I pointed to the pictures of our two girls that we had pinned up.

Dolores was about our age and spoke very clear Spanish, although because of our poor language skills we lost much of what she said. We needed our Spanish lessons. We did learn that she had a son who was at university studying international relations. La Venta was an ancient Oaxacan village of the *la raza Zapoteca*, or the Zapotecan race. The Zapotecans were a Mexican tribe that coexisted with the Aztecs, but were independent of them. Dolores was Zapotecan and obviously proud of it. She said that there was plenty of work in the community, but the politics had prevented the area from growing. It seems that the government had selected this area for a power plant, but our hostess felt the government came up short on providing social services for their community. She also wanted to know our opinion of America vs. Iraq and the war. We promised to send her a copy of the picture of herself and her daughter in front of her shop as soon as we returned to the U.S.

Driving back down the hard packed, windswept, dirt road we thought what an interesting place we had discovered and had a whole new insight on the little town of La Venta. Our hope is that other tourists will pause and visit the Refresquería Lolita in La Venta and say *hola* to Dolores and her family.

Back on the Pan-American Highway we headed east towards Chiapas. We stopped for lunch near a wide shallow river where we gave the dog a run and I cooled my feet. Brindle immediately lay down in the water. Then along came a couple of *vaqueros* bringing a herd of cattle for a drink. The horsemen were full of smiles, one wearing a cowboy hat and the other a wonderful drooping mustache, a baseball hat on his head and flip-flops on his feet. The horses wore bridles, which were made of rope tied around the nose and held up behind the ears.

We had read about the *Hogar Infantil* orphanage and it sounded worth a visit. The home, or *hogar*, is an orphanage that houses seventy-five girls and boys varying in age from six to twenty one years. They all go to the local school in Ocozocoautla and do chores about the place. It is a very pleasant establishment and the children were polite. It is definitely a good spot to camp with power and water (both rather weak) at a half dozen places. We had a cool spot under a tree close to the buildings. There are acres of grass with trees and play equipment for the children as well as a soccer field. This was where we parted with the first of our soccer balls and we felt it would be put to good use.

LEFT: Dolores (right) and her daughter in La Venta, Oaxaca
RIGHT: Hogar Infantil in Ocozocoaulta

I must have made a balloon animal for each of the boys and ended up breaking my pump, which really slowed me down

for the rest of the trip. I had to blow up the balloons with the pump since the long thin ones are far too difficult to blow up by mouth. I'd then hand one to each kid and then John or I would twist them into animals. If the audience isn't too large we sometimes taught the youngsters how to make balloon dogs for themselves. It is fun for us as well as the children and we found it a great ice-breaker with both the young and old. We didn't see much of the girls in the orphanage and wondered if they had been told to keep away from strangers.

Day 9
Wednesday, January 22, Hogar Infantil to San Cristóbal de las Casas, Chiapas

The children, now smartly dressed, climbed onto a little school bus first thing in the morning.

Brindle also learned a lesson this morning. This was another sheep encounter.

The flock here must have been used to being harassed by the children because when the dog approached them and barked they just looked at her. She pranced about trying to encourage them to play. They chased her. She came running back to the bus with a flock of sheep in hot pursuit! Some sheep dog!

We heard Tuxtla Gutierrez was an "ugly, hot" town, but it did have its charms. Among other things it had an

we left the States we had tried to buy some used bikes, but the cheapest we could find were at the after-Christmas sale at Wal-Mart. We sort of expected to lose these bikes.

Tuxtla marked the end of the flat country. East of town we immediately started climbing into the hills for which Chiapas is famous. To begin with we had a brand new divided highway that too quickly changed into a narrow, winding

interesting taxi system using bicycles towing little carriages. The taxis were lined up at the bus stops on the highway waiting for clients returning from town with their shopping.

The friendly people in Tuxtla waved to us and we waved back. Many boys and young men asked if the bicycles tied to the front of our motorhome were for sale. They were shiny and pretty and we could have sold them many times over at a profit, but they were not good and the gears were lousy. Before

mountain road. There are two vast artificial lakes in this area that are worth visiting, to say nothing of the 3,300 foot deep Sumidero Canyon, which is a National park. It was here that Indians facing the Spanish conquest jumped to their deaths rather than live under Spanish rule. This illustrates the independent nature of these highland people who even the current Mexican government continues to find a challenge.

ABOVE: Taxi in Tuxtla Gutierrez

CHAPTER 2

Meeting the Maya

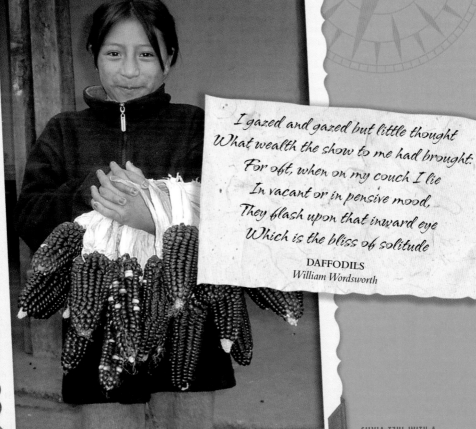

I gazed and gazed but little thought
What wealth the show to me had brought:
For oft, when on my couch I lie
In vacant or in pensive mood,
They flash upon that inward eye
Which is the bliss of solitude

DAFFODILS
William Wordsworth

SILVIA TZUL WITH A
GIFT OF MAIZE FOR US

UNDER BRILLIANT SUNSHINE we climbed the pine-covered mountains. The small Indian villages we stopped at along the way were not much more than clusters of homes, but this was where we did the first of our Mayan shopping.

There was a stall selling brightly colored woven fabric at the side of the road. John pulled over and there was just enough room for vehicles to pass. There were hand-woven place mats of various colors with big bold embroidered pictures of local things

21

like sunflowers, birds and lilies. The colors were predominately strong blues, greens and golds. Although they were individual, they all had a similarity and I was able to select a dozen made by different hands in various colors that mixed and matched to create a set.

The Mayans are shy in this area, but this lady said she would show me how she did her weaving and walked us up the steep hill to her home. As we walked we passed a piece of intricately woven fabric on the ground. I thought she had dropped it so I picked it up for her. She laughed and returned it to the ground, as an artist might have cast a work of art into the trash can.

All the ladies were wearing hand-woven fabric with a glint of silver thread throughout. I purchased a very special piece that looked oriental in its design and detail. It is a shawl with silver thread in the weave and elaborate embroidery over the shoulders and two ties with long tassels. It is a work of art that could hang on a wall or be worn with an evening dress. Here it is everyday attire.

As we drove through other villages there was a greater mixture of woven items; some in strong colors and others in the natural grays and browns of the undyed wool. Fresh tangerines and other citrus grown in the area were offered at roadside stands in neat piles, their colors complementing those of the weavings.

We arrived at the Hotel Bonampak in San Cristóbal early in the afternoon and parked in their walled grass campsite. What a treat, they had all the hook-ups! There were four other motorhomes that were traveling together, so we could compare notes. We found that trading stories with fellow travelers was one of the best ways to find out where to go. These folks had traveled from the Yucatan by way of Palenque. Route 199 from Palenque to San Cristóbal is a tough mountain road covering about 100 miles. It takes about eight hours. One rig burned out a transmission on this route, but fortunately there was a good Ford dealer in San Cristóbal who was able to service his vehicle. The little caravan was heading west to return to the States via the Pacific route, so we regaled them with our stories of *Hogar Infantil* and the windy town of La Venta.

Once we were settled at the trailer park, we unloaded our bikes for the first time and headed for town. San Cristóbal was vibrant and full of people, including

LEFT: Weaving a shawl, Chiapa de Corzo, Mexico
ABOVE: Fruit for sale in Chiapas

a fair number of *gringos* and Mayan. Gringo is a term locals use to describe people of European descent. There were shops of all variety. We found the local artisans' market for more souvenirs, and the local food market where we stocked up with fresh produce.

When we returned from our bike ride we took advantage of the restaurant at the hotel and enjoyed our first decent restaurant meal since we left home. We both enjoyed nice tender pieces of steak. This would be the last tender beef we would find for the entire trip.

Day 10
Thursday, January 23, Tour from San Cristóbal de las Casas to two incredible villages.

We woke up to a deep frost and confirmation, thankfully, that our heater really worked. When we opened the door there were three charming ladies waiting,

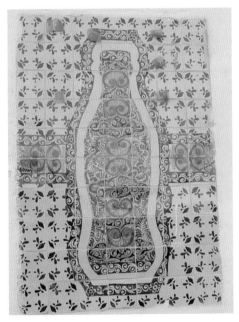

ready to sell us macramé belts and woven shawls. They were full of smiles, knotting their macramé belts as they patiently waited for the occupants of the other RVs to open up.

We had decided to stay in San Cristóbal for another night. It had been pleasant wandering around the town the

previous evening, and we wanted to see more of the villages in the surrounding mountains. We made reservations through the hotel for a tour as we didn't know the condition of the roads, or how to get to the interesting places. Our maps did not even show the roads.

Our guide arrived twenty minutes late in a mini van that was packed to the gills with Americans, a Canadian and a lady from Venezuela. Unfortunately, the guide was not as informative as he should have been, but the places we visited were fascinating.

The first village we visited was San Juan Chamula, named for St. John the Baptist. This is a Tzotzil Mayan village. Like other highland Mayan villages, the Indians settled here to escape the Spanish conquest. They speak their own Mayan dialect. Many don't speak any Spanish.

We drove the narrow winding road through fir and pine trees to our first stop on a hill, which overlooked the ruined church of San Sebastian. It was a

ABOVE: Tiles on a wall in San Cristóbal
RIGHT: These charming woman were selling their handmade wares at the Bonampak Trailer Park

shell of a church with an expansive active graveyard. The grass was cropped short around the mounds and at the head of each grave there was usually more than one cross. It is customary to bury a husband and wife together along with other family members. Many of the crosses were of plain wood, while others were painted light blue. Many graves had branches of fir in place of or alongside crosses.

This church is only used on *Dia de los Muertos* (Day of the Dead, November 1st) when the graveyard is the center of a large celebration. During those celebrations graves are cleaned and dressed with new flowers and the townspeople spend the day at the graveyard visiting their deceased relatives.

When the Catholics originally came to the area to teach the Mayans about the one God, they built their churches on the sites that the Mayans had used for worship over the centuries. All over the region there are Christian churches with all the Saints and religious trim, where the local Mayans burn incense on the steps outside as they did on the temple steps in pre-Columbian times. They have taken what they wanted of the Christian religions and made it their own.

San Juan Chamula is a special example. The Spanish missionaries built the church in the 16th century. However, the congregation later cut their ties with Rome in order to worship in their own way. Then the evangelical missionaries moved in and thought they could fill a void and make the Mayans see God through their eyes. They did not leave so easily and lives were lost in the conflict. We ascertained that evangelical missionaries were still *persona non grata* in San Juan Chamula. The locals still use this charming church built by the Catholics and filled with holy figures. But that is only half the story.

The church is painted white with blue trim, the same blue as was used to paint the crosses in the cemetery, and embellished with colorful painted flowers. Over this were masses of real flowers and sprays of pine and fir.

A small fee had to be paid to the town elders in order for visitors to enter the church, and photographs were not permitted inside. The locals are shy and believe that a picture steals the spirit of a person. This concept is thought to have come about when their forefathers first saw a negative film that showed the black and white reversal of an image, and thought that it pictured the soul. To take a picture in church would be an attempt to steal the spirit of God.

I stepped inside the church and was speechless.

The first impact was light. Thousands of candles of all sizes flickered in the gloom from every ledge and covered large areas of the floor. The worshipers placed a row of candles to represent each of their family members and the prayers they had for them. They have

LEFT: The ruins of San Sebastian church, with its well tended graveyard in San Juan, Chiapas
RIGHT: San Juan Chamula, Chiapas

large families so there were many rows of candles. Different colored candles have different meanings, so a colored candle or one with a band of color might be placed at each end of the row. Families sat in groups on the floor next to the blocks of flickering candles. There were dozens of statues of Christian saints around the perimeter of the church, mostly in glass showcases, but they could hardly be seen for the brilliantly colored ribbons cascading around them and the profusion of fresh and plastic white flowers stacked before them. In front of each saint was at least one table covered in candles, dozens of them. Some of the candles were as small as the ones you see on birthday cakes, others were almost as thin but twelve inches tall.

The paved floor was covered in a deep layer of pine needles that, together with the smell of the burning wax, created a heady aroma. On the floor in front of the saints and throughout the church there were more candles. Families were kneeling and children were crawling about in the pine needles. One mother was nursing her baby and another had her child sleeping on her lap. They were chatting comfortably together.

Shafts of sunlight angled down, cutting through the drifting smoke and illuminating patches of floor or family groupings. Three women sitting in a pool of light were knotting macramé artifacts. Almost everyone was in traditional handmade woven clothes of various colors. There were toddlers playing and old men were chatting. Four large faded swags of diaphanous fabric, swooping from the ceiling, gave the church a more intimate and friendly feeling. It was awe inspiring, but casual at the same time.

Two ladies came in to pay reverence to a statue. One cleared a space in the pine needles on the floor with her hands as the other opened the paper wrapping around bundles of thin white candles about four inches long. She melted the bottom of the first with the flame of another candle, and with a practiced stab plunked it on the tile where it stayed upright. In no time she had fourteen in a row and began on a second row. Then she made two rows of six before both women together began to light them all.

Other things considered precious to the Mayans were being offered to their gods. There was a neat row of three brown eggs. There was a dead chicken.

In addition the worshipers were offering *posh,* the local corn liquor. The drink was poured into small glasses and moved in three circles above the candles before being shared with the family group, adults and children alike. Coca-Cola is also considered a precious item that has become part of the offerings.

Adding to all this was live music. A minstrel group, including an accordion, drums, and an acoustic guitar, played ponderous music with a heavy beat. The musicians wore unusual flat hats and the heavy, black woven poncho jackets that are traditional in the area. This group hung around the church altar, where *posh* was being distributed to the worshipers. The musicians walked around inside, then out into the sunlight and toured the village playing all the while.

The Mayans believe that the church is the funnel to God's energy, and they try to capture a little of it to take home to their home altars. This really felt like a funnel of spiritual energy.

I could have stayed for hours absorbing the warm mystical feelings and the welcoming friendliness of the congregation. I was pulled out as the tour bus was going to leave for the another of the mountain Mayan villages: Zinacantán.

Education is compulsory in Mexico, but in many parts of Chiapas this is not enforced. However, in Zinacantán the children go to school, many progress to college, and are encouraged to return as professionals. This is reflected by the affluence of the area.

As part of the tour we were invited into a typical home in the village. The front room and the garden were filled with woven materials and some ceramics for sale. This was obviously designed for tourists, but it was also a glimpse into the lives of the indigenous people.

The young girls invited us into the smoke-filled main room of the house. With a practiced flip-flop back and forth between her hands, the eldest made a lump of mush, or corn paste, into a flat tortilla. She tossed this onto a griddle made hot by an open fire beneath. A few minutes later she turned it over with her

LEFT: Children cooking tortillas in Zinacantán, Chiapas
ABOVE: A back strap loom

fingertips, careful not to burn herself. When the tortillas were cooked she put them in a gourd that served as a bowl and offered them to us. We were invited to put salsa on them and try the traditional fare together with a sampling of the potent posh.

The women were weaving on back strap looms. These traditional looms consist of two wooden rods between

around the village and admired the church and checked out the small gathering of vendors selling vegetables. Women of all ages, and some with babies on their backs, strolled in groups down the wide dirt streets. They each wore their black hair braided with a purple silk ribbon, which was tied into a big bow at the back of the head, plaited into the hair and tied together in another big floppy

which the threads are secured. One end is secured to a post and the weaver steps into a belt that passes behind her. The women kneel on the ground leaning back to keep the threads taut. They lean forward, relax the vertical threads and pass the shuttle back and forth.

The girls wore the same traditional length of heavy fabric wound around their waist and brought forward, bundled in front, and held up with a woven belt. It didn't look very comfortable to me, but the women have been wearing skirts like this for hundreds of years. We walked

ABOVE: A young sales lady, Zinacantán, Chiapas

bow at the bottom. They obviously didn't want their photographs taken, but were friendly as soon as we put the camera away. They wore fabric woven in the same pattern, traditional to this village, with green, purple and blue wool. It was a fine weave and attractive enough to be made into an evening dress back home.

Day 11
Friday, January 24, San Cristóbal to Huehuetenango, Guatemala

The three gracious ladies were there again very early in the cold morning; sitting in the weak sunshine against the wall at the back of the camp.

While I prepared breakfast and readied the motorhome for our departure, John and I discussed our next plan of action. We had intended all along to do a total immersion Spanish course. Antigua, Guatemala is noted for its culture and Spanish schools, and our friends there recommended one that offered one-on-one instruction. (See section on Languages and Language Schools in the reference section for more information.)

The problem was that we needed to find a home-stay family that would accept Brindle, but the school in Antigua couldn't come up with one. Our friends there found a bed and breakfast that would accept the dog so we could have the total immersion experience. However, their rates were $240 per person per week. Additionally, we would have to pay $125 for the Spanish lessons, so it would cost us $365 per week per person in addition to the purchase of lunches and dinners. Although that may seem like a decent price for room, board and intense language training, it was more than we wanted to spend.

Today was Friday, and we hoped to begin class on Monday. John had read that there were total immersion schools in Quetzaltenango, Guatemala. Before we left San Cristóbal and entered the country we thought we better check this out. It would be useful to know which city to drive towards!

John used the satellite phone to call every Spanish school in Quetzaltenango listed in the *Lonely Planet* guidebook. The first several schools didn't answer, or the phones were not in service. Finally, we got Nora and Rolando at the Guatemalensis Spanish School, and they were most helpful. By the time we had finished breakfast they confirmed that there was a family that would take the dog, and they knew a secure place we could park our motorhome. The cost was $120 for each of us per week plus the vehicle storage. This would save us almost $500 a week by staying in Quetzaltenango over Antigua. It was a no-brainer. We arranged to meet Rolando the following afternoon, Saturday, to get oriented and check in with the family. We would start school on the Monday.

We needed to make a quick shopping trip since we were getting to the end of our U.S. perishables. After all of this we left San Cristóbal at 9:30 a.m. We took the high road to Guatemala through La Mesilla. The map lists this as Route CA1, so we assumed this was the Pan-American Highway, however most travel guides show the main route into Guatemala through Tapachula near the coast on Route CA2. We are still not sure which is the "real" Pan-American Highway.

The route from San Cristóbal to La Mesilla is a winding two-lane road with a smooth surface with just the occasional truck and the numerous *topes* to slow us down. Passing was not much of a problem and the trucks either traveled faster than we did or we found a stretch where we could pass.

The homes in this part of Chiapas are made of plank wood, adobe, or cement blocks with roofs of tile or corrugated iron. The towns seem bustling and busy. We particularly liked Teopisca with its narrow street flanked with brightly painted houses and shops. The combination of colors was glorious and creative. The main square, or *zócalo,* was filled with carefully trimmed trees and the park benches had colorfully painted ceramic tile. The tiles lined the benches and the walls around the flowerbeds creating designs that were prettier than the scant blossoms struggling in the dry dirt.

The mountain scenery was spectacular. A mountain range appeared like an impenetrable wall growing out of the flat farmland. Some peaks reach as high as 12,000 ft.

At 1:15 p.m. we approached Mexican customs and turned in our Mexican tourist permits. We kept the car sticker as around, but the one I wanted was in a deserted shop. We asked the merchant in the next shop and he said the owner would return after lunch. We sat down at a nearby food kiosk and ate tacos. Finally, the shopkeeper returned and I bought a beauty of a hat for $9 that would be 2-3 times the price in the U.S. Most other things we had seen for sale from bread to melons seemed to be about the same price as back home.

it was good for three months and we would need it for our return. Brindle was not mentioned.

The Guatemalan border was a ways beyond Mexican immigration and between was a kind of "no man's land," with a rather chaotic duty free zone. Dozens of small shops lined the road and spilled into it, selling leather goods, typical clothing *(Ropa Típica)* along with some local food kiosks. I needed a Mexican cowboy hat. We browsed

ABOVE: Aproaching the highlands of Guatemala from Chiapas

We returned to the road and came to the Guatemala border authorities. It was a two-lane road covered with pedestrians, families with bundles of possessions, trucks, cars and bicycles, and more pedestrians walking in-between everything. We were directed over to the left-hand side of the road and told to park. Here they sprayed the wheels of the motorhome and those of the bikes with some kind of disinfectant or insecticide. A friendly border agent invited us inside a little office and asked for the dog's papers. We showed him the health certificate completed by our vet and certified by the USDA official in Houston. I had subsequently taken it to the Guatemalan consulate and received the *permiso* stamp for a ten-dollar fee. The border-crossing agent studied it with care. He read each page and examined the assortment of stamps from the other Central American consulates. He then stamped each of the six original pages including the "carbons" and asked us for a copy. I produced a color computer scanned copy. He repeated that he wanted a copy and not an original. I assured him that it was a copy so he stamped that too and put it in the drawer of his desk. No problem, just 49 quetzals (about $6.13) for the spray and dog charges.

We then moved the motorhome from its parallel parking spot on the left, to a right angle spot across the road down about twenty feet. This was for our passport check. Again no problem, it just cost 20 quetzals ($2.50) per person.

There were about a dozen helpful men and boys all telling us what to do every step of the way, with slight variations.

Now we had to drive another twenty feet, through the chaotic traffic, and parallel park across the road on the left, again, for the vehicle papers. We had a slightly longer wait here with more paperwork to fill out. We had to pay our vehicle fee of 46 quetzals ($6) at the bank, ten paces away. It was interesting that the immigration fees were paid directly to the immigration personnel, agriculture were paid directly to them, while the vehicle fees (customs or *aduana*) required a trip to the bank to make a deposit into their account. This pattern was repeated at every border in Central America. We always got receipts.

After paying our vehicle fee, John escorted the customs official to the bus with the sticker for the windshield. He applied the sticker while John held the dog back. Brindle had become a very

good deterrent. I was stopped right outside the customs house door by a uniformed customs agent who requested all the documents. Sitting in a chair in the shade he copied the information from the documents and entered it in a large ledger on his lap. So much for the computer age.

We climbed back in the bus and drove to the barrier across the road, which was lifted just high enough so we could pass underneath. We had crossed in one hour and fifteen minutes at a cost of 175 quetzals, less than twenty dollars. We thought that if all the crossings were like this one, it would be a breeze. What was all the fuss we had read about? We saw none of the bribery or *mordida* that we had read about. That would come later.

Once through the border we had to contend with more chaos on the road ahead. It was packed with traffic of all forms taking up both lanes in front of us, going every which way. Shop wares overflowed onto the road, and vendors were everywhere trying to sell things to those stuck in the traffic or walking to catch a bus. It was 3:15 p.m. and we were beginning to think that we might be stuck there for the night.

When at last we got out of town, the Pan-American Highway suddenly deteriorated as we climbed into the mountains. We were back to thirty miles per hour. There were some good patches where we were up to Mach speed (55 mph) and then we would hit a patch that had been washed out or hit by a landslide. Coffee was growing all along the hills and in front of many of the homes.

It was spread out to dry or piled in heaps by the road in front of houses.

The road narrowed as it wound between steep mountain passes. The scenery was magnificent. It was the kind of road you see in car ads on TV with sleek new models flying round the verdant hills. Great cliffs jutted up covered with rich undergrowth and pines, when they could catch their roots in the soil. The rocks were also used to express political opinions and some very diligent, enthusiastic supporters had painted their party's logo on many protruding boulders. We would turn a corner and see one or even ten rocks facing us, painted white with a red emblem. In another area a different supporter would paint his blue emblem all over the place, sometimes over the symbol of the opponent. It is interesting how politically savvy the Guatemalans are.

After an hour we found a little stream by the road to take a break. Our routine was to change drivers every hour, and to give Brindle a chance for some exercise. It was approaching 5:00 p.m. and we didn't want to drive after dark, so we took the turnoff for Huehuetenango, the first major city south of the border. Chaos! Rush hour! The roads were too narrow for our RV and when we met another truck it would take several minutes of maneuvering to get around, usually with a couple of police helping. We knew of no place to stay. Fortunately, we suddenly saw the police station, and found just enough room to parallel park in a no parking zone directly in front of it. We had planned on going into the police station to ask if they knew a place where we could spend the night. Instead, the police poured out and pressed their faces to the windows showing far more curiosity than most people. As we were trying to communicate with the policemen, two college age youths came by. They looked American (we use the term "American" to refer to anyone from the U.S. or Canada, although technically it applies to Central Americans as well). One of them began translating our questions. We quickly got directions to the Hotel Cuchumatanes, a few miles out of town. The police assured us that this was the place to go. Once we were settled on the directions, I asked our interpreter where he was from. It turned out he was a college student from the States and a frequent visitor of Huehuetenango, where he was studying Spanish with the family of his companion. His companion didn't speak any English.

We arrived at the hotel about two-and-a-half hours after crossing the border. We had the soccer field behind the hotel to ourselves and we parked there next to the small conference center. We were allowed to plug our extension cord into one of the outlets inside a meeting room, and we took advantage of an irrigation water outlet. This was almost like staying in a real RV park. If you are not traveling with your own bed, then this would also be a classy place to visit, with good rooms and pleasant facilities. We opted to eat in the motorhome although the hotel had a tempting restaurant.

Day 12
Saturday, January 25, Huehuetenango to Quetzaltenango (Xela), Guatemala

Armed with directions from the hotel manager, we set out to find an easy way back to the highway. John got out his hand-held GPS and recorded each intersection. In no time we were completely lost. Well, John wasn't lost, he knew our exact position on earth, but he didn't know the way out of town!

The road "to the left, up the hill, to the cemetery", didn't appear to exist. We stopped to ask two workmen for directions. They didn't seem to understand the hotel's directions, but one of them offered to get in and show us the way. Great!

Our guide sat in the front seat while John drove. I sat in the back, at the dinette table, taking frantic notes still trying to log our route as we bumped along on the cobblestones. We seemed to be in a maze. Left turn, right turn, two blocks, two more turns right. We did make it back to the main road out of town without passing through the narrow streets we had to negotiate the night before, but it was hopeless to try to reconstruct any kind of directions. We failed in our first attempt to provide meaningful directions for friends who might follow. At least we have the GPS coordinates.

Our advice for finding this hotel, or in fact most places in the larger cities of Central America: get to the outskirts of town and find a taxi or volunteer guide. Someone will be happy to show you the way for the price of a bus ticket back plus a little change. We paid $1-2 for this service. If you are worried about letting a stranger into your vehicle, just pay the fare for a taxi to lead the way.

In spite of our difficulties, we were on our way back to the Pan-American

Highway by 10:00 a.m. We only had seventy-four miles to cover to make our rendezvous in Quetzaltenango, so we had plenty of time to visit the ruins of Zaculeu on the northern outskirts of Huehuetenango.

Once again, getting there was a challenge and it took us asking numerous locals for directions. Mostly they said *directo*, straight-ahead. This either meant that the place we wanted was on the road ahead, or the guide wanted to be helpful but didn't know the way.

We deduced that getting directions was the problem of the Conquistadors. Every time they asked where the gold was, they were told "straight ahead," even though there wasn't any treasure! Everywhere people were friendly and wanted to help.

The maps showed a route to the ruins from the center of Huehuetenango, but at the hotel we were told to return to the highway and head north to another turnoff, past the military base. They explained that this was a better route for a large vehicle. We took this turnoff and after skirting the town on a dirt road that kept dividing, necessitating continuous requests for directions, we eventually found a blacktop road and then the ruins.

The walls of the temples at Zaculeu had been restored and plastered over, which gave them an ugly appearance. This was as they would have originally looked but with paint over the plaster. There were several local school groups learning about their own history even though it was a Saturday.

These charming young ladies said I could take their picture.

RIGHT: Local young ladies enjoying the ruins at Zaculeu, Huehuetenango, Guatemala

We left the ruins at about noon and backtracked through an alternate route to the highway. The turnoff to Quetzaltenango is about sixty miles south of Huehuetenango at a place called *Cuatro Caminos,* (Four Roads.) This is a chaotic confluence of roads, vendors, buses, trucks and pedestrians going to all parts of Guatemala. Quetzaltenango is seven and a half miles west of the Pan-American Highway.

Quetzaltenango actually has two names. Xela, pronounced "shay-la" is the Quiché Mayan name for the city, and the name most commonly used in and around the city. All the bus signs read "Xela."

We were supposed to meet Rolando at the language school, but we met that challenge with another mixed adventure of wrong turns and one way streets. After driving in circles for about a half-hour, we gave up and sought refuge in a parking lot of a university situated across from a large park.

We had passed it twice before and it was about the only place we could pull up and stop. I drove straight in waving at the guard as though I knew what I was doing, and parked. This was a gated parking lot and the guard ran up frantically waving at us to turn around and get out. It was his job not to let strangers park there; and here was this strange vehicle in the middle of his lot. John got out the satellite phone while I engaged the guard

We found out that she was a student at the university studying international relations. She deserved an 'A' from us.

Rolando showed up a few minutes later and we followed him to the school, which was less than a mile away. So close and yet so far! We could park temporarily right outside the school on the cobbled street. There were rows of adjoining blockhouses that fronted directly onto a narrow sidewalk.

in conversation, trying to explain our predicament. When John got Rolando on the phone, he turned to the guard and asked if he would tell Rolando where we were. The guard didn't want to help us; he just wanted us out of there. I think the guard believed he would get fired if his boss found us there. Fortunately, a nice lady noticing our predicament came by to help. She couldn't speak English, but wanting to assist struggled with our pidgin Spanish and understood the situation. She got on the phone and told Rolando where we were and relayed that he was on his way to meet us. Then she talked to the guard and settled him down a little.

Rolando and Nora showed us around and then led us to the auto repair and machine shop where we could stow the motorhome. Doña Mariana, a delightful and friendly lady, ran the place with her son Hector. When they were closed for business, a high steel door secured the motorhome, but they would let us in any time, and always had a friendly smile. We had a few minor repairs to do on the motorhome, which were easily handled by Hector. The constant bumping up and down had caused the microwave to pound a hole in the wood of the cabinet

ABOVE: The road to our school in Xela

liked this as she could sleep with her nose almost touching whomever slept there. We took turns in each bed as the lower one had a scoop in the middle larger than the scoop in the other bed. We needed to fetch our own linens to augment what was there and no towels were made available.

Day 13
Sunday, January 26, First Day in Xela

There were ten people living in the house when we arrived: one other student and ourselves, and the family. The family consisted of Mario and Patti, their four children and Mario's mother Julia, who was there on an extended stay from her apartment in Guatemala City.

The oldest son Marito, or little Mario, was a lanky red headed fourteen-year-old boy who was into sports. He had a huge Los Angeles Galaxy soccer poster on his wall. I asked him why he liked them and he said that Carlos Ruiz was

below. Hector cut out a piece of sheet metal in five minutes, which we placed under the microwave. He charged us all of fifty cents. We also had a badly bent step to the door of the motorhome, caused by a close encounter with one of the many high curbs. He fixed this for about the same price. We wanted to take him home with us. The parking area is on 7th street, next to a small park, Parque Calvario, just a block from the Spanish school.

We packed a couple of bags and walked to our host family's house with Nora, Brindle trotting at our side. Nora introduced us to the de Palma family and we settled in. The school, the motorhome and the home of our new family were all within a ten-minute walk of each other. We were ready for our "total immersion."

Our room had two twin beds, one that was six inches off the floor. The dog

ABOVE: The Garage: Dona Mariana and the motorhome in Xela, Guatemala
RIGHT: The de Palma family in their kitchen
(Left: Marito, Mario carrying David, Ricki and his little sister Melanny in front of Patti, and grandma Julia on the right.)

his favorite player; Ruiz is from Guatemala. The middle boy was Ricky. Really it was Ricardo, so we called him "Ricky Ricardo." He laughed at this. Ricky was a smart, quiet eleven-year-old. He was good with Brindle and made a real effort to learn how to train Dino, his grandmother's spaniel. Melanny, a cute eight-year-old, was always smiling. She loved Brindle. David was a typical four-year-old, curious about everything. He would stand outside our bedroom for hours waiting for Brindle to make an appearance. Brindle would stay inside to avoid him. Sometimes David would knock on the door to make Brindle bark. OK, so he was a bit of a brat, but

and Mario were well educated, intelligent people. Patti could understand some English, but she never spoke it in our presence as we were only meant to be speaking Spanish in their house. Mario had his degree and taught in the public school. He also held a second job in a private school to bolster the meager salary. Unfortunately we rarely saw him. While we were living in Guatemala, all the public school teachers were on

no more than other boys of his age. All of the children were extremely well behaved. We didn't see many toys around, and Melanny didn't seem to have what I would call a decent doll.

Mario's mother, Julia, was a delightful character. She was well educated and interested in everything. She had had a career in radio as a news broadcaster. We learned that it was common to refer to a person with Julia's type of character as Chispa, which means vivacious.

La Señora de Palma, "Patti" was in charge of the house and our care. Although the family might be considered poor by our standards, both Patti

strike. Mario participated in various strike actions each day, and there was obviously a lot of stress in the house. His school was a two-hour bus ride down the mountains towards the coast, and he was expected to show up at the school each day even during the strike. Patti would never know when he was coming home and one night he didn't come home at all because of the roadblocks that the strikers caused.

The house was L shaped with a courtyard making up the square. The rooms also had windows into the hallway that opened into the courtyard. This kept the house cool, especially so in winter.

The master bedroom was in the front corner. It was equipped with two single beds and one double bed. This was where the television was and where the family spent most of their time. Five people slept there. Grandma Julia and the teenager, Marito shared the next room.

The small kitchen was filled by the table, which sat eight. When everyone was seated no one could pass around it on either side. There was no hot water in the kitchen but there was an assortment of appliances like a blender and a pressure cooker that Patti used to make *frijoles* (beans).

Another student had a room down the hall, but she left two days after we arrived. She said it was too cold for her.

In the passageway in front of the kitchen there was a free-standing concrete sink. I had seen these for sale along the side of the roads and had wondered what they were. One cold tap fed into the center sink and it seemed to be left running or dripping almost all day. Dishes were washed in the cold water and they used the other side with the ribbed bottom for laundry. Against the wall was a wash basin where everyone brushed their teeth and washed their hands, again in cold water.

The toilet had a pull chain that released the flushing water from the overhead tank like the ones I used when I was a kid in England. The occasional mosquitoes would visit. All over Central America the city plumbing is only good enough for human waste, so everything else, including toilet paper, is supposed to go in the little waste bin next to the toilet. This practice was a little hard to

LEFT: The courtyard of the de Palma house, Quetzaltenango, Guatemala
RIGHT: Grandma Julia washing dishes

get used to, but it was important to remember since paper clogged the plumbing systems.

The shower has a little anteroom where we could balance our towel and dry clothes on a little stool. There was a large shower with the showerhead hanging from the ceiling. The hot water was the interesting factor here. There was a cylindrical heating element on the pipe, between the ceiling and the showerhead,

with electrical wires going in and out. A switch on the wall activated it. When you turned the water on it automatically passed through the heater and came out hot. First you had to trust that you weren't going to get electrocuted, and then you had to turn on as little water as you could for the temperature you needed. Considering the amount of energy available, the more water that passed through the heater meant a lower temperature for the water. It was also temperamental, and we sometimes had to wait for Patti to come in and turn the water off and on again in order for it to work. There was also a knack to keep your feet in the same spot that the hot water fell on or you ended up treading on very cold, bare, unfinished concrete. It could be done, but it was not a relaxing shower.

The formal sitting room to which we were first escorted was only accessible through the master bedroom. There was a stiff couch and a couple of chairs in this room. It was freshly painted in white with a six-foot rainbow arching over one wall and an artificial Christmas tree still standing in the corner. It was all very different from the house I'm used to, but it is home to the de Palma family.

John and I went out to explore the neighborhood and found a nearby flower market, and an internet café to reconnect with our families.

That evening, after dinner, there was a parade that passed outside the house. It was the firecrackers and music that drew us into the street. First came two long lines of ladies in colorful traditional costumes and wide fabric headwear. Cloth, as wide as the rim, was wound around their hats, but still showed the crown of the head at the back. Then there were two lines of men, well dressed, many in suits and ties. These men took turns carrying a large platform with the Baby Jesus on their shoulders. The statue had all sorts of embellishments, and a canopy with spotlights illuminating the Infant. Each person with a free hand carried a candle or sparkler and there were fireworks going off all over the place. Everyone in the procession was walking and swaying to the dirge-like music, similar to the kind you would hear at a New Orleans funeral. The band consisted of a tuba, about four trumpets, a trombone, a

clarinet, a couple of drums, a cymbal and perhaps other instruments that were hidden in the dark.

Between the illuminated dais and the band was an elderly man pushing a wheelbarrow. In the wheelbarrow was a generator to power the lights. More people in costume followed; children with firecrackers were darting about, and others in various garb, followed in the procession. There were quite a few spectators standing along the narrow road. The procession filled the narrow road. There were local police for stopping traffic at the cross streets, but most of the cars had already paused because of the firecrackers.

We returned to our room, tired and our minds filled with the day's events. We spent our first night away from the motorhome.

Day 14
Monday, January 27, Language School Begins

More firecrackers awakened us the next morning. Patti said it was probably someone's birthday.

It must have been freezing during the night. We were cold and unaccustomed to the beds and played rocks, paper scissors to see who would get up and have the first shower. John won. We needed the shower just to warm ourselves. John had trouble with the hot water, and returned disappointed and cold. I asked Patti to help, and she magically got it working. Brindle needed a walk so I took her outside while John took another shower. I wore two sweaters, as we had not brought coats.

At 7:00 a.m., with showers, shaves and dog walk under our belt, Patti presented us with a breakfast of hotcakes, juice and coffee.

This was our first day at the school. The school building was a drab two-story cement block structure with re-bar sticking out of the top of the roof. I understand owners are taxed on a building once it is finished which means that many people complete a building just enough so they can use it, but never admit to actually finishing construction.

The school consisted of two floors. The front of the first floor had a small cubicle for Nora and Rolando to conduct business. There was a large foyer/sitting area next to this and a stairway leading to the second floor. Behind the stairway was a table with coffee and, at the 10:00 breaks, some cookies from the *panadería* down the street. When John went for coffee he discovered there was no cream or milk. Nora quickly went to the store to buy their equivalent of Creamora. I think it is only the Americans who take cream in their coffee.

We both had pleasant young women teaching us. There was no textbook. Each teacher tailored the lesson to fit the needs of the student. We each had the book *501 Spanish Verbs* (Kendris), and it was an invaluable help. It contains full conjugations for almost any verb you might want. We of course had dictionaries, but one of our dictionaries was a small pocket dictionary for travelers in Spain. It had the European vocabulary and was often deficient in Latin American words.

Five hours of private instruction is a long time, especially for those of us who have been away from formal schooling for decades. There was a pattern to the lessons, with conversation, grammar and reading. This class regimen was tiring but good. I believe that if we could have invested three or four more weeks here, we may have reached some level of fluency. As it was, we might be considered "conversant" Spanish speakers. I still

have to do a lot of pointing and gesturing, but between us we could usually get along. We came with some previous Spanish skills. If someone were to start from scratch, I would recommend a minimum of three weeks of this training to be able to communicate.

We returned to our *familia* for lunch at 1:00 p.m., starved. Patti served us a combination of tortillas, rice and beans for lunch. The afternoon was free so we set out to find the Central Market. We ended up in the Mercado de la Democracia, which was right next to the University and the parking lot where we first stopped in town. We did not go and visit the guard. Although this was the wrong market, it was very interesting and had a variety of indigenous clothes available for the locals to purchase. There was an intoxicating mixture of aromas with fresh produce and the accompanying smell of the occasional rotten item, the pungent aroma of dried herbs and spices mixed with fish and straw goods. The merchandise was in specific areas but overlapped. A plump lady sat with a lap full of onions for sale at one intersection while a teenaged girl tried to sell brooms at another.

The premier indigenous costume of the Mayans in these parts is the *huipil,* or *guipil.* It is a rectangular piece of colorfully woven fabric with a hole for the head to pass through. The sides are sewn together. Around the neck there is usually an amazing amount of embroidery in a blaze of color competing with the rest of the fabric. I have seen very few where one set of colors actually complemented the other. It is not tailored in any way and neither is the skirt, which is a strip of woven fabric usually in subdued colors of black, blues or gray stripes wrapped around the waist.

This skirt is sometimes colorfully embellished and wrapped around much like a sarong with the excess fabric brought forward at the hips, and all this bulk is cinched together round the waist with a *faja,* or sash. These long woven belts are frequently seen in the U.S. in international shops. It is a practical souvenir gift as they can be used as belts and headbands. A heavily embroidered apron is often worn over the skirt.

At one particularly colorful stall selling *huipiles* I asked if I could take a picture. The lady said yes, and then bent down so I could not see her behind the counter. She was half the charm but the picture is still interesting.

Hanging up on the right is a selection of skirt fabrics and next to that are scarves. These scarves are also used as shawls or to carry babies and other items tied onto a woman's back. There are *huipiles* with circular neck embroidery and patterns for those who want to do their own embroidery.

were in western style clothes, but there were always people in sight wearing traditional costume.

There was another parade at night but it was during dinner, so we didn't go out to see it. We were warm under our own bedding, which we retrieved from the motorhome during our school break that morning. We were tired and slept well.

Day 15
Tuesday, January 28, First "Chicken Bus" Ride

Today we had our first ride on a "chicken bus." Nora from the school had arranged a trip to the home of a family in the mountains, near the village of Momostenango, where they weave

At last we found Plaza Central Americano, and I sat and watched the people pass as John drew money out of the bank. I also had a $0.21 shoe shine from a little boy. Most of the people

LEFT: A huipil and shawls for sale in the Mercado de la Democracia, Xela, Guatemala

ABOVE: Two ladies proudly showing off their traditional clothes in Central Park, Quetzaltenango,Guatemala. These ladies have unusually colorful skirts. They are probably from the same family because the clothes are so similar. The lady on the left has a child tied to her back in one of her shawls, and is carrying something on her head wrapped in another shawl. In the heat of the day the shawls are folded and used as hats to shade the eyes.

floor mats and rugs. The purpose was for us to talk with our teachers and work on our Spanish as well as absorb the cultural experience.

After the morning class we raced back to our *familia* for lunch and back to the school again. From there we joined other students and were taken for a brisk fifteen-minute walk to the street corner where the buses stopped. The buses are retired Bluebird school buses. School buses never die, they end up somewhere in Central America. Some were their original cheesy yellow, and it looked like they still had the original tires, but they all had a couple of modifications. I don't think the schools would have approved of the ladders up the back to the luggage rack on top, although the kids would have loved the air horn. Most of the buses were painted a splendid riot of colors, but they never hid the Bluebird logo.

Each bus had a driver and a conductor. The buses paused at the bus stops and the conductor would get off and yell out the destination, encouraging passengers to board. You often find people yelling in the streets in Central America. It took us a while to realize that they were either conductors announcing the bus's destination, or vendors calling out their wares.

If a passenger had big bundles they were taken and usually thrown onto the roof of the bus. Sometimes there was a third person on the bus just to help with the luggage, and for crowd control.

It was almost an hour before our bus came. It was full, but that didn't seem to matter. It had Weld County School District painted down its sides. We later looked up Weld County; it was from Greeley, Colorado. The dozen or so of us

from the school and Thelma, the lady of the house we were to visit, were encouraged on board and then told to go to the back. People were sitting three to a seat on both sides and there was no room to pass. Well, it is amazing what can be done. This was a forty-passenger school bus, but I counted seventy-three people on board! A little later a few more crammed on, including two men with cartons of baby chickens that they wedged into the overhead storage racks, which were already filled with bundles wrapped in colorful fabric, and scarves containing goodness knows what. No wonder they called them "chicken buses." Now that the whole world was on board, sitting or standing, holding bundles and babies, the conductor slid through like an eel to collect the fares. When he reached the very back, where John was standing up against bunches of fresh flowers for market, the conductor waited for the bus to pause in the traffic, opened the emergency door, jumped out, and ran to the front to start all over again.

These bus drivers drive like crazy. Consider the fact that an ordinary highway coach ride from Xela to Guatemala City takes four hours and costs around $9. The chicken bus, with all its stops, only takes three hours and costs around

RIGHT: Life on the chicken bus, Xela, Guatemala

$3. We later learned that the chicken bus driver is rewarded for the number of passengers he carries. Since there doesn't seem to be any control on the number of buses going between two destinations, there is a race between buses to see who can reach the next bus stop first. The winner gets the passengers. While driving the motorhome we often were passed by chicken buses on blind corners. We never saw a serious accident with the chicken buses, but I'm sure they had their share. Another reason they are called "chicken buses" is because you can't be chicken to ride in one.

Our ride to Momostenango took us out of Xela along the road we had driven to enter town three days before. We branched off our path at *Cuatro Caminos* and began climbing into the mountains. The last part of this hour-long trip was up extremely winding mountain roads that climbed steeply around pine filled canyons. We were still driving at full throttle. I began to feel sick. At last we reached our stop and our teachers waved over the crowd signaling for us to get off. We squeezed out; I took a deep breath of mountain air and recovered my color.

Pine trees climbed up to the right and there were more on the steep slope down to the left. Pine needles lay deep on the rust colored dirt and added to the fragrance in the air. If Momostenango was a village, we must have been some distance outside of it. We climbed down a progression of steep dirt paths and steps cut into the mountain, between adobe houses. The occasional curious pig or dog appeared to inspect us. Goats and sheep were tethered or in small pens.

Thelma then stopped and waved us into her home and showed us around the small courtyard. There were several woven rugs, in the Navajo style, but not quite as heavy, hanging up and piled about on show for her customers. A dog that was lying on the display was quickly sent running by one of the children wielding a stick. There were two large looms and one small one outside under tiled overhanging roofs. Wire coat hangers with more woven merchandise hung under the eaves beside dried corn on the cob that was being stored for later use.

Her ten-year-old son was working a pattern into a rug on the smaller loom. He had the design drawn on a sheet of school paper resting at his elbow. He told us that he went to school in the morning and worked at the loom in the afternoons. His dad was at a large loom with an enormous turkey strutting at his feet.

Thelma showed us how she carded the raw wool to make the threads line up for spinning. She called her younger son over to prepare little wads of it for her to card. She used two paddles with metal bristles that she stroked against each other drawing the hairs into line. It was hard work and took some muscle power.

Then the man of the house left his loom to demonstrate how to spin the

LEFT: Thelma's son weaving a rug, Momostenango, Guatemala

freshly carded handfuls of wool. He had a homemade spinning wheel that required him to turn a crank with one hand. He began by drawing threads from the wool, then catching them into the end of the already spun thread. He was constantly turning the handle while touching the new wool to the old, blending it together into yarn onto the twisting spindle. As a skilled craftsman he made it look easier than it was. Some of our fellow students tried, illustrating that it takes a practiced hand to turn a bunch of raw wool into smooth thread.

The next process was dying the wool. Thelma showed us the natural plants she used to extract the colored dyes. She could get three distinct colors from one

ABOVE: Thelma carding wool
RIGHT: Thelma's husband demonstrating spinning, Momostenango, Guatemala

bark, varying from a cream to a rusty brown to a rich burgundy brown, depending on how long she soaked the wool. She also showed us the berries she uses to get a deep soft purple dye and the

leaves she uses for the green. From what looked like "witches hair," a long stringy yellow-orange vine, she extracted a yellow shade. Finally, she used a mix of ash from her hearth and chalk from local hillsides to "fix" the dyes so they wouldn't leach and run. It takes about two days to weave just one of these rugs that they sell for $10.

At this point we heard an air horn blasting. Thelma had sent her children up to the road to stop the bus for us. This was the last bus of the day so we made a mad rush scrambling up the precipitous dirt steps to the road, and were hoisted on board through the emergency exit at the back. We were at an altitude of about 8,000 feet so this scramble was quite breathtaking.

That evening after dinner the sound of firecrackers alerted us to another parade in the streets near the house. This time they were carrying a glass showcase in which was depicted a prostrate Jesus after he had descended from the cross. He was carried on a dais at shoulder height, illuminated with neon lights. There were not so many participants, and the women wore different outfits. They had the same band and the same generator in the wheelbarrow pushed by the same old man. There were fewer spectators than before, standing shoulder to shoulder holding candles, on the narrow sidewalk.

Day 16
Wednesday, January 29,
A Visit with the Tzul Family

Before we left Houston, we offered to carry some things to Guatemala for Consuelo Tzul, who cleans our house for us. Her parents didn't have a phone, but Consuelo gave us the number for an aunt who lived next door. We didn't feel fluent enough to try to make an initial contact by ourselves, so Patti agreed to call them and to arrange a rendezvous. This didn't help too much, however, as the aunt was not fluent in Spanish either. The Tzul family's first language is Quiché, a Mayan dialect. They lived in a small village called Totonicapan, not too far from Xela.

After a few calls back and forth, we found someone Patti could communicate with. The Tzuls could not see how we could find their house, and insisted that they come over to see us instead. I was deeply disappointed, as I really wanted to visit them in their home. But I looked forward to meeting them anyway. They were scheduled to arrive at 3:00 p.m. I was not sure what the etiquette was when entertaining in someone else's house, so I dashed out to get some cookies at the nearby *panadería*. I returned at ten past three and the Tzul family was already there, seated in the formal sitting room with John and the family. They had arrived at three, right on time.

Santiago, Consuelo's dad, was a wiry, vibrant man with a rich brown face and pointed chin. He came with his wife, Francesa, their teenage son, and two daughters who were still living at home. Maria, Consuelo's eldest sister, was very pretty and they looked very much alike.

LEFT: Local plants are used to dye the wool various colors.

The family was full of smiles and all the women were in their traditional Mayan clothes. The men wore slacks and knit shirts. Patti had prepared some tea for everyone and served the cookies I had bought. We gave them the two large bags packed full of new clothes. There were sweaters of every color and size, and a couple of pairs of jeans. We went outside into the courtyard to take photographs that I could take back for Consuelo.

Now Santiago offered to take us all back to their house. I hadn't realized that they had driven, I had presumed that they had all come by bus. I so wanted to visit their home, and now we wouldn't have to struggle to find the place driving the motorhome. Our host family was also invited, and to our delight, seventy-six-year-old grandma Julia accepted the invitation.

To my surprise Santiago drove an extended cab pickup truck. John sat up front next to Santiago; Francesa, Grandma Julia and I sat behind, and the rest of the Tzuls piled in the covered bed in the back. It was about a forty-five minute drive to their village of Paqui, near Totonicapan. We would never have found it on our own.

We turned off the paved road onto a dirt road. My next surprise was when we pulled up to a new two-story house with fresh white paint and a high iron fence. This, we were told, was the house of Consuelo and her husband. It was built with their earnings in the States. Consuelo cleans houses and he waits table. The house is not furnished and has no fittings that could easily be stolen, but it is ready for them when they want to return to live here. It sits empty, with just

a guard dog waiting for them to move in. Consuelo has never seen the house, as she has not been to Guatemala since she left nine years ago.

After visiting the new house we all piled back into the truck (perhaps bought with Consuelo's earnings as well) and stopped at the Tzul family home where Consuelo was born. We walked between corn and squash patches, which were idle as it was the dry season and nothing was growing. The names of the seasons are reversed here. The dry season, which is during our winter, is called summer *(verano)*. The wet season, during our summer, is called winter *(invierno)*.

We walked to the courtyard of another L shaped house closed in with a bare cement block wall creating a courtyard. The corrugated iron roof extended over the courtyard to create a covered patio. There was a wonderful display of black and gold corn hanging under the eaves that was being stored for later consumption. Here more extended family members, all in colorful traditional outfits, greeted us.

We were invited inside, but the doors were made for the comfort of the residents and we had to bend low to enter. John didn't make it and acquired a sizable bruise from not reacting fast enough.

RIGHT: Sisters Simiona and Elaida, with their mother Francesa Tzul

The first room we went into was very large. There was a bed pushed into the corner; about a dozen chairs were stacked up and a bench was in place, as though they were ready for a grand fiesta. The walls were freshly painted cream and covered with picture boards with family photos and vacation snapshots. Among family portraits were numerous picture calendars from various years and a couple of paintings on velvet. On a

small table was a brand new tin bucket overflowing with enormous bunches of yellow and white flowers.

The second room was the kitchen with a large freestanding gas stove, with a bright blue tiled food preparation surface around it. Santiago explained that their other wood burning cooker was specifically for tacos. I was shown foods that I'd never seen before like the green leaves they use to wrap their little tamales. We were invited to sit for traditional hot chocolate and local *panecitos,* which were little sweet bread rolls. Then they gave us instruction on the Quiché Mayan language. It was all I could do to remember the Spanish so I'm afraid I didn't remember much Quiché. There are numerous Mayan languages, but if you want to learn one, the language schools in Xela and Antigua offer courses.

Photos were taken in all directions and (a third surprise) a young relative

arrived with his video camera. We went outside again for more pictures. They were laughing at my height; yes, I'm tall at six foot. When I knelt down I was the same height as the women!

Santiago climbed on a stool and gathered up bunches of the corn he had grown, from under the eaves. We were presented bundles of black corn dried on the cob for Julia to take back to our host family. I was given some of the disks of chocolate and instructions on how to make the beverage that has been traditional to the Mayans for centuries.

Santiago said we should have a *calabaza,* or squash. The great aunt produced an enormous one, but Santiago didn't think it was good enough and he sent one of the little girls into the squash patch for another one. She reached up for one that was still hanging from a vine, almost taking her feet off the ground before it came free, and she brought it to us. We were then told to take them both.

I produced a packet of tomato seeds from my pocket and Santiago was delighted. I always carried packets of seeds in my pocket for just this sort of occasion. When the great aunt Julia saw the packet of lupine seeds in my hand she almost made a diving leap for it. After returning home we mailed them some more seeds along with pictures of the Texas countryside covered in wild lupine: the blue bonnet. I was so glad that I had some seeds with me. We were then shown with pride the vegetable patch where beans, cabbage and cauliflower were thriving. They took us on a walk to see the little stream that ran nearby with tall white lilies growing wild on its banks.

LEFT: Drinking hot chocolate inside the Tzul kitchen with Santiago, Aunt Julia, Grandma Antonia, and Francesa (left to right)

It was time to go. Francesa took my hands in both of hers and said, *"Gracias por visitar. Gracias por visitar. Gracias por visitar."* Over and over again she repeated her thanks to us for visiting her, all the while clutching my hands. My eyes teared-up because I was the one who was grateful for the hospitality and the wonderful experience, and yet she was so grateful that we had visited her.

We climbed back into the truck and this time all the aunts wanted to come for the ride as well as any of the cousins who had missed out before. When we reached the town of Quetzaltenango, we made a slight detour to visit another of the Tzul daughters, and more family photographs were taken.

It had been a wonderful day. One I will never forget

I must add that Julia, grandma of our *familia,* was great to have along. She acted as our translator from their Spanish to ours. She was equally enthralled by the

ABOVE: The Tzul family with Harriet. From left to right, Santiago and Francesa with their granddaughter Silvia, Harriet, Francesa's mother Antonia, and her sister Julia. Francesa's daughters Simiona and Elaida are wearing their new sweaters. Young cousin Jose is on the end.
RIGHT: Santiago Tzul giving away his precious gift from the gods

visit with the Tzul family and constantly asked questions of her own. She is quite a lady, *una mujer muy chispa*.

Day 17
Thursday, January 30, Quetzaltenango

It was cold in Xela with a frost overnight. An indigent person died of hypothermia outside a hospital in Guatemala City that night. When we took the dog for her run in the open area behind the house our breath created clouds.

We bundled up our dirty laundry and took it to the *lavandería* on the way to school. It was washed and dried and folded for two dollars, and ready for us when we walked home.

There were several different routes to the school that passed a variety of homes and businesses on the way. You couldn't tell from the outside what is going on behind the doors. One housed a typing school with twenty typewriters (yes, manual typewriters) lined up in rows on tables. One was a cobbler, and several were *molinos,* with little mills for grinding maize into *masa*. Others were *tortillerías* where thin pancakes of *masa* were cooked on hot griddles to become tortillas. Behind some doors were courtyards full of flower gardens whereas others hid cars. Some doors opened directly into private

homes. Many homes had been made into little shops. It was all fascinating and all close enough to reach out to touch and smell.

Day 18
Friday, January 31, San Francisco
El Alto market

Friday is market day in San Francisco el Alto. Our language school suggested that our teachers take us there to give us some on the job training. Unfortunately, my language instructor hardly said more than two words to me so from that angle the morning was a complete loss. However, I would not have missed the experience for the world. It was incredible.

First was the chicken bus. You could clearly see the Bluebird logo that had survived all the other creative embellishments. Very little of the windshield could actually be seen through, what with all the bric-a-brac and tassels that hung around the driver's viewing area and was glued to the dashboard. To block out the glaring sun the top of the windshield had been painted over. On one bus the only clear space for seeing the road ahead was in the shape of the Batman logo. A truck we saw had two

LEFT: A street in Quetzaltenango
ABOVE: The chicken bus

hearts clear on an otherwise obscured windshield.

Like our other chicken bus ride, this bus became very, very crowded. There were five or six adults to a row plus a couple of babies. We were packed absolutely

solid. Of course there was still room for the lady who wormed her way back and perched as the fourth person in the row in front of me. She put a sack on her lap and carefully opened the neck whereupon a chicken popped its head out for a breath of air. Did I say these were called chicken buses?

We arrived in San Francisco el Alto and our bus lined up with a hundred or more other retired school buses. This market is supposedly the largest one in Guatemala although the one at Chichicastenango is more famous with the tourists. Friday at San Francisco el Alto is the local wholesale market, not designed for tourists. We climbed a succession of steep alleyways and steps crammed with merchandise. Vendors had erected shades and hung their products in every possible ledge, selling every conceivable item.

Some people only had a few bananas to sell; others had stacks of clothes or baskets of ducks that they carried on their heads.

ABOVE: Stairs in the San Francisco El Alto Market, Guatemala
RIGHT: Buying a machete in San Francisco El Alto, Guatemala

I was on overload. In hot weather the women of Mayan heritage wear a lighter blouse, frequently of a shimmering factory-made fabric that was heavily embroidered, usually by sewing machine. The blue tarp that was hung for protection from sun and rain gave some areas a blue light.

We continued up the hillside until we came to a plateau above the town where things really got lively. This was the animal market, and also where those without a regular spot to display their produce could sell their wares. It looked like most of the critters were young, and they were handled with great care and individual attention.

We wandered around for ages and I thought my camera would give off steam from all the pictures I was taking. There were a couple of people selling a selection of *huipiles* and fabrics on a tarpaulin on the ground. I went over and browsed through the embroidered items. They were all second hand and had that familiar warm feel of used clothes.

We walked on to the edge of the plateau where there was a wall overlooking the town center and the lower market area. Below we could see where new

fabric items were sold. Many of the fabrics were packaged in bulk for entrepreneurs to resell elsewhere. After enjoying the atmosphere and animals, and a shoeshine,

we made our way back down through the passages and stairwells passing many ladies selling *huipiles* and aprons. When we reached the lower level, where the new fabrics were for sale, we came to a cooler and quieter colonnade filled with vendors with full length skirts.

Each village had its own vocabulary of colors and patterns. I was in seventh heaven meandering through the market with all the wonderful fabrics and intoxicating colors. All the nice ladies in colorful embroidered outfits would do anything to encourage me to take just one more of anything home with me. Thankfully John's sanity prevailed or I would have returned home with twenty sets of placemats. It was a blaze of color and smiling faces.

We returned to the bus parking lot and were swept onto a chicken bus with a crowd of other shoppers. Big packages were thrown on top and away we went. I wondered how passengers were able to reclaim their bundles in the very short time that the driver paused at each bus stop. We were half way home when I noticed a lady on the curb by the bus

looking very distraught. She was talking with the conductor who then climbed the ladder onto the roof. The lady re-boarded the bus and walked through, obviously searching for her bundle. She wasn't permitted to hold up the bus for very long. As we pulled away she was standing alone in her colorful garb with her hand to her forehead shading her eyes from the sun watching the bus leave. She had lost her day's purchases.

Day 19
Saturday, February 1, Chichicastenango

There had been quite a debate at school and between our host family members as to which market was the more interesting: San Francisco el Alto or Guatemala's most famous market, Chichicastenango. Many told us that we needn't bother going to Chichicastenango if we had visited San Francisco. Actually, in my mind there was no question that we were going to go to Chichicastenango. It was on my list of places to go before we left the U.S. San Francisco el Alto was an extra bonus.

LEFT: Animals for sale in San Francisco El Alto
ABOVE: Skirt fabric in San Francisco El Alto, Guatemala

ABOVE: Footbridge in Xela, Guatemala

The trip to Chichicastenango involved an overnight stay even though it was only sixty miles away. It was up in the mountains and we didn't want to be rushed. The weekend seemed ideal. Also, and most importantly, Sunday and Thursday are market days. Julia, our family's grandmother, had actively joined in the discussions as to whether San Francisco or Chichi was the best market, but had not been to Chichi for years. After enjoying her company so much before, we invited her to join us. We were delighted when she said yes.

This morning we showed her around our little motorhome and explained how things worked. She was most amazed when I insisted that the toilet paper must go in "la taza," the toilet

bowl. She seemed to fit in immediately and was never in the way in our cramped quarters.

We also hoped that she would be a guide to help us get out of the city of Quetzaltenango. We were wrong on that account, but at least she was able to translate the directions we received at each street corner. Not only did we need the way out of town, but a route that the motorhome could navigate. We made it, but only after deliberately going the wrong way down a one way road because the right road led under a charming little footbridge that would have decapitated the motorhome.

Once on the Pan-American Highway we began to climb the hills and could see the tiny patches of farmland surrounded by houses. There would be a house, a second and perhaps a third added to create

an L or an open E when the family grew. All over the countryside there were small clusters of homes with tiny plots of land. At this time of year there was hardly anything growing, but you could see the large *calabaza* still sitting on the dry earth. This was the dry season and nothing was going to be planted until the rains came. Some of the roofs were covered with corn on the cob where it was drying and being stored.

The people of the Quetzaltenango Valley are an independent lot. They once declared themselves an independent nation.

Two volcanoes look down on the valley. Santa Maria is the highest, and you can also see the still active Santiaguito volcano shadowing the city and emitting the occasional plume of smoke.

It took about an hour to drive from *Cuatro Caminos* to the turnoff for Chichi at *Los Encuentros*. Once we made the turnoff from the Pan-American Highway, the traffic was much lighter and the road surface smoother, although the climbing became more pronounced. Eventually, after some hefty uphill hairpin bends, we arrived in Chichicastenango.

We took the first place we could find to hold us: the Shell Gas Station. The management was agreeable and for a small fee we could sleep over. Even better, because we filled up with gas there, we would get the motorhome washed for free. That was a treat. We were also able to hook up to their power and refill our depleted fresh water tank.

We usually have an audience when we set up camp, and this family parked their truck next to us. Like us, they had come early for a parking spot and to attend the

ABOVE: The countryside east of Xela: Quetzaltenango Valley
LEFT: A family who arrived early for the Chichicastenango market

market. Eventually we were completely closed in by various trucks.

Although this was Saturday and the market was not meant to be open until the next day, there was plenty of action. We grabbed some quick food for lunch and the three of us went for a stroll through town to see where the market was and how the town was laid out. Brindle tagged along as usual.

The visitors' part of the market is held in the plaza between two churches. You have to make an effort to find the market stalls where the locals purchase their everyday items like vegetables and plastic bowls. It is there that inexpensive food stands serve tasty, inexpensive meals.

The Santo Thomas Church was built by the Spanish in the 1540s, on the site of an ancient Mayan religious site. The current residents use the steps outside as much as they do the interior. The Mayans of this area are Cakchiquel, and can trace their lineage back for centuries. Ancestors are buried below the church so candles and *maize* offerings are lined up on the pine-strewn floor in

remembrance. Originally, only high priests used the main steps and entrance so it is polite to use the side door.

As offerings were left on temple steps a thousand years ago, so little fires burn incense on these church steps today.

The smoke of copal resin drifted in all directions. At the other end of the market square was the little white El Calvario Church where a man on the steps was swinging a censer. His eyes were closed and he was fully absorbed in his ceremony.

We started the serious business of looking at the merchandise. Although this was the day before the market was meant to be open, many of the stalls were overflowing with color and eager merchants.

Grandma Julia was interested in everything. Glorious bed spreads and table cloths were made from three hand woven blue, or green, or purple strips of cloth sewn together. We had interrupted the sales lady in her embroidery but she was happy to show us what she had been doing while waiting for customers.

The colors everywhere were unbelievable. Each stall was predominately one product, but you were just as likely to see bananas stacked up together with

ABOVE: Looking across the market square to Santo Tomas Church from the steps of El Calvario Church, Chichicastenango
RIGHT: Incense burning on the church steps, Chichicastenango, Guatemala

skirt fabric. The local vendors have worked out that the gringos don't buy many *huipiles*. Like me, they can't find a way to use them. Here the craftsmen and women have taken old and new *huipiles,* cut them up and made patchwork bed spreads, pillow covers, and every kind of bag. They have taken scraps of everything and made trim for clothes. They have made woven items that are useable. Here were patchwork shirts and dresses made from blends of blues or browns created from fabric lengths that might otherwise have been hard to sell.

After shopping and browsing and enjoyable bartering all afternoon, we took Julia to dinner at the Hotel Santo Tomas next to where we had parked. It was a classy place that would charm any

gringo. Trailing bougainvillea drooped over the whitewashed interior colonnade. Parrots perched among the fountains and great pots stuffed with dozens of lilies filled shaded alcoves around the courtyard. They had some good guidebooks in their little shop and a nice clean lavatory.

It was a great meal in a first class restaurant, and cost about $36 for the three of us. The wait staff wore very unusual colorful costumes. Julia reached across the table and took my hand with tears of gratitude in her eyes. We shed a couple of tears together. It was such a treat for us to have this intelligent, vibrant, inquisitive woman with us.

That night ours was the only vehicle in the parking lot. I could not sleep. My mind was whirling with all the colorful sights and sounds I'd experienced. I was on overload. It was wonderful. And tomorrow the real market would open!

Day 20
February 2, Chichicastenango Market Day

Pickup trucks packed with vendors and their merchandise began arriving early to set up their stalls for market day. Unlike what I had expected, the market really didn't begin until about ten in the morning. We were pretty well boxed in by pickups when buses spewing gringos began arriving. They were coming from places like Guatemala City, Antigua, and Lake Atitlán, which were each a few hours away. The town was a glorious riot of colors and friendly faces. Most of the merchandise was definitely created for the gringo market. It was very appealing.

TOP LEFT: A vendor showing her embroidery to Julia
LEFT: Patchwork bedspreads and other colorful merchandise for sale in Chichicastenango

We walked down the main street with little shops on either side overflowing with merchandise. Additional enterprising vendors covered every inch of the sidewalk. They were packed so closely together it was hard to tell who was selling which items. Women and children in colorful outfits, some carrying merchandise on their heads and

We wound our way to the Mercado in front of the church of Santo Thomas. The steps were mostly being used as the flower market but there were still little incense fires burning.

At the other end of the market there was even more activity on the steps of El Calvario Church. There was a fog of incense burning and drifting into the

babies on their backs, came up to us to offer their products. Little children held out beads and woven belts and masks whereas the women had the more valuable fabrics stacked high on their heads like multicolored sandwiches. Between it all were ice-cream carts and wagons full of oranges.

The bank was open on Sunday, and so were the internet cafes, but the latter were too crowded to tempt us. Besides, who would want to be inside with this blaze of color assaulting you in the clear bright sunshine outside?

stalls. Below the steps, the stalls selling masks had a much better selection than on the previous day. We bought another mask so we had one for us and one to give to the youth who was watering our houseplants back in Houston. (Oh dear, I hope everything was OK back at home. This was such a different whirling world that I had forgotten about the little problems of home.) I concentrated on shopping. We needed to buy two of everything, as I was afraid I might otherwise be tempted to give away something that I couldn't live without!

The local women from Chichicastenango could be identified by the up and

ABOVE: The main street in Chichicastenango on market day

down zigzag pattern embroidered on their *huipil* in bright rainbow colors. Each area or village, and sometimes family, is known for the special pattern or color scheme of their weaving and embroidery. Therefore, their *huipil,* skirts, or shawls could identify them. I was again on overload; my mind bursting with the colors.

There was so much color and activity. In one stall they specialized in materials and bags and *huipiles,* all in subdued browns and rust colors. Next door there would be nothing but deep purples and blues and I'd do another flip. Other stalls were a riot of every color.

It was crowded and we had been warned that pickpockets might be about, so we had taken precautions and kept our money as inaccessible as practical. However, we only got warm feelings from the merchants and locals crowding the streets of town and the paths

between the market stalls. The day before, when we had done most of our purchasing, merchants had told us that their products were cheaper and that tax wasn't charged on non-market days. We didn't notice any difference in price between the two days. There was a lot more competition on the Sunday with many more stalls, with many selling similar items. We were glad we had done most of our shopping on the Saturday because it was less crowded and the sales people could spend more time with us.

We decided that the San Francisco el Alto market was more for the local clientele, and Chichicastenango was for the tourists. That is not meant to be derogatory. In fact, if I was only able to go to one, I would probably choose Chichi, but it would be a difficult decision. They are both fascinating and anyone in the area should really try to spend time in each town.

The drive home seemed quite serene although it was by the same tortuous road. Houses sat quietly scattered among

TOP: Two photos I took from virtually the same spot but looking in a different direction.
LEFT: A stall in Chichicastenango selling only brown fabrics

small terraced fields. A thin stream of smoke drifted into the sky from the Santiaguito Volcano.

Day 21
Monday, February 3, Xela

John had to return to the U.S. for a business conference in New Mexico and would not be back until Sunday. This was his last day at the language school, so after a morning of classes he bade his farewells and we went back to the house for lunch.

We found the place on the other side of town to buy Guatemalan insurance for the motorhome. We purchased the maximum available, which cost a hundred dollars for six thousand dollars coverage. It didn't seem worth it, and we had to wait until the next Monday to pick up our policy. Across the road from the insurance office was a large modern mall. It was just like many in the U.S. The same brand name stores and fast food restaurants. They didn't sell milk-shakes though. There was a large "discount" *supermercado* called Hiperpaiz that would rival any Wal-Mart superstore. They allowed RVs to park overnight, which is useful to know for travelers like us.

ABOVE: Buying chiles in Chichicastenango
RIGHT: The country between Chichicastenango and Xela

After a supper of beans, soupy stew and tamales there was time for a little more Spanish homework before bed. John did his packing and wrote a list of things to bring back from the States.

Day 22
Tuesday, February 4, Xela

The van was on time at 6:00 a.m. to take John to Guatemala City from whence he would catch a flight to New Mexico. There he would have a steak, a good bed, unlimited hot running water, TV and news of the world, coffee with cream, bacon for breakfast, and milk-shakes. All those little things we had come to miss in the past month. He would be gone for five days.

After John left I walked the dog, had rice and beans for breakfast and walked to school. The streets in our part of town are narrow, cobbled, but mostly clean and the buildings are colorful. There was a mass of character in this old part of Xela. I stopped to buy a couple of cakes at this very nice *panadería* that I passed each day on my way home. I had found that quite often after dinner I would still be hungry, and rather than ask Patti for more food I decided to have a snack in my room.

Marito was ready with their dog Dino to go for a walk as soon as I returned. I

had been encouraging him and Ricki to take Dino for walks with Brindle and me. Before we came to visit the house, Dino lived on a six-foot chain in their courtyard, seldom had any attention and never went for walks. Now he gets one or two walks each day, which of course he loves. Patti likes it too because she doesn't have to scoop up his droppings all the time. I usually let Marito and Ricki use our expandable leash as it provided them the means to train Dino. In the short time we were there they taught him to come to them when they call, well, most of the time. I have also

provided some doggy treats as encouragement. The family had been most surprised at Brindle's good behavior. I don't think they had ever seen a dog that could run and play and then return when called. Of course she does the other usual things like sit and stay, shake and lie down. And she is house trained. She quickly became possessive about our room, and also barked when anyone rang the front door bell.

Day 23
Wednesday, February 5, Milling the Maiz

I had been asking Patti when she was going to prepare the black corn we had been given by Santiago Tzul. I would have been sad to miss trying it. I noticed that it had been shucked off the cob, and the kernels had been soaking overnight in buckets of water. It was now swollen and tasteless. This afternoon Patti came to my room and said, *"Esta tarde vamos al*

ABOVE: 16 Avenida, Zona 1, Xela, Guatemala (Down to the left is the street were we lived.)
LEFT: Taking the gold and black corn to the **molino** was a family affair

molino." They were going to the mill. It was going to be a family event and at five in the evening Patti, Melanny, Ricki, Grandma Julia, little David and I set off to the *molino.*

The water had been drained from the corn, but the buckets were heavy. We wrapped cloth around the handles and took turns carrying them between us. After walking for about five minutes we arrived at the house that was also a *molino.* To the bewilderment of the family it was closed.

No problem, there was another lady who had a mill in the front room of her home around the next corner. She started the little motor. Belts whirred and the black corn was poured in the top funnel with a slow stream of water. The storekeeper used a little whisk brush to sweep it down the chute evenly and grind every last kernel. Grandma Julia scooped the clay-like paste from the receiving shelf, and dolloped it back into her bucket.

The belt that ran from the little electric motor to drive the grinding machine stretched across the room and the pipe that brought water to the mill was pretty basic, but it all worked. Grandma Julia made sure that she had every last scraping of her *masa,* or corn paste, in her bucket and gave it to the children to carry home.

The storekeeper then turned off the motor and carefully wiped down and covered up her equipment until the next client arrived. I insisted on tasting it first. It not only looked like clay it tasted like clay. I was looking forward to eating it cooked up into tortillas, but I would have to wait another day. The *masa* was placed in the fridge covered with a damp

RIGHT: The proprietor of the **molino** and Grandma Julia milling the black maize into masa

cloth where, it was explained, it would be OK for as long as a week.

Day 24
Thursday, February 6, The Processional Party

My back had been giving me problems. It is probably because the bed had an antique mattress that provided no support and springs that sagged almost to the ground. I made some inquiries about getting a massage, and the school proprietor made me an appointment. It was just a few minutes walk from the school, and the masseuse's house was like so

many others presenting a flat wall to the street. I looked for a yellow home with her name next to the bell.

She welcomed me in and asked me what my problem was. She invited me to take my shoes off and gave me a nice foot rub. I said "nice." This did not seem to be what I would call the work of a professional masseuse. I asked her how long she had been giving massages and she said she had recently retired from being a social worker for the government. Her family said that she gave good massages, so she took a course and hung out her shingle. I resigned any idea of therapeutic massage. I enjoyed a "nice" back rub and paid her the requested thirty quetzals for the half-hour of her time. I should not have expected more for four dollars.

When we took the dogs for their evening run we met some young women dressed in their finery. I surmised that they were dressed for a procession. It is customary for a woman to put on her finest outfit and wear her best woven shawl over the shoulder as the one in the center had done. They were flattered that I requested to take their picture, and happily waited while I adjusted the settings. Their friend who was dressed in a leather jacket quickly stepped out of the picture.

Tonight the ladies of the house were making tortillas from the black corn masa. Little Melanny had her lump of clay-like *masa* from which she was making doll sized tortillas.

I returned to do some of my homework, but firecrackers and music from outside disturbed my studies. There had been processions most evenings,

sometimes more than one. I determined that this evening I would get some good pictures. I had also noted that the doorway to a house just a block away had been decorated with palm leaves, and thought that it might be involved. I grabbed my camera and went out. My timing was great. They were coming toward me down the narrow street and were about to turn left right in front of me.

It was the usual solemn procession, but there were many more people in traditional clothes lining the cobbles and dozens of boys running about lighting fireworks at the intersection. The dais swayed while those carrying it rocked from side to side as they shuffled their feet in time with the dirge being played behind them.

This procession was different from the others I had seen because there were costumed women carrying the platform instead of men. Most of the men wore business suits and ties. This was obviously a very important event. The candles carried by the crowd in procession, and those watching, illuminated the street.

LEFT: Three ladies dressed for the evening's procession
ABOVE: Melanny helping make the tortillas

The atmosphere was full of excitement and everyone was having a great time, spectators and participants alike. I had not seen costumes like these before and some of the women had shawls over their heads, while others wore hats with a wide two-inch thick brim and no crown. There was plenty of incense drifting in the air from the censers that were being swung in time to the slow music, as well as smoke from the constant firecrackers.

There must have been over a hundred people following the decorated and illuminated dais and the band. Bringing up the rear was the elderly gentleman with his generator in a wheelbarrow providing the electricity for the dais.

They all continued past me and through the doors I had seen decorated with palms. I squeezed along through the crowd of spectators and saw the dais being taken to a tent at the far side of a large courtyard.

As I was watching, a slightly inebriated gentleman in a suit came up to me and said *"Bienvenido, te gustaría comer la cena con nosotoros?"*

I declined his invitation to join him for dinner, but he insisted *"Nuestra casa está abierta, invitamos a todo el mundo."* He said his house was open and everyone was invited.

"What is the celebration?" I struggled in my Spanish.

"Ha llegado el niño," he said smiling. And then broke into English, "The baby has come. The baby has come."

I congratulated him, and it crossed my mind to ask him if it was a girl or a boy. Thank goodness I didn't. He meant of course the religious statue of the Baby Jesus had arrived!

ABOVE: Almost every night there was a procession that was heralded by fireworks and a band
RIGHT: The dais at the end of the procession

I allowed myself to be swept into the courtyard and saw that I was one of a couple of hundred people. Most guests had found themselves a seat in one of the rows of blue painted chairs facing the marquee. Many guests were in colorful outfits and I was sure that the three ladies

I had photographed in the afternoon were in there somewhere. The religious icon was at the back of a raised stage at the far side of the courtyard surrounded by fresh flowers. There were great floral displays everywhere rivaling any I have seen in posh hotels in the U.S. There were a few well-dressed individuals on the stage that I later learned were family members.

A young man approached me and started a conversation in English. "My name is Sergio. Please come in and join us. This is my uncle's house. He works in Los Angeles," he stumbled with his English. "Where are you from?"

"I'm from Houston and my name is Harriet. I am pleased to meet you." I held out my hand and we shook. "Would you explain what is happening?"

"We have the Baby Jesus here tonight and we have a fiesta. Everyone is invited. You are invited. Please take a seat. Have dinner with us."

"I have dinner waiting for me with my *familia*. They are expecting me. Thank you so much though. The costumes are different to others I have seen. They are beautiful."

"Yes. They are very old and only worn for special occasions. We call this *nimpot*. Please wait." Sergio darted off into the crowd. A few minutes later he returned. "These are my cousins. The children of my uncle."

I was introduced to two ladies and a gentleman all in wonderful colorful ceremonial dress. These were three of the key figures in the procession. At Sergio's insistence they paused long enough for me to take their picture and we exchanged greetings before they excused themselves. They were the hosts and were serving food and drinks to the guests.

He continued to tell me, "My uncle can't be here. These are his children. He lives in Los Angeles. Do you live near Los Angeles?"

"No, Houston is a long way from Los Angeles. He couldn't come for the celebration?"

"That was not possible, but he sent the money for the fiesta. It is a big honor that we have the Baby Jesus here. It is a very important time because our church is seventy-five years old. The Baby Jesus goes to many houses of important people in the church." I learned later that some elders go into serious debt to live up to this honor.

"Sergio. You speak very good English. Have you lived in America as well?"

"Thank you. Thank you. No, I learn it here. I am at University. I study

LEFT: Three siblings in Nimpot costumes
RIGHT: After the religious icon has arrived at its new home, the host throws a party for the whole neighborhood.

International Law at University. I want to practice my English."

"That is wonderful."

"I like to travel. I spent the summer in a kibbutz in Israel."

The gentleman who had originally invited me to join the celebration joined us and he was introduced to me as another of Sergio's uncles. I was handed a plastic fork and a napkin and again invited to stay for dinner.

"You must stay to see the dancing," Sergio insisted. "It will begin soon."

All this time the band had continued to play the same sad tune they had played during the parade. Once at the house, two marimbas enhanced it. They played continuously and monotonously the whole time.

Sergio pointed to the stage. "Look they have begun. That is my aunt and she is dancing with her son because her husband is not here."

They were walking side by side, she with her hands clasped in front of her, and he with his hands clasped behind his back. They were keeping time with the music and with a singular lack of intricate steps they walked haltingly together, very slowly across the raised platform. They turned and "danced" back in the same manner.

"You see she has her hands in front like this," Sergio demonstrated, "and he has his hands like this. It is tradition."

This was supposed to be a celebration but it looked more like a funeral. I made my excuses and dashed back to my *familia*.

Unfortunately dinner hit a new low this night. Patti's cooking was not to my taste at the best of times. This meal consisted of two thick gray tortillas served with a mix of scrambled eggs and tomato.

These tortillas were thicker than usual, probably because of the less experienced family hands that made them. Apparently the propane tank ran out of gas half way into the cooking which explained the raw centers.

I eagerly tried the tortillas as I had been looking forward to them after following the whole process. The outside was crispy and dry, but the interior was still raw and soft and oozed gray mud when I squeezed it. Imagine two disks of dry, gray, tepid clay oozing warm clay from the inside. I could

hardly swallow the greedy mouthful I had bitten off. The eggs were great. I ate the eggs on my plate as we chatted about the parade. We could still hear the music playing.

Brindle was underneath the table next to me in her usual position against my leg. I pinched off a little piece of tortilla and let my hand drop below the table. I felt her bristly nuzzle touch my hand and the scrap was removed. I never looked down, just broke another morsel off my tortilla as though I was going to eat it, and continued to struggle to converse in Spanish. I let my hand relax to my lap and then hang down beside the chair. 'Thank you, Brindle,' I thought as little by little all of the tortillas I was given disappeared below the table. We never feed the dog from the table and she would not usually eat pieces of bread or chips she was offered. I just hoped that she was not dropping them at my feet.

This was one of the rare occasions I was offered second helpings. I declined politely. I said I was eager to return to watch the festivities across the street.

When I returned to the fiesta there was a different couple dancing in exactly the same walk to the same tune across the platform in the twenty-foot illuminated tent.

I had a chance to look around to see that the courtyard had been freshly painted and strung with little lights. A tarpaulin canopy had been hung over the main area where everyone was seated. Fresh palm fronds decorated the walls.

Sergio approached me and again urged me to have dinner and this time I decided to accept. It was a good-sized piece of chicken in a cinnamon sauce served over rice. It was the best food I'd had in a while and certainly the largest portion I had been served.

"It is tradition to have dinner for the whole village when the Baby Jesus comes to visit. Now the village is too big but we feed as many people as we can. We give everyone who comes a bag of bread. They take it home and can share it with their family. Like sharing the bread. This way everyone can be part of the sharing. It is a very important night for us."

With that he handed me a brown bag with two little loaves of sweet cake-like bread. Our house was dark when I returned except for the flickering glow from the TV in Patti and Mario's room. I kept the bread to share at breakfast in the morning.

That night I lay in bed feeling the excitement that Sergio's family had felt at having this precious icon in their home, and feeling the warmth of a stranger who had been given a real welcome. I could hear the familiar melody of the marimba playing the same continuous tune long into the night, gently putting me to sleep with a smile on my lips.

Day 25
Friday, February 7, The Teachers Strike

The routine was becoming established with me getting up to walk the dog before breakfast, and then the brisk ten minute walk to school. At one o'clock school took a break and I would wander home via the pastry shop and get my snack for later. Then there was time for another walk with Brindle before lunch. Marito and Ricki would come along with Dino and we would work on his obedience training. After lunch, Marito had his typing class. It was interesting to me that Mario considered the ability to type so important for his son, especially when the family is so strapped for money.

RIGHT: A religious procession with a military edge

The atmosphere in the house was not always very comfortable. They were under great stress because of the teachers' strike. The school term in Guatemala usually begins in early January, but the teachers were on strike and hadn't worked since the winter break. The teachers did go "to work" every day, however. They went to their respective schools and held a lock-out. Sometimes they created road-blocks and closed main arteries into the cities, or they blocked the Pan-American Highway. Occasionally they converged on the capital, Guatemala City, and staged a demonstration in front of the legislature. Mario earned the equivalent of two hundred dollars a month. His wife brought in about the same amount of money having Spanish language students like us stay in their home. The strikers were asking for a $100 per month increase in their pay; the government was offering $10 per month. To understand the income comparison, groceries here cost us about eighty percent of what we pay in the U.S. I appreciated that Patti went to less expensive shops, but we did eat a lot of rice. For dinner there might be a piece of chicken, no larger than an inch or two square in a thin stew.

I had the afternoon to work on my Spanish and to perfect my siesta skills. That evening there were more fireworks and another parade passing the street corner.

They were moving the statue of the Baby Jesus from the home of the party I attended the previous night to a new respected family in the parish. The musicians, who were all in army fatigues, distinguished this parade. Perhaps the homeowner was in the army. The music was different, but still a baleful dirge.

Day 26
Saturday, February 8, The Cemetery in Xela

There was no school on Saturday so I took a walk to the old city cemetery. I had been warned that robbers and drug dealers hung out there, but it was a bright clear morning with plenty of people about and I had the dog. Our teachers had taken us there previously, as part of our Spanish immersion training. John's teacher, Tania, had told us stories about growing up in Xela when she and her friends would spend hours in the cemetery playing games.

The cemetery took up over a hundred acres right in the middle of town surrounded by a high wall. Unless you

knew it was there you would not notice it. We had seen the flower sellers in the park but had not realized they were at the gates of this enormous cemetery. It was only a block from where we kept the motorhome.

Immediately beyond the gate were walls of crypts for the ashes of the deceased. Many of the doors were painted pink, yellow, green or shades of green as though that was the favorite color of the deceased. Some had fresh flowers while others had dead flowers or little plants struggling to survive.

Shading the well-traveled path were grand old pepper trees, which drooped over the crypts. On either side, other paths led between hundreds of above ground crypts. They looked like dollhouses of various colors disappearing into the distance, some on paved lanes others with well-worn grass paths between them. These miniature roads went on forever. Those to the south lead towards the distant volcano. Some of the crypts were intricately carved, topped with little spires and filigree carved in the stone. Unfortunately, much of the statuary has been vandalized and stolen. There were many torsos with stunted arms reaching to the brilliant sky for new hands. Apparently there are homes in town with marble statues of angels stolen from the graves.

Just to the right, as I entered, I noticed a crypt with a solid wrought iron gate. Beyond the gate, away from the reach of the vandals, was the figure of a smiling, chubby one-year-old baby boy in marble lace trimmed clothes. He had died in the eighteen hundreds and yet there were fresh flowers on his grave.

There were all sorts of people walking through the cemetery, some briskly on their way somewhere, perhaps wheeling a bicycle, others meandering with children in the pleasant setting away from the exhaust of the traffic. Half a mile down the central path it led up wide paved steps to a plateau beyond. Here the graves were much smaller and some had no headstones at all. In death as in life: money counts.

John phoned from Guatemala City in the evening. The school had arranged for a local family in Guatemala City to pick him up at the airport when he arrived that evening, and to house him for the night. It is not practical to try to get to Quetzaltenango at night. The cost for this service was $50 including coach fare to Xela the following morning.

LEFT: The cemetery in Xela
ABOVE: Looking across the cemetery at the hills surrounding Xela

CHAPTER 3

Atitlán

Still around the corner there may wait
A new road or a secret gate,
And though we may pass them by today,
Tomorrow we may come this way
And take the hidden paths that run
Towards the Moon or to the Sun.

LORD OF THE RINGS
J.R.R. Tolkein

Day 27
Sunday, February 9,
John Returns and We Leave Xela

Today was my birthday and much to my surprise there was a little gift from the family at the breakfast table. It was a souvenir wood and straw doll of a Guatemalan woman with baskets of beans and maize. It was very kind of them.

John arose early today in Guatemala City and caught the coach for Xela, but even these highway coaches are not immune to flat tires. The driver and conductor were obviously very experienced in changing tires and the bus arrived almost on time. John was at the de Palma household soon after noon.

We originally were going to leave Xela on Monday, but our hosts had another student family who wanted to move in today. The couple had two small children, so the de Palmas would also be paid for baby-sitting during the day. The de Palmas needed the money and I was ready to move on. I had prepared the motorhome, dusted it down again and bought perishables at the market. When John arrived we were ready to go. Marito and Ricki helped bring the bikes from the house and we bade our farewells.

We could not collect our hard fought-for insurance papers because it was Sunday, but we decided that if something dreadful happened we had the temporary letter stating that we did have insurance, along with the agent's phone number. We actually passed their office as we left Quetzaltenango on the good, new, wide road we had discovered, that passed through the modern part of town, *Avenida Las Americas.*

We made a brief stop at the Hiperpaiz for the supplies that I couldn't get in the mercado: bottled water in particular. They didn't have the little bottles so we got big bottles, which we could use to refill the little pint bottles we had saved anticipating this problem. We needed the little bottles for drinking as we drove.

We were now familiar with the road out of Xela, through Cuatro Caminos then eastbound on the CA1. An hour after leaving Xela we left the main road and headed for Sololá on a slow winding lane that climbed into the hills. We passed through modest villages and little farms and past stalls selling their produce at the side of the road.

Sololá is a bustling town, high on the hillside with incredible views of Lake Atitlán. There was just enough room for us to navigate around parked cars and donkey carts on the narrow streets and under the low cables hanging overhead. Then we met a great big, yellow, earth-moving Caterpillar truck. We acquiesced and backed around the corner to let him pass.

We had to drive between market stalls that overflowed from the main square. I could almost reach out and pick the bananas off the stalls. It was tempting to stop and see what else the market had to offer, but we couldn't see any place to park. Leaving town, there was a very

steep descent down to Panajachel and the lake. Low gear all the way and I was glad we had good brakes. Near the bottom of the hill we saw the sign to the Visión Azul Hotel where we planned to camp.

The manager pointed to the field between the hotel and the lakeshore, and said we could park wherever we wanted. He unlocked the gate and showed us the power hookup behind the pool bar. The swimming pool and swim-up bar might have been a highlight of some hotels, but this setup was a little run down.

The pool and bar situation was irrelevant, however, as Lake Atitlán captivated us. The sharp peaks of three misty purple volcanoes looked down on a pool of blue water. The water was flat and close. A couple of little skiffs were darting across the lake, leaving a white line, like a ghostly tail of the elusive (and perhaps illusive) quetzal bird.

There were three other RVs in this large terraced field when we arrived. We were also sharing the place with a donkey, two horses and a herd of cattle. I learned that cows really like watermelon rind. This was paradise for Brindle.

We went to visit our new neighbors. Carol and Bill in the other Class 'C' motorhome like us, were on a four-month trip covering Mexico, Belize and Guatemala. I guess it goes with the territory that everyone we met on this trip was the adventurous type. They were also doing their first motorhome trip, but they used to own a sailboat in the Bahamas and had spent many a winter sailing the Caribbean. They work all summer in Montana producing woodcrafts, which are sold throughout the

world. But as soon as the cold winds start to blow across the State, they head out on a trip.

There was another strange looking custom-made van driven by a couple from Switzerland. It was all corners and angles and resembled a small tank. We didn't get to meet them, but Carol told us later that the vehicle had been shipped over from Europe and they were touring the entire continent.

There was also a pickup truck camper parked near us, but the owner wasn't around. We had a peaceful cocktail hour alone, watching the sunset over this serene lake and listening to the animals munching grass. Later we cooked supper and treated ourselves to an episode of M★A★S★H on the VCR. Although the de Palmas were nice people, after two weeks of total immersion it felt good to be in our own 'home' with familiar things around us. And this setting could not be beaten.

Day 28
Monday, February 10, To Antigua

We spent the morning wallowing in the beauty of Lake Atitlán.

A storage area with a door on the inside and the outside became Brindle's doggy-door. When we parked the

LEFT: Saying goodbye to our host family in Quetzaltenago, Guatemala
RIGHT: Lake Atitlán, Guatemala

motorhome and left for the afternoon the dog had her own way in and out. This system worked well, and she was always back in the driver's seat when we returned.

We made contact with our friends in Antigua. We hoped to camp at their place on our way home during *Semana Santa,* Easter week. These festivities in Antigua are meant to be one of the most interesting and colorful pageants in Latin America. Our only chance of seeing our friends during our southbound trip was if we went to Antigua today, so we left Lake Atitlán at 1:45 p.m. We should have left earlier as once again the drive took longer than anticipated.

We climbed back up the steep hill and passed through the town of Sololá, the reverse of the route we had just taken the day before. It was nice to have a big V-10 engine for these hills, although we paid the price when we arrived at a gas station. Once back on the Pan-American Highway at Los Encuentros, the drive was through the countryside with very small plots of land terraced and farmed to an inch of the edge. Houses were nestled up against them. This was the dry season, so the corn stalks stood stiff and dry in some plots beside others of bare dirt that had been tilled and ready for the rain.

The road became very rough as we approached the town of Chimaltenango, slowing us down to about twenty miles an hour. There were at least two turnoffs to Antigua, the first of which was right in the middle of Chimaltenango. We had been told to look for a very small sign on the side of a hardware store at the traffic light. Fortunately, there was only one traffic light in town. Without these directions we would not have made it. When we reached the ancient city it was after 5:00 p.m., and we had told our friends we would be there about 4:00 p.m. Late again. We had no idea how difficult it would be to navigate through Antigua. The main problem was that the city was closed to heavy traffic. Of course we thought we should be an exception. We didn't consider ourselves a truck, but the concrete bollards don't negotiate with anyone. After considerable twisting and turning on the outskirts of town we found our friends' home at dusk. They offered their fenced-in lawn and garden for us to camp in. We contributed the bottle of Chivas Regal purchased in Matamoros, Mexico, and had a nice visit.

Day 29
Tuesday, February 11, Antigua Guatemala

We rode our bikes the couple of miles into town, on dirt and cobbled roads (I much prefer the former). You can't imagine how it jolts one around riding a bicycle on cobbles.

Unfortunately, once we arrived in the center of Antigua, John broke the derailleur (gear changing mechanism) of his bicycle. I went to the local market while he tried to find a bicycle repair

LEFT: Visitors to our campsite in Panajachel, Guatemala. Perhaps we were really the visitors.

shop. After being directed in various directions and walking around for a while, he was finally sent back into the mercado area where I had been happily spending my time and money. The market contained two areas: one consisted of outdoor stalls and one was a maze of shops inside. It seemed the bicycle shop was in the basement of this indoor maze. John had to wheel his bike through a series of narrow, crowded aisles between stalls selling everything from *huipiles* to freshly butchered animals. Finding the stairway to the basement was a real puzzle. Once there he had to leave the bike to be fixed, hoping he could find the shop later that afternoon. I hung my bike on a public hook across the street and locked it.

Antigua is not at all like Quetzaltenango or any of the other Guatemalan towns we had visited. It was bustling with tourists from all over the world. We ran into Carol, our RV camp-mate from Lake Atitlán, while walking around. We

agreed to join forces and hire a guide to give us a city tour. There were willing candidates everywhere.

The Spaniards built Antigua, Guatemala as the capital of the area, and they had erected some spectacular colonial buildings. Unfortunately, several earthquakes in 1773 destroyed the city and caused the capital to be moved to the current Guatemala City. Much of the area of the central square had been rebuilt, and the Palacio de Los Capitanes is still used as the government center for the area. This famous fountain is a replica of the original.

ABOVE: Camping in our friends' garden in Antigua
RIGHT: Palacio de Los Capitanes, Antigua

Throughout the city there are the remains of the churches, some standing like elaborate skeletons. The Hotel Santo Domingo envelops a convent that was destroyed in 1773, in a very classy balance of deluxe restoration. There is certainly plenty of interest and lots of international visitors were enjoying the sights. The town was very clean and quaint. There weren't any of the dogs that are usually trotting about other parts. We left Brindle back in the garden campsite. Antigua had been very well restored and maintained. As I already mentioned, there were no trucks or buses driving through town. There were loads of shops with English speaking clerks for the tourists.

All of this was very nice, but somehow lacking some of the real lived-in quality I had become used to in Quetzaltenango. We were glad we had not chosen Antigua in which to study Spanish.

Day 30
Wednesday, February 12,
Finding our way back to Atitlán

We left the walled-in garden sanctuary of our friends' home around 9:00 a.m. Their gardener unlocked the narrow door in the wall, and lifted the low telephone line with a long stick. We made our way to the street. From the outside it looked just like the other walled-in gardens. All we had to do was find our way out of town, but this was not as easy as it sounded. We followed directions we had been given until we came to three concrete stanchions, one on either side of the road and one in the middle.

There was a sign saying that the road was closed to trucks, but we started through anyway. We provided amusement for the locals who came out of their homes to watch, or paused as they easily slipped around us in their little cars. I got in front to direct. Inch by inch, John was able to get the front wheels through, then the infamous doorstep, which we had trashed on a Xela curb, then, the generator exhaust. The engine exhaust pipe was half an inch too long. If we had had a hacksaw with us we could have made it. As it was we had to admit defeat and John backed out of our tight spot admirably.

We backtracked and found a street heading toward Guatemala City. We wanted to go the other way toward Lake Atitlán, but we figured any road out of town was good. A little further along we again asked directions. A young man tried valiantly to explain how to navigate around town toward Chimaltenango. We started out and immediately made a wrong turn. Another young man who was watching our plight ran over and offered to guide us through town. We gladly accepted and welcomed him on board. He took us through a maze. We didn't seem to follow any main roads. We turned left, then right, then straight for a few blocks, left again, right again. We were finally released onto the highway out of town.

LEFT: Fountain in Central Park, Antigua, Guatemala
RIGHT: A street in Antigua, Guatemala

If you think it was unwise to permit a complete stranger on board I wouldn't agree. First of all, we like to think the best of people and have not been disappointed. Secondly, he took the passenger's seat up front and I held onto a barking Brindle in the back. Anyone who did not know better might think that we could set the vicious dog on him, but he was as trusting as we were.

We returned to Panajachel to find our tranquil campsite on Lake Atitlán waiting.

Day 31
Thursday, February 13, Atitlán

What was it about Lake Atitlán that made it so special? It was like a fantasyland. Crystal clear air and a year round spring climate made this one of the world's most pleasant places. But it was more than that. Before the sun rose from behind the volcano the lake was still, with a fisherman or two sitting motionless in their dugout canoes. Then the sharp line of sunlight opens up the valley like a door opening, and the birds start to sing. Ripples appear on the water enhanced by the motorboats plying their way to the various villages hiding out of sight in bays across the water. The water feels as deep as the sky is high, it goes on forever. There is something magical about Lake Atitlán.

The people who shared this field with us on the edge of Lake Atitlán were most interesting. Thor Janson spent most of his time in his little camper traveling Central America. He makes his living by photography and has produced some splendid books of the people and the wildlife. The pictures are classics and the information is thoughtful and interesting. He left the University of San Francisco to establish a manatee preserve in Lake Izabal, near Rio Dulce on Guatemala's Caribbean coast. His mentor and guide, Mario Dary Rivera, a professor at the University of Guatemala, was assassinated in 1981, as part of the guerilla wars down here. Now, Thor has fallen for the indigenous Mayan people. He is a free spirit, into Buckminster Fuller's synergism philosophy and all things of nature and Mayan. His next

project could be on such diverse subjects as Green Lighting, the quetzal, or on Maximon, an unusual Mayan god. He had two Mac computers and John spent some time trying to help him get them connected.

We spent an interesting evening with our new friends Carol and Bill and their friends visiting from California. We enjoyed cocktails and a potluck dinner, while watching the lake change colors. As the sun went down, the little white stallion whose field we shared went to the lake for a drink. He pawed the water and then took a roll in the shallows to cool off. Brindle was right there when he stood up. Brindle wanted to play. The horse ran off with the dog in hot pursuit. Then the horse turned in a circle and began chasing the dog. They started chasing each other. It was incredible to watch. The horse bucked and kicked up his heels high in the air as the dog raced after him. Then the stallion swung around and chased the dog. At first I thought Brindle was going to get trampled until the horse stopped and changed direction and ran away with the dog at his heels. They were jumping over ditches and leaping up the terraces and going in circles so we couldn't tell who was chasing whom. They were definitely

playing and we laughed so much we had tears in our eyes.

Sitting by Lake Atitlán at sunset, sipping good wine with new friends was one of the highlights of our trip.

Day 32
Friday, February 14,
Valentine's Day on Lake Atitlán

On the edge of Lake Atitlán we were surrounded not only by the volcanoes, but also by the high rim of the crater. The lake is in an ancient *caldera*. This meant that the sun didn't touch us until about 8:30 a.m., a very civilized hour to get up. I was suffering from the cold that John brought back from New Mexico, and decided that today would be my day for sleeping in.

When we first looked out of the window there were a dozen or so people blowing up balloons around the pool area fifty feet away from us. Others arrived as the balloons multiplied and chairs and equipment arrived. Then at 9:00 a.m., the colossal loud speakers burst into life and destroyed the tranquility of the lake. It was a Valentine's Day party for about a hundred young teenagers from a local private school.

LEFT: Afternoon at Lake Atitlán
ABOVE: Volcán San Pedro at sunrise

It was appealing to watch a couple of young teen girls, one in traditional costume and dress shoes with heels, holding hands with her girl friend wearing jeans, a T-shirt and sneakers. They all vied in spirited games and competitions. There was a costume parade; they had made Mayan outfits from feathers, tin foil and brown paper. There were dance competitions and several heats of lip-sync singers. Later they took turns standing up and making well-rehearsed presentations, explaining the importance of the traditional Mayan ways of life.

I went to use the toilets that were located near the pool, forgetting for a moment that there were over fifty teenage girls about. They had completely taken over the facilities. True, there was no indication as to which room was for men and which for women, but they were using them all. When I did eventually make my way to the only cubicle that had a door, I found six backpacks stashed around the john. I had pity for the boy who was waiting to use the toilet, and I left before he gained access. The girls were changing out of their traditional ankle-length woven skirts and *huipiles* into shorts and T-shirts. They were transforming themselves into twenty-first century kids right before my eyes. They then headed for the improvised soccer field for an all girls' game.

I was later disturbed by the kind of scream that only a teenage girl could emit. The teachers were throwing buckets of water over anyone who they could get close to. The boys had taken over the soccer field and the girls were having a ball at the pool. By the end of it everyone, boys, girls, teachers and all landed

RIGHT: Teenage girls watching the action at the Valentine's party, Hotel Vision Azul, Guatemala

up in the pool with their clothes on. I only saw one swimsuit.

So there we were, sitting in the shade of a willow tree with the most spectacular view of tranquil Lake Atitlán and her volcanoes in front of me, our little motorhome behind us buffering us from the din of music enjoyed by an audience of local adolescents. By this time they were re-clothed, some in their dry ancient styled costumes. A few of the youngsters were paddling barefoot down in the lake and others were playing soccer. Pairs of girls were innocently holding hands and couples, perhaps not so innocently, sat enjoying the view. It all seemed such a strange mix.

Day 33
Saturday, February 15, Panajachel

Today we were going to explore Panajachel. We opened Brindle's doggy-door and left her in the motorhome with admonishments to "look after the bus." Then we walked up the hill to the road and down into the town. This is a thriving little town that expects visitors, especially gringos. All along the street to the water were stalls selling colorful woven articles and other craft items. Numerous women, in the same style of dress that their ancestors wore, carried

their multi-colored wares on their heads and approached us with items for sale. Most of their products were similar to what we had purchased in Chichicastenango and a little more expensive, but they were nice; both the ladies and their products. The price variation is so small that if I had seen anything I wanted, I would have bought it.

We made note of the ferry schedule to the villages around the lake. While by the waterfront we went into the restaurant where locals were eating lunch. While waiting for our food we were sitting ducks for the children selling small items. I bought a hatband for my new hat. The trinkets were so inexpensive that I was buying them to please the children rather than because I needed them.

While waiting for our lunch I had a shoeshine. There is a definite advantage in wearing sandals: you don't get hassled by the shoeshine boys. On the other hand, who could resist this little chap? He asked for seven cents and he used his bare hands to apply the polish.

Panajachel had a surprisingly large and attractive church dating back to the middle of the sixteenth century. Unfortunately, the 1976 earthquake had taken its toll on the town and the church was the only building with any old charm left standing. The town of Panajachel itself doesn't have much

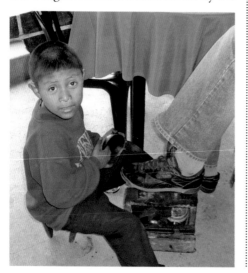

ABOVE: Panajachel Church
LEFT: Shoe shine boy, Panajachel
RIGHT: Locals on the ferry across Lake Atitlán

appeal to us except for the climate and the lake of course. It is overrun with so many tourists and foreigners who have moved in that it has become known as Gringotenango! There are language schools aplenty and students everywhere.

Wandering into the part of town where the locals shopped we found the mercado. There was nothing of interest and the produce was not very fresh. We looked at the meat in the butcher shop and, not being sure how to prepare the typically tough beef, we decided to buy some *carne molida,* ground beef, for our spaghetti dinner. The butcher selected the cut of meat and went across the street to another vendor to have it ground. Milk was our next challenge but we found some and stuffed it all in our backpacks for the climb back up the hill and down again into our secluded campsite.

Brindle was right where we had left her. She jumped out of her little door to welcome us home and we were happy to learn that she had been in and out of the motorhome all day in our absence.

The afternoon breeze over the lake is called Xocomil, and it had created little waves that rippled on the shore below us. We had another magnificent evening as the sun set and the stars came out over the valley of Lake Atitlán.

Day 34,
Sunday, February 16,
Exploring Villages around the Lake

We opened Brindle's doggie door, made sure she had plenty of water, and told her to look after the bus. She watched us wistfully as we walked away.

Knowing that it would be a full day of walking, we took a taxi up the hill from the hotel, and down to the pier at the foot of town. From the Panajachel dock we rode the ferry for a couple of dollars to Santiago Atitlán on the other side of the lake. The boat ride itself was glorious with magnificent views in all directions of the volcanoes, and the bays, and a sky so clear and blue that it felt like a dome was holding this little piece of heaven in place.

As we approached Santiago, the shore was brushed with the green crops growing in patches up the hillsides and reeds growing in and near the water. Where reeds softened the rocky shore, dugout

canoes with flat prows were lined up waiting to be pushed back into the water.

As soon as we set foot on the shore we were approached by a Tz'utuhil Mayan man in the local traditional costume wanting to be our guide. He wore pajama-like white pantaloons cut off at the knee and held up with a long woven belt wrapped around a couple of times and decorated with tassels on the ends. The time-honored pantaloons are one-size-fits-all and are embroidered with little figures or patterns that make up stripes either up and down or around the legs.

It is these distinguishing designs that identify in which village the men live. Many hours of work goes into the embroidery but none into tailoring. We frequently saw women in traditional costumes accompanied by men in jeans and T-shirt. We also came across a woman in colorful traditional clothes and a NY Yankees baseball cap.

We retained Alfredo as our escort because without a local guide you cannot find Maximon's current home. Maximon (mah-shee-mōne, with emphasis on the last syllable) is quite a character. He is a god, or perhaps he would be better described as a blend of deities who was worshipped long before the Conquistadors arrived. Now he is described as a Mayan god who has become partly the fierce Conquistador Pedro de Alvarado, who fought in Guatemala against the Mayan, and even part Judas Iscariot who betrayed Jesus. He is worshipped, perhaps with trepidation, throughout the Mayan lands and can usually be recognized by his lack of limbs, his Western style hat, and his penchant for tobacco and hard liquor.

Some people look down on him as the god of drunks and prostitutes, but here in this little village there are a whole lot of people who respect him, ask favors of him, and leave him offerings. His favorite gifts are rum and cigarettes, which might tell you a little about his character. Not knowing this ahead of time, we brought Werther's hard candies. Someone there will enjoy them, we reasoned. Each year this Maximon is moved through the village from the home of one honored town dignitary to another. This way he shares his blessings, and the material gifts no doubt, among the town elders.

We could tell by the smell of the incense down the lane that we were approaching his current home. We entered an ordinary dirt courtyard of a home of no distinction except for the pervasive incense, to find the washing line filled with colorful silk-like scarves that had been left for him. Ahead and to the right were the living quarters of the host family. Maximon was in a dark room immediately on the left with a dirt floor illuminated by candles and an unusual collection of Christmas lights.

There was a strange mix of religious emblems. On the right was a life-size figure of the crucified body of Christ lying in a glass coffin. The figure and the coffin were draped in purple and almost completely covered in gaudy silk scarves.

LEFT: Tz'utuhil Mayan man in Santiago Atitlán

There was a large, very old embossed leather chest suspended from the ceiling that was big enough to hold a corpse, but it was beyond my imagination as to what was actually in it. Sausage-like, rather phallic purple gourds, holiday lights, tinsel and plastic bunting hung all around overhead. None of the lights were on so the room had a gloomy feel to it. Against the left wall were large biblical figures that appeared to be several representations of Mary, Jesus and some of the saints. It was hard to identify them as they were all draped in uniform purple robes and smothered in multi-colored silk scarves. Just their faces and the occasional hand were visible. There were thirteen figures from two to four feet tall in this grouping, but I don't know if there was any significance in the number. There were candles and masses of fresh flowers everywhere. Great bunches were in vases and others were strung into necklaces and looped about. Further offerings were on a table in front of the biblical figures.

In the center of the room was Maximon with a cigar in his mouth and

a brown leather Stetson-styled hat on his head. He was carved from wood and didn't look very old. His features were Western and he was smothered with so many silk scarves that the rest of his body was completely hidden. Candles or other offerings could be placed in front of him or in little dishes. We put our caramel candies in the little dishes. At either side of him sat a serious looking man with his arms folded.

Other locals milled about the room and in the courtyard, but there were no local women. The over all feeling was definitely one of respect. We paid the required five dollars to take one picture of him, and placed our cash in his offering dish along with the candies. It was the dense incense that drove me out in the end, as I would have stayed longer to absorb more of the details and the atmosphere.

Back in the brilliant sunshine we continued our tour of Santiago Atitlán. We were interested in the old Franciscan church where the Mayan builders carved an ear of corn transitioning it into man. As the Bible says that man was created from the earth, the Mayans believe he was created from an ear of corn. It is not known if the missionaries noticed what was being carved, or as so often happened,

ABOVE: Franciscan Church in Santiago Atitlán
RIGHT: Maximon with attendants in Santiago

that they turned a blind eye to the blending of beliefs. There was a service going on in the church with an overflow congregation kneeling outside on the steps so there was no way we could explore inside.

In the monastery behind the church there were children playing, so I got my balloons out and we had some fun. It was pleasing to see some of the young boys and girls wearing traditional clothes, but most had the less bulky western style tailored jeans and shirts.

We left the monastery and toured the center of town. There was a large two-story market with excellent produce. It was much better than the one in Panachjel, but we didn't want to carry produce around all day. It was very hot.

Along the main street were shops and stalls that sold woven articles. One corner shop was filled with particularly finely woven and embroidered huipiles. Many were secondhand, some probably antique, and were imported from all over Guatemala. They were not cheap, some were priced at several hundred dollars, but it was the best collection I had seen. It was like a museum where you could touch everything and even try them on. The oldest had the finest stitching on thin, sometimes threadbare fabric, whereas the more modern ones had embroidery in thicker thread. Although

ABOVE: Children in the courtyard of the Santiago Monastery

LEFT: Produce market in Santiago Atitlán

some of the newer versions were machine embroidered they were just as attractive. The patterns often included the spiritual Quetzal bird, which is so important to the Mayans, and other easily identifiable representations.

Once again I couldn't bring myself to buy one of these treasures; there was no way I could use it and I have too much on my walls already. We did however make a large purchase: a six-foot purchase. A man was selling wooden birds whose bodies, necks and heads were created from the natural sweep of a tree branch. The bark was removed or left according to the preferred coloring and legs were attached separately to create a charming crane. They came in various sizes. We went for the tall freestanding version. The legs and stand detached so it wasn't too hard to carry, and with the motorhome it was a rare opportunity to take some large souvenirs home. Oh yes, the finishing touch of this tall wading bird was the little fish in its beak.

We left Santiago Atitlán and took the ferry to San Pedro La Laguna, the next village going west around the lake. This did not have as much charm, although I learned that they give classes there in traditional back-strap weaving, which I was interested in taking. There are also several language schools there and I can't imagine a more picturesque setting than to have classes under the *palapas* in this outdoor classroom.

We had lunch and took the ferry back to Panajachel. We staggered in the heat up and over the hill to our camp. From the top there was a good view of the

Hotel Vision Azul with our motorhome under the trees. We couldn't pick out the dog but that was probably because she was waiting behind the wheel.

Day 35
Monday, February 17, A Day in Panajachel

We went back into Panajachel and did a little more shopping. An English lady operated one of the first shops on the right at the beginning of town. When Prudence retired she moved to Lake Atitlán with her husband. We English like a good cup of tea and she couldn't buy it there. She also found that the numerous U.S. gringos missed their comfort foods like peanut butter and Cornflakes. She opened a shop to provide these items as well as quite a good selection of wine.

TOP RIGHT: A collection of high class huipiles in Santiago Atitlán
RIGHT: A language school in San Pedro La Laguna, on Lake Atitlán

She seems to be doing a good trade even though her prices are way too high for the indigenous residents.

While we were wandering around the town another English lady bicycled up to us. Margaret had lived there for twenty years supporting herself by baking and selling bread to visitors. From out of her bicycle basket she produced an admirable selection along with some cookies. A gathering of expatriates quickly surrounded her. Good bread is hard to find in Central America, as there aren't many of the *panaderias* that are found throughout Mexico. We usually had to be content with sliced, packaged white bread. Margaret's baking was a treat.

The craft shops and stalls overflowed into the streets and there was plenty to amuse me until John decided that it was time for a cool beer and lunch back at the bus.

Day 36
Tuesday, February 18, Departure from Atitlán

This was our last morning on the lake. It was another serene dawn followed by a picture perfect sunrise. The sun rose behind the rim of the *caldera* and lit the far volcano and then the south side of the lake long before it reached our shore or the fisherman in his little dugout canoe.

We were sad to leave, but at 8:30 a.m. we were driving up the hill from our campsite promising that we would return. We were heading for the Copán Ruins across the border in Honduras. On the recommendation of Thor Janson we decided to make a detour and visit Esquipulas in Guatemala near the border.

Our route took us back up the very steep hill, through the narrow streets of

ABOVE: Looking down at the Hotel Vision Azul campsite
RIGHT: Terraced Fields West of Guatemala

Sololá, to the Pan-American Highway. We had to transit Guatemala City in order to take the eastbound highway toward Puerto Barrios and the Caribbean. We were lucky to have received specific directions from Thor on how to by-pass the city. Tour books and maps do not do justice to the problem of navigating through or around Central American cities, and they don't show the one-way streets. Guatemala City is one of the worst. There are two big problems: most roads do not have street signs; and many of the roads are one-way. In our case Thor's directions helped us avoid the pitfalls of most travelers. We've included these directions in the reference section. We deliberately avoided the big cities of Central America. If we wanted to visit them or see them again, we would fly in without the motorhome or the dog.

The narrow road towards Guatemala City wound through steep hills rich in vegetation. The hills were dotted with homes, each with its plot of land under cultivation that had been cut from the wooded slopes. Steep terraces had been sliced into the mountainsides, and as they stepped up they would change in color from green to deep green to bare dirt, or brown with dead corn stalks. Livestock was tethered at the roadside, as this was grass that was not to be wasted.

The homes were small and of adobe with tile roofs, some clustered together in little pueblos and others scattered on the slopes. Some had tin roofs, which did not look as charming, but they would have been considerably safer during an earthquake.

On the northern outskirts of Guatemala City we were looking for the by-pass, or *periférico*. We found it at the large suburban city of El Progreso, and to our pleasure we found a Hiperpaiz supermarket at the turnoff. We took full advantage and stocked up on the items that we couldn't find in the little mercado. John likes his Raisin Bran for

breakfast and we could also get cheese, yogurt and other luxuries that we missed from back home.

The *periférico* lasted about five miles before we were forced to exit and make our way through typical congested Central American city streets, but we quickly found ourselves on highway CA9 leading to the east.

The highway was a narrow two-lane road clogged with 18-wheelers carrying goods to and from the deep-water port of Puerto Barrios. We were still in the mountains and being passed on the winding roads was hair raising. Eventually the mountains became hills, and the hills became plains, and the driving became much more tranquil and civilized. Ninety-four miles east of Guatemala City we came to our turnoff at the small village of Rio Hondo. We turned south on CA10 towards Honduras and El Salvador.

The roads in this part of Guatemala are in perfect condition, not like the pothole filled roads in the highlands. We enjoyed the journey; it was some of the prettiest scenery we had passed through and it was a pleasure to be able to relax and look up from the road surface to enjoy the views. But once again the drive took longer than anticipated. Perhaps we had taken too long shopping. Our rule was to not drive after dark, but on this occasion we pressed on to reach Esquipulas. Thor Janson had told us we could camp behind the local chicken restaurant in Esquipulas, *Pollo Campero;* the Colonel's counterpart for fried chicken in Guatemala. Actually it was only really dark for the last twenty minutes or so, but this bit of road was very dark and winding as we were coming into mountainous terrain again. We didn't feel comfortable at all

driving in the dark. There are too many obstacles on the road and we were tired after one of the longest driving days of the trip. We had gone two hundred and twenty miles.

When we reached Esquipulas there was a fork in the road. It was very dark and there were no signs. By chance we drove left and immediately John saw the sign for *Pollo Campero.* We pulled into the parking lot behind the restaurant. After confirming that we could stay there overnight with the ever-present automatic rifle toting *vigilante,* or hired guard, we dropped our blinds and relaxed.

Day 37
Wednesday February 19, Esquipulas

Called by the ringing of the Basilica bells a block away, the dog and I set out to explore early in the morning. The only people around were the variously uniformed and armed guards, some carrying nasty looking big guns, and the orange juice salesman. The guards must have reported to different forces because the uniforms varied significantly from light and dark blue to tan. I asked one if I could take his picture, as he looked smart in his clean pressed military uniform and a New York Yankees baseball cap. He declined. I guess the uniform doesn't include the headwear. He was friendly in spite of the two-foot machine gun he hefted.

I ordered two orange juices from the vendor. He whipped off the tops of eight oranges with slashes from a small machete and squeezed the juice out of them in a great crushing machine and strained it into parfait glasses. Then he poured it into plastic bags and popped a straw into each. I delivered John's to him in bed, gathered my camera, and returned to the Basilica.

The town is named after the Mayan chief who welcomed the Spanish instead of fighting them. In 1595, a figure of Christ on the Cross was carved from black wood and installed in a church built on a site that had been the center of Mayan pilgrimages. In 1737, the Catholic Archbishop joined the many pilgrims and was cured of his ailment. He subsequently built this basilica (a church with a broad nave ending in a domed roof) that has withstood many earthquakes. Receiving pilgrims is the main industry here: even the Pope came.

There were a couple of large fields to accommodate cars and buses. If we had arrived earlier they would have made a better campsite away from the lights and the pedestrians, although there would have been a small fee to pay.

English speaking Benedictine monks from Louisiana care for the facility but we couldn't find one to ask why, or to delve into other interesting aspects of the area.

In the touristy mercado they sold a multitude of religious articles and also silly straw hats with all sorts of colorful baubles hanging from the wide rim. No one could tell us the significance of the hats, but numerous visitors were buying them or having customized ones made. Fortunately I had my new cowboy hat so was not tempted. The visitors to the area were mostly from Guatemala and neighboring countries, and no one was evident who spoke English.

The entrance to see the Black Christ was at the side of the basilica.

They were obviously set up for large numbers of pilgrims but we were almost alone and walked zigzag around the Disneyland-like queuing area. We

entered the church and climbed a ramp leading to the figure of the Black Christ. We came into the church behind the figure as though through a back door. Heavy stone walls closed in on us.

I was particularly taken by the grouping of women figures around him within the glass case. The women must have been made at a later date and were not quite to scale. That didn't detract from the caressing manner in which Mary Magdalene embraced the cross. The devotion displayed by the pilgrims around us was humbling. When leaving the statue they walked backwards, down and around a long ramp until they were out of sight of the figures.

Even though the Mass was over, most of the few pews were filled. There were more candles than I'd seen in the morning. The reverence was palpable. Family groups sat in clusters all over the floor praying and talking. A man in his farm clothes, with a woven bag over his shoulder and a machete in his belt was standing candles in rows on the wax covered floor

RIGHT: Black Christ in the Basilica of Esquipulas

and lighting them. A deep layer of candle wax covered the stone slabs.

It was striking, but it didn't have the impact of the little church in San Juan Chamula in Chiapas where the floor was covered in pine needles and crowded with people in costume. This was a large basilica with a larger congregation operated by Catholics, where these locals had found their own way to worship.

After leaving town just before noon we hit our second misadventure of the trip. We were stopped by the *Policía National Civil Guatemala.* They examined our papers in a grumbly sort of way. We had been stopped before by much more pleasant *Policía* who checked our papers. These guys were not so friendly but let us back on our way. Not ten minutes later we heard a hissing noise above the usual rattles of the motorhome. We decided that it was crickets or the wind in the window until

we heard the familiar flop, flop, flop of a flat tire. We were close to the town of Quezaltepeque, on a wide two-lane road and had room to pull off on the right shoulder. It was time to see if our preparations for this sort of problem were adequate.

It was very dry and hot. John was great and declined any assistance; he changed the tire in about an hour. Not bad seeing it was a first time and there were a lot of instructions to read. It took me almost that long to work out how to assemble the reflective triangle to put out on the road behind us.

He had just about finished when two cars pulled up with four men. One man came to the window and looked in. I didn't like him and neither did Brindle.

ABOVE: Man at prayer and inside the Basilica of Esquipulas, Guatemala
RIGHT: Interior of Basilica in Esquipulas

I heard John saying *"No gracias"* to the other men, so I waved the man looking in the window away. He then went to the back of the bus and started to climb up the ladder at the back, and was peering in that window. He was rocking the bus all over the place and I was worried about John under the jacked up vehicle. I went outside and firmly told the man we didn't need his help and to get down. The dog was going wild inside. 'Good dog!' I thought. I really think that Brindle deterred them from any nefarious thoughts they might have had.

On the road again. It was only about ten miles to the turnoff for the El Florido border crossing into Honduras. We were anticipating an easy border crossing and an early arrival at Copán Ruinas. This was not to be.

The highway from CA10 to El Florido was, until recently, a dirt road.

Many of the older tour books warned against passing this way in anything but a 4WD vehicle. Now the road is paved and it provides a pleasant winding route through a series of hills and valleys. Many day-trippers pass this way from Guatemala City to see the Mayan Ruins at Copán.

We found a spot for lunch overlooking a river just beyond the little town of Jocotán. We were parked in a clear patch of land where workmen were constructing a building. There were boys swimming in the river and I might have joined them in spite of the brown water if I had been able to climb down the twenty-foot cliff. The owner of the property came up and explained that it was his motel across the road with two swimming pools and that he was building a restaurant where we had parked that would be open for *Semana Santa*.

Later, a young Peace Corps volunteer from the States came up a path along the river. Robby was spending his time wandering the local hills teaching the locals about sanitation. We learned from him that the area did have fresh potable water. The owner of the hotel, Sr. Romilo Daniel Sandoval, made us very welcome and insisted that he wanted other motorhomes to stop there or at his hotel.

After lunch we headed off to the border a mere dozen miles off. John then realized that he didn't have his wallet. No amount of searching helped. We returned to the lunch stop. We thought maybe John dropped it there and that one of the kids picked it up. Sr. Sandoval assured us that he and one of the laborers would check with the boys who had been hanging around to see if they had picked it up. We feel that it must have dropped out of John's pocket either when changing the tire or at this location when he was trying to re-inflate the tire. Anyway, no wallet. Sr. Sandoval told us to call him at home the next day and he would have word on whether any of the children in the area had picked it up.

We turned around again and continued to the border. Aside from a few credit cards and personal family photos, the most valuable item in the wallet was John's driver's license. The credit cards could be easily cancelled, and we had backup cards from different accounts stashed in the RV for just such an emergency.

CHAPTER 4
The Sands of Honduras

SAILING IN
LOS CAYOS COCHINOS

*I shall be telling this with a sigh
Somewhere ages and ages hence:
Two roads diverged in a wood, and I—
I took the one less traveled by,
And that has made all the difference.*

THE ROAD NOT TAKEN
Robert Frost

IT COST US $1 EACH TO GET OUT of Guatemala, and they raised the gate that blocked our exit from the country. We had lost a lot of time backtracking and looking for John's driver's license, however, we still hoped to speed through this border and make the town of Copán Ruinas before dark.

Fifty yards beyond Guatemala we approached a string across the road that marked the Honduras line. It had little strips of plastic dangling from it so you could see it more easily. The immigration, customs and quarantine departments were housed in an old wooden plank building. To conduct our business we had to bend down to

89

talk through little windows to the officials inside.

Immigration was easy; we just completed the same form all Central American countries use at all the crossings and had our passports stamped. Customs was most interested in the vehicle and just wouldn't believe it had ten cylinders. The clerk needed to complete his form. *"Cuantos cilindros?"*

"Diez," I replied

"No. Seis u ocho? Cuantos cilindros?" He kept repeating. He wanted to know if it was six or eight cylinders. He would not believe that our little motorhome had ten cylinders. Eventually I showed him what was written on the hood. Fortunately we didn't have to remove the bicycles and lift the hood for him to count the actual cylinders.

He also wanted to know if we had air-conditioning and a radio, and how many doors and seats. He needed to make sure that we are not importing car seats and that we took out whatever we brought in.

We had decided not to mention the dog to see what would happen, but she was hard to miss when the official came to count the seats and cylinders. He called his colleagues from quarantine.

While John handled the car documents I was led to a fourth office in the building and this time I was invited inside to do my business. The short story of a long hour is that we could only get a two-week transit pass for Brindle and that the eighty dollars I paid to the consulate in Houston didn't mean a thing. I had to show the USDA documentation and pay this agent 150 *lempiras* ($10). Most important, I had to show the agent the paperwork from the Nicaraguan consulate giving permission for Brindle to enter that country once we left

Honduras. I think we might have been able to get a longer transit had I said in the beginning that we were going to take three or four weeks instead of two. Also, they told us we could get an extension at an international airport within Honduras if we decided to stay longer. The agent also documented the border crossing where we said we would be leaving Honduras.

During these formalities John saw several mangy stray dogs wandering between Guatemala and Honduras. When he questioned the quarantine official on this point he shrugged and said, "but they are local dogs."

Once again we were looking for a place to camp in the falling darkness. Copán Ruinas, the town adjacent to the Ruins of Copán, is quite charming, but again the streets were narrow and cobbled. As we worked our way into the central square, several young men approached us asking if we needed a hotel room. They apparently weren't aware that this big bus we were in doubled as a bedroom, and they wanted their commission for finding us a room.

We spotted a tourist information office off the main square and I was able to pull over and leave just enough space for a car to pass. The young girl in the office was very helpful and even spoke some English. She told us that we could camp at a small establishment outside the cemetery. We were given the name of a lady whose house we were to look for, Doña Belia. Following directions down the narrow lanes in the darkness, we failed to notice a low hanging telephone wire, which we snared on our air conditioning housing. We pulled over too late. John was about to climb on the roof of

RIGHT: Cemetery in town of Copán Ruinas

the motorhome and try to fix it, when a policeman came by to survey the damage. A lady came out of the house, arms waving, complaining that her phone didn't work and pointing accusingly at the fallen line and us. I was wondering what the jail cells would be like in town. John tried to understand the rapid conversation between the policeman, the lady and several supposed witnesses, more of which were gathering as we spoke. There was much discussion and pointing. In the end, the policeman declared that the wire was hung too low and that we were in the clear. He urged us to move on. We did.

We found Doña Belia's home and she showed us where to park on the flat gravel three feet in front of her porch. She had a little shop, and the first thing we did was to ask her for a couple of beers. Bottles were 10 *lempiras* (60 cents) each and cans were 20 *lempiras*. I got the bottles. It was good to relax after a taxing day, even if we were between a village shop and a cemetery. After finishing the first beers, we were ready for a second. I returned the bottles and had to buy cans, as she didn't stock more than two bottles. She was really nice, and we made balloon animals for the six children who were running about. She offered to fix us up with a guide and horses for a ride in the countryside for the next day. We accepted.

Wandering back towards town with Brindle following along, we quickly passed the scene of the broken phone line and found a little restaurant for dinner. We were the only customers. The restaurant had a satellite TV hookup and the owner agreed to change the television channel from a Spanish soap opera to CNN in English. Brindle under the table never attracted a second glance.

Day 38
Thursday, February 20
Horse Ride at Copán Ruinas

While I was taking Brindle for her morning walk through the cemetery adjacent to our campsite, I met one of the workers sitting on one of the mausoleums eating his breakfast. He told me that the Mayans used to sleep on the graves of their ancestors. They would

build the sepulchers in their homes and use them for their beds. According to my new friend, the original graves in that cemetery were below ground, but when people had the means they started to built sepulches above ground. Today they build above ground if they can afford it. Unfortunately the age of plastic is with us and besides the plastic flowers, the locals decorate the graves with plastic strips that become tattered and faded.

Back at the bus, our priority was to get the flat tire fixed. But yesterday had been a long day and somehow time passed and the guide we were promised would take us for our mid morning ride arrived before we could deal with the tire.

While we were relaxing before our guide arrived we had another mishap. A scrawny young chicken had been scratching about in the dirt beside the motorhome. Doña Belia's grandson, a three year old toddler, yelled out, "¡El lo mató!" (He killed it!) The toddler was pointing to the pullet while looking accusingly at Brindle.

Doña Belia didn't seem at all concerned. We offered to pay for it but she would have none of it. We felt very bad, but it seemed that she wasn't really worried. She just walked off saying "pobre pollito" (poor little chicken).

I hope some of our readers will visit her and purchase from her shop. It was a good place to camp. We felt very bad and determined to keep a closer watch on our killer dog.

Alfredo, our young teenaged guide, walked us the couple of blocks to where the horses were waiting and we mounted up. Alfredo set off on foot to lead the way. It was very hot and I was not comfortable with him walking up into the hills while we rode, but he insisted it was fine. Five minutes later while we were walking through town on the cobbled road we heard a great clatter of a horse running on the cobbles. Alfredo's grandfather, who had tended our animals, was cantering up to us. He dismounted and gave the new mount to our guide. We were all relieved.

I have been on better rides as it was a little uncomfortable walking on the rough stone road; it was more of a trek.

During the ride we could see a small part of one of the Copán temples,

LEFT: Doña Belia's flower covered store and home, Copán Ruinas.
ABOVE: Our horses are waiting, Copán Ruinas, Honduras

showing white against the green under-growth, as well as the town of Copán Ruinas below us. The Copán River was diverted by University of Pennsylvania archaeologists because it was eating into the ruins every time there was a flood.

Our trip of about an hour-and-a-half took us to Hacienda San Lucas, an attractively restored Spanish colonial house high on the hill. It had thick walls and high ceilings and a long deep veranda, all contributing to keeping the house cool. We relaxed in hammocks, watching the exotic birds.

At San Lucas they still use the old oven to cook outside, but they have solar power and hot water. The oven was away from the house to keep the home cooler. The rooms run $60 per night and you can make your own tortillas to eat with the traditional meals.

ABOVE: Hacienda San Lucas in the hills above the Copán Ruins, Honduras
RIGHT: In the mountains behind Copán, Honduras.

Alfredo led us, on foot, along a jungle walk, down a well maintained path following a little stream, and out into the sun. We passed a watering hole that the local Mayans still use and came to the area known as *"El hospital."* There was a carved toad and lizard, and a clear depiction of a woman giving birth, all carved into the boulders embedded deep in the hillside. This is a 1400-year-old maternity ward. Pregnant women were meant to put their stomachs on the stone toad in

order to have a healthy child. It might have lost something in the translation but I'm glad I have my OB/GYN.

We reclaimed our mounts and rode slowly back down the rocky road, the horses going carefully on the uncomfortable footing. We were following the river and we could look down to where cars had been driven into the water and were being washed. A pickup truck was being loaded with river sand by a couple of men with shovels.

We had to move the horses off the side of the gravel road when a car came along. I was just saying to John to hold on and be alert when his horse shied and slipped down the drop to the bank of the

river. John said he decided to slide off! In any case, in an instant he was lying in the grass with this surprised look on his face. The horse stood over him. Fortunately both were completely unhurt. John remounted and we walked back through the village to the motorhome.

The ancient ruins are a couple of miles away from the town, so in order to be sure of a parking place, and be there first thing in the morning ahead of the tour buses, we elected to move that afternoon.

Again we tried to pay Doña Belia for watching the bus for us, and for the young chicken, but she wouldn't take our money. They are really nice people around here. I was glad that I had bought some things from her earlier and given the children balloons the evening before.

Looking around for something else to buy from her I asked about the long pointed green buds of an agave on her counter that I hadn't seen before. She showed me that inside the sheaf were the buds of a myriad of little flowers clustered on fronds. She said they were best chopped up and cooked with scrambled eggs. I bought them and prepared it for dinner just as she described. It might need an acquired taste, or a better cook. We didn't cook up a second batch.

We moved to the Texaco station next to the Ruins entrance, and parked in a corner. It wasn't pretty, but it was close and secure. They also fixed the leaky valve on the spare tire for $2.

Day 39
Friday, February 21, Copán Ruins

There were several guides hanging around the ticket booth for Copán

TOP LEFT: Grinding the maize into masa for tortillas in the outdoor kitchen of Hacienda San Lucas
LEFT: 1400 year-old toad and lizard carvings at Copán

Ruins when we arrived at opening time. We decided to hire one to get full advantage of our visit.

The park entrance is about 200 yards behind the ticket booth and meeting place. Dogs were not permitted in the park. We took Brindle up the long walk to the gate with her bucket of water in hand. We couldn't leave her running about the garage as there was too much traffic, and the motorhome was too hot.

There were several scarlet macaws squawking near the entrance and flying about freely. They attracted Brindle's interest. Not wanting another dead bird incident we backtracked a ways and tied her under the trees away from the footpath but where she could watch people. We asked the guard to keep an eye on her and when we returned a few hours later he said she had been *"muy tranquila"* (very tranquil or calm).

It is the stone stairs and stelae that make the ruins at Copán so important. These are the only Mayan ruins that contain a written history. Most of the hieroglyphs are about one dynasty, and the history they kept on these stelae and other carvings now enable archaeologists to decipher their lives. The discovery is an ongoing process. First signs of civilization here date from about 1200 B.C. and the place seems to have been deserted by 1200 A.D. The dynasty of particular interest was from 628 to 755 A.D. One of the rulers commissioned a stairway as a record of his family history. Those cleverer than I, can trace the family and the exact dates by linking the dates the stelae were dedicated with celestial events. The historians can be chronologically exact because of the Mayan counting system. In their numerical system there are

RIGHT: Macaws at Copán Ruins

drawings of various heads that represent units of tens, bars represent fives and dots are ones. But you don't count it if the dot has a hole in the middle. As I said, someone far cleverer than I worked it all out.

A recent study of some bones found here has revealed that the early people who lived here were very healthy, whereas the later inhabitants were not. This has led to the theory that over population, over farming the delicate soils, and the failure to rotate the crops led to chronic malnutrition and depletion of

calcium. The result was shorter people who didn't live as long. Life expectancy towards the end of the period decreased so much that children between the ages of five and fifteen were dying, and these normally would be the most resilient population. This was the current theory for why the Mayan Civilization had vanished around the thirteenth century.

The T-shaped main ball court is small in comparison to those in other parts of the Americas, and is therefore thought to be for just two players. At the top of the sloping walls, three stone Macaw heads are the goals. The ball, shaped like an oval US football, was made of solid rubber and weighed about eight pounds. It had to be propelled by legs, hips and elbows.

This was not an easy sport and each game is thought to have lasted several days. Players truly gave their all as they were frequently sacrificed at the end. There is debate, however, as to whether it was the winners or losers who had this privilege.

For the past thirty years an ugly green tarpaulin has protected the precious inscribed stairway from the elements. The stairway is like a giant open book and doesn't lead anywhere, but the inscriptions take us back in time. The canopy detracts from the impact but is obviously necessary.

Among other buildings at Copán is one large pyramid that is great in itself, but it was built over another temple that was considered so important that the builders made sure that they didn't damage it. This original temple is the carefully preserved Santa Rosa Temple, that was only discovered about ten years ago. We could have paid an additional $10 each to grovel through the tunnels that led to the buried temple, but we decided

to visit the reconstructed life-sized model in the museum instead. Our guide had a chat with the *vigilante* and reported back that if we returned later we could slip the guard a "fiver," and get in.

The ruins were grand. They are not as grand and imposing as Tikal, but the carvings are very intricate and well-preserved. They are like filigree in stone. It was hard to believe that someone with primitive tools two thousand years ago could carve all those loops and swirls so delicately into stone. It must have been quite a society to have artisans this skilled dedicated to stone carving.

Our guide, Juan, had been interesting, but not for the right reasons. He was tall, lanky and had a wizened face, which he kept shaded by a broad brimmed straw hat. He had been around for a long time, and moved slowly and deliberately. He kind of reminded me of Boris Karlov. He spoke five languages and could greet people in a couple of dozen others. He

ABOVE: The Ball Court at Copán

claimed to be in the *Guinness Book of Records* for most languages spoken. Juan knew the archaeologists on a first name basis and he had translated scientific articles for them. While we were walking around he greeted the head scientist of the current research project and had a little discussion with him. I think Juan knew his stuff, but unfortunately, he said very little of interest unless we asked him. It was like he was out for a stroll with us and if we wanted to know anything we had to ask him.

We reclaimed the dog and wandered over to the museum and tethered her up again. This time she wasn't so happy and for about five minutes we could hear her yelps echoing throughout the museum, which was open to the sky. We disclaimed her during this performance.

The entrance to the museum is as the Mayans might have constructed it. You walk through the gaping jaws of a serpent along a tunnel that winds underground until you turn a bend and are suddenly confronted by the Santa Rosa Temple.

It is a replica, of course, but it has quite an impact. It is about 25 feet high by 80

feet wide 30 feet deep and it is painted in the original colors of burnt red with green, yellow and white trim to emphasize the designs. It was awesome. This was how the inhabitants of Copán would have seen it two thousand years ago.

We left the Ruins and headed for the motorhome. We needed to resolve our first medical situation. John had a most uncomfortable lump on his behind and needed to see a doctor. We had seen a doctor's office in town. Not wanting to move the motorhome, as shaded parking was at a premium and feeling that the dog deserved a walk, we went on foot the couple of miles into town. We walked along the pleasant pathway noting the occasional stelae at the side of the road and in the pasture with the cows.

The doctor's office was along the street but it was locked. As we headed away the doctor came running from the hardware store across the road. He was more than happy to help us. No appointment was necessary and no waiting, which is normal for private clinics in Central America. The public clinics are always crowded.

Unglamorous but true, John had a "boil on his butt" which is locally known as an absceso. Dr. Cuevas gave

ABOVE: Copán Stelae
RIGHT: Replica of the Santa Rosa Temple

him a supply of penicillin tablets and a prescription for ibuprofen and sent him on his way. The total cost was $10. It was all very clean, efficient and inexpensive.

Day 40
Saturday, February 22,
Copán to Tela on the Caribbean

We were up and ready to make an early start. Today we were finally going to encounter the Caribbean. We were anxious to get to our goal: Tela, a town recommended to us for its casual Caribbean atmosphere and beaches.

We were about to move into a position where we could fill our water tank when I discovered the fridge was not working. The fridge was the one thing that we felt there was no chance locals could repair. This could be grim. I didn't look forward to warm milk and having to buy it each day. Ugh! No ice in John's Scotch! Really grim! I put the one piece of meat that had thawed into the crock-pot with some veggies to cook, piled the frozen stuff into our bed with

the pillows and bedding as insulation and defrosted the freezer. I was done in an hour and the fridge worked again. Phew! We never had another problem with it.

In the meantime, John discovered that the city water was not on, so we couldn't refill our tank. The water was running the night before. Lesson learned: top off the water tank whenever you can, even if you don't need it! Also, don't let the "snow" build up in the freezer, which happens so quickly with all the humidity.

We still managed to pull out at 8:40 a.m. We had a good road surface to drive on which makes all the difference for us, even though it was a narrow two-lane road winding around the hills. There were few cars so it was a pleasant easy drive. We were doing about 35 mph most of the time through steep, verdant hills. We wound down a gentle gradient with precipitous grassy slopes of green rising and falling around us. Trees were dotted about, adding rich emerald patches of shadow. Green hills beyond

green hills faded into soft blue ridges in the distance and blended into the sky. It was hard to take it all in and the camera certainly didn't do justice to the scale.

The dog was relaxed traveling with us. Her favorite place was lying on the couch when we were moving. The problem was that today she had to fight John for it, as he was more comfortable reclining than sitting because of his boil. So Brindle road shotgun with her head out of the window; ears flapping, nose pointing.

As we descended out of the hills, it became hotter and more humid. I was happy to notice that women were wearing shorts in Honduras. That was enough for me to break out mine, and give my white slug-like legs some sun and air. John was a day ahead of me.

Coffee groves gave way to corn and tobacco, which in turn yielded to fields of sugar cane as we came down out of the mountains. There was a lot of livestock.

LEFT: Hills south of Copán
ABOVE: Tela, Honduras

Great looking cattle and horses were being used for transportation. This was really lush land compared to yesterday up in the dry mountains around Copán.

We almost totally missed the town of Tela, as there is no sign for it. We were backtracking on the main road looking for the propane dealership when we saw the sign from the other direction. We trundled into the little community of about six thousand people. The town consisted of wood and cement block two story buildings abutting the narrow streets. Roofs overhang the streets to protect pedestrians from torrential rains.

Tela has about ten square blocks bounded on the north by the Caribbean Sea. We parked and explored on foot and soon felt we knew where things were. Thor Janson, our author friend from Lake Atitlán, told us we could park in the Tourist Police parking lot in Tela. This is a large enclosed parking lot near the beach. Baking cement with no shade was not very appealing. There was a small building next to the parking lot that housed an office, storage room and a restroom. We poked our heads into the office. A young officer was behind the desk next to a fan. When he saw us he sprang to his feet and greeted us with a friendly smile. This was Officer Carlos of the Tourist Police. He was a typical short, stocky officer in an immaculate uniform. Yes, for five dollars we could park in their lot for the night. Carlos wanted to do anything he could to make our stay enjoyable. We could hook up for water and electricity in their bathroom (water from the sink faucet). Only problem was that these utilities were shut down at night. When we told Carlos that we were hoping for a location with more atmosphere, maybe on the beach, he jumped to the phone and quickly found us a place about five miles west of town at a beach resort. He offered to lead us there.

We said we would be back with the motorhome. Walking back to the motorhome we passed a launderette (never miss an opportunity) and found the offices of Garífuna Tours that Thor had recommended. We signed up for a trip the following day to Punta Sal National Park that is noted for animal spotting and snorkeling opportunities.

Returning in the motorhome to the police headquarters, Carlos and his friend told us to follow them. They led us in a truck for thirty minutes down a dirt road to the Tela Beach Club, a.k.a. Honduras Shores Plantation. We could probably have found it without them, but it was very good of them to make the effort. Then they disappeared before we could tip them. Most unusual! Tela was the only place on the trip that had "Tourist Police." Their job was to help tourists. We were most grateful.

An armed guard greeted us as we arrived at the club. They had been expecting us.

The Beach Club has a pool in pleasant surroundings with shade and palms, and a very pleasant beach and masses of security. We had decided before arriving at this "resort" that it would be nice to spend a night in a real bed, with cable TV. We were prepared to pay for a room for the night. We were escorted into the offices of Señor Roberto Lazarus Lozano, *Presidente Ejecutivo*. The Honduras Beach Plantation is a housing development. They were looking for gringo investors to buy real estate and we sure looked like candidates. Mr. Lazarus was a distinguished gentleman with a friendly businesslike manner. We had been out of civilization for a while and our encounter was a welcome glimpse of "reality" again. His English was about as good as our Spanish, so we switched between languages as we spoke about the project.

The home-sites are situated on a narrow isthmus between the sea and a large lagoon. They had some cottages near the lagoon which were for rent by the night, but we were disappointed to learn that they were sold out. There were not many places to park the motorhome out of the blazing sun, but they directed us to a secluded spot near the cottages in the shade of a mango tree. It was a five-minute walk back to the clubhouse, pool and bar.

The surroundings were decidedly pleasant. We could see the lagoon at the back of our parking spot. There were connections outside the cottages for water and electricity. Armed vigilantes regularly visited us as they did their rounds.

There are *vigilantes* everywhere for anything that might need protecting. The supermarkets usually have a couple *vigilantes* and of course all the banks have them oozing out of the doors. They are very polite and open doors for you with their automatic rifles casually slung over their shoulders. They nod a greeting as you are hit with the icy blast of the air-conditioned interior. Most are veterans of various conflicts in Central America. Not quite the Wal-Mart greeters we are used to.

We spent the rest of the day sampling the beach, the pool and most importantly their great piña coladas. We later awarded the prize to the Tela Beach Club for the best piña coladas on our trip. Dinner was waiting in our crock-pot.

Day 41
Sunday, February 23, Exploring Tela

The wind was up and the day was gray and overcast. We left Brindle with the motorhome, with the doggy door open, hoping that there weren't any hungry crocodiles in the lagoon. We walked to the road at the clubhouse. We had ordered a taxi for the trip into town, but it was late. This gave us the opportunity to socialize with the gaggle of *vigilantes* gathered around the guard-shack by the road. The night shift was getting off and the day shift was arriving. Although in fatigues with automatic rifles slung across their backs, this was a congenial, friendly lot. The day crew was drinking coffee. They all assured us that our RV and our dog would be safe while we went off to town.

The tour involved a one-hour boat ride along the coast to Punta Sal. When we arrived in town we found out the tour was canceled because the wind had whipped up the waves and the ride would have been uncomfortable in a small boat. There were about eight tourists in addition to us, and the tour-

company offered to substitute a tour around the Lagoon instead of Punta Sal. We opted to pass on this. We had gathered for the tour in a bamboo hut on the river's edge above the small boat dock. They had a little internet café, so we had breakfast and then tried to relay some messages home. It was a struggle to send anything as the machines were old and the connections were slow. We were trying to send long narratives along with pictures to about forty people. It just wasn't happening. We got something through so the family at least knew we were still going strong.

It was still early morning, so we took a walk on the beach in front of the town. Families were gathered in clusters, children were running around and everyone seemed to be cooking something. Then we heard music. It was Sunday morning but it wasn't church music. Down the beach there was a building emanating a Latin beat. There was a big burly bouncer outside and loads of folks of all ages inside doing the Salsa or its Honduran equivalent. This was a Saturday night party that hadn't broken up yet! We were not into that scene, so we decided to head for the market. The market didn't

RIGHT: Sign at the Tela Beach Club, Honduras

have any fish that looked appetizing or produce that looked very fresh, so it seemed this would be a good evening to eat at the Club.

We caught a much less expensive taxi back to the club and found Brindle sitting in the front seat waiting for us. We spent the afternoon poolside relaxing under filtered sun and enjoyed a pleasant dinner by the pool.

Brindle had a fun time on the walk from the clubhouse back to the motorhome in the dark. She just couldn't make out the fireflies. She kept going further and further into this grassy field, prancing and bounding like Bambi, but could never quite get to one. She had never seen fireflies before.

Day 42
Monday, February 24
A Boat Ride to Punta Sal

We hadn't ordered a taxi to take us to town today because we were unsure about the weather and would not go into town if it was cloudy and rough again. And we knew there was a bus that left soon after seven. It was a glorious day. We waited for the bus. It didn't come! Then along came a taxi. We asked him how much to town, and he said 30 *Lempiras*. This was interesting as the taxi the previous day cost two hundred! The bus was seven each but we splurged at an extra expense of about a dollar US.

This time John was ready for the internet café and had brought a disk with our correspondence on it. We were early at the bamboo hut and he was able to dispatch two more of our reports before the tour. We were almost up to date with our dispatches. We had time to explore the little hut before our tour left. Upstairs was a museum of the Garífuna people. There wasn't much to show, just a few photos and a dusty reconstruction of a hut.

The boat ride to Punta Sal was exhilarating in the early morning sun. We sped across the water and could pick out

Tela Beach Club as we passed by. The peninsula looked like the tropical island of my dreams. This was straight out of the picture books. The first bay we pulled into was where we would return for lunch. The guide needed to alert the residents to catch fish for our lunch. There was no phone and their only access to the outside world was by boat. The residents lived in a couple of thatched huts nestled in the shade of the palms at the foot of gentle jungle-covered hills. Palms lined the curving beach where a couple of skiffs rested on the white sand. The deep blue water complemented the sky until the water became shallow and turned turquoise as the white sand shone through.

The residents acknowledged us and we motored along the peninsula, where the jungle growth came down the gray rocks and drooped towards the sea. Little palms were growing out of the cliffs wherever they could sink their roots between the smooth layers of rock. We pulled into a tiny bay and clambered out into the water and up the sand for a walk through *el bosque* (the jungle). The peninsula was narrow at this point and we were going to cross it and pick up the boat again on the other side.

Yes, we saw monkeys, howler monkeys in fact, which are usually very reclusive. The noisy male looked pretty big and responded on cue when our guide howled.

The park on Punta Sal is named for conservationist Janette Kowas, who was killed by those who didn't appreciate her efforts. This is the second person we were aware of who has met the same sad

LEFT: Punta Sal has beaches and a rocky cliff
RIGHT: Swampy jungle with spike covered palms on Punta Sal, Honduras

and violent fate in Central America while working for conservation.

Parts of the park were swampy and filled with prickly palms while other areas were lush with thick tangled jungle growth. We had flagstones to walk on most of the way so it was an easy shaded walk. The two families who had lived on the peninsula for 15 and 20 years respectively have the responsibility of maintaining the paths and they do it well.

The guide was great and explained about various plants like the wild banana with little black seeds that is a sure and drastic remedy for constipation, and the palm nut that has been used for centuries for oil. There was also the fluffy kapok that could be spun or used as a soft filling for pillows. And he showed us a giant multi-colored spider that was right out of the original Swiss Family Robinson movie.

We came out into the brilliant sunshine at a little lagoon and had a quick dip before getting back into the boat. We then returned by water for lunch with the local family. This was an ideal spot for swimming although there wasn't a great deal to see underwater.

We had time to chat with some interesting retired Americans on the tour. Tom, with his wife, Carol, spent his time

volunteering for Rotary International, finding places and supervising where his organization's assistance was needed. Maurice was there with his wife, Jean. He was a civil engineer with an organization from Canada which placed professionals where their volunteer skills were needed. He had just concluded a month around Tegucigalpa working on water, sanitation and road construction. We invited them all to join us for dinner at the club that evening and continued our conversations late into the night.

Day 43
Tuesday, February 25, Corozal

Things didn't go too well this morning. Our plan was to leave Tela early. We were heading for La Ceiba farther down the coast but we were still debating whether we wanted to make a trip out to the Bay Islands. Flights left from La Ceiba.

It had rained last night. This was the first time since we had fixed a leak in our roof back in Houston that we had experienced any amount of rain. Back at home we had used cups to scoop the water out from the cavity next to the bed. It had made sleep a soggy proposition. Fortunately, the caulking we had done held up and we were dry. Rain on the roof made a heck of a din, but we were soon asleep again. Everything was refreshingly dust-free when we went out in the morning.

ABOVE: Beach on Punta Sal
LEFT: Fishing boat on Punta Sal, Honduras

I went to start up the generator so I could use the microwave to make oatmeal: nothing happened. The shore power here wasn't strong enough to run the microwave. I pressed the button again, still nothing. It was not all that bad, as this would be a pleasant place to wait for repairs or parts. I resigned myself to another day at the Beach Club. John was quickly on the satellite phone to the place in the States where we bought the motorhome, to the manufacturer, and who knows else. In the end he changed the fuse and all was well. We were real novices at motorhoming and learning all the time. We had only lost about an hour, and nine thirty wasn't such a bad start.

We were off. Instead of backing out the way we had come in, I started to drive forward and got about six feet before getting stuck in the sand. The rain had made it look hard-packed, but it was not. We got out our wood blocks and dug them under the wheels then tried again and sank deeper. The security guard was watching and through the use of his radio called for help. A minute later a team of workers, who were building a house on one of the lots, arrived with long shovels and more planks of wood. A little tractor also arrived as if that would help pull us out. They didn't realize what a big vehicle we had. We were so deep in the sand that we were worried about the exhaust pipe and the drainage tank valves getting damaged. We badly needed to empty the tanks so this would not have been a good time to break the fitting.

The team dug so deep that one man was able to get under the motorhome.

RIGHT: Stuck in the sand in Tela, Honduras. Note the man digging underneath the bus, and vigilante with his gun.

He put boards down to support our jack, and jacked the RV up. They then put boards under the wheels and lowered us onto them so we could get traction. They then dug a path and laid planks and boards behind us so we could back out. After several failed attempts, more digging and jacking, we finally got out.

We reversed all the way to the paved road. Phew! A few minutes before we were free their boss turned up. We gave the *trabajador* in turquoise, the one who had been digging right underneath the motorhome, a tip to share with the six co-workers. He handed it straight to his boss without looking him in the eye. After all, they had left their posts building a new home to assist us. We did note one of them carrying several liter bottles of Coke from the club as we departed five

minutes later. I hope they got more than that for their labor. For us, it was typical of how locals are ingenious at solving problems and they were always eager to offer us assistance. This whole episode took about two hours, but one nice thing about not having to be anywhere for months is that it really didn't matter.

We made an executive decision to bypass La Ceiba. Its main claim to fame seemed to be transportation to the Bay Islands: Roatan, Utila and Guanaja.

These are well-publicized tourist destinations, but the folks we met in Tela had just come from Roatan and they were not too thrilled. Sand flies are a big problem, which makes relaxing on the beach impossible. If you want to learn how to SCUBA dive, the islands are the place to go. This is apparently one of the real bargains of the Caribbean. We were encumbered with Brindle, which would have made the journey difficult and we also had to get Brindle through the country in two weeks. Our dog permit was technically only for transit. We decided to skip the islands.

We found an extensive supermarket on the through road around La Ceiba that had everything from peanut butter to teriyaki sauce and irons. We stocked up on soft drink and juices. They didn't have the large bottles of water that were convenient for us to refill our individual bottles, so drinking water was the next thing we would need to replenish.

There were two dots on the map east of La Ceiba that looked promising for a camp location on the beach and we pulled off towards the first: Corozal.

The road quickly became cobbled. We had to wait for a bus to pass so we could use the left side of the road to avoid the great old trees that were shading it and would have taken off our roof. This was a

Garífuna village. I felt so ignorant that there are whole collections of people that I just didn't know existed. The Garífuna are descendants of slaves brought to this coast by the British after they rebelled in St. Vincent at the end of the eighteenth century. They intermarried with Arawak Indians from the mainland and additional slaves who were shipwrecked or who had escaped. The Indians opposed the "white man," and had been hiding in the hills. They welcomed the slaves who, needless to say, also needed somewhere to hide. This is a little over simplified but covers the basics. All along the Caribbean coast of Central America as far south as Nicaragua are villages of predominately black culture where English and Spanish are spoken. In some cases their own Garífuna language survives. It is a very interesting culture that blends the African with the indigenous, together with a touch of British.

As we drove through Corozal everyone was very friendly, sitting in the shade in front of their homes and smiling and greeting us with waves. Several children were still in their school uniforms doing their homework in front of their houses while their parents looked on.

The road became dirt as we followed directions to the beach with assurances that there was parking there for the night. We went down the main street between one-room houses of adobe and others that were of brightly painted cement block. Frequently, the homes were also places of business, which sold local necessities like batteries or soft drinks. The road was narrow and there were a lot of low wires overhead and roofs that jutted out into the street.

By now I was walking in front to aid John in making turns and to avoid the obstacles. There was a gazebo in the

center of town with a group of men who looked a little spaced-out enjoying a smoke. We eventually came to the end of the road and parked facing the beach. Along came the children, the cow and a couple of pigs.

I went into a covered area that had a restaurant sign on it and asked if we could stay the night there. "No problem, maan". No problem, that is if Brindle could keep the cow from scratching itself on the motorhome.

We locked up and went for a stroll, not altogether comfortable with our location because there were so many people just hanging around. We found Linda, from the U.S., sitting in front of the restaurant enjoying a drink with Francisco who was visiting from La Ceiba. Linda suggested that we not spend the night there, and suggested that we would be safer down the beach at the Brisas Del Mar Hotel. Her friend Francisco was staying there and he jumped up and offered to escort us. He climbed into the passenger seat and became our guide for the next two days.

Francisco Vivas was the quintessential tour guide and wheeler-dealer. He and his American wife, Judy, operate a tour business, La Ceiba Tours (+504-4434-207). They were in Corozal for a holiday weekend but as soon as he met us he was ready to go to work. He had lived in the States and spoke perfect English.

Francisco led us to the hotel that was just a mile east of the town of Corozal. The hotel wasn't glamorous, but there was enough space for us behind a rickety barbed wire fence that drew the line, but little more, for anyone who was not staying at the hotel.

The hotel rooms were concrete block painted bright turquoise and the small bar and restaurant next to the beach was in a thatched building called a "Chamfa." The fence kept the cows out but not the pigs, which Brindle kept away in her eagerness to play.

It was right on the Caribbean. The owner was pleasant and his wife cooked us a good dinner. Francisco and Judy joined us and he told us about the local villages and the islands.

Francisco was eager to have us see the small Bay Islands called the Cayos

---

LEFT: The Garífuna village of Corozal, Honduras
ABOVE: Brisas Del Mar Hotel, Corozal, Honduras

Cochinos, or Hog Islands, which were just offshore. Where the guidebooks had failed to persuade us to go to these islands, Francisco succeeded. He said he would have transportation there in the morning to deliver us to a boat that would take us to "the most beautiful little coral cays off the Honduran coast." He kept disappearing into the town of Corozal and returning with more information. By 10:00 that evening he had made the necessary arrangements with friends and fishermen for our transfers and the boat trip.

Day 44
Wednesday February 26, Cayos Cochinos

We were ready at six in the morning for our ride in his friend's truck to take us to Sambo Creek where a fisherman would take us out to the islands. We left Brindle in the motorhome with the doggy door open so she could play with the pigs.

Everyone seemed to be Francisco's friend around here. John rode in the back of the pickup truck. We stopped to pick up someone in Corozal. He accompanied us to Sambo Creek but we never figured out why he came with us. After a few minutes on the beach at Sambo Creek, Francisco found our fisherman. His boat was a sturdy, 20-foot fiberglass

runabout with a 25 horsepower outboard motor. Nothing fancy. Many of these boats lined the beach. The Japanese government had donated them to assist the local fishermen, but the locals preferred their smaller dugout canoes carved from a single tree. At least this boat was to be put to good use. It could be chalked off to a fishing day too, as we would find out. Francisco saw that we were safe in the hands of the fisherman and his young assistant, and waved goodbye as we headed into the surf.

The Hog Islands are not set up for tourists. They consist of two larger islands a few miles across, and a number of smaller cays barely out of the water. There is a hotel on the larger island, but we never got that far.

It took us about an hour from Sambo Creek to the first island we visited. It was called Cayo Culebra and was owned by a wealthy Italian. Francisco told us the story of how he had arranged the purchase, so we felt we had a chance of being welcomed, but the owner was not there. A lady walked leisurely out from the main house to where we had tied up on their pier and told us that there would be a five dollar charge to use the beach. With advance notice you apparently can stay on the Cayo Culebra, which would be pleasant if you want an island retreat. Francisco can set it up for you! I would make the arrangements ahead of time, however. I'm sure he could also sell you another island if you wanted one.

We decided to swim off the next island, which they called Chachauate Cay. We walked from one island to the other as they were only separated at high tide. Later, looking on a map we

LEFT: Sunrise at Corozal

couldn't identify any of these islands by these names. I assume we really were at the Cayos Cochinos, but we couldn't prove it.

Chachauate was about the size of a football field and was covered with thatched huts. They were either made from faded planks of wood or cane stalks. The bamboo kept it shaded and kept prying eyes out, but would permit the wind and a little light through. The only other openings were the doors.

The water was clear and teeming with fish. I lay in the shallows with my mask and snorkel on, looking over an eighteen-inch ledge and was in the middle of hundreds of little fishes about an inch long twisting and dancing in the filtered sunlight. Then along came a larger fish with blues and yellows and then a larger one, and then a really big one. All this was within feet of dry land and within reach of my hand. The really big one was probably

six inches but through the goggles and to the little fish he looked massive.

Unfortunately the coral there was mostly dead. Hurricane Mitch seems to be blamed for anything negative. We asked if we could go to another area where we would see more live and colorful coral but first we took a stroll through the houses. These huts are only occupied during the fishing season, but someone has taken care of the sanitation, if not the modesty of the residents.

Upper Key was our next stop. Talk about a deserted desert island. This one had half a hut and seven palm trees. It was the kind of desert island you read

ABOVE: Cayo Chachauate off the Caribbean Coast of Honduras
RIGHT: Island style lavatories and dog (We could have brought Brindle!)

about with wonderful soft sand, nothing in any direction but clear blue water. The coral was better here. A person marooned on this island would really have a problem.

I was in the middle of reading Bill Bryson's *Down Under* where he describes the Great Barrier Reef where one jellyfish can zap "a room full" of people. This didn't make me feel comfortable swimming between the little floating globs, but we came to no harm. We did see a couple of massive sea stars (starfish) that were much bigger than my hand. Also, there were some strange little critters that coiled to look like pairs of miniature Christmas trees in soft burgundy and orange. When you disturbed them they completely disappeared into minute holes in the coral.

When we returned to the little island from our swim, honeybees had discovered us. My hat must have had a dozen on and in it. You have to look at it from the bee's point of view. There was very little potential for them on this little island, no flowers that I could see, so they were searching for a drink or anything they could turn into honey. We were careful and respectful, which was more than the co-pilot of the boat, who was stung for his thrashing. We escaped unscathed, leaving the bees to their desperate search, and moved on to another island.

We paused to eat the picnic lunch we had brought, on Cayo Bolanos. It was idyllic. A few resident fishermen sailed past in their little dugouts. We propped ourselves against a giant piece of driftwood, ate, read, snoozed, and contemplated how lucky we were. Ash-blond sand melted into the crystal water that blended from turquoise to deep blue and then faded into the horizon to blend into the sky that held the blazing sun overhead. It wasn't unpleasantly hot, as there was a constant breeze and always the water to fall into.

On the return trip to the mainland, our captain and one-man crew fished in earnest. They had caught a couple of decent sized ones on the way out. While we were enjoying the beach they had used nets to catch the schools of little fish I had been admiring, to use as chum. A sad fate! Now they were seriously trawling.

Suddenly they cut the motor altogether and hauled in a great yellow-fin tuna. This was a whopper. They immediately backtracked to pass over the same area again. Unfortunately, they were more interested in the fishing than in where they were going. We came to a sudden halt. We had run aground on the coral. John and I looked at each other. The closest island was infested with bees and a long swim at best. (Bill Bryson has a great story about a couple who went for a day trip on the Great Barrier Reef and never made it home. My imagination was warming up.) All we could see

in any direction was flat water and Bee Island. The captain jumped over the side and stood on the coral ledge. We used the paddles to push off and with less weight on board we freed ourselves and made it back safely.

Back at Sambo Creek we were on our own to take a bus back to our home at Brisas del Mar. Buses are the way to travel in Central America, and this was much more comfortable than the pickup ride in the morning. We also got to meet interesting characters.

That evening we asked Francisco and Judy where we could get the time-honored Garífuna dinner of fish cooked in coconut milk. We invited them to join us and we all walked down the railway line from the beach community where our hotel was to the town center. We didn't worry about a train coming. Standard Fruit Company had laid the tracks, but since they had removed their headquarters to La Lima and shipping to Puerto Castilla, there wasn't much business in town. The tracks were used by all as a convenient path. I had a hard time finding out what people did for a living

LEFT: Upper Key
ABOVE: John being "helped" by some Garífuna children
RIGHT: The potent drink guifity

besides survival fishing. Apparently family members working in North America send down most of the income.

We walked on through town. It was lively at night and there were people going every which way. Francisco seemed to know everyone. This was Wednesday night, but on Saturday night the Garífuna villages are full of music and traditional dancing. This was one pleasure we missed.

We stopped at the very restaurant where we had originally parked when looking for a camping place two days earlier.

When we arrived at the restaurant Francisco insisted that we try the local specialty: *guifity*. This is a traditional Garífuna drink made from a bottle of rum filled with twenty different roots and bark and percolated for a while. It looked grim. I looked for critters swimming between the roots. I hoped the alcohol killed anything nasty that went in with the vegetation. It didn't taste bad, especially when washed down with a couple of local beers.

Frank and Judy made for an interesting couple. She had been through culinary school in the States and had come

to Honduras with her then husband for a scuba trip. She liked the country more than the husband and stayed to open a restaurant in Corozal. This is where she and Francisco met. He is in tourism and real estate, and offers rafting trips, horse rides into the mountains and just about anything a visitor might be interested in doing. He knows his stuff, and just about everyone there is to know. His father is in Congress and his uncle in the Department of Natural Resources. Francisco tried hard to get us to go on a three-day excursion into the remote part of Honduras known as La Mosquitia. In spite of the name, this is supposed to be a remarkable destination, unspoiled by tourism. The trip would have entailed a plane ride to Palacios and a boat trip through rivers and lagoons to an outfitting camp of some sort. We were tempted, but we were beginning to feel the need to move on towards our ultimate goal, Panama, before we had to return to our daughter's graduation.

John had lobster, fish and conch for dinner at a cost of 110 *lempira,* about nine dollars. I just had the lobster. Then we were shown how to do a Garífuna dance and we showed the locals a couple of our swing moves so all in all it was a good exchange.

The *guifity* did not make it any easier to walk back over the sleepers on the dark narrow railway tracks, but Brindle kept us in the right direction and we returned safely to our little motorhome.

Day 45
Thursday, February 27, Pico Bonito Park,

Once again we planned an early start and once again we were thwarted. This time it was Francisco who insisted upon a detour, as he wanted to show us the highly acclaimed Pico Bonito Park. We all took off in the motorhome on this adventure.

We never would have found the park at all without Francisco, as there was no signage to this entrance of the country's largest National Park. We were east of the town of La Ceiba and turned onto the road that was signposted for Urraco, immediately east of the new bridge.

The floods caused by Hurricane Mitch had destroyed the old bridge. Francisco told us how, after the hurricane, he had fetched his boat and was charging five lempira (about $.25) to ferry people across. He made sixteen hundred lempira a day (about $320) He insisted that was without charging old women and rescue workers. Francisco is resourceful. He said that there were a hundred boats there by the end of the week, but he was the first.

We turned the motorhome onto the dirt road for an interesting trip into the park. Pico Bonito, as its name implies, consists of peaked mountains that formed a jagged skyline. It is filled with waterfalls, rivers and streams all wrapped in dense jungle.

The river was glorious and ideal for rafting, which of course Francisco could arrange. He could also produce a string of horses for those who wanted to ride through the park. One could easily have stayed a week and had plenty to do in the area.

We paused at a farm with big old cacao, or chocolate trees with strange seedpods growing directly from the branches.

If you break one of the ripe yellow-orange pods open, the half-inch black seeds are packed in and covered in a sharp, sweet, white slime. It is pleasant to suck this coating off the smooth seeds, but the taste is nothing like chocolate. As with the coffee, the cacao bean has no flavor until it is roasted. The Mayans would bury their esteemed dead with cacao beans. The beans were used in trade all over Central America and up into the Yucatan. It was their currency.

Hurricane Mitch had done a lot of damage in the area but new growth had covered the scars left by landslides, and all you could see now were the new bridges. The German government donated one of them.

We continued on and then parked the bus for a stroll through the jungle. Unfortunately, the suspension bridge over a canyon had a few too many planks missing so we decided not to try to cross it. We did have a great dip in a pool below, even though we hadn't come prepared to swim. It was hot so none of us minded the walk back to the motorhome in our wet clothes.

It was time to continue on our journey so we returned Francisco and Judy to Corozal and headed on for Trujillo. We had made new friends and had experienced a taste of Garífuna life. This was the kind of experience that is hard to acquire on the usual tourist trails, and exactly why we preferred to move around off the beaten track.

LEFT: Pico Bonito Park, Honduras
RIGHT: Coco pods growing on the trees

The road from La Ceiba to Trujillo goes away from the Coast through the bustling plantation towns of Jutiapa and Saba. This was a really pretty drive—one of the nicest we have been on. I feel as though I keep saying that, but the scenery really was very picturesque. Some of the sharp little hills looked like they hid Mayan pyramids waiting to be discovered. Mud and wattle thatched huts were along the side of the road, but then there were new ones made from cement block and built in the same design that might have been more comfortable but lacked the charm.

Orange, palm oil and banana trees clustered around the homes in each pueblo. Sacks of oranges were piled at the side of the road waiting for transport to the packers.

Suddenly, a great flat valley opened in front of us and all we could see was bananas, bananas, bananas! Vast rows of banana plants, each with their fruit covered in a blue plastic bag to encourage even ripening and to protect it from the elements and the bugs. These are bananas for export and they don't have half the flavor or nutrition of the chubby little

ones eaten locally. The local ones don't transport well. We saw men riding bicycles with enormous sacks of bananas, as big as themselves, across the handlebars.

It was time for a change of driver, lunch and perhaps a short siesta. I found a level spot well off the road where we could park in the shade of a tree. I had hardly begun preparing the food when the local children surrounded us. Most of them were standing at a respectful distance, but we felt we were under scrutiny as we ate our lunch. Then one barely touched one of the bicycles locked to the grill of the motorhome. The dog

went wild. She leaped to the dashboard with her teeth pressed against the glass of the windshield. The kid bolted into the woods and his friends stepped back. Brindle kept up a near constant growl and occasional bark when the children moved, but there was no chance they would touch the bus or the bikes again. Unfortunately we didn't feel comfortable taking a siesta with a dozen children watching, so we moved on. I am sure that they were just curious and meant us no harm.

As we motored on through this glorious scenery we dropped in altitude and bananas gave way to palm oil trees as far as the eye could see. There was this great sweep of dark green all the way to the smoke-blue mountains in the distance. The road was hot and as straight as an arrow cutting between the palms and under the palms was a deep cool shade.

ABOVE: Thatched homes along the road between Corozal and Trujillo
LEFT: Kids watching us through the screen door.
RIGHT: Our office in Trujillo, at the Christopher Columbus Hotel

We were in the sun. It was hot. The native palm nut that the Mayans used to extract oil is no longer harvested commercially. The palm tree imported from Africa produces five times the amount of oil from each nut and has much larger clusters of nuts.

By late in the afternoon we were still driving through picturesque green hills covered with various palms and scattered with homes hiding in the shade of mango or banana trees. Tall coconut palms laden with their golden nuts stood at the edges of small dirt plots. The mango trees were like giant clouds of green, the kind of tree that a child might draw. Part of the green was brushed in yellow from the myriad little blossoms that in season would become clusters of fruit that would cause the branches to droop.

We made it to Trujillo by half past five and found the disproportionately large airport runway. This was the runway built by Oliver North to supply the Contras with personnel and equipment in their battle against the Sandinistas in Nicaragua.

There were buildings between the runway and the beach so we couldn't see the water, and it seemed it might be dangerous to park actually at the end of the runway, although we had heard some people had camped there. In addition, our motorhome would be more conspicuous than we liked. We opted for the Hotel Christopher Columbus parking lot where we would blend in a little. We went in and asked if we could park there, off to one side, out of the way, for a couple of days. The front desk clerk could not or didn't want to make that decision and the manager was away until Saturday, two days hence. We asked the clerk if she could call the manager while we enjoyed a piña colada at their pool side bar. We returned a little later and she still didn't have an answer, so we said we would wait in the motorhome until she heard from him. She seemed happy with this arrangement. Two days later and we still hadn't heard!

Day 46
Friday, February 28, Trujillo

We enjoyed an idle day at one of the nicest locations you could desire. There might have been half a dozen rooms rented in the Christopher Columbus Hotel, but we hardly saw anyone. The beach was deserted and clean, with lounge chairs waiting in the shade of *palapas* evenly spaced along the white sand. We even had our own private office. It was a *champa* set up with a bar for busier times. It was here, under the palm thatched shade with a breeze wafting through and the glorious blue waters beyond the white sand, that

we spent the day writing home. Well, we were writing between a siesta, reading, swimming and sampling piña coladas. I think we went south to do that.

The town of Trujillo has plenty of historical interest. This is where Christopher Columbus limped ashore with a ship badly damaged after hitting the coral reef, making this the first place he touched the mainland of America. The Spanish shipped gold to Europe from here. Trujillo is the oldest town in Honduras and was the first capital on the Central American mainland. In 1860, the infamous American, William Walker, met his end at a firing squad here in town. Walker was an enterprising North American who decided that he wanted to rule all of Central America, and did in fact take over Nicaragua. The Hondurans would have none of it, and after kicking him out of

ABOVE: Sunset at Trujillo, Honduras
LEFT: Christopher Columbus Hotel on the Contra Airstrip
RIGHT: Brindle hunting for grave of William Walker, Trujillo, Honduras

the country twice, sent him to his Maker after a third attempt to run their country. We crossed his historical path several times on this trip.

From our exotic "private" *Champa* we could see Puerto Castilla across the bay. This is the port Standard Fruit built to ship fruit, mostly bananas, to the lucrative northern markets. For better or worse, the fruit companies became the most important economic entity here and thus became a major, political force in shaping this Banana Republic. They provided employment for thousands of people.

Day 47
Saturday, March 1, Trujillo, Honduras

We are having way too much fun!

The sand in front of the hotel arced around the clear azure water of the bay in a long sweeping curve. In the morning neither of us made any effort to move, so we didn't. We stayed an extra day. This was not only a restful place; the weather and the water were great. We could have stayed here a lot longer and

might even come back and stay in the hotel. That would mean flying in!

We set off to walk across the runway and the couple of kilometers into town. We were in search of an internet café. We found the only one in town an hour after it closed for the weekend. This place is not set up to serve tourists and we hardly saw any.

People were milling about the town square and sucking frozen juice from bags a local entrepreneur was selling from a battered cooler chest. It was mellow in this hilltop town and everyone moved slowly in the heat of the day. There was a small market and a church with a tall spire with the date 1525 engraved in the stone. That was when the town was established by Juan de Medina.

William Walker was shot a block east of where I was sitting with my bag of juice, and there is a marker for it in the hospital garden. We left the square to hunt for his grave. We found the graveyard after making numerous inquiries but could not find the stone we wanted.

There were all sorts of markers of wood or stone in romantic disrepair, covered with creeping flowers softening the scars of time and neglect. Some markers were just of faded wood and the inscriptions quite illegible. I can't imagine the marker of an expatriate, executed revolutionary being very grand.

We learned that there were some good trails through the hills to waterfalls and rivers to swim in but we didn't have our things with us. It was the hottest part of the day and we were beginning to wilt. We didn't even make it up the hill to the old Spanish fort. Two miles beyond the fort is the museum containing artifacts from the fort as well as the wreck of a C-80 in situ, along with a swimming pool!

We wandered back to what seemed like our private resort. We ordered a couple of piña coladas from our personal waiter who brought them to us in our *champa,* and then wallowed in another gorgeous sunset on a pristine beach.

Tomorrow we really had to move on!

CHAPTER 5

The Elusive Quetzal

CENTRAL HONDURAS

*To travel hopefully
is a better thing than to arrive,
And the true success is to labour.*

Robert Louis Stevenson

Day 48
Sunday, March 2, La Union and Muralla

What a glorious day! I wonder why I should be so lucky. The road from Trujillo to Saba and Olanchito was a good two lane black top with little traffic, but several nasty potholes. We could drive 40-50 mph with a watchful eye for the holes.

We were heading across Honduras toward Tegucigalpa and on to Nicar-agua. When we arrived in Trujillo we had no clue which route to take across the country. We had to cross a few mountain ranges on dirt roads to accomplish this, unless we were to backtrack all the way to western Honduras and take the main highway between San Pedro Sula and Teguci-galpa. We did not like backtracking. We had three maps: the ITMB travel map of Honduras, a "treasure map" put out by the tourist office, and the American Automobile Association map of Central America. They were not consistent. Each showed roads that didn't exist on the other. In the end we discovered that the ITMB map was the most accurate. The most interesting route appeared to us to be the eastern highway, which would take us through the heart of the Olancho district, and close to the jungles of La Mosquitia.

We asked several locals in Trujillo about this route and were consistently told not to go this way. There were apparently gangs of robbers lurking in the mountains of Olancho who would routinely stop people driving on this road. We were encouraged to take the paved road west toward Saba and cross

the mountains on the dirt road to La Union and Limones. I am sure one of the reasons we never had problems on this trip was that we always sought local knowledge about our routes, we never drove at night and we always camped in areas with some security. We opted to backtrack as far as Saba and take the central "highway" through the mountains.

The drive from Trujillo across the mountains of Honduras was magnificent.

We passed about fifty miles of palm oil trees, a few rice paddies and glorious scenery before reaching Saba. This was the center of the local agricultural industry. There is an intersection where one road leads to La Ceiba and the coast, and the other to Olanchito and the interior of the country. Like most major intersections of this sort, there was a big gas station with loads of cars and large trucks. We stopped here and made another inquiry as to the status and security of the road we were about to take across the mountains. The gas station attendant made a brief inspection of our tires and suspension system and said that we could make it. He assured us that buses travel this road all the time and that there were no "bandidos." He directed us to the road toward Olanchito and assured us that the turnoff for La Union was about 15 kilometers away. We were going to go into uncharted territory.

As we continued we noticed that there were no signs with route numbers or destinations on the road. We were told later that the locals steal the flat metal signs to use as pans to cook their tortillas.

After a while we came to a bus stop and numerous people hanging about at a junction. Who better to ask about the condition of the road and where it went than a bus driver? I waited while John went over to the bus to solicit all the information he could get. While he was doing that, a charming round faced lady came up to me with her arms out, greeting me as though we were long lost friends. She clasped my hands and was so pleased to see me. She burbled along asking where we were from, and where we were going, and how many children we have, which is always the next question. I struggled to chat with her and get information on the road. Great conversations

The scenery we passed through was magnificent. Every turn presented new dramatic sweeping vistas. I could stand and turn in a circle and be in awestruck wonder in each direction. We were following a little river through valleys between sharp green mountains that cut irregular shapes in the skyline. Little plots were cultivated on the level patches but it was mostly uncultivated with broad-leaf and pine trees covering the slopes.

Herds of horses that didn't look like they had ever been ridden, and cattle, were wandering all over the place. Immense Brahma-cross bulls with sleek coats had ears that hung to their jowls and other appendages that hung to their knees. They don't seem to have any steers here and they keep the males as bulls. We watched a couple jousting. There were cows and calves in the roving herds wandering across the road or lying in the soft dirt and mingling with the horses. With the good fodder, we thought, they might raise the horses here for sale down the mountain. We did see a dead horse that had been hit by traffic: just another reminder of why never to drive at night.

We were climbing gradually and the dense undergrowth gave way to pine trees, with hills stretching forever with

ensued and more assistance was offered from others waiting for their bus. In no time there was a crowd of people all talking at once. Then someone asked if they could get a ride with us. It is common practice for civilians to give rides, and the hitchhikers are expected that they pay the usual bus fare. We weren't quite ready for this. With good old Brindle growling and straining at her collar we were able to say no. In retrospect we both regretted not sharing our transportation.

We turned south leaving the paved highway for the dirt one. It was 10:00 o'clock.

Our speed was cut to 25–30 mph with much bumping and shaking. Later we became bolder and realized that if you could get up to about 40 mph you rode over the corrugations and not into them. At that speed you also had the opportunity of diving into the great ruts created in the rainy season or hitting the boulders scattered about, or running over cattle lying resting in the dust, or falling head first into a big hole.

LEFT: Cultivating the hills between Trujillo and Saba.
ABOVE: The countryside leading south towards La Union, Honduras
RIGHT: The mountains north of La Union, Honduras

their unusual jagged peeks. It was cooler and pleasant driving, even though we were chugging along slowly in the dust.

It was Sunday, and during the morning we had seen many people dressed in their Sunday best walking and riding to church clutching their bibles. Later in the day others dressed in their favorite soccer team uniform replaced them. It shouldn't have been a surprise when we turned a corner in the middle of nowhere and came across a soccer field with a match in full swing. They lost some of their spectators when we stopped to change drivers and were swarmed by children. It did seem incongruous though, that here, where transportation was often by horse or donkey and where the norm was a dirt floor in the home, that there would be fully equipped teams in smart uniforms playing soccer on an undulating field that it must have taken hours to reach. The nearest town was Esquipulas del Norte, 15 miles away.

The country was so appealing that we didn't really mind the dirt road and the occasional herd of cattle blocking our way. Frequently we had to pause and make the cattle stand up and move over to let us pass. This was the richest forest I'd seen. It was an explosion of color: all different greens. Some trees were tinged with peach colored blossoms and others were covered in bright yellow or pink flowers.

The road deteriorated and we had to slow down. We resigned ourselves and settled down to twenty miles an hour. We hoped to camp at The Muralla National Park, near La Union, half way to Tegucigalpa from Trujillo. This park is

ABOVE: Playing soccer in the Macupina Mountains. Note the undulations in the field.
LEFT: Town of La Union, Honduras

said to have a lot of critters. We had seen no wildlife in Honduras other than a few birds and butterflies and we looked forward to seeing some real wildlife in this park.

We pulled into La Union at half past one in the afternoon. It was a pleasant little village with hand painted paper plates strung across the road spelling out *Bienvenido a La Union* along with colorful strips of plastic. There was just enough room for us to pass under the decorations without catching the top of the motorhome. There were dozens of donkeys and pigs meandering along the road and foraging throughout the pueblo or resting in the shade.

La Union was lively with people everywhere celebrating a week-long festival. We parked and explored the town. We wandered past some temporary booths selling roasted strips of meat and chicken that we were about to buy for lunch when a crowd under a roofed-in area caught our attention. It was a cockfight.

We stood in the street beyond the fenced-in area, but being taller than everyone else we could clearly see beyond the circle of men and boys. Most were standing, but some were sitting around the planked thirty-foot ring. The men inside the ring were holding up their prized birds and challenging those around. No, I was not going to watch a cockfight, but I was curious about it and the preliminaries. Other men entered the ring with their roosters treating them with care and respect, holding them up and showing them off and stroking their feathers.

Someone brought out a set of hanging scales and a bird was laid on it. The

ABOVE: Sharing the road
RIGHT: Preparing for the cock fight in La Union

critter must have been very used to all the handling and excitement as it lay quietly on the scales while the weight was called out to the spectators. A second bird was weighed and a disagreement ensued, which was settled with a second weigh-in. It looked like something might be going to happen and I was ready to move on when a policeman entered the ring and spoke to the crowd. We thought he said something about those under age eighteen not being permitted, but everyone began to leave and money was returned between gamblers. I thought that perhaps we had stumbled on an illegal event and my picture taking had alerted the police, who would otherwise have ignored it. No one gave us more than an occasional glance, so we really don't know why it was broken up. There was not a woman anywhere near. None of the birds wore spurs.

We wandered on and found a restaurant where we could sit in the shade for lunch. There were half a dozen tables and chairs but no one was eating. Everyone was seated in chairs around the perimeter watching a soap opera on television. The town had only received electricity a couple of years earlier and TV was still a novelty. We wanted to see if they could get CNN so we could catch up on the world situation, but we didn't think changing channels would make us very popular.

According to our maps, Muralla National Park was just outside of La Union, but we found it difficult to find anyone in town who could tell us how to get there. After asking several people we eventually felt comfortable enough to set out. Comfortable meant that we had at least three instructions in the same direction and what was equally important they all said that we could drive it *"no problema."* Then as confirmation there was a sign just outside of town saying that it was sixteen kilometers to the National Park. It was mid afternoon so another sixteen km of dirt road should be OK.

The first thing to slow us down was the local car wash, otherwise known as the place were the road fords the river. The car ahead of us was getting a wash, and there were kids splashing and women washing their hair and clothes a little further up stream. It was not deep

LEFT: Fording a river between La Union and Muralla National Park in central Honduras
ABOVE: In the mountains of Honduras on the way to Muralla.

but you wouldn't want to try it in the rainy season. We discussed the need for a prompt evacuation if it started to rain.

We were now on a dry, narrow, dirt lane that wound around sharp bends. The hillsides were dry with sparse pine trees covering the slopes. There were a couple of very nice coffee *fincas* (farms) along the way, where workers were shucking and drying the beans. It was a very slow road. Over an hour later we came to a sign with a big cat painted on it informing us that we had entered the park. There were no gates or park headquarters. There was dense undergrowth and we had seen very little signs of human habitation except at the little *fincas*.

The road was hardly a road. We did meet an occasional vehicle, two pickup trucks full of workers, but we just took it slowly and climbed or crawled off the road to pass. The motorhome really handled admirably. The shadows were getting

long and it was beginning to get late. We felt that we should stop for the night before it got dark. Perhaps there was no park headquarters building and nowhere to turn around. The road could go on forever climbing into the mountains. We found a wide place off the road that was level and would work well enough so we pulled in. I walked up the road with the dog to stretch my legs and came to a better place. Then we decided that we would drive a little further as there seemed no shortage of stopping or turning places. Three minutes further on, surprise! We came to the park headquarters.

We pulled up onto the flat piece of land next to the park buildings. It was carved into the hillside and sliced into the deep forest. The naked silver tree trunks that used to reach upwards towards the light amidst the dark of the jungle were now exposed to the bright light of the sinking sun. The park ranger, Eduardo, came to greet us as though he had been waiting all day for our arrival. He made us welcome and immediately said that this was the best time for a two-hour walk in the cloud forest. He would be our guide. Unfortunately, because of the poor lighting, and because I was out of breath from the hike at five thousand foot elevation, my hands were shaking and none of the pictures came out.

The virgin cloud forest was thick with vegetation and could be impossible to walk through. It would be easy to get lost. Eduardo had kept the path well maintained with stones marking the edges. We walked quietly over little bridges spanning gullies, but beyond the path the undergrowth was dense. We heard a quetzal. This is the beautiful bird of Central America that was revered by the ancient Mayas and is the namesake of the Guatemalan currency.

We heard it again. It was more of a call than a song. Eduardo got all excited and asked if we wanted to see it. "Of course." He then turned off the maintained path and swam through the undergrowth. In his enthusiasm to find the quetzal he almost lost us, disappearing into the vegetation. Under branches, over fallen trees our feet sank deep into rotten undergrowth. I don't think I actually trod on dirt. I was either balancing on fallen limbs or suspended on rotten matter under green twigs and dead wood and leaves. There were plenty of mosquitoes. We were really stirring up the bugs. I realized that with all the crunching of dry leaves and snapping of twigs no shy bird would hang around. Only the insects were not scared away! After several minutes of crashing through the jungle, I suggested we give up and return to his nicely maintained path.

It was quite a relief to have firm ground underfoot. I would never have found the path without Eduardo. He was so keen to show us the birds. He

said that in another month, in April and May, there was a ninety-percent chance of spotting a magical quetzal. This time of year the birds were in the lower elevations.

After the sun set the jungle became black and still. The stars were brilliant and so close you could touch them above our little clearing. The night was cool and peaceful. It was a good place for sleeping.

Day 49
Monday, March 3, Muralla National Park, Honduras to Valle de Angeles

As I lay in bed and the light of dawn grew, so did the bird sounds. The cloud forest had been very quiet during the night. Very, very quiet. No jaguar screeching, no howls, no freeway hum, not even insects or frog singing. Just quiet. Then there was the dawn chorus of all these strange and wonderful bird sounds. We were in a clearing in the jungle and I kept expecting to see some great animal appear, but none obliged. Just birds warbling. Some sounded like they were singing under water, others were whistling and calling.

We heard reports that they were having a cold and snowy winter up in the U.S.,

ABOVE: Flowering trees like this were everywhere.

but you must forgive me when I say it was cold! We cuddled up during the night, a nice treat, and we needed a blanket and were still cold. It was 57 degrees. Don't laugh, but the day before we were sweltering on the Caribbean coast, and this morning I wrapped myself in the blue woven wool shawl I had bought in Chiapas, Mexico. The only way John could get a GPS fix was to do it outside with a direct shot at the satellites, so there he was sitting on a bench with his business jacket on he was so cold. It was the only jacket he had.

On our return to La Union, we decided to copy the locals and wash the motorhome in the ford. I really just did the windows, but it made a difference. It was fun to have lots of water to splash around.

The donkeys were still in the streets as we passed back through La Union, and southward towards Tegucigalpa. The scenery was magnificent. There were wonderful great hills, mountains and valleys in varying shades of greens. As we traveled it became drier.

We were very glad that we had taken this route, even though it was a slow dirt road. The road surface south of La Union was even worse than the stretch to the north. Dirt road? It was a dust road. Not just because of the surface, but because of the dust we took with us. I opened the drawer for a cooking pot that evening and found a thick layer of dust covering everything. The entire top layer of clothes had changed color. Every space, and there are a lot of them, was caked with dust. Now try to get that out with a very limited amount of water? I managed one drawer a day. A week later and I still hadn't tackled some of the cupboards. If we didn't need the corkscrew I didn't tackle that drawer. I didn't get it

really dust free until we returned home. New dirt roads made it pointless.

The country was drier with pine and other trees all around, but there were still herds of free-range horses and cattle wandering along the road and in the pastures. The houses were colorfully painted and better maintained even though most were made with thick adobe walls. Concrete blocks were becoming more evident the closer we came to the capital.

There were not any wild flowers at the roadside, but there were trees in bloom. I particularly liked one kind that must be a hundred feet high. It had no leaves at that time but it was dusted with masses of blue flowers. They always seemed to be on distant hills adding this bright smoky blue hazy patch above the other trees. Then there was a much smaller kind of tree that was frequently near the road that had bunches of pink flowers. Others had large brilliant yellow flowers and some trees were covered with tiny orange blossoms. Bougainvillea and poinsettias and colorful shrubs were in the villages embellishing even the simplest home.

Near the southern end of our dirt road, we climbed out of the Valle de Lepaguare into heavily pined forest. There were still magnificent views at every turn. Suddenly, we came to a stretch where the road was carved through pink rock. It didn't last long but the road and the embankments were bright pink; and of course there was pink dust that made up the road. A few miles further on, just as abruptly, the road and the rocks became yellow ochre and then it returned to that dust-color we had come to know so well. So now there was a rainbow of dust layers on everything inside the motorhome.

We came across a road crew laying the road. There was great activity all around and more heavy equipment than we had seen in all of Central America. There were a few interesting moments as we followed behind the grader and then had to pass him, but thereafter the road was great. This road was brand new, two lanes of black top and no traffic. We might have been the first to drive on it. When they lay it all the way to La Union it will be an excellent route.

We could relax and happily truck along at 40 mph through pretty little peaks of hills with pines all around. The countryside continued to get dryer and there was always smoke somewhere to be seen in the distance.

When we passed through the villages, there were children in uniform going to or from school. They operate two shifts to take advantage of the facilities so there are children from the very young to teenagers with their books and various uniforms walking along the road at all times of the day. They looked so clean and neat one minute, and then ten minutes later a kid would change out of his uniform and become a scruffy urchin. One boy on horseback was dragging his siblings along on the dirt on a homemade sled tied to the horse's tail!

In the town of Limones we reached the road to Tegucigalpa. The new road was such a pleasure to drive on as we wove through pines shaggy with Spanish moss. The driver, however, needed to maintain constant vigilance because of the freerange cattle and horses cropping the grass at the roadside: they could suddenly think the grass was greener on the other side.

The lower we drove in altitude the hotter it became. Sugar cane surrounded us again and there were fields of those little red chile peppers that look so pretty, but carry a hefty punch. There were commercial plantations of bananas and papaya, and donkeys wandering everywhere. It was as though we had driven into a picturesque oven.

We were heading for a charming town called Valle de Angeles. The Spanish originally built the town when they were mining for silver in the area, and it was now restored to an appealing area for tourists. It is busiest on weekends when Hondurans visit from Tegucigalpa, half an hour away. Not many other people come except for Peace Corps and NGO (Non Governmental Organization) members who are here to assist in the post Hurricane Mitch rebuilding effort. I had visited the area two years earlier on an American Red Cross training mission. To get to Valle de Angeles, we turned off the paved road at Talanga and were again on a dirt road leading through steep mountains. It was a long trek with no signs and we constantly had to ask pedestrians whether we were on the right road. The road wound around precipitous mountain curves with breathtaking views of the valley stretching towards the east and Nicaragua, our next destination.

We finally entered the village of Valle de Angeles. As soon as we parked a couple of scrappy young boys came up to us. One said, "¿Lava su caro? Nos gustaria lavar su carro." One was dressed in a bright yellow shirt and they looked as if they had just come from a soccer game. My attempt to wash the bus that morning had just succeeded in providing wet places for the new dust to adhere to. These entrepreneurs were offering to wash it for us. They did a great job considering they had to carry every bucket of water from a nearby house.

ABOVE: Valle de Angeles, in the hills above
Tegucigalpa, Honduras

The town square was the traditional little park with overgrown trees providing shade to numerous benches where the elderly and the romantic could ponder the passers-by. The branches of the ancient jacaranda trees were so laden with bromeliads, that their orange flowers rivaled the purple of the jacaranda. The weight of the guest would surely bring branches of the host to the ground.

Small, whitewashed, adobe houses with thick walls and terracotta tiles lined the square. Most of the homes were now little shops offering locally made works of art and trinkets imported from other parts of the country. There were little restaurants and places to sit and enjoy good Honduran coffee. Next to an antique shop selling dilapidated household items that at one time might have been precious, was an elderly gentleman selling photographic prints. He had photos of Che Guevara, the revolutionary, and of Germans in military uniforms when they visited the capital in the late 1930s. He said his father had taken the pictures. There were some interesting shots of cars and airplanes of that era.

The guitar maker I'd met there on my previous visit was still at his trade making various stringed musical instruments. He told us about a public park that would be a suitable place to overnight just two kilometers down the road to Tegucigalpa.

The Parque Turístico was perfect for us. This was obviously well used on weekends with its soccer field with bleachers and all sorts of picnic tables and barbecues, restrooms and even a swimming pool. Altogether the park must have been a couple of hundred acres. The *vigilante* was not used to overnight visitors but decided to charge us $1.20 and he assured us that he and his *compadres* would be there all night to keep an eye on us. He then completely disappeared and left us to the horses that were grazing the soccer field.

We spent a pleasant evening enjoying the gentle climate among the pine trees feeling completely safe and having the entire park to ourselves.

Day 50
Tuesday, March 4
Visiting Colonia Santa Rosa

Hurricane Mitch had caused devastation around Tegucigalpa. The United States's National Oceanic and Atmospheric Administration calculated that there could have been over seventy-five inches of rain in the mountains. One group of survivors who had lost their homes banded together and purchased land high on a hill just out of town. With the help of the Red Cross they were able to build a new *colonia* they called Santa Rosa. The Spanish Red Cross provided the means for them to purchase the cement blocks that they built into homes, the Japanese Red Cross built the road up the steep hillside and the American Red Cross provided the water and sanitation expertise and materials. The future homeowners provided the labor. After the construction, a lottery was conducted to determine who in the group would get each house.

One of my goals in Honduras was to re-visit the *colonia* that I had seen two years earlier. When I was there before it was under construction and I wanted to see it inhabited.

The narrow streets of Tegucigalpa were like a maze and we got lost. Nothing new! We were trying to meet with Andrew, the head of the American Red Cross Delegation in Honduras. The American Red Cross does great work there, not only providing immediate relief after disasters like earthquakes and hurricanes, but they also take on long term projects providing water and sanitation in stricken areas in addition to health and safety projects. Here, they helped the locals with materials and expertise to pipe water four miles from a spring to their *colonia*. They designed and helped construct the sanitation system. In other *colonias* they teach mitigation so that families can take action before a disaster to improve their chances of surviving with their belongings. On TV in the States you sometimes see someone with a Red Cross on their back handing out food and water after a disaster. You seldom hear about the continuing work they do. Preventing loss of life and destruction of property is better and less expensive than trying to fix things after a disaster. It is a major challenge and they are very committed to it.

We used our satellite phone to call Andrew from the parking lot of a supermarket. He kindly rescued us and led us to their offices that were only a few blocks away. We thanked him with a large jar of peanut butter that I had been saving, knowing that this was a delicacy that most expatriates appreciate.

Santa Rosa had been dedicated only nine months before this visit, and the homeowners were making the gray concrete boxes into homes. The roads were still a jumble, but as their income permitted, the residents were beginning to show their individuality in their houses and some planted shrubs and vegetables.

The semi-detached block homes were lined up in rows on either side of the streets. Each house had a main living area with sink and stove; a bathroom and shower; and two little bedrooms. Each home shares one wall with its neighbor. These are far better than the houses they lost, but I don't intend to de-emphasize the trauma of losing a home, however humble, and everything that was in it.

There have been some challenges that people living in first world countries might not have imagined. In their old homes these families needed to buy drinking water by the bottle or jug from a vendor who came to their street. Now it comes out of a tap inside their home. They still have to pay for it even though it is much less expensive by the gallon. Some of the residents are having a hard time with the concept of saving up to pay for something they have already used, and to monitor their consumption. It is a new system for them.

Several residents had opened little shops, or *pulperías,* in their front rooms and were selling general merchandise and a wide variety of necessities. There were also several *refresquerías,* which sold mainly refreshments like soft drinks and chips. One enterprising homeowner had invested in a couple of pinball machines that he installed on his front patio!

School was currently being taught in sheds leaning together and made of tin, sheets of hardboard and anything else that provided a wall and shade. The incessant chatter of youth could be heard through the thin walls. The new school was being built from the ubiquitous, gray, concrete blocks. We were introduced to the headmistress. We had brought a soccer ball for the school, but the headmistress didn't seem very interested. as they didn't have a team. The kids seemed very attracted, however, and I hope they get to use it. Then I pulled a

LEFT: Shop on the main street of Santa Rosa, a community built with Red Cross assistance.
ABOVE: A back street in Santa Rosa with a view of Tegucigalpa, Honduras

couple of packets of seeds out of my pocket. That got her attention and she gratefully accepted them to grow in class. They have four hundred and eleven children enrolled and expect more when the facility is finished.

Our drive out of Tegucigalpa started by descending down a winding two-lane pothole riddled road. Perhaps the potholes contributed to the next flat tire. It was only another valve stem leaking, but it caused a flat just the same. Some missionaries pulled over and offered assistance, but John managed to change tires and we continued.

Throughout the trip we did a fair amount of driving with a flat spare tire. We would not have been stranded if we had had another flat because we had double wheels on the back. It was like having two more emergency wheels. If we had a flat in the front we could take one from the back and put it on the front. We wouldn't want to go any distance like that, but it would be a last resort. This time we decided to continue to Danli and have the tire worked on there after we had found a place for the night.

Now we were flagged down at another police stop. John was driving and since his wallet was lost in Guatemala he had no driver's license. He could only produce a photocopy. Somehow this satisfied them and they let us continue. The police were not so agreeable in Nicaragua, but that's another day.

The road deteriorated. There was very little traffic but what there was caused some interesting moments. There would be an eighteen-wheeler approaching in the distance that would suddenly move over to our side of the road. We kept on trucking, attention fixed on it while glancing continually at the pothole riddled surface in front of us. "The truck is

coming closer right at us," I gasped. Then the driver casually returned to his side of the road, waving as he passed us. Then we realized that his side of the road was almost impassable. A minute or two later our side of the road became so pocked, that to avoid demolition, we steered to the left side in spite of the other tractor-trailer approaching us from a distance. And so it goes on. Needless to say, you can't drive very fast or relax, and there are numerous stretches of bad surface you just have to struggle through.

When we had the courage to look up from the on-coming traffic or the road surface, the countryside was not very interesting. We were in the valley that provided a spectacular view for us two days earlier as we approached Valle de Angeles on the mountain road. The valley was dry and barren, with scattered pine trees. As we descended there were more bananas growing around the homes and more pines. It also became warmer.

We liked Danli. It was a busy town filled with active people and a variety of shops and businesses. In among the two-story buildings were older adobe homes and shops with cool thick walls and undulating tile roofs.

Our first mission was to get our clothes washed. The laundry was not easy to find. The Texaco man told us that it was just down the road and he pointed. As we left the station, we turned in that direction only to find we were going the wrong way on a one way street. We went around and back, and parked right outside a little shop that did photocopying. Two men and a lady were working in this small but efficient office. No one had a clue about a laundry but the lady said that some people would do laundry in their homes if you asked. We decided to utilize their business and have them copy our documents for the next border crossing, and went back inside our motorhome to get passports, car papers, etc. Copies cost just a few cents each, cheaper than in the U.S. and much easier than at the borders.

In the meantime, the shop lady had made some phone calls and had located a laundry for us. This was another example of people going out of their way to help. It was just a few blocks away so we gathered our dirty clothes into pillowcases and set off. The laundry consisted of a small storefront that was closed with a corrugated sheet metal door. The word *lavandería* was scribbled on the sheet metal. There was not a soul in sight. I waited with Brindle and the bags of laundry while John walked down the street and asked the shopkeeper next door when the laundry would be open.

"*Toca,*" she said, knocking with her hand in the air to demonstrate. "*Toca fuerte en la puerta.*" John did as he was told and knocked hard on the corrugated door. It is not uncommon for a shopkeeper to close up for a siesta in the middle of the day. It is apparently acceptable to bang on the door if you need something.

A young lady looked over the balcony of the house over the shop and gave us the universal *momentito* sign, the thumb and forefinger held a little bit apart. She reappeared downstairs, opened up and was quite happy to take our laundry. She promised to have it done early in the morning. "*Sí. Temprano,*" she assured us.

Our next stop was to find a place to fix the tire. The motorhome was also due for a lube and oil change. The Texaco station didn't do oil changes or fix tires, but directed us to a Dippsa gas station, the national oil company located in the middle of town. They had a modern service bay right next to a place with a water hose where all the taxi drivers in town seemed to be washing their cars. I went off to find an internet café while John stayed with the vehicle. They didn't do tire repairs either but John arranged for the oil change. All went well until when he went to pay he found out that the little signs in the window with Visa and Mastercard logos didn't mean that that they accepted credit cards. They wanted cash. We were preparing to leave the country and had few Lempiras remaining. John tracked me down and between us we managed to come up with just enough cash with a couple of U.S. dollars thrown in.

John wanted a hair cut so when we passed a barber's shop we went in. I was made welcome among the male audience who insisted that John have the next cut ahead of those waiting. The *barbero* trimmed his hair and then, after sharpening his razor on a leather strap, gave him a close shave on the back of his neck. The other customers wanted to know our history and our opinion of the war with Iraq. The only pictures on the walls were of three demure Japanese girls in traditional costume.

It was getting dark and none of the places we had been to so far could fix our tire. We backtracked to the outskirts of town where we had spotted an Esso station. They did not repair tires either but they did have a large area where we could camp. It was away from the traffic and actually had a pleasant view of a canyon and the hills. It was a big enough field that we could let the dog roam. In the U.S. there are frequent rest stops on the highways built to accommodate travelers and truck drivers who need a break. In Central America private enterprise has filled the need. Most of the gas stations, especially those away from the cities,

provide enough space to get well off the road and away from the traffic. Occasionally there would be other trucks, but most often we were on our own. Sometimes the manager would welcome us to a power point so we could string our extension cord and enjoy an episode of M.A.S.H., or he would let us fill up our water tank. Of course we would fill up on gas as well. There would always be a *vigilante* there who was being paid to guard the place, and he would be more than happy to watch out for us, for a couple of dollars tip.

Day 51
Wednesday, March, 5 Danli to Nicaragua

We were only forty miles from the Nicaraguan border and we hoped to make an early crossing, after picking up our laundry, of course. And we still needed to get the tire repaired.

We were recommended to a *llantería* in town that would fix the tire, so we went there first not knowing exactly when in the morning our laundry would be ready.

We turned off the main road down an unmade dirt lane and into the courtyard of the *llantería*. They were very professional and knew big truck tires. We only needed a valve stem replacement and for the tire to be re-inflated. This cost us about $2 and about an hour.

Now that we were familiar with the town, we pulled the motorhome up in front of the laundry and our things were ready, all fluffed and folded. We also picked up some perishables for dinner at the stalls across the street.

Three miles south of Danli we found a cigar factory. Actually there were two, but the larger one didn't welcome visitors and we wanted to see cigars being made. I enjoy seeing skilled craftsmen and these worked so fast I could hardly follow what their hands were doing. One worker took a leaf, stripped the tougher center strip out and tore the leaf in two. Gathering more tobacco and bunching it together he wrapped and rolled the bundle into a cigar inside the half leaf. This was then put in a wooden box with cigar sized grooves. When all the grooves were filled it was covered with a lid that was pressed down in a vise. This was just the first stage. Another

---

ABOVE: Danli, Honduras
RIGHT: Indio Cigar Factory south of Danli, Honduras.

worker would trim the ends and wrap the tips. Yet another worker in a different room added the bands, graded and boxed them. It sounds simple but it was obvious that the men and women there had been doing it for a while. There must have been two hundred workers in the main room making various sizes of cigars. For entertainment there was a man sitting in a rostrum overlooking the large room full of workers. He was reading the newspaper over a loud speaker.

Everyone was friendly and appeared proud of what they were doing. We received welcoming smiles wherever we went but the hands never stopped. They were paid by the hour but they never slowed down.

Our timing was off as we arrived at the Nicaraguan border at Las Manos at 11:15. We ran into conflict with the noon lunch hour. It didn't really matter as we had to eat too, and we decided not to let the border crossings get to us. Great eighteen wheelers loomed over us as we waited, squeezed between them for our turn for inspection. It took two and a half hours including lunch, and as we pulled out there was a sign in English that read, "The Nicaraguan immigration wishes you a pleasant trip." A nice touch.

For the past couple of days I had been suffering from the same affliction as John. I had a boil. Not only did the boil hurt; it made me feel dreadful. The poison had got into my blood stream. I just lay down in the back of the bus and wished I could die. If I had an amused smile at John's complaint before, I didn't now. Boils are nasty. I needed a doctor. When we reached the town of Estelí, John pulled over where he saw a *farmacia* sign. I didn't care where he took me.

John went in first to ask where he could find a doctor. There was a pharmacy counter facing the road and two ladies dispensing medicine. One of them volunteered that she was a doctor. As John came to fetch me from the motorhome the doctor donned her white surgical gown and welcomed us as we entered the pharmacy. She showed us into a clinic through a door at the side of the pharmacy counter. There was a small examination room and we all crowded in. She invited me to sit down: *"Siéntese."*

I laughed and replied, *"Ésa es mi problema. No es posible. Tengo un absceso."* I explained that if I could sit I wouldn't be there. She took a look and immediately decided it needed lancing. She went to lengths to make sure all the surfaces and her equipment were sterile, but there was no anesthetic. She made two cuts across the boil and proceeded to squeeze all the nasty stuff out that she could. She squeezed very hard. It hurt. Poor John didn't know what to do. I was screaming through clenched teeth and crushing his hand until I hurt him.

I left the clinic feeling immediately better, but boy had it hurt! She prescribed antibiotics and an anti-inflammatory. The total cost of my medical treatment and medicine was 314 *córdobas*, or $21. The Cipro antibiotic she prescribed was actually available over-the-counter anywhere

in Central America for about a fifth of the cost in the States. She told us that if it wasn't better in the morning I would need to go to the hospital. That wasn't appealing so I decided to get better immediately. At least I could sit and that was an improvement.

Feeling better, but still groggy, we looked for a place to camp. After searching unsuccessfully in town for a camping place, we headed south on the Pan-American Highway and saw a restaurant high on a hill with a dirt road next to it. It looked promising. We turned down the lane, but instead of leading to the restaurant parking lot, a couple hundred yards down there was a private school with a large field beyond. The field was perfect. John went into the school to ask permission to park there. In the meantime school let out and there were all these children about, so I broke out my balloons. Some of the parents waited patiently while the children took turns for a sculptured balloon animal. The girls and boys were all polite and fun, and comfortable chatting with us.

We were made welcome and Ronaldo, the administrator, insisted that we stay close to the school so their *vigilante* could watch over us. We would have preferred to be in the field but it was hard to say that. Everyone was so kind to us. The *vigilante* even helped us top off our

water. We walked back to the restaurant and climbed up to their top floor for a great view of the valley. After enjoying a nice meal with some wine, I, with all my drugs, went to sleep extra early.

Day 52
Thursday, March 6, Managua

We left the school after the children had settled into their morning classes and headed south on the Pan-American Highway towards Managua.

There was a hodgepodge of vehicles on the roads, and this would peak in the small towns. Waiting at the bus stops along the way were three wheeled bicycles. The driver peddled at the back and there were at least two passengers up front often under a colorful little shade canopy. The more affluent workers modified the system and had motor scooters pushing the carriage and thus they could carry heavier merchandise.

The traditional horse and trap could be seen everywhere. Many of these two-wheeled carts had car wheels, which must be considerably more comfortable than the plank wheels that are still around. And then add to the traffic, second hand school buses from the U.S. painted with psychedelic scenes and used as regular public transport; and the ever present eighteen wheelers all over the road, trying to get from one end of the country to the other as fast as they could. Traffic jams were made up of any or all of the above mixed in with a healthy scattering of pedestrians and dogs weaving in and out of the vehicles. There weren't traffic lights in the small towns, just speed bumps so it is just good manners that seem to prevail at the congested intersections.

LEFT: Making balloon animals for the school children, Estelí, Nicaragua

We were stopped by the military again. There were orange cones in the road and two young men in army fatigues with guns slung over their shoulders flagged us down.

"May I see your driver's license." I handed it over and he examined it. I looked at John. We were both grateful that I had been behind the wheel, as John didn't have a license to produce.

"I need to see your car documents." Even though I couldn't understand every word, his gestures made his meaning clear. John got these down from the file box where we carried all our documents. I handed over the car papers. He walked away to examine them and to discuss the situation with his *compadre.*

He returned, and holding them away from me said, "You cannot have the bicycles tied to the front of the vehicle. It is against the law and you must pay a fine." John helped me with this translation.

"But we had them there when we came across the border," I protested. "The police at the *aduana* didn't say we couldn't have them there." I'm not sure he understood my scrambled Spanish but he got the gist of what I was saying. "No," can usually be understood in any language.

He repeated, "You must put them inside and pay a fine." The idea of traveling with two bicycles inside the little motorhome was most unappealing.

John said to me, "Why don't we just give them the bikes?" We had thought all along that there was very little chance that we would bring them home with us.

"What! No way! They are trying to rip us off and you want to reward them with our bikes! No way!" I retorted something like that in a sotto voice to John.

"You need to take them off and put them inside and pay a fine." The young soldier now had his friend at his side.

"No," I said. "Look at the papers we got at the border. They say we have two bicycles. Look. It says so right there. The police at the border saw them on the front of the *casa rodante* and said they were OK." Well they hadn't exactly said they were OK, but they hadn't told us to remove them.

He retorted "It might be legal at the border. but it is against the law in this town. And there is a fine."

"No." I said in my best Spanish. "We were told that we could drive with them there through Nicaragua."

At this point I think the young man realized that he had met his match and he muttered, "We won't fine you then, but you must move them inside."

I held my hand out for the precious papers, which he passed to me and I said, *"Gracias.* We will find a place off the road where it is safe to stop and we will take them off." And at that he stepped back and allowed me to drive on. We never did remove them and they stayed on the front of the bus until we returned to Texas.

Managua had more traffic than we had seen in a while. While stopped in traffic we were approached by the usual flock of vendors but instead of selling fruit for pennies, as we had become accustomed, here they were selling small electronics and cell phone attachments.

We planned to head right through Managua, as we don't enjoy driving the motorhome in the cities. We were on Avenida Bolivia asking directions when I saw a magnificent and unabashed statue. Here was a colossus of a man brandishing an axe in one hand and an automatic rifle with a Sandinista flag stuck down the barrel in the other. I learned later that the inscription reads "Workers and campesinos onward until the end." Regardless of politics it is a grand statue.

The roads through Nicaragua were considerably better than the roads we had seen in other parts of Central America. They looked as though they had just been built and in the same style as the U.S. roads.

We did a shop in a supermarket in Managua, then continued on the Pan-American Highway towards Costa Rica. Once again we saw the cones in the road and were stopped by uniformed men toting automatic rifles. This time John was at the wheel and again he didn't have an original of his license. These guys didn't like it and suggested that we could return to Managua, an hour behind us, or pay them twenty dollars each. We took the easier more expensive option as this time we didn't have a leg to stand on. One of them had his badge hidden and the other showed it very briefly to me when I asked for it. I asked for their badge numbers and they wrote some figures on a scrap of paper, clearly not their ID numbers. It was not worth the hassle with them, although I think we could have pushed back on the negotiations. We had one twenty on hand, that the first man took and he walked off leaving his accomplice waiting for his twenty. We logged it in our expenses under "tolls." It was clearly a rip off. These guys never mentioned the bicycles on the front.

Continuing south, we came to the town of Rivas. The map showed Lake Nicaragua just a few miles away so we decided to take a quick detour to check it out. We found our way to the lakeside resort town of San Jorge. We passed a statue of him slaying the dragon as we arrived. It was a surprise to suddenly come to a beach in front of the lake. We pulled over and parked next to a restaurant and went in for a cool beer and to ask if we could stay the night.

The sun was sinking behind us and casting its orange light on the lake and the volcanoes on Ometepe Island. Along the shore were rows of poles for holiday-makers to hang their hammocks and frames for shade. Posts marked the firm ground for cars or horse drawn carts to drive along the water's edge. The occasional pig meandered past us and rooted around for a snack, dogs trotted by, and a horse went down to the water to drink. Brindle enjoyed it all. There were a few families relaxing in the late afternoon sun with children digging in the sand. We had dinner at the little restaurant and some good cold beer before turning in for the night.

ABOVE: Lake Nicaragua and Ometepe Island, San Jorge, Honduras

CHAPTER 6

Cloud Forests

MONTEVERDE, COSTA RICA

Day 53
Friday, March 7
Lake Nicaragua to Costa Rica

It was strange to have such a large body of water and no tide. People park their cars in the shallows to wash them. Pigs and horses wander in for a drink. We plan to take the ferry across to the island on our return trip north. Accounts from locals as well as friends far away say it is worth a visit.

*A lizard ran out
on a rock and looked up,
listening no doubt
to the sounding of the spheres.
And what a dandy fellow!
The right toss of a chin for you
and a swirl of a tail!
If men were as much men
as lizards are lizards
They'd be worth looking at.*

LIZARD
D.H. Lawrence

An hour or so after breaking camp we were at the border between Nicaragua and Costa Rica and being

swarmed by *transitos* holding up their licenses and offering their services to guide us through the formalities. Because this border was on the Pan-American Highway it was very busy and there were a large number of trucks. As usual, we had not rushed to get away from our overnight camp, so once again we arrived at the border so our transit would be interrupted by the lunch hour. We were eating at the *aduana,* but at least we could turn on our air conditioning and keep comfortable on the scorching concrete.

There was a couple of dollars to pay to the local municipality to exit Nicaragua and six dollars for immigration. As I had the motorhome listed on my passport, it was important that it was counter stamped saying I was taking the vehicle out of the country, otherwise I would be sent a bill for the sales tax. We also had to have the dog's papers stamped showing that she left the country. We wanted to get the formalities right for our return to Nicaragua.

To enter Costa Rica we had to pay a fee of U.S. $4.50 to have our car disinfected.

It was like driving through a very poor car wash with a fine spray. We then had to buy car insurance for three months at a cost of about U.S. $17. We could not find out what it covered and I hoped we would never have to learn. The Costa Ricans stamped the dog's papers with little more that a cursory glance and no money changing hands. On top of all that we paid U. S. $14 to the *transitos,* the three young men who guided us through the maze and confusion on both sides of the border. They were worth it.

Nicaragua had been very dry with a constant wind, but almost as soon as we crossed the border the countryside became greener with sweeping hills and generally much more pleasant scenery. There were fields of cattle, one of exclusively white livestock that looked lovely against the dark green grass. It must have been part of a very large ranch, because across the road I saw the most colossal bull. There were also fields of horses, but

ABOVE: Sunrise over Ometepe Island

it was the cattle that looked particularly fine here.

As the view improved the road deteriorated measurably. Just when you want to look around you have to keep your eyes on the road. We were driving 40 mph at best.

Because of John's lack of a license, I drove across the border, and soon after we saw orange cones and we were pulled over by *federales*. We dutifully showed our papers and asked if there were more stops so we would know whether we could put our passports and other documents away.

"Hay mas. Hay cuatro mas." "There are four more check stations?" We didn't believe there would be five, but there were. These young men sit in little self-constructed shelters until a vehicle comes along and then come out and check either a driver's license or the car papers or something. The last guy must have realized the futility of his position, as he just waved us on from his perch in the shade.

As we approached the town of Liberia, John spotted another motorhome in a field behind some bushes. We decided to turn around and investigate. We hadn't seen another motorhome in a while so it was worth checking out.

I made a U-turn.

A motorhome! There were twenty of them! We had come across a well laid-out motorhome campsite where a caravan was staying for the night. If they hadn't been there we never would have seen it. There were water and power hook-ups in neat rows that had long since been disconnected, but there were shade trees and plenty of space. Most important, there was a dumpsite.

We spent quite a while chatting with the gringos and the wagonmaster who gave us some useful and interesting information. John Plaxton was the wagonmaster and together with his wife Liz, had done a trip similar to what we were attempting a couple or years earlier and had written a book about it. This experience had helped them get the position of wagonmasters. They freely shared information on what to expect and some good places to camp. We were happy to buy an autographed edition of *Mexico and Central America by Campervan* from them.

The caravan was organized by Adventure Caravans. This is the same outfit that organized the Mexican caravan we ran into in Veracruz, Mexico. All the motorhome occupants went over to the swimming pool for a meeting on transiting north into Nicaragua. They had been to Panama and were on their way home. We felt that we were just beginning.

Day 54
Saturday, March 8, Puntarenas

The caravan of motorhomes was scheduled to pull out at 6:30 a. m., and I heard rumblings at about five. I got up and went out to keep an eye on the dog. The RVs were gathering and then the leader started to pull out. Although there were only twenty, it seemed like a hundred of varying sizes from a little camper on a truck to a forty-one foot class "A" colossal coach. They all circled for their place in line. I called John to have a look, but by the time he climbed down from the bunk and came out into the sunshine at 6:33, the caboose was pulling out! We had the place to ourselves until the horses wandered over.

We topped off our water tanks and were able to empty our holding tanks in the first dump station since Mexico; we were out of there before nine. The roads were not good. They were surfaced but full of potholes. All sorts of vehicles overtook us, including eighteen wheelers, but we could catch them again on the uphill. I was able to use cruise control for the first time since leaving the U.S. I set it at forty mph and just steered around the holes and ignored the guys behind me. I occasionally glanced up at the scenery.

There were miles of pastureland. The animals looked well-fed, although the land was dry and the grass brown. There were herds of sleek white cattle grazing with a background of the blue volcanoes, hazy hills, and cloud forest beyond.

There were more trees here than there were north of the Nicaraguan border, which offered occasional shade on the road and provided silhouettes against the skyline. These enormous trees at one time would have needed their height to reach the light through the dark jungle. Now they spread their branches as though they were stretching their arms in the sunshine and offering shade to herds

of cattle and horses. The shadows also hid the potholes on the road!

There was some large-scale irrigation and some lush green rice paddies, providing contrast to the dry grass, and always there was something burning. Either the dead crops were burning in the fields, or the grass verges, or trash, but always you could see smoke.

We crossed over a couple of fast moving rivers where appealing rafting trips were being offered. If it were not for the boils on our butts we would have had a go. We would have to wait and do it on the return trip.

We were in a quandary as to how to plan the next phase of our trip. When we left Honduras we decided it would be best to drive directly to our ultimate destination, Panama, leaving sightseeing in Nicaragua and Costa Rica for our return trip. The wagonmasters of the caravan told us that if we re-entered Costa Rica within three months of our departure from the country, we would only have three days on the return trip

to transit the country. We had also been told that we couldn't take a dog into Panama, but we couldn't confirm any of this. John also needed to replace his lost driver's license. Our attempts to get a replacement from Texas were stalled, and the Costa Rican authorities said we could obtain a Costa Rican license in San José. We changed our plans and headed directly for San José where we thought we could find out the real story while John got his license replaced.

So there we were chugging along with about two hours to go to the capital when I saw a sign for Puntarenas and remembered our daughter, Tanya, saying something about it. This was Saturday, and we couldn't do any of our business until Monday, so what was the rush? We made another change and headed for the beach. Fifty-four days after leaving Houston we'd be on the Pacific Ocean at last!

Puntarenas is a resort community where the locals crowd during weekends in the dry season. We drove the five miles to the tip of the peninsula and meandered about until we came across *Paseo de los Turistas,* with tall palms, shade trees, and 100 feet of sand to the water. We pulled over under a tree. We put our chairs on the sand in the shade of the same tree, cracked our new bottle of rum and poured it over ice, added some coke, and watched as the sun cooled and set. A review of boats sailed past us from pleasure craft to ferries, to tankers, to a tuna fishing boat. There were a dozen families enjoying the beach and the Gulf of Nicoya. Other families and couples were strolling up and down the beach, or on the sidewalk, which had become our front porch. Is this why we came to Central America?

After the sunset we took advantage of the convenient public lighting to continue to read and absorb the atmosphere and the sea breeze.

Across the paseo a choice of restaurants offered *plato típico* (typical dinner). We chose the closest place since the rum didn't encourage us to walk far. The motorhome glowed under the street light across the way, the dog lay under the table, and the food was good.

Day 55
Sunday, March 9, Puntarenas to
San Antonio de Belén, San José

Puntaranas was a pleasant surprise. There we were on Sunday morning with the best parking spot on the strand with an expansive view of the beach.

Joggers ran along the sand just out of the waves and families swam. Yes, they were in the water at six in the morning. It was that warm and pleasant. A golfer practiced his golf swing as he strolled along the beach. He played a few balls along the wet sand just above the gently breaking waves and then gathered them up. When he reached the furthest ball, he set up his tee and started all over again. A nice way to exercise on a Sunday morning.

A bedraggled man who looked like he had not slept in a bed for a while came up to us offering a handful of cashew fruits for sale. He had probably just picked them off a tree further down the road. He had a friendly black-tooth smile. The somewhat imperfect yellow and orange kidney shaped fruits still had their nuts attached. He only wanted a few pennies for them all, so I gave him what he wanted but only took a couple. I peeled back the thin smooth skin which revealed a very juicy flesh with little black specks that might have been seeds eons ago. They were bitter and neither of us liked them. We couldn't crack the nuts that protruded from the bottom, as the shells were like solid rock.

After lunch we packed up and drove back along the peninsula with a railway track separating us from the never-ending beach. There were other areas we could have pulled off the road to enjoy the sun and sand, but we were heading out and had business ahead.

We made the short drive to San Antonio de Belén, a suburb of San José, and to one of the few real trailer parks in Central America. What a relief to be able to take advantage of the facilities. They have a string of good hot showers. Ahhhhhhhh. My major chore was to begin scraping, scooping and brushing out the dust inside the RV. Then, with unlimited water tapped right into the motorhome, I could wash everything in the drawers, shelves, and cupboards. It was an endless chore that I never finished.

With the good electrical hookup we lay in bed and treated ourselves to another episode of M★A★S★H★.

Day 56
Monday, March 10, San José

The entire day was spent cleaning, surfing the internet, and attempting to get John's driver's license. John spent ages on the satellite phone to Houston trying to get his Texas license replaced and then gave up. He might as well get a Costa Rican one.

The proprietor of the trailer park called us a cab, which wasn't really a taxi but a friend of her son who had a car. We figured this out when the police stopped him and as Nicasio was slowing down he turned to us and pointedly said, "You are my friends. You are just my friends and we are driving together. OK?"

"*No problema,*" John responded. We learned that there was a crackdown on private car owners making money charging for rides. We were happy to play along but were never questioned by the police.

Nicasio was a great help and took us to the correct authorities to get John his Costa Rican driver's license. Going through these formalities is not usually simple in any country, even when you speak the language. This was particularly confusing. There were long lines and people waiting in corridors at different windows with little or no signage and it was very hot. Nicasio led us from one location to another within the building and eventually to the chief of the department. He helped plead our case that it would be very nice if they issued us at least a temporary emergency license. No. John would have to take the tests, both written and practical. He paid for the written test and made an appointment to take it as soon as he could, which was two days hence. John bought the textbook of the local rules of the road, available in Spanish only, so he could study for it. Then it dawned on us that he would have to take the practical test in the motorhome. That would be quite an experience for both John and the examiner. Then Nicasio offered John his car to drive for the test. That was very generous and another example of how kind everyone was. Yes, of course we would have paid him for the use and for his time; nevertheless, I can't imagine anyone lending a stranger their car like that in the U.S.

When John visited the Panamanian Consulate in Houston he was told that the dog's papers must not be more than three days old. We had also heard more than one rumor that we could not take a dog into Panama at all. Just to be on the safe side we asked Nicasio if he would take us to the Panamanian consulate here in San José.

I slid the papers under the glass window to the bored young lady saying, "Are these papers all OK to take our dog into Panama?"

She looked at them for a while. She flipped through the several pages, and went back to the cover page. Her face was expressionless. I don't think she had ever seen the likes before. She took a breath and said, *"Son buenos,"* and passed them back under the glass separating us.

I did not feel very comforted even though she had said they were OK, but we had done our best. Just to make sure that she was actually alive I asked her if she had any tourist information on Panama.

She raised her eyebrows as though surprised that we were really driving there. *"Momentito,"* she said and disappeared through the door behind her cubicle.

A minute or two later another lady appeared. Maria was warm, voluptuous, middle aged, and full of smiles. She presented us with a book solid with information about Panama. We wanted to know if we could transit the Canal. She repeated what we had heard about the weekly tours and found the advertisement in the book for us.

Nicasio was being such a good guide that John decided to attempt one other chore while in the city. We were passing very modern and upscale shopping areas and John asked Nicasio if there might be a computer shop close by. Nicasio knew of one and took us there. We had taken hundreds of pictures and stored them on our laptop's hard drive. John wanted a backup system so he purchased an external CD burner from this small shop in San José.

The trailer park had a washing machine and I must have done a dozen loads. What wasn't dirty was dusty. The brisk breeze dried the clothes on the line so fast that by the time I had hung up the last item I could take down and fold up the first.

John was back on the phone and internet and in the end determined that sending a replacement Texas license to Panama would be the most efficient after all. I think he was nervous about taking the tests in Costa Rica and I don't blame him. Also there was not much to do where we were, apart from cleaning, so I was happy to continue on.

Day 57, Tuesday
March 11, Belén Trailer Park,

This morning John re-confirmed disappointing news, this time with the border agent of a tour operating company. He verified there was a limit to the length of stay customs would permit for a vehicle on a second visit to Costa Rica within a ninety-day period. This explained why caravans schedule their trips to tour when heading south, and passed directly through Costa Rica in three days on the homeward journey. When we later reentered Costa Rica from Panama we found this information was **completely false.** We had **no** limit put on the length of our north-bound visit.

At the time we believed we would only have three days on our home bound transit, so we needed to explore Costa Rica then. There were places we didn't want to miss, so we changed our plans once more and turned back north to the mountains and the Arenal volcano. Changing our plans was nothing new; we did it almost on a daily basis.

The scenery was picturesque and lush. Tomatoes were for sale along the road

and each vendor tried to make theirs look more appealing than the next, displaying them attractively in tiers in boxes. There were tight little fields of sugar cane edged by dark green acres of coffee bushes with their tall shade trees. There were countless shades of green.

We backtracked on CA1, as the Pan-American Highway is called down here. We left the highway at the industrial town of San Ramon and headed for the hills. I inherited from my father an interest in knowing what the crops were that grew along the roadside. Now I noticed something that amazed me. Here was a field of scraggly plants with leaves of five saw tooth fingers. It looked for all-the-world like marijuana, even though most of the leaves had seven fingers. Not marijuana in Costa Rica, surely! Who would grow it so brazenly in fields next to a main thoroughfare? I recommend our fellow travelers not to get excited and leap out of their cars to grab a smoke. We learned later that this was the plant of the root crop yucca.

Our speed dropped to twenty miles an hour, and now that we were out of the city, cattle began to appear grazing at the side of the road. Suddenly ferns and tall trees surrounded us. It was a dramatic change. Masses of impatiens flowers created verges of pinks prettier than the lushest of gardens.

Local residents took advantage of the rich soil and had carefully planned gardens of colorful foliage shrubs; translucent royal-purple bougainvillea draped over flaming poinsettia bushes. Perhaps they were all gardeners because the fields around were filled with decorative plants. There were hundreds, perhaps thousands, of acres of ornamental plants coloring the hills in shades of green and yellows.

ABOVE: Fields of ornamental plants, Costa Rica
RIGHT: Wallowing in the hot pools of Tabacón, Arenal, Costa Rica

The road was slow and winding with verdant hedges of the kinds of plants I struggle to keep alive in my home. The workers just chopped off the tops and transported them somewhere else to be potted for sale. The stumps then grew back into new plants. Many of the plants growing in the fields were for export to the U.S. as tropical indoor plants.

It was a slow but attractive drive to La Fortuna, the gateway to Arenal. This town is famous for the fiery displays of the most active volcano in the Americas. Unfortunately, it is usually obscured in clouds.

The campsite listed in one of our tour books, where we planned to stay, didn't materialize. It was here that we added a new item to our departure checklist. We had carefully followed directions and arrived at a little hut, but it only advertised tours and was closed anyway. We peered through the window searching in vain for a clue to the promised campsite. There was nothing so we moved out. All of a sudden something seemed wrong. No dog! We

looked back and there she was doing what dogs should do in the bushes, but with a slightly more strained expression than usual. She was usually the first on board. She became the first item on our checklist.

We kept going, looking for a camping place, until we reached the Tabacón Resort, but there was hardly a place to pull over along the way. Fortunately, the *vigilante* at the resort said we could stay in their parking area for the night. We maneuvered the motorhome so we could watch the volcano from our window, hoping for a fireworks display.

After dinner we changed into our swimwear and walked across the road to the resort. It was now completely dark. The volcano produces hot water springs and one of the main reasons for visiting Arenal is to indulge in the hot pools and streams, and this famous resort that surrounds them.

The clientele consisted exclusively of international tourists. While waiting, as John purchased the tickets and recorded the price in his palm pilot, I heard squeals

and shouts from a gaggle of North Americans who were waiting for their bus back to San José.

"There! Did you see it? Did you see it?"

"No. Where?"

"Right up there on the right. Over there!" She pointed into the sky. "No, it is gone now. You mean I drove all that way just for that!" Her package tour from San José was a four-hour drive in a minibus over dirt roads to get here, and she was looking at another four hours on the dark bumpy road back to her hotel. At least she had caught a glimpse of hot lava between the clouds and I hoped she

had enjoyed an afternoon in the hot pools. We didn't see any glowing embers. Our current intent, however, was to wallow in the warm waters.

The exotic plants have been there a long time and were developed into lush and well tended gardens. Streams had been coaxed to wind around the vegetation and over waterfalls of various sizes. We sat in a little hot pool by ourselves in the dark with the clear water pouring over a little cliff and bouncing off our shoulders. The streams have loose river-pebbles on the bottom and the banks have been built with the same smooth stones. The only dirt is in the flowerbeds.

Gathering up our towels, we walked down the winding path to a much larger pool where there was a twenty-foot waterfall tumbling down the round boulders, steaming and streaming around us with the water pounding on our backs. Climbing up a way we found level perches where we could watch a group of Germans frolicking and laughing as the steam hugged them and swallowed them in the hot mist. We moved on, preferring to loll in a quiet pond with ornamental vegetation hanging atop of us while frogs croaked in the undergrowth. (I know what you are thinking but if there were a frog foolish enough to hop in he would surely cook.) I am not a person who usually indulges in a hot tub, but this was all most enjoyable.

We wallowed in the natural streams and river pools and then went to one of the ten or more western-style blue walled swimming pools. This one had a

LEFT: Lost deep in the Costa Rican jungle
RIGHT: Through breaks in the trees there were magnificent vistas across Lake Arenal

bar in the middle that was surrounded with bar stools that were all under water. These pools ranged in temperature from various shades of hot to cold. We swam up to the bar and sampled their piña coladas, which rated a "B." The second one was a B+. We played like children on the long slide at the far side of the pool.

The Tabacón Resort could be called a jungle paradise, but it is not in any way primitive. There is a fully equipped spa offering mud baths and massages, a shop, restaurants, and seventy-three rooms. It is a long way from any other accommodations, so if you plan to stay at the hotel I would recommend making reservations. Costa Rica is much more developed than its neighboring countries, and this resort is an example of that.

We walked back dripping wet in the warm damp night and settled into our little home. I took a long look at the volcano before drawing the curtains. She stayed serenely shrouded in the clouds.

Day 58
Wednesday, March 12, Arenal to Castillo

I didn't sleep well. I kept waking up to look out of the window for a lava flow or hot sparks to appear. I had this nagging feeling that this active volcano might put on more than a show. I could not see any glowing flow through the cloud, or was it smoke or steam, that sat over the volcano?

John had learned about a place on the other side of the lake where we could park with a full view of the Arenal Volcano. We set off to find it. This is the only time we really got completely and utterly lost, (other than in big cities) and we enjoyed the entire ride.

After leaving the main road we tracked a dirt road for an hour or more through a really intimidating rain-forest

in a light rain. The narrow damp dirt trail sliced through the ultimate jungle that reached so high it was as though the clumps of green at the top were in a different world. This was a wonderland of green on green, with dragonflies and beetles, and critters with eight legs, and others with four, and birds and butterflies flitting by. This was jungle at its best. There was no one for miles and we were completely lost.

It flashed through my mind that we could break down and be stuck for a week. Then I smiled and thought that it didn't really matter if we did break down. We were self-contained and could just sit in the middle of the road, in the middle of the jungle, enjoying our surroundings for at least a week. The men in Central America are so used to keeping their ancient vehicles running that I was confident that someone would come along who could repair it or fetch help. In the meantime I would just admire the dripping leaves and lizards.

John could pinpoint where we were with his GPS, but that wouldn't help us find the main road because of the vague map coordinates. We weren't even sure the road we wanted was on the map. We also had a compass and could always retrace our tracks. It wasn't as if we had been driving for days.

The lack of dust was also a relief. Although it was warm and very muggy, the fine rain and moisture in the air made the road damp and dust free.

Then we came out of the jungle at the main highway almost where we started. I have to admit that it was a bit of a let down to be back on the two-lane road with the occasional car passing. I had enjoyed being lost.

We were rewarded for our happy misadventures by a coatimundi wandering about on the road. He seemed completely unafraid and in fact curious about the motorhome, so much so that I though he might be sick. He sat down and scratched, looked at us and then wandered past before we headed on our way. From subsequent experiences I learned that these critters of the raccoon family can be very bold and although they are usually nocturnal, the lone males frequently wander about during the day. It might not have been an unusual encounter, but it was very special to us. He was all the more cute as he browsed next to the bank of wild impatiens that blossomed along the road.

We had driven in a full circle. We tried again to find the road to the other side of the lake, and once on the dirt road we made a left turn where we had gone right before, and were immediately swallowed by jungle again. This time we came to a forestry station where there was a gathering of backpackers and enough locals to give us some encouraging advice and directions. Coming out of the forest we were presented with wonderful views of the Arenal volcano. Without the trees around us we could always see the volcano, so although we

LEFT: A coatimundi exploring the wild impatiens on the Costa Rican mountain road

were lost again, we knew where we were, sort of!

After an hour driving on these very slow roads we came to a lodge high up on the pinnacle of a hill. We took a deep breath and charged up their very steep, narrow, concrete driveway and came out on a little flat parking lot with magnificent views all round of the lake and volcano. We thought that this would be one time that it would be worth staying in a hotel. That was until we learned that their midweek rate was $70 a night. Cost Rica is not backwards in their pricing. We put the bus in low gear and crept back down their drive and meandered along the dirt road until we came to a little village right on the lake. There was a soccer field and a parking area next to it that looked like it was made for us.

We had found Castillo, but don't try looking it up on a map. (We have

included a map of our own in the "Camping Section" if you want to try it.) Castillo is on the edge of Lake Arenal and there must be, ooh fifty residents at most. We were three-and-a-half-hours by horse from Monteverde. It is eight hours by car even when you know the way.

On our walk down to the lakeshore our path crossed another path, that of a leaf-cutter ant colony. It is amazing to see these little critters carry as much as fifty times their weight in unwieldy great flakes of a leaf. They bump into each

ABOVE: Cloud shrouded Arenal volcano, Costa Rica
RIGHT: The view from Castillo across Lake Arenal to the volcano

other, seem to have the occasional chat with a friend, but always scurry on waving their vast load over their heads. The innumerable little feet going back and forth had worn a path in the grass. It was incredible to think that a myriad of minute feet had actually worn a clear path through the grass. How many little footprints would it take to wear this path and keep the grass from growing back over? It has been calculated that the leaf-cutters harvest twelve percent of the rain-forest. They bring the leaves below ground and turn them into mulch where they grow fungus that the ants eat. The mulch also provides nutrients for the trees above and so the cycle continues.

On a previous visit to Costa Rica, I remember sitting down to rest on a tree

root in the middle of a jungle path. I watched leaf-cutter ants devour a cluster of leaves that had fallen on the dirt. In the quiet I realized I could actually hear the ants munching on the dry leaves. They have major jaws. The local Indians used them for medicinal purposes. If someone had a cut the ant was positioned so that it bit the cut together like a suture. The ant's mandibles biodegrade in the skin as the cut heals.

We made new friends. A couple with four girls came out to enjoy the adjacent soccer field as the sun was setting. It turned out that the man had a string of horses that he rents for the trek to Monteverde. We wished we could have given him the business and taken the horse trek, but then what would we do with the motorhome?

Once again we found a most glorious place to spend the night. I sat in the shade of the bus with Arenal Volcano filling the skyline in front of me. John made grilled ham and cheese sandwiches for supper and Brindle wandered about visiting with new friends. We had a view of the lake and I could lie in bed and watch the volcano without my nervousness of an eruption.

Day 59
Thursday, March 13, To Monteverde

We left the pueblo of Castillo on the Arenal lakeshore early for what we expected to be an arduous drive through interesting scenery. Where the sun shone on the side of the road the verges were rich with every shade of pink where wild impatiens were blossoming. We were driving through deep rain-forest. It was intimidating jungle, towering overhead. The wind kissed the tops of the very

TOP LEFT: Children in Castillo, Costa Rica
LEFT: On the main road between Arenal and Monteverde

tallest trees where the clouds had rested overnight. The rustling leaves scattered drips of delayed rain onto the dirt road below. The trees leaned over the narrow damp gray road as if they wanted to embrace. Some had gray trunks and others were so wrapped in creepers you couldn't see the trunks. Vines and creepers tied it all together to make it an impenetrable all encompassing green. A fern pierced through with delicate fronds to drip water onto the elephant ear leaves below. It was still, and gray, and green, and the moist leaves shone in the misty light and dripped, dripped all day. We were in rainforest and the clouds drifted, dripping softly round us. The jungle could have swallowed us and it wouldn't even notice.

We came to another dirt road that we thought was the "main" road around the north shore of the lake. It was two lanes wide and our assumption was confirmed by the mini buses full of tourists that darted, bucking and swaying, past us. The passengers didn't look too comfortable crammed in as they were, but at least, I would hope, they were being given a guided tour as they went. For us it was another gray, wet, dirt track with many more potholes, because of the additional traffic. Nevertheless, it was absorbing.

In case we hadn't realized the road was in a bad condition, there were signs telling us: *Carretera en mal estado*. At some corners half the road had been washed away down a crevasse in the rainy season. We carefully followed the tracks of the last minivan. It was slick packed mud, but there was no chance of us skidding at the speed we were going. There were

water-filled potholes to slow us down and to keep us guessing as to how deep they were. The little tourist minibuses splashed through them. You would really need four-wheel drive if you were to attempt this in the rainy season. We rumbled on at a steady pace reveling in a great, wet, green wonder.

We broke out from the forest to dramatic views of Lake Arenal. Little green-gray islands rested on steel-gray waters, reflecting the blue-gray sky with a ghostly shore looming in the background. The sky was still dripping and so were we. It was swelteringly hot and muggy.

The views were dramatic at every turn. Either we were looking at dense jungle, or the lake, or the volcano or all

TOP RIGHT: Sign on the main road to Monteverde, warning that the road is in bad condition
RIGHT: Lake Arenal from the north shore

three. We had plenty of time to look because of the necessity to drive so slowly. We were making about twelve miles an hour, but speed didn't matter. We were there to see the country.

There were also farms and villages along the way in areas where the jungle had been cleared. Some were advertised as being Swiss or German. We stopped in one village for lunch to buy some fresh bread and apple strudel at a German bakery. We chatted with a gaggle of tourists resting on their buttocks. This was definitely a more affluent part of Central America than the other countries we had traversed. There were nicely painted little block-houses with fenced gardens. The snack cost $12, illustrating their effort to be on a par with first world countries.

It took about four hours to encircle Lake Arenal and reach the town of Tilarán. This is an important crossroads. A short paved road from Cañas on the Pan-American Highway climbs the mountains to Tilarán and the Arenal area. If you are driving from Liberia this is the best approach to the Monteverde cloud forests and the volcano area. There are good bus connections on this route to either Liberia or San José, about three hours away. We were a little embarrassed when we asked someone which way to Tilarán when we were actually in the middle of it. We pressed on towards Monteverde and found ourselves on an even worse and bumpy dirt road. Fortunately it was the dry season. Eventually, in the afternoon we came to Santa Elena, the village near the Monteverde Reserve. We did a little shopping and made inquiries as to tours we could take in the morning. Most importantly, we needed a place to park for the night. The tour operator who ran his business from a little building in the

parking lot of the bank, assured us we would be welcome there, but it was not our kind of place; too noisy and right in the middle of town.

Continuing through town toward the Monteverde Reserve the road got even worse. It was three miles over **very** bad broken rock road. I was not looking forward to having to drive back to park in town if there was nothing at the Reserve. There were plenty of pedestrians with sensible shoes or hiking boots. Families strolled with children, and couples walked holding hands. Ornithologists strode glancing up, and every other kind of "—ists," that this overabundant land could attract, were wending their way to their varied accommodations for the night. We were going against the flow.

John had spent some time in Monteverde a few years earlier. He was chaperoning our daughter and her high school friend who were taking total immersion Spanish at the Centro Panamericano de Idiomas. He knew this area, and thought we might be able to overnight at a place called the Cheese Factory. They were willing to let us stay but they needed to lock the gate for security reasons, which would lock us up and keep us safe until nine the next morning when they opened. We

thanked them but decided to move on. The Cheese Factory has an interesting history having been established by a group of Quakers who moved here to farm the area fifty years ago.

We finally arrived at the end of the road and Monteverde Cloud Forest Biological Reserve. This Reserve was established by a group of North American Quakers who settled in the area in 1951. It has been added to over the years, and now consists of 3500 hectares (8650 acres) of pristine jungle. There are many miles of trails and guided tours are run every day. We were hoping to take a tour and to find a place to stay overnight, in spite of the fact that the tour books clearly state that there is no camping in the park, and that pets are not allowed.

The parking available at the entrance to the Reserve was at right angles along the approach road. The park was closed for the day, tourists were leaving and guides were closing the place up. We asked some of the guides and found the manager. We asked him if we could join the night tour, park overnight, and join the early morning tour. We were made welcome. He recommended that we move to a lower parking lot where we would be out of the way of the evening traffic. The manager called a guard who opened the chain that blocked the road to the lower lot. We were allowed to pass and the chain was locked behind us. We trundled down past the entrance buildings to a little clearing of hard packed wet dirt with a tree in the middle that someone had decided was more important than a comfortable turn-around. We were the

only people there in this small opening in the jungle. It couldn't have been more pristine. The only condition the authorities made was that we must keep the dog on a leash. We parked as tight in the corner as we could with the foliage brushing the windows on two sides.

Dinner was in our own private little jungle clearing.

At seven o'clock we walked up the drive to the park headquarters and joined a group of half a dozen others for the night tour. Each person was provided with a high powered flashlight. We saw giant tiger-striped tarantulas lurking next to their lair waiting to pounce on dinner as it passed. There was a rare tanager perched in the branches with his head tucked under his wing, showing off

LEFT: Tucked into the Monteverde parking lot
TOP RIGHT: A bird hiding in a hole during the night.
RIGHT: Monteverde in the rain

his red chest. Another bird was hiding, but not concealed in a hole in the trunk of a tree. The frogs that make so much noise are actually very small, just half an inch long. There were bats hanging on the underside of branches and lizards in frozen animation on twigs.

There are no "beasties" of the Central American jungle. Perhaps the very rare panther, that would prefer to avoid people, could be considered dangerous. The tarantulas are not interested in humans; we are too big to bite! So we slept well in this very quiet rain-forest listening for animals, but only hearing the drip of the constant damp of the rain-forest.

Day 60
Friday, March 15, Monteverde and Sta. Elena

We reveled in The Monteverde Ecological Reserve. When we woke up we were the only people in the jungle. There was not a sound other than the gentle movement of wind through the humid trees above. Then there was a rustle or the flitter of wings. Was it a hummingbird or an insect? It was too fast to see.

Our morning tour started watching a group of howler monkeys swinging in the trees over our campsite. Although we walked some of the same jungle paths we had seen the night before, the early morning tour was very different. Fortunately we avoided any real rain. The tour took us between the trees and ferns and other plants growing from the trunks of the trees. Some of these plants sprout upward with flowers, like bromeliads and orchids, others have tentacles that go to the ground to become roots and even strangle their host. The clouds draped everything like a warm wet blanket. Sometimes clouds snuggled around the trunks and then drifted up above the canopy to show a glimpse of a brilliant "… little tent of blue, we prisoners call

the sky" (Oscar Wilde). It made the sky seem all the higher because of the height of the canopy. Most of the time the low fog obscured the middle distance and created a luminous damp glow.

There were ferns so small that little lizards trampled them underfoot. Others ferns were tall, like lofty creatures from another planet, uncoiling tentacle arms that spread out and become feathery wings once they had absorbed enough light. The tree trunks and branches were saturated with damp moss and vegetation of every kind.

Our guide pointed out many plants and animals and birds we would have never otherwise spotted, making the viewing much more interesting. The information and the sights were overwhelming. At the end he invited us to go on a bridge suspended over a canyon that brought us eye-level with the middle of the giant trees, showing us yet another world. There are three divergent levels in the jungle, the floor, the canopy, and this mid-level. Each level is distinct and some plants and critters never cross from one to another. With this bridge we could visit the mid-level. Later, we would enjoy other bridges that took us through and above the canopy to see the part of the rainforest that enjoys occasional sunshine.

When we returned to our camp we found that it wasn't so secluded, as there were other cars packed in and an old yellow school bus struggling to turn around and not hit the tree. We were then visited by another coatimundi. We refrained from feeding him but he was right outside the motorhome and very curious. Wanting a better look, and perhaps

LEFT: At mid level of the jungle in the Monteverde Reserve
RIGHT: Within the canopy of the Monteverde Cloud Forest

smelling our good German bread he stood up on his back legs. Neither the coatimundi nor the dog was particularly interested in the other. The former was not familiar with animals that could hurt it, and the latter, well, it was too hot for Brindle to want to run around and play.

Reluctantly we left our special little camp and headed for the Butterfly Farm back in the town of Santa Elena. This was a little disappointing, perhaps because there wasn't the variety of insects I expected, but they offer great volunteer opportunities for anyone interested in entomology or for someone who needs an excuse to live in this part of Costa Rica. They had an undeveloped parking area across the dirt lane, which would have been ideal for an overnight stopping place for us. It was a flat dirt lot cut out of the hillside that could handle about a dozen cars. It had a pleasant view of the valley and no buildings nearby, but it was near enough to town that we could walk. Alas, they said we couldn't camp there. We were amazed and disappointed. It turned out that a North American operated it, and he was worried about insurance! It was the only time in all of Central America we were turned down.

But good fortune was again on our side. We found temporary curbside parking in town. A man then approached me from the U.S. who had retired to Santa Elena. He wanted to know how on earth we got the motorhome down there. We chatted for a while and I asked him if he knew of any level ground where we might over-night. He suggested the Bar Las Orquídeas just outside town on the road to San José.

It was perfect, with good-sized grass patches on either side that would be used for parking when the bar was busy. The owners, Danilo and Nidia Zamora were a delightful couple who made us more than welcome.

Danilo was our instant friend. He was an energetic and engaging host. "No, don't park there," Danilo waved his hand. "Over here will be quieter. In the evening we have live music and it will be quieter on the other side."

The view was staggering. There was a little picket fence separating us from a deep precipice of perhaps two or three hundred feet. We had a wide-open view across a jungle valley to the far, tree-covered side with a distant waterfall cascading to the canyon floor.

They encouraged us to plug into their power and to use their water. We settled in and joined them in the bar for a beer. We were struggling for quite a while in Spanish until we learned that they had lived in the States for 20 years. Their English was perfect, but they preferred that we stick with the Spanish as we were trying to learn it. They told us that when they first moved to the U.S., they would refuse to speak Spanish, even to each other. Continual practice is the only way to learn a language. Unfortunately, John and I didn't follow this rule when we were together and our

ABOVE: The canyon behind Bar Las Orquídeas, where we saw the sloths
RIGHT: Inside a strangler ficus tree, years after the host tree inside had disintegrated

language skills didn't develop as much as they might have.

The Zamoras went out of their way to make us feel welcome. All they asked in exchange was our company, and to phone their sons when we returned to the U.S. Nidia and Danilo used to live in Mississippi and Louisiana where their now-grown sons were born. Their children still live in Mississippi.

Nidia would have preferred to live closer to a more developed area as it is a long uncomfortable run to shops other that the limited ones in Santa Elena. Nidia was a nurse in Mississippi and returned to Costa Rica to be with her elderly mother. Her mother is restricted to her wheelchair, but she wheels about the dance floor where they teach the salsa in the evenings. Danilo ran a catfish farm in the U.S. and was a mechanic.

We highly recommend that tenters and RVers check in with them, at least for a cold beer and local information. We did suggest that they charge for the privilege of camping, so it might not be free. We enjoyed their company and their beer, and watching the dance lessons. We were to become good friends.

Day 61
Saturday, March 15 Sta. Elena

When Danilo saw me in the morning he approached very excited with binoculars in his hand. The Bar Las Orquídeas sits on a cliff overlooking a very deep canyon lush with undergrowth that is part of the reserves. There was a very large white sloth with a baby on her back in a tree not far away. It was enormous with coarse scraggly hair, wedged-in between a branch and the trunk of the tree. It looked like some cream colored prehistoric monster with two great finger-like claws clutching the branch. Then with an exclamation Danilo spotted another one, this time a brown one, feeding in a tree together with a coatimundi. I could have watched them all day. The big white one never moved, but the brown one went, can I say, "slothfully" from one branch to another, grasping the branch ahead and

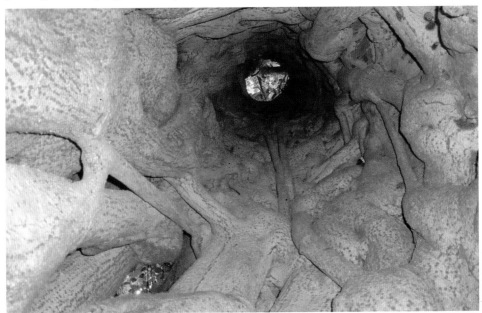

gently shifting her weight to it and moving over. The coatimundi on the other hand, moved like a large clumsy monkey to the ends of the branches, which weighed them down so much I thought they would break, and then grabbed the little leaves at the tips to eat.

There is another rainforest preserve we wanted to visit, the Santa Elena Reserve, and Danilo and Nidia offered to take us there. They were going to go to their little *finca,* or farm, and it was in the same direction. The drive was an experience. The roads were as bad as the ones we had traversed during the past couple of days, but he hit them at thirty miles an hour. Our bus would have shattered. His truck just bounced and bucked like a bull. I almost shattered!

The Zamoras had been buying land around Monteverde for many years, and now had some prime real estate all over the place, some right in the middle of town. If the road is ever paved into Santa Elena and Monteverde he will have some valuable land. They took us to one plot they keep for themselves. It is a small acreage of primary jungle forest with wonderful great old trees. It was an island of dark trees in the middle of pastureland. Like the skyscrapers of Manhattan in the middle of the Hudson River the

trees shot up to the sky. He had seen a big cat there on other occasions and showed us where she had made a nesting place overnight.

One of the ancient strangler trees stood tall, leaving the space inside where the original host had once stood. It had been engulfed and strangled by the little seed that had taken root in its high branches. I felt I was standing inside someone's intestines with the roots intertwining to form the walls around me.

Right in the middle of all this there is a clearing where Danilo has a small vegetable garden. This was what he called his *finca.* The space was cut into the forest before he bought the land. He had healthy crops of potatoes, beans, sweet potatoes, squash, choco, and other vegetables along with numerous herbs. We picked a large bag of fresh green beans that we were still enjoying a week later. They also provided us with cilantro and some mint to make into tea.

We wanted so much to thank them when I suddenly remembered the seeds in my back pocket.

"Danilo, would these tomato seeds be any use to you?"

"Who is it that carries seeds in their pocket? Do you always have seeds with you?"

I laughed. The answer was, "Yes."

We walked through their island of old growth jungle to the far side of the trees where he had built a little gazebo to enjoy the incredible view over the valley. What a place!

Danilo convinced us that the "Sky Walk" was as good, or better, than the Santa Elena Reserve as you explore the jungle on a "Tree Top Tour." This involves walking on bridges to experience the vegetation up in, and at times, over the tops of the trees. They dropped us off and we had lunch at a pleasant restaurant and were entertained yet again by a wild coatimundi wandering around the tropical flowerbeds.

Throughout many jungle areas in Costa Rica "canopy tours" are available and they had one here. These are not really tours; they are thrill rides. They are not for the faint of heart and didn't interest me. There was a long cable, high in the air stretching over the road and the adjacent jungle. Participants are harnessed onto the cable and slide over deep canyons and over the jungle canopy in a manner that a teenager might love, screaming in terror all the while. They were right out of the "reality shows," but without the cameras.

We wanted a more peaceful walk through the canopy on their Tree Top walk. This hike followed paths through dense jungle and across thirteen suspension bridges that span the canyons. These suspension bridges proved to be sufficiently high to produce enough adrenaline for the day! It is not so much that the bridges are high, just that the canyon floor drops precipitously as you walk out on the bridge. You start out at ground level and then as you progress onto the bridge the jungle floor falls away. You are suddenly at the mid-level of the trees awestruck by the plant life that grows in this semi-light, clutching onto the trunks and branches. Then as you walk on, the ground drops below you until you are walking over the tops of the very

tallest trees. You are looking down on the trees rooted in the canyons over 200 feet below.

Several of these upper branches of old trees had died through age or from other plants sucking their sap. But these branches did not look dead, although they were completely rotten. Each branch was like a garden filled with hosts of vegetation, drawing in the rain and the sunlight. These plants and flowers were in turn home to insects, reptiles and birds that live on the top of the world; an entire ecosystem contained on a branch. One day all this will be too much for the rotten branch and it will break and drop to the jungle floor taking with it the hundreds of plants it hosted. As I watched I expected to see one crack and fall in front of me.

The bridges varied in length. Several

LEFT: Danilo and Nidia Zamora showing us around their property, Santa Elena, Costa Rica
TOP RIGHT: A break in the jungle where the sun shone at the mid level of the jungle.
RIGHT: One of the suspension bridges over Santa Elena Cloud Forest

took us exclusively through intermediate level to view plants that grow out of the trunks and branches of the large canopy trees in dappled sunlight.

Other bridges were suspended for great distances over the cloud-like treetops. We were walking over a steaming, billowing blanket of green blushed with red or purple, or tinged in blue or yellow. Very rarely we could see the streams far below even though we could often hear them.

Tired and hot after the hike, we relaxed for a while in the hummingbird garden and then caught the shuttle back to town. We walked to the motorhome to be greeted by Brindle bouncing towards us.

Nidia had arranged for us to take a sunset horseback ride. We had missed so many other opportunities to go riding I didn't want to lose this one. Yesterday had been clear with a dramatic orange sunset. As luck would have it, today was overcast. No matter, we were going.

Across the road José was saddling up our mounts. Both the horses and equipment were as good as I've seen anywhere. The bridles were of attractively braided leather in an unusual design, and they didn't have a bit in the horses' mouths. The Western style saddles were very new and in excellent condition.

We were the only ones on the ride, and José took us through the pasture and into the dark forest beyond. We watched a silver gray fox out prowling. José told us they are known locally as *"gato del monte"*, or cat of the mountains, because they can climb trees. Ours silently trotted along ignoring us for a while and then disappeared as if by magic.

ABOVE: Playing Carrera de Cinchas, Santa Elena, Costa Rica
LEFT: The view through the windshield on the route from Santa Elena back to the Pan-American Highway

I noticed that a pencil-like dart was tied with a leather thong to each of our saddles. The darts were like sharp little spindles and I couldn't work out what they were for. Eventually I asked José and he tried to explain but the vocabulary was too challenging.

He laughed. "*Espera*.... Wait and I will show you."

A little further down the trail we came over a hill and ahead of us was what looked like a clothesline strung between two posts about seven feet off the ground. This was where they played the sport of *Carrera de cinchas*. As knights of old would use a twelve-foot lance to pluck a ring off a pole, these *vaqueros* use little hand-held spikes to spear little rings clipped with clothes pins to a line.

José charged under the line aiming the miniature spear at the ring, showing us how to hook it. The first time I knocked the ring off the line. The second time I hooked it. Brilliant! This was fun. I think I should have been riding faster though.

It would be quite a skill to spear the little rings with the pencil at a full gallop. It was a fun game where competitors win big prizes, like saddles, at competitions around the country.

Day 62
Sunday, March 16, Santa Elena to San José

It was a grim drive back to San José. We took the road directly south from Monteverde back to CA1, the Pan-American Highway. The surface was so bad that in the first ninety minutes we had covered eleven miles. If you had a car you might go faster and rely on your

ABOVE: Sweeping hills south of Monteverde
RIGHT: John with a rock he removed from between the tires

shocks, but in the motorhome with our house on our back we traveled like the proverbial snail.

We had plenty of time to enjoy the scenery. There were great peaked hills that could have been mistaken for California. A few dark trees in the gullies emphasized the brown of the pasture.

Once back on the Pan-American Highway we saw another motorhome like ours, but with Mississippi plates, going north. While driving our motorhome we only encountered two motorhomes on the entire trip other than the caravans in the camp sites we mentioned. Both of the ones we passed were on the same stretch of road between San José and Pantarenas in Costa Rica.

It took us most of the day to get back to the Belén Trailer Park near San José where we could clean up, take a long shower and attempt to clean the interior of the bus yet again. We also tried to catch up on our email. John still hadn't any news about his Texas driver's license.

Day 63
Tuesday, March 17 Belén Trailer Park

We found other travelers of interest at the Belén Trailer Park. William and Niny were a Dutch couple who had no time limit on their trek. They had a truck onto which they, themselves, had built a home that had everything. It looked a little like a tank, but it was well equipped for living in any climate and for just about any emergency. After seven years of preparation the truck had been shipped to the U.S. where they had driven from Alaska to California. They had explored Central America and were now waiting for a boat to South America. The ship they were to sail on with their truck departed four hours before the

scheduled time, so they missed it. The second booking a month later suddenly couldn't accommodate their height. They now had yet another month to wait. They had found an inexpensive shipping rate; $500 on a roll-on roll-off ship from Puerto Caldera, Costa Rica to Guayaquil, Ecuador. But it might have been worth paying a little more.

During the morning, as I worked on the interior, John worked on the exterior of the motorhome including his constant checking of the tires and other basic mechanical parts. It was a good thing he did. To illustrate the kinds of roads we had been on he wrenched out a rock like an ostrich egg that had lodged between the two back tires. Heaven knows how long it had been there.

The road south of San José took us up into the clouds again. It was winding but there was little traffic. For the first time there were a great number and variety of roadside flowers along the Pan-American Highway. There were bushes of purple blossoms and eight-foot shrubs covered in yellow cauliflower-like flowers. There were splashes of red that sometimes were paintbrushes and other times were leaves. There were plants with elephant ear leaves on stalks growing out of the ground and two-foot tall flowers, like deep burgundy pointed bottle brushes. They were very strange.

We drove along a ridge between steep valleys and on either side clouds dusted the hills like puffs of smoke. At times we were driving in the clouds, which reduced our visibility of the road not to mention the magnificent vistas.

We were late in stopping again. There had been a few places to stop in the mountains but we wanted to put a few miles behind us. There wasn't much around for camping so we took advantage

of the large Shell station in San Isidro. There was plenty of space to get back from the road and we received a friendly welcome.

Next door was a restaurant so we could treat ourselves and eat out. It was a little outdoor *comedor* with no menu. We had trouble understanding what was available so Maria invited us into the kitchen to see what she had. We should have known; rice and beans with chicken or pork or beef. It wasn't a complicated menu and this was *gallo pinto,* the traditional Costa Rican fare. Dinner was $2.50 each regardless of which meat we selected.

Maria was the hostess and co-owner with her husband, Jorge, who was also the chef. She expressed an interest in the motorhome and wanted to know if it could accommodate herself, her husband and their seven children. I said no, but she was very interested to see it so

ABOVE: Landslide on the Pan-American Highway south of San Isidro

we gave her a tour after our meal. She called over her teenaged son who dragged along behind us as we walked back to the bus. Her son stuck his head in and showed the lack of interest prevalent in teens all over the world. But she wanted to know everything.

There is a market for motorhomes in Central America, Costa Rica and Panama in particular, but they need to build the facilities, e.g. dumpsites. It was surprising to think that the owners of this little food stand should seriously consider such an expensive vehicle. They did have a big new truck though. How many $2.50 meals would they have to sell to buy a motorhome?

Day 64
Tuesday, March 18 Panama

Our stay at the Shell station in San Isidro was uneventful and we left in good time in the morning. We changed our minds again and decided to go straight to Panama City. This was primarily because in the literature that we had been given at the Panamanian Embassy in San José, it said that the tour boats only transit the canal on Saturdays.

We stayed on the Pan-American Highway and headed south for the border. It was mostly a two-lane road that hugged the hills winding above a little river. Passing was nearly impossible but there were very few other vehicles. There were some interesting moments when we had to negotiate landslides but someone ahead of us had always cleared the way. Boulders in the road were another reason to negotiate the corners slowly. I would not have wanted to be the first along the road after a heavy rain.

On another occasion the two-lane road suddenly become one dirt lane with a triangular yellow *ceda* sign telling us to yield to oncoming traffic. Half of the road had fallen away where a temporary road-fill had been washed out.

Even though this was the main road transiting Central America, there were little one-lane bridges crossing back and forth over the river. We stopped to cool our feet in the swift shallow water. Brindle stretched out and cooled her belly as well.

We were afforded wonderful mountainous views and along the road were groves of coffee and fields of sugar cane. The cane can be harvested twice before it has to be plowed in and re-planted. It looks like it is a year-round crop as we saw it in all stages of growth, as well as dropping off trucks as they headed for the processing factory.

We drove down out of the mountains into the fertile Valle de General where there were acres of pineapples growing. The neat rows of silver gray-green leaves made a lovely contrast to the rich red soil. Someone had made a major investment here, judging by the irrigation.

There were plenty of good looking horses as well as bicycles that were being used for transportation now that the land was more even. There was a lady with a young child on her knee who went up and down with every push of the pedal, and a man pedaling with a weed-eater over his shoulder when everyone else had a machete.

The traffic lessened as we approached the border. There wasn't any signage to say we had reached the border, and we actually drove right through. We had to walk back to go through the formalities. We processed out of Costa Rica, bus, dog and us in no time, and at a cost of U. S. $22.75.

CHAPTER 7

Sailing the Panama Canal

*It's enough for this restless wanderer
that we got this far
Can you feel the love as I lay to rest?
It's enough for kings and vagabonds
to believe the very best*

Elton John

LOCK OF THE PANAMA CANAL

IT TOOK A WHILE TO GET INTO Panama, as it was lunchtime again when we arrived at the border. When will we learn? They didn't close the immigration office, but just one man was working both the incoming people as well as those exiting the country. He served one person leaving the country, and then moved over to the *Entrada* window to process the next person wanting to enter the country.

The clerk in the quarantine office didn't know how to handle Brindle's papers. He made a phone call, and then after a conversation on his two way radio, he walked me to Dr. Felipe's office about five minutes away. Dr. Felipe was in charge and although he agreed that the papers were OK he wanted to charge us for a dog license. After I insisted that we were **transiting** the country and therefore didn't need to license the dog (I had learned the importance of *tránsito* at the last border crossing), he conceded and we didn't have to pay anything. The clerk walked me back to his office where it took him about fifteen minutes to complete a five line form in duplicate. He said I could go, and was again bemused when I asked him for a copy of the permission, or at least a stamp on our already heavily endorsed USDA form. He found a clean spot next to the Panamanian consulate stamp and stamped and initialed it. It was a good thing I had insisted on this or we would have had a problem taking Brindle out of the country.

In spite of all the stories about not being able to take a dog into one or more of the countries of Central America, we had done it. We just had to suffer more than the usual bureaucracy. On no occasion had anyone wanted to look at the animal to compare her to the papers, not even the USDA official who had approved the papers back in the U.S. We could have been traveling with a completely different *mixta,* or mixed breed, to the one our U.S. vet had examined. It was all a bureaucratic farce! However, all the legwork I had gone through before we left home had paid off. We had brought Brindle to Panama. Now we just had to get her home again.

The total border crossing into Panama took two hours and forty minutes, which is about what we had come to expect. All the while the dog kept vendors and scurrilous looking people away, and encouraged inspectors to abbreviate their inspections. We had signs in the windows warning people that there was

a dangerous dog on board. Now she announced herself, and those who weren't baiting her kept well away. I don't think anyone would reach into the bus to take anything.

As so often happened, there were some interesting people waiting with us at the border crossing so we exchanged useful tips with them on road conditions and camping locations. On this occasion we met Catherine Woodward, an American student living in Panama. She needed to make the trek from Panama to Costa Rica four times a year to take her car out of the country just to renew her car's tourist permit. This is a classic example of the bureaucracy of the area. She gave us all sorts of tips and told us to call her when we got to Panama City.

Catherine's first useful tip was to be on the lookout for speed traps. Once past the first twenty miles of broken concrete slab road, we found an excellent divided highway with plenty of police waiting. Speeding was not a problem at the rate we trundled along, but this stretch of road has netted the municipalities plenty of money from foreign travelers. East of David (pronounced with the stress on the last syllable), the road was again a two-lane blacktop, where breaking the speed limit was not so tempting.

In the area just south of the border we saw an unusual number of iguana crossing the road. Not all of them made it. Beside the road there were vendors selling little parakeets; they held them out into the traffic on sticks. There were always watermelons for sale and occasionally other items like some wooden platters. I would have liked to inspect the wood products, but unfortunately there wasn't always a place to pull the motorhome off the narrow two-lane road.

We were happily tripping along when at about 5:30 p.m., we had our fourth flat tire. We managed to pull off the road and park in the shade of a mango tree. The tire had a great gash in it and couldn't be repaired, so we would have to replace it in Panama City. By now John could change a tire blindfolded, and we were on our way quickly. It was after 6:30, the dark was hanging over us, and we had about fifteen minutes of useable light left. Once it is fully dark we wouldn't be able to see enough to know if the ground was solid, or what the environs were like. I saw a sign for the village of Tolé, three kilometers off the road just, as John said, "Turn left." We do tend to think in unison some times.

I was mostly keeping my eyes on the road for potholes, people, and dogs when John called out that there was a church on the left that we could return to if necessary. Around a couple more turns the road opened up and revealed a stretch of cropped grass, a hundred yards wide, which ran along the road for a quarter of a mile with houses on either side. It was just like an English common sitting in the middle of a village; a perfect campsite for a hundred RVs. We drove beyond the soccer goals and parked under a tree.

The first thing we noticed about this village was the music coming from the far end of the grass area. We then saw a gathering of people, and horses. Climbing out to stretch our legs, we walked over to a family seated outside their home across the street near to where we had stopped.

"Would it be all right if we parked on the grass over there for the night?"

RIGHT: Many of the locals didn't even dismount to enjoy their beer

"Of course, of course" the papa replied. "Bienvenido. Everyone is welcome to join the festivities. Tomorrow we celebrate our patron Saint, San José."

Wonderful! What a welcome to Panama.

We strolled down to the activities with Brindle following along. There was a small "ring" about fifty feet in diameter surrounded by spectators, standing on the railing or hanging over the top. Men were watching from horseback, with reins in one hand and a bottle of beer in the other. Others were gathered in the back of pickup trucks sitting or standing to see the activities. We wended our way through the crowd.

There were also some indigenous locals in traditional costumes that I hadn't seen previously. The women and girls wore long colorful dresses with big loose collars and short sleeves. Each dress was of a single bright color with rick-rack trim along the edges. Later we saw similar outfits for sale along the road.

There was a bullfight in progress. We had learned previously that these animals are far too precious to be hurt in village celebrations, so we went over for a better look. A dozen or so cattle were penned off in a corner of the ring. In the ring were two men on long-eared mules, another on horseback, and a bull. The bullfighter wore jeans, with no shirt, and waved a red plastic raincoat at the animal. The animal was unimpressed. The spectators were doing all they could to excite the bull and get it to charge. It made a couple of passes, and then stood looking around at the crowd. This animal had no killer instinct. I then noticed that this well kept beast with its great horns was a cow!

With great maneuvering they put this animal back in the pen, and got another one out for another local to "fight." The results were about the same. Everyone was having a great time. Then a gate was opened and the animals were herded out and away down the grass, past our motorhome, with the men on mules following.

Then the serious drinking started.

The center of activity was a small building that opened out on three sides for serving drinks and food, mainly drinks. Beyond the bar there was a large concrete slab with basketball nets at either end. On this occasion it was a

dance floor. Huge speakers were blaring out Latin rhythms and a few people were moving around the dance floor. There were not many couples around.

John went to the bar and found that he could buy a pitcher of beer for $1.50. He really did buy the pitcher; it was part of the deal. Refills were $1. Also, he discovered that U.S. dollars were the currency in Panama.

We found a seat at one of the cabaret tables encircled by a little, temporary, picket fence, just like the beer gardens set up at fairs in the U.S. There were a couple of pretty, busty girls in scanty tops serving beer. We ordered our second pitcher. The barmaids, who were only in town for the Saint's day celebrations, were serving cups of ice along with beer. We noticed locals adding ice to their beer, which really didn't look very appealing. It didn't take us long to work out that the beer was getting warm before we could drink it. The ice made it cooler, and after the first pitcher it tasted just fine. We were very thirsty and it was very hot.

Brindle was under the table, and then disappeared off in the direction of a local dog. She had trouble finding us again and couldn't hear our whistles because of the din of the music. She sat under the wrong table and was booted out. I knew she was getting stressed out after this happened a couple of times. She crawled up onto my lap, which was a sure sign that she was unhappy. John took her back to the motorhome so we could wait for the band to start. While I was holding the table for his return, I noticed that I was almost the only woman there, apart from the bar girls, but no one took any notice of me and I felt quite comfortable. The local women were getting ready for the dance.

By now I had no intention of cooking dinner, so we bought some skewers of very flavorful chicken for twenty-five cents each. We later had a few beef ones at fifty cents as well. By the time we decided the band wasn't really going to start at nine o'clock, there were eighteen of the wooden skewers lying across the table, and we had consumed four pitchers of beer (plus all the ice we had added to it!)

It began to rain, and there was no sign of the band beginning, so we walked 200 yards back to the motorhome in the cooling drizzle. We could still hear the recorded music very well. We thought about moving further away from the noise, but it was very dark and we didn't want to drive further down the grass stretch in case we got stuck or encountered something we couldn't handle. It began to rain hard, which made a lovely sound on the roof and drowned out the music. Unfortunately it didn't rain all night. At around midnight, we're not sure of the exact time, the live band

LEFT: Tolé woman in traditional dress

started playing at twice the earlier volume. What made it worse, between every song the master of ceremonies would make a long speech. As the night progressed he had more to drink and his speeches became more animated. Every hour or so the music would stop, and we would think that we could get to sleep, only to be awakened again with another raucous salsa 15 or 20 minutes later. This went on until dawn. Ugh! In the clear light of day we realized that we could have easily driven a couple of hundred yards farther away from the noise with no problem.

Day 65
Wednesday, March 19,
Tolé to Playa Santa Clara

I really wanted to stay in Tolé and revel in the celebrations, but we couldn't find out what was going to happen or when. Also, the brochure said the only boat rides through the Panama Canal were on Saturdays, and we thought we needed a couple of days to get there and make the arrangements.

We drove for a mile into Tolé, and found the center of town, a charming, well-kept place. There was a very nice church and affluent homes. The locals were dressed in their best clothes. Bamboo covered in flowers was arched over the road and in front of the houses in celebration of their patron saint. We circled the square and returned to the main road.

As soon as we were back on the Pan-American Highway there were stalls selling the local products. Families dressed in bright dresses I had seen in town the night before were selling them, but unfortunately their merchandise was a poor imitation of the real thing. However, they did have some interesting bead necklaces for sale. The workmanship

was excellent and the colors ranged from blacks with silver to various mixes of colors. Most of them were far too exotic to wear every day, but I bought a couple that could be worn with a cocktail dress in black, and a little multi-colored one for me to wear on the trip. It cost all of three dollars, and must have taken several hours to make. I understand that this beadwork is the specialty of the Tolé Indians.

As we continued south there were dramatic vistas right and left of the road. It seemed that we were driving along the top of the continental divide. There were stalls along the side of the road selling everything from mangos to bananas, orchids, and whatever else the locals had to market.

The crickets or cicadas or whatever the insects were in the trees around there, made an amazing sound like a space ship. There we were driving happily along when this weird, metallic, whining noise grew louder and louder like aliens were about to land on top of us, and then as we passed from under the trees the sound faded and we were not lifted to another planet. We frequently passed under these alien creatures but we always remained safely on earth.

It was an easy two-lane road with no traffic so we were able to keep up a good pace, watching, as ever, for the nasty

ABOVE: Driving out of town past the beer tent and our camping place in Tolé, Panama
LEFT: Tolé Indian bead necklaces and dresses for sale along the road
RIGHT: The Balneario at Playa Santa Clara, Panama

potholes. The countryside opened into a big, wide, dry valley with short stunted trees and a few scattered villages. At times there were long stretches of straight concrete slab road disappearing over the hills for miles ahead. It seemed strange to be heading down Central America with a compass reading of due east.

We had heard from fellow campers that there was a good place to camp on the beach in Santa Clara, and there was. Apparently it is full of locals during weekends, but we were there mid-week with only one other couple swinging in hammocks as the sun went down. We pulled up under a tree on the hard packed sand, within reach of a power plug, and stopped there for the day. Somehow we felt like we needed a rest although we hadn't really done anything. It is a very nice idle life. The roads had been good, we had gone a hundred and fifty miles, and were only sixty miles out of Panama City. We should be able to arrive in plenty of time to find a place to stay and make arrangements for the boat ride through the Canal.

This was one of our better camps. We had electricity, so we could watch another episode of M★A★S★H★ and we

were able to fill up with water. There wasn't a dump station, but we were able to position the motorhome on the rise behind the lavatories, and with our extra long hose we could empty our tanks right into them. What a relief!

The waves were warm and whipped by the evening breeze, and fun to swim in. We sat on the beach under a full moon and enjoyed a beer.

I love to lie in bed listening to waves washing onto the sand. They sound like the rhythmic breathing of a fat man exhaling through flabby lips. Pruusssss. Pruusss.

Day 66
Thursday, March 20 Panama City

Fancy waking up to a walk on this beach? There were a lot more song birds in this part of the continent than farther north. This would be a good place to stay for a while.

An hour and a half after we left Santa Clara Beach we were driving across the Bridge of the Americas. You should have heard me hoot'n and holler'n as I drove over the Panama Canal. "Yahooooooo!" I hollered to the world. We had done it! We had driven all the way to the Panama Canal and had a wonderful

time doing it. And, we had gotten the dog there.

We followed signs for Balboa, as we understood we could park at the Yacht Club there. By chance, John suddenly saw the Chadwick Travel Service that our friend Catherine had recommended to us. We pulled into the parking lot and asked how we could get tickets to transit the Canal. Sadly, they confirmed that excursions that go all the way through the Canal only operated once a month, and we had just missed one. They did

have boat trips available every Saturday that would go through the first set of locks, into Gatun Lake, and back, at $108 per person. It was a whole day's tour and you could buy lunch on board. I had so wanted to transit the Canal, but it looked like this was the best we could do. We could book as late as Friday afternoon, which was the following day. We decided to procrastinate purchasing the tickets, as we really wanted to experience the entire Canal.

Behind the white Y.M.C.A. building housing Chadwick was an interesting barn, and inside was a wealth of souvenir shops. The merchandise was most interesting, but I prefer to make my purchases from the artisans rather than from a shopkeeper. We did plan to return though, as there were some masks made in the Darién Province I wanted and we were not going that far south.

We easily located the Balboa Yacht Club and discovered it was little more than an open-air bar. They did have a hut on the pier for the yacht business,

and an office behind the bar for swimming pool business as well, but it seemed that most of the business was conducted in the bar. We could have joined the club for an annual fee of $20 and used the pool. They used to have a lovely old wood building with a veranda, but it was destroyed by fire some years back. Patrons have to make do. Everyone who walks up is a patron.

John went to make a phone call back to the U.S. as he was still desperately trying to get his U.S. driver's license replaced. After the forty-dollar fine, and a dance with the police in Nicaragua, he didn't want to risk driving again. This put a heavy load on me. The Texas license was still not in the hands of his secretary, but it would be "any day," and then she would Express Mail it to our friends here. It had been almost three weeks since she had begun trying to get an "emergency replacement." Bureaucracy abounds everywhere!

I wandered into the bar and approached a gringo-looking couple.

"Excuse me." I just went straight to speaking English. "Do you need line handlers?"

"Well...." She looked rather blank and surprised.

"My husband and I are interested in transiting the Canal and would like to work as line handlers. We used to have a sailing boat so know a little about it."

"Yes." She said. "We are going on Saturday at five in the morning." That was the day after tomorrow!

Now it was my turn to look surprised and blank. I wonder if my jaw dropped open. "That's fine. Let me get my husband and introduce you." I stammered. "Would you like a drink?" We were in a bar after all.

"No, we must go" She had a strong, clipped, Finnish accent. "But we can meet you here at between four and six tomorrow night. That is when they confirm our transit."

"Great. We will see you then." We exchanged names and I watched as they walked out into the sun.

"That is our boat over there," She called back, pointing to a flotilla of yachts scattered to the left of the long pier. "The Sophia II. Can you see it?"

"Yes," I said squinting into the sun. I could see about a hundred various boats. The Sophia had to be one of them.

They walked off towards the long pier carrying their supplies.

I ran back to John and couldn't wait for him to get off the phone. "We are going to transit the Canal. We are going to do it." I couldn't believe that I had just walked up to complete strangers and with a simple "Yes," they had granted me a dream of a lifetime. This deserved another "Yahooooooooooo," but I restrained myself in the colonial atmosphere of the yacht club. Holy cow!

TOP LEFT: Santa Clara Beach at sunrise showing some of the eating and drinking establishments that are busy on weekends.
LEFT: Bridge of the Americas crossing the Panama Canal
RIGHT: The Balboa Yacht Club, where you need to check in if you plan to work as line handlers through the Canal

All boats transiting the Canal must have one person to handle each line, or rope. On the yachts this meant that they needed four people dedicated to working the lines. If the vessel is tied up to the side of the lock, the lines need to be let out or pulled in as the water lowers or rises. On the other side there might be another vessel tied up to you. When a gringo walks up and offers to do the work it saves the yacht owners fifty dollars per line handler. Gringos do it for free. Heck, I would have paid to do it! I would imagine it is more fun for the yacht owners to have someone they can talk to rather than have four local handlers who might not be comfortable mingling in the confined space of a yacht. Many of the private yachts are crewed by a couple on a round the world trip.

We returned to the motorhome a little overwhelmed by our exciting prospect. We had to make preparations to sail the Panama Canal. A *vigilante* we had talked to earlier came up to us and said that we could not stay where we were overnight. Big problem. It was an enormous parking lot that could handle about a thousand cars, with big old trees providing patches of deep shade. We walked over to the adjacent Country Inn Hotel and asked there if we could possibly stay the night in their parking lot. We were prepared to take a room if necessary. The manager was called and kindly said that although they don't usually do it, he would permit us to park in the back of the parking lot for three days. Phew!

We did some research and kept a watchful eye out for other places over the next days, but could not find anywhere else in Panama to park a motorhome. The group caravans stay out near Santa Clara in a real campsite, near where we were the previous night, and commute in by coach. If other motorhomers follow us and are permitted to stay at the Country Inn, I hope they are very respectful of the establishment so they will continue to welcome RVs.

Our next dilemma was the dog. Even before we left Houston I knew that Brindle would be a problem in Panama if we wanted to transit the Canal. We called Dr. Nora La Penta at Veterinario La Penta, the vet that had been recommended by Catherine. After visiting her clinic in the pleasant El Dorado suburb, we were assured that Brindle would be comfortable enough. The fact that the proprietor was a veterinarian gave us added comfort.

John had made contact with Bert Shelton, a fellow engineer from Houston. Bert's dad lived in Panama City and there was a good chance that we would find Bert visiting his dad. Now we made contact and he was going to pick us up to see the city and to meet his dad. Importantly, he would first help us locate a good place we could buy a replacement tire for the one that had been shredded.

Bert met us and we got the tire at about what it would cost in the U.S. He took us on a brief tour of the city that concluded at his dad's home. His father is an eighty-two year old Panamanian of British, Colombian and Spanish heritage and proud of every bit of it. He is a wonderful old gentleman, full of stories and highlights of his life. He wanted to share everything from the name of the colorful birds at his feeder to the attributes of his late wife. He had taught geology at the University of Panama, and really knew the country and her people. His mother was Colombian, as she was born when Panama was still part of Colombia.

Bert Jr. returned us to the motorhome parked behind the hotel. There was a little shade from an enormous old mango tree that was dropping its fruit. I collected several mangos that lay scattered across the hotel's sweeping lawn. They were lying all over the grass, and I just had to hunt for those the birds hadn't found first. We were eating them three at a time for days afterwards.

There was a TGI Friday restaurant within the hotel, and the two of us had a very nice, very North American dinner, with the same North American décor and the same menu shared at all the TGIF, and with the same standard of North American service. We watched world news on the TV there and caught up with the distressing war news. It was just like being back in the U.S. We were happy to retreat to the motorhome.

Day 67
Friday, March 21, Touring Panama City

This morning was our time to see Panama City. We had met this friendly taxi driver, Carlos, who had adopted us as soon as he saw us pull up in the Balboa parking lot. Carlos was one of those enthusiastic taxi drivers you find in almost any foreign city who wants to take you under his wing and show you everything. He became our alternate chauffeur for our short stay in Panama City. Bert was our primary chauffeur and guide. Carlos said he spoke English and offered to take us on a city tour. It was a mistake, as neither his English nor his local knowledge was good enough. We did get to see Panama City though.

First of all we went to see the Mira-flores Locks, the first locks on the Pacific end of the Canal. There is a visitors' area and a little show and tell. The show was

RIGHT: Traditional Panamanian dress, called the **pollera** on display at **Mi Pueblito**, in Panama City

out of date by about ten years, but it was good enough to give us our first lesson on the workings of the Canal. We wanted to see a ship pass through, but decided not to wait the two hours for the next scheduled vessel.

We met a young North American who was very interested in transiting the Canal. I told him what we had lined up. When I saw him later that evening at the Balboa Yacht Club, he said that he had secured a position on another boat. It is obviously not a difficult thing to do.

The next stop on our tour was *Mi Pueblito,* or "My Little Village." It is a replica of a village from the interior of Panama in the early nineteen hundreds. The most interesting room had some of the traditional *pollera,* the Panamanian national dress. These magnificently embroidered white dresses looked like they had printed patterns, but on close inspection it was finely embroidered or appliquéd. The embroidery was in dark green or blue or purple, and then to top it off, there was a great wool pompom in

a contrasting color that looked like a strange afterthought.

Carlos then took us to San Felipe, within which is the old walled city known as the Casco Viejo. It was full of atmosphere with its charming narrow streets. This is one of the older quarters of Panama City, reminiscent of the French Quarter of New Orleans, only much larger and very much lived in. It makes New Orleans look like Disneyland.

Stone as well as brick houses had wrought iron balconies, which hung over narrow cobbled streets. Many homes were charming, with carefully restored ironwork and pastel paint, others were in great need of love to restore them to their glory. There were wooden balconies with neat little railings supported by trusses that were rotten right through. The first person to step out might be met with a nasty fate. The roads were so narrow and the balconies protruded so far that neighbors could have reached out and almost touched across the way. Restored buildings had elaborate sconces under the balconies, and brackets for torches or coach lights along the front. Pots of flowers spilled greenery and bougainvillea like brilliant spots of manicured light. The next building was abandoned and had a young tree growing from between the stones of the wall. The balconies all had shade either from their own little awning or from an extension of the roof to the building. This allowed for little direct sunlight to hit the narrow lanes except at high noon. The front doors were solid wood and defensive, whereas the balconies were friendly, with flowers and clothes giving clues about occupants.

It was high noon, and as fascinating as all this was I was beginning to cook in the back of the little unair-conditioned taxi as it rattled and bumped over the cobbles. I was relieved when we stopped in Old Panama. It was built in 1519, as the first Spanish settlement on the Pacific. It was destroyed by the pirate Henry Morgan in 1671, when the population could have been as high as ten thousand. We seem to frequently be in the wake of this knighted pirate who harassed the Spanish. Being the narrow point of the isthmus, it was here where gold and silver transited the continent to the Atlantic for shipment to Europe. There are some great old stone ruins, but as so frequently happens, most of the stone blocks have been scavenged over the centuries to construct other buildings.

Adjacent to the old ruins was a building where souvenirs were for sale, and I always love to have a look. They were mostly locally made hand crafted items. In one of the little shops was a lady of the Kuna tribe selling *molas*. These are very finely stitched appliqué and reverse appliqué squares with embroidered highlights. The sewing was amazing, and the designs bright and intricate. Traditionally, the *molas* are patches that are sewn to the fronts and backs of their blouses. We bought one that had been set into a tray, which was more practical for our purposes. The woman who sold it to us was less than five feet tall and had the traditional bracelets around her wrists and ankles. She had straight, cropped hair and the all important and distinguishing gold ring in her nose. Some women also draw a black line from their forehead to the tips of their noses. The Kuna are obviously very

good with the needle. However, their skirts are just fabric strips, which wrap around the waist, but aren't hemmed.

The Kuna are usually shy about having their picture taken but this lady gave me permission. She was very serious, and non-smiling, throughout the entire encounter and let her wares speak for themselves. She looked out of place among the gringo tourists, so petite in her unique dress.

We returned to the Country Inn. Carlos took John and Brindle to the vet where the dog was going to stay while we transited the Canal. We had arranged to meet the yacht owners, Suvi and David, back at the Balboa Yacht club at 4:00p.m. to make final arrangements for the morning. We also invited the Sheltons and Catherine Woodward to join us there for drinks before dinner. This was the most civilized socializing we had done since leaving Guatemala.

Bert Shelton Jr.'s mother was from Finland and he was fluent in the language. We thought he and Suvi would

LEFT: The old district of San Felipe in the city of Panama
RIGHT: A Kuna lady selling **molas** in Old Panama

enjoy meeting each other and in fact, they started chatting in Finnish as soon as they were introduced. Here we were sitting in the tropics of Panama and two Finns had found one another.

Unfortunately, as soon as Suvi saw us she told us that their passage had been postponed. Talk about a disappointment! The new schedule was to sail at the same time on Sunday morning. We had just taken the dog to the vet's. We considered trying to fetch her before the office closed but decided it was too late. She would just have to be there for two days instead of one.

We enjoyed the company and chatted with our friends who had numerous things in common. Then Suvi was paged for a phone call and returned to announce with a smile that the passage was on again for the morning. She had previously contracted with an experienced line handler who was going to show us how to do it. He had already left the extra long lines and the additional fenders they would need on the Sofia II. Once Suvi learned that the trip was postponed she had contacted him. Now she had the challenge of reaching him again to let him know the trip was on again as originally scheduled.

Catherine and the Sheltons joined us for a great dinner at a local open-air restaurant. We sat under the thatched umbrella and the evening was filled with conversation. Catherine was working on her doctorate on: the "inbreeding" of trees in isolated patches of rainforest. There are quite a few people and groups in Central America that have preserved various parts of the rainforest. Her thesis asks whether tree species are headed for extinction in small forest "islands," because of the disappearance of pollinators and a failure to successfully reproduce. We thought of Danilo and his little patch of old growth forest near Monteverde, Costa Rica. Catherine spends a lot of time in Monteverde and in fact knew the Orquídeas Bar where we had stayed. She was interested to hear that Danilo owned large isolated plots of cloud forest. This was the kind of land that Catherine's organization is looking for.

Day 68
Saturday, March 22,
Transiting the Panama Canal

There was no one around the hotel parking lot at five-thirty in the morning. We walked across to the yacht club and down the long pier in the dark. There was no sign of dawn. It was pitch black. David had told us that there was always someone on the pier to provide rides out to the yachts, 24 hours a day. I was prepared to swim if I had to. No need, as we found two sleepy *trabajadores* sitting in the small shack at the end of the pier. I think we woke one up with the sound of our feet on the planks, while the other was engaged in some paperwork. We were scheduled to pick up Stephan and Nancy in their yacht at 5:45 en route to the Sofia II. We were a little early, so

LEFT: Bert Shelton Sr. in front of the Balboa yacht basin at the Pacific entrance of the Canal

we told the workers we wanted to depart in ten minutes. Stephan and Nancy were a couple who owned another yacht and had their Canal transit booked in a couple of weeks. They had become friends with David and Suvi, and because they wanted experience going through the canal, they offered to work the lines on the Sofia.

We peered across the dark water looking for any yachts with a light on. All the boats we could see in the water appeared to be sleeping shadows, perhaps waiting for us to wake them up. Black shadows rested on black water with a lighter shade of black overhead. In spite of the numerous specks of light everywhere, there was the overwhelming feeling of being wrapped in darkness down by the water. It was like being in the middle of a dying fire, surrounded by sparks. It was a clear, tropical morning, and we were anxious to get this adventure underway.

At 5:40 we boarded the little *panga* for the short dinghy ride out to the yacht of Stephan and Nancy. They were sitting on their yacht waiting for us, completely invisible in the dark. Their disembodied voices were surprisingly close and friendly. They climbed down into the boat to go the fifty yards to the Sofia II. We arrived right on time.

Suvi and David had not been able to make contact with Luis, the local experienced line handler to tell him that the transit was back on for today. They had left messages and hoped that he would arrive any minute.

David asked if we would return the cables and fenders to Luis that evening when we returned by bus from Colón. It would be a heavy load, with half a dozen old tires and 100 yards of line, but it was the least we could do for the trip through the Canal. We felt sorry for Luis, for missing a day's work. Stephan, Nancy, John

and I would be the line handlers for this trip. Suvi kept the refreshments coming while David never left the helm.

Suvi had coffee and snacks ready when we boarded, and then we all sat back and waited for our "advisor" to arrive. A vessel longer than fifty feet requires a pilot, but a smaller vessel only requires an advisor. Advisors are usually Canal tug captains who don't currently have a tug to master.

The Sofia II was a Beneteau First 47.7. It was 47.7 ft long with a beam of 14 feet. Her draft was 7.7 ft and, for those interested, had a total displacement of 25,000 lbs. She was finely crafted, inside and out. There were two sleeping cabins aft, a shower/bathroom and a main cabin with well appointed kitchen and dining area. All interior surfaces were exquisitely finished in deeply polished wood. There was about ten times the living area that we have in our motorhome. I looked with envy at her stove on gimbals and wished that I could cook while on the move.

Eventually our advisor came on board. Señor Carmelo Gonzalez was a young, hardened tug captain assigned to the "advisor" roll on this occasion. He was pleasant enough, but as the day wore on he became a little surly, and it was obvious that he preferred commanding a tugboat to this assignment. Whenever we tied up to a tug in the locks, he was off chatting with the crew.

A vast cruise ship, the Seven Seas Navigator, black and dotted with warm lights, loomed over us. She sailed past us as we sat waiting in the dark. As we rose and settled in her wake I thought of her passengers in their comfortable beds, bloated from the limitless midnight buffet, and wondered if they would sleep through the crossing.

Dawn turned the world gray and I could see the silhouette of the city. Still we waited for word on the radio that we could move out. Streaks of pink hit the steel sky and were reflected in the flat black water. The water looked like treacle, so thick that I could walk on it.

At last Carmelo's radio crackled again, and an unintelligible word from the Canal Authority told him it was our turn. We leapt into action, and at 6:05 a.m., we cast off from the buoys at the Balboa Yacht Club. Three minutes later we passed between the Panama Canal markers and passed under the Bridge of the Americas.

Sr. Gonzalez told us that we were going to enter the lock chambers behind the Queen Ace, and tie up to her tug. This was good news as it is preferable for a small boat like ours to have something of similar size to attach to. The tug would be responsible for monitoring the lines tied to the walls of the locks and make the necessary adjustments as we all went up. In one of the Gatun locks, when we were being lowered to the Atlantic, the tug ahead of us did break a line like this. The crewman was slightly injured when the cable snapped back, but perhaps he was more humiliated than anything. His captain went over and had a word with him.

The Queen Ace was like an enormous rectangular shoebox full of cars. Although she was of Panamanian registration, we speculated she was coming from Japan on account of the flag she was flying. She must have had thousands of cars on board. We could see the long gangway that she could lower from her stern so they could drive off from different levels.

Carmelo told us that there was a web site for the Canal, and that you can watch the vessels passing through the first locks we were to come to: the Miraflores locks. If we had known about this a day earlier, we would have called our family in the States, but at 6:30 in the morning we left them alone. We frantically called my family members in the U.K. though, to encourage them to watch us on the web site at www.pancanal.com. Suvi borrowed our satellite phone to call her family in Finland.

We passed along the docks where great derricks and cranes jutted from the horizon like monsters on skeletal legs with long headless necks. The superstructures of ships, from tankers to tuna boats, studded the skyline between palm trees. Suddenly, the sun burst over the horizon and everything was bathed in gold. What a magnificent way to start the day. Then the gold light and the gray sky and the black water were gone. In their stead was an intense tropical sun in a clear sky turning the waters of the Canal a vivid blue.

Although the Sophia II was a sailing vessel, she was required to go through the Canal on her motor so she could maintain the speed and position required.

LEFT: Dawn under the Bridge of the Americas as it crosses the Panama Canal
RIGHT: The Queen Ace about to enter the left chamber of the Miraflores Lock

We arrived at the first lock on schedule, but were told to wait, so we cruised in circles. Our captain was anxious; he wanted to be in the right place at the right time. He had to do what Carmelo told him, as Carmelo was his only means of communication with the Canal Authority. We could hear all sorts of conversations to and from the Queen Ace on Sr. Gonzalez's little radio. They were having problems with the big ship's stern lines.

Suddenly Carmelo sat up and told us to move. We had been diverted to the parallel set of locks. It seemed that the Queen was stuck half out of the western ones. The locks are 110 ft wide. She was 105.92ft wide and 654.63 ft long. This gave the Queen Ace about two feet clearance on either side. Not much when you consider her overall size. The lock chambers are over a thousand feet long, so there would have been plenty of room for our boat and the tug behind her. We were just happy to be moving.

Entering the lock was like going into a canyon with vertical damp walls showing

where the water had been just minutes before. There were little electric locomotives, called mules, on either side running back into position ready for the next ship. They were like tugs on land, responsible for keeping large ships in position in the middle of the chambers. We approached the gate, which was an immense steel barrier 82 feet high holding up a wall of water. The chamber felt very strange and big. The Queen Ace's tug was already snugly up at the next gates. We motored over to it and tied up alongside. I smiled to the deckhand in the hope that he would alert me if I was doing something dreadfully wrong. He passed back our line after he had looped it around his stanchion, and watched me clumsily turn our line in a figure eight and secure it. He said nothing.

The first gates closed behind us at 8:40 a.m.. These are the tallest of all the gates, and weigh 1,460 tons so they can handle the Pacific tidal fluctuations.

As soon as the gate closed, water gushed in, coming up from the depths around us. There is a series of underground

culverts and valves that controls the water. The water seemed to push us up from the bowels of the canyon, bringing us up to the level of the top of the lock. Just seven minutes later the gates ahead of us were opening and we were moving into the next chamber, already free of the tug we had tied up to.

It amazed me to think how little all this had changed in the ninety years since these blocks of stone had been laid. All the gates are the original ones. I thought of Richard Halliburton, who swam the entire Canal in 1928, and

imagined looking up from the water at those forbidding walls and swimming past the miter gates with teeth like jaws waiting to crush him.

Nine minutes later we were secured to the same tug again in the second lock chamber with the gates closing behind us.

Once the second set of gates had opened in front of us we were raised up to the level of little Miraflores Lake, which we needed to traverse before we came to Pedro Miguel, the last lock on the Pacific side. There are two gates at the top of the Upper Miraflores chamber to lessen the opportunity of a disaster should a ship ram one and drain the precious fresh waters from the lake. Pedro Miguel locks, and the Gatun Locks at the Caribbean end of the Canal, have the same double gate arrangement to protect against what could be disastrous flooding.

ABOVE: Approaching the first lock with the wall of the second gate ahead
LEFT: Our pilot directing us to the tug where we tied up in the second chamber

This process of raising vessels up to the level of Lake Gatun takes its toll on the water supply. Every time a lock is filled, the water comes from the lake and is subsequently lost to the ocean when the water level is dropped for the vessels coming the other way. Water conservation is one of the biggest issues facing the Panama Canal Authority, or ACP, as it is known here. A lot of planning is required to schedule the operation of the locks to minimize water loss. The most efficient plan is to fill each lock with one enormous large ship before flooding, to maximize the amount of cargo transited for the water used. That is the main reason they try to schedule yachts with ships that don't fully occupy a lock. In 1935, the Madden Dam was built on the Chagres River above the Canal to control the river floodwaters, to replenish the supply of water for the Canal, and to generate power.

It was exactly another nine minutes when the double gates opened. We were out of the last of the Miraflores double locks and motoring forward to the Pedro Miguel single chamber lock. It amazed me how fast all this was going.

I can see why the Authority requires a line handler for each of the four lines. It takes an inexperienced worker a minute or two to loosen the lines and you have to go from secure to free very quickly. I just had enough time to make my line secure and stand up to take a photo before I had to cast off again.

Now we sat and waited for half an hour below Pedro Miguel Lock. In the meantime, the Queen Ace caught up and went into the west chamber ahead of us. Suddenly we were given the order

to proceed and were directed to enter the eastern chamber. Once safely tied up, I had time to watch as several other boats joined us, including the party boat with all those happy tourists we had almost joined. They would be going as far as the great Gatun Lake before returning to Panama. We waved and they waved back. I smiled and thought how close we were to booking the same trip. Instead, here we were on a yacht about to go the whole way through all the locks and across the lake to the Caribbean Sea. We were crossing the continent. How could we be so lucky?

A tug suddenly came rushing in stirring up all sorts of waves. The commotion awoke me from my daydreaming and reminded me to check my line. The

TOP RIGHT: Tugs and the party boat making secure
RIGHT: Looking up at workers at the Pedro Miguel Lock

gates started closing as soon as the tug was in.

The tug crews handling the lines next to the lock wall had a long way to throw their lines up. The tug we tied up to spent a while hollering and whistling for these two workers to come and lower a line for them to attach theirs to so it could be pulled up and secured.

It was 9:37 a.m. when the gates opened and we went forward into the Gaillard, or Culebra, Cut. This part of the Canal is where most of the excavating was done, as it is here the Canal was cut through the Continental Divide. Over a million cubic yards of material was removed, half of the entire dirt that was taken from the entire Canal was dug up at this point. The Cut had just been widened to theoretically permit two

maximum sized vessels (called "Panamax" vessels) to sail by each other. The shore was newly scarred, and unattractive, and the water here was muddy, whereas most of the way it was clean and blue.

We now we had four or five hours of cruising to get through the Cut and across Gatun Lake. The Cut was like a deep river, but it was unusual to come so close to the enormous container ships. Then it opened out into Gatun Lake. It was a shame we couldn't break out the sails and let the wind take us, but that was out of the question. We had a fixed schedule to keep and a path to follow between the buoys. I also don't think that these ships, with their containers stacked six high on the deck, would think kindly about giving way to a little sailing boat. Vessels of every size were passing us and overtaking us, but always between the marker buoys.

Once we entered the lake the scenery changed. The banks and islands were covered with dense vegetation. The bulky container ships and tankers seemed out of place in such an attractive setting on the lake dotted with green islands, and a jungle-covered shore with tall flower-covered trees. The yachts and pleasure craft looked so small and vulnerable against the monsters from Holland, Japan and Sweden. Many of the ships had refrigerated cargo, and we speculated that they were carrying bananas to Europe.

Carmelo directed us to starboard, to a channel on the east side of the lake, which would take us away from the larger vessels. The old locals refer to this as the Banana Channel, as it was intended for small vessels. It was also a short cut. Our

TOP LEFT: Passing ships on Gatun Lake, the Panama Canal
LEFT: Larger Vessels on the other side of Gatun Lake

best cruising speed was about 7 knots. The larger cargo vessels could cruise at 15 to 20 knots. We could see the giant ships between the little jungle islands as we each went our separate ways. At times I could hardly see the other side of the vast lake, and then we would almost be brushing the shore. There were small clusters of trees that had been drowned when the water had risen after the sealing of Gatun Lake. Those skeleton trees had been standing there like sentinels for almost a hundred years.

Suvi was a great hostess providing lunch and all the refreshments we could want, but this was no pleasure sail for the owners. After going flat out by motor for four hours we arrived at the top of the Gatun Locks. We had reached the Atlantic end only to be told that we

ABOVE: The Queen Ace going through Gatun Lock ahead of us. In the picture you can see the Paz pushing at the wall of the lock, and the closed gate with the yellow handrail. Notice how little clearance the Queen Ace has.

would have to wait two or three hours before we could enter the locks. The Queen Ace, the cruise ship, and several other vessels were all waiting their turn. If we had known there was going to be a delay, we could have paused to watch the monkeys that we had spotted in the trees on one of the islands. I took a nap.

There we were moored in the lake, gently rocking up and down, being entertained by the sounds of a steel drum band drifting from shore. The band had been provided by the cruise ship company to entertain their passengers who, we were told, had taken the train from Panama to Colón.

We began to get concerned that we would not make the locks in the daylight. It was prohibited for little boats to go through after dark, and there would be an additional charge if we took two days for the crossing. Historically, transit charges are based on displacement. Small yachts pay about $500 and the big ships pay as much as $45,000 while Mr.

Halliburton paid just 36 cents for his swim. There are a variety of other charges for the advisor, the rental of lines, and the like.

At last we saw the Queen Ace move and enter the western lock, and we knew we would be next. We were instructed to tie up to the left wall outside the eastern lock until the gates opened. Meanwhile, behind us, the Marillo, a refrigerated cargo ship was pulling up with the assistance of a tug, and getting her lines attached to the locomotives on either side. All vessels must go through the locks under their own power but the fifty-five-ton electric locomotives on their tracks at the sides of the locks, keep the bigger ships aligned. The biggest ships need as many as eight locomotives.

The tug Paz then came in front of us and held her position by turning at right angles to us and pushing against the chamber wall with her engines revving at full belt, as though she were trying to push it down.

At quarter to four the gates in front of us opened and we headed in at full speed in the choppy wake of La Paz.

Looking at the schedule Sr. Gonzalez provided, the Marillo should have been three hours ahead of us. She was not nearly as big as the Queen Ace, but appeared daunting from our angle. She was held neatly in the middle of the lock by the little locomotives.

At 4:45 p.m., we had been lowered to the Atlantic, out of the last of the locks and steaming towards the Panama Yacht Club where the Sofia II was to berth for the night. Before finding the yacht club, a pilot boat came by and quickly removed Carmelo. He left with hardly a good-bye, much less any guidance on how to find the yacht club. We were on our own.

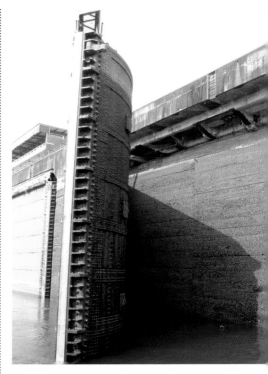

With the help of Sofia's charts we did finally find the yacht club hidden behind a quay. Luis, the missing line handler, was there to greet us. His day job is driving a taxi, and he had driven his taxi all the way to Colón when he learned we had sailed without him. He was probably concerned about his valuable lines. We were grateful that we didn't have to carry them back on the bus. Instead he put his taxi to good use and gave us a ride back to our motorhome.

It took us twelve hours to transit the Canal from Pacific to Atlantic. It took one and a half-hours to return to our motorhome in Luis's taxi.

What a day!

Day 69
Sunday, March 23, Crossing the Peninsula Again

I woke up thinking I should feel let down now that we had achieved our ultimate goal. Far from it! I couldn't wait to get going, to see more of the country. The Sheltons had advised us not to venture south into the Province of Darien, as there was not much to see along the road and it was renowned for not being safe. That was the clincher, although I had dreamed of driving to the end of the road.

John went with our chauffeur, Carlos, to fetch the dog and I readied the motorhome for departure. I also collected a bunch more mangos from the lawn of the hotel. The people at Country Inn had been great hosts with a wonderful swimming pool and a good gringo restaurant. They deserved our heartfelt thanks.

We left Panama City and went northeast, back across the isthmus keeping the Canal to our left. We passed spreading railway yards where the trains load and unload containers from the ships, avoiding the canal transit fee. The road passed the Miraflores Locks and I smiled with a feeling of superiority. A couple of days earlier we had been gawking into the museum chambers and examining the faded model in wonder.

We took a side trip off the main Boyd-Roosevelt Highway (CA 3) to get a glimpse of Madden Dam and Lake Alajuela. We went through a pleasant park, winding through thick undergrowth and old trees. Then we crossed farmland with small villages. At the village of Sabanita, we turned to the east towards Portobelo, and the beaches of the Caribbean. This is a busy intersection filled with colorfully painted, retired U.S. school buses. Here they have really

good paintings of pop stars. They are still gaudy colors, but some of the artwork is excellent.

Once we hit the north coast we could see it was an area frequented by holiday traffic, but somehow, even though it was Sunday, we seemed to have missed the crowds. We explored the first beach town we came to, Playa Maria Chiquita. Turning left off the highway we found ourselves on a dirt road passing through a small town square and behind small wooden houses lined up along the beach. It was Sunday afternoon, and the distinctly Caribbean populace was lounging on porches and strolling along the roads. There didn't appear to be any particularly attractive places to camp. We pulled up in front of a house that had a Coca-Cola sign in front. The house had a front porch but nothing that looked like a shop. When we climbed the steps to the porch, we were looking through a window at an elderly lady, a younger woman, and two young boys sitting at the kitchen table. They didn't seem surprised to see us, and one of the young boys came out with a friendly greeting to see what we wanted. Yes, they had Coke. A bottle cost 25¢ provided we returned the empty. He collected two bottles from the refrigerator in the

LEFT: The gate at the Gatun Locks on the Atlantic end of the Canal
RIGHT: Lowered in the Gatun Lock. The locomotives positioning the Marillo in the center of the lock can be clearly seen.

kitchen. They kindly offered us a place to camp next to their house, and even pointed out an electrical plug we could use as a hookup. We didn't feel this was our ideal Caribbean campsite, so we thanked them and continued driving down the coast. If it had been later in the day we probably would have accepted their offer, and I'm sure we would have had another remarkable cultural experience.

A few miles down the road we pulled onto the grounds of Las Palmeras, an isolated open-air restaurant overlooking the water. There were tables with thatched sunshades available for rent where a couple of families clustered watching the children playing in the sand. We drove right up to the water's edge and parked. We had found our Caribbean beach.

This was one of our shorter days on the road. We departed the Country Inn parking lot on the Pacific at 11:20 in the morning and stopped on the Atlantic coast fifty-five miles later at 2:15 p.m.

A fisherman worked his net right in front of where we were sitting. He used his teeth to hold the net while he gathered it, made it ready to throw, and then flung it so that it would land as a flat disk. Pulling the cord he retrieved it, but there were no fish in front of us. Other fishermen lined up in the water and worked as teams with their nets. Others were standing precariously balanced in little dugout canoes. The water was as warm as the air and whole families were working and playing together.

We later wandered to the restaurant for a piece of local *corvina* for dinner.

Day 70
Monday, March 24, Las Palmeras

I think this is why we came to Central America: to indulge on a "private" beach a few feet from our door, with the Caribbean sun to warm us and gentle breezes to cool us. Rustling palm trees sang a counterpoint to the waves spilling on the beach. And then there was the restaurant behind us any time I didn't

want to cook. We enjoyed it here so much that we decided to stay an extra day. We didn't so much come to that decision, we just didn't move. This has happened before. It must be something to do with the climate.

The motorhome was parked about twelve feet from a two-foot drop down to a narrow beach, where waves gently flopped over each other. The sand was a dark slate-green and off to the right there was a plateau of rocks. A couple of men caught lobster over there and approached us, offering a monster for sale. I love lobster, but neither of us could cope with a live one.

It is much cooler here than the Pacific side of Panama, just fifty miles away, which makes it much more comfortable. The water is lovely. It is warm and very clear.

All day long locals had been walking past us on the sand, many with fishing lines. As the sun set they seemed to gather off to our left, where a fresh water stream emptied into the Caribbean. If

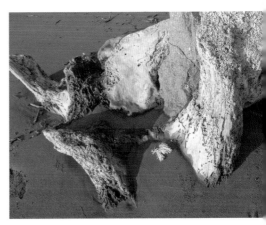

they didn't have a boat they waded into the warm water. There were families playing on the beach waiting.

Imagine me sitting on a log in my sarong, waves bubbling at my feet. Fishermen in dugout canoes sit silhouetted against a gentle pink sunset, and I'm picking mango from between my teeth. Yes, this is why we came.

The setting sun paused above the water, propped up by the fishing boats, as if to take one last look.

Tomorrow we will move on.

Day 71
Tuesday, March 25, Portobelo and Isla Grande

The Caribbean coast of Panama is very attractive, and the residents of Panama City take advantage of it. Two miles east of the black-sand Maria Chiquita Beach we came to the pretty, clean, white beach of Playa Langosta. This was another ideal place to camp on the spacious parking lot of a restaurant. We pulled up to make inquiries. The manager quickly came out to greet us.

"We are not able to stop here at this time, but are interested to know if motorhomes are welcome."

"Yes," he said in good English, "Oh yes, you are very welcome. Would you like breakfast?"

LEFT: Fisherman throwing his net near Restaurante Las Palmeras
ABOVE: Sunset over the Atlantic, an unusual sight in America. Las Palmeras
RIGHT: Driftwood on the green-gray sand at Las Palmeras, east of Maria Chiquita.

"No thank you. I didn't realize that your restaurant was open." We had already eaten before we left.

"I would be happy to open it and make breakfast for you."

"No. Thank you very much. We are just looking for places that motorhomes could park. We want to encourage more people to drive here from North America."

He then let loose on all the attributes of the little white sand bay. The water is good for snorkeling, and there really are lobsters you can catch, which is why it is named Playa Langosta. The restaurant is good and there is fresh water available. Unfortunately there is nowhere to dump. We liked the place, with its tight little cove lined with thatched umbrellas that they call *bohíos* in Panama.

We continued west, along the coast on an easy road, and less than an hour later we came to Portobelo. This was another one of Christopher Columbus' ports of call. He was reputedly the first to call it "Beautiful Port." For two hundred years the Spanish used it to ship Peruvian gold that had been carried across the isthmus, back to Spain. The trading of gold and silver for local merchandise was held at great fairs that lasted for weeks in the 1630s. It is said that the gold and silver was stacked up like

firewood in the customs house. The customs house is still there, but not the treasure. One of my countrymen, Sir Francis Drake, used to make regular calls here relieving the Spanish of whatever loot he could. He met his fate here too, and died of dysentery. It is said he is buried in a lead coffin off Isla Drake. We could see the island among others that dotted the azure waters. I remembered reading the gory tale of Henry Morgan's raid here in 1668 as dramatized by James Michener in *Caribbean*.

We suddenly saw some major fortifications and pulled over just barely off the road. The fortifications were well maintained, and it was easy to imagine the Spanish soldiers standing behind their ramparts manning their cannons, watching for the buccaneers. Looking up at the hill behind us, we saw a path to a lookout, so we clambered up the steps for a great view of the bay, the forts and the town.

After a short walk we continued into town, and found a very large parking lot right in the middle that was conspicuous for its lack of cars. We had it to ourselves, so we parked across the lines in the shade

LEFT: Fishing along the beach at Las Palmeras
ABOVE: Playa Langosta, Panama

and walked into town. They expected tourists here, and during festival times there would be hundreds. This is only a few hours by car from Panama City on the Pacific Ocean. It would have been only five or six days by horse and mule on the Royal Road during the height of the Spanish rule. Exploring a little, we sat and rested on a breakwater built by the Spanish about four hundred years ago. Brindle happily flopped into the water, lying on the pebbles, cooling her belly, with her head held up out of the water. I began to long for a swim.

Not only are there extensive, well preserved, Spanish fortifications or *castillos,* and an interesting restored colonial customs house, but they have the "Black Christ." This is a life-sized crucifix carved from local wood. Legend says that the ship that was to transport it to Spain had to turn back because of bad weather. Four more attempts were made but the bad weather prevailed. The superstitious crew decided that the Christ was bad luck, and it didn't want to leave the New World, so they threw it overboard. It floated ashore and the villagers reclaimed it.

ABOVE: Spanish fortifications at Portobelo.
RIGHT: A vulture pauses on the ramparts of the Spanish fort overlooking Portobelo Harbor

The colonial church of San Felipe was relatively large but not particularly interesting. There was not the awe-inspiring feeling we felt in the Guatemalan and Chiapas churches. The figure of the Black Christ stands behind glass off to the left of the main altar. They say that it mysteriously turned black. Some skeptics say it was the smoke from candles that caused the "miracle," but believers know it was the hand of God. I am a skeptic, but it did not look as though it was stained by smoke, as the coloration was very uniform. He was of a shiny dark wood, but not dark enough for me to really call Him black.

He has been credited with several miracles, particularly of curing cholera. People visit him from all over the country, especially on the 21st of October. On that date the Christ is moved through the streets by men who march in a procession, taking three steps forward and two backwards.

Back into the brilliant sunshine, we walked to the old customs house. There is a relief of the Spanish fortifications in the lobby, and a small museum. I was more interested in the Kuna women and the *molas* they were selling in the cool of the colonnade.

The Kuna people preserve their tradiional ways and they govern their own territory, which includes almost four hundred islands of San Blas, about fifty miles east of Portabelo. The Kuna won autonomy for their lands, or Kuna Yala, after a short conflict with the Panamanian government in 1925. If you want to visit the Kuna Indians, access is by air or by boat.

They have permitted visitors since Columbus, but do not allow them to buy the land. It makes me smile to think that this shy, matriarchal society continues to live in its own way, permitting outsiders to visit only on Kuna terms.

The Kuna have survived for centuries on the fruits of the sea and coconuts.

They now also grow other produce like yams, yucca and bananas on the mainland where the soil is better. The women make overlaid appliqué *molas* for sale to the visitors.

We returned to our motorhome, driving east toward the town of La Guaria and Isla Grande, a popular spot we had been told to visit. The town was filled with children in their school uniforms returning home for lunch. Smiles and waves were exchanged as we left Portobelo. The road diverted inland and we drove through ranchland. There was a large place that looked like an equestrian center, but it was run down and not too inviting. John took a GPS reading thinking that it could house a caravan of motorhomes if they wanted to venture this far.

We were thinking of staying the night in a hotel on Isla Grande. Near the dock on the mainland, we found a very large grassy parking area with enough shade for the motorhome. A man came over promptly and offered to watch the vehicle, and we were under the misconception that his charge also covered the parking. We found out differently when we returned. Oh well! One person owned the land while the other watches the vehicles.

It was still only noon and the island was very close, just a few hundred yards off shore. I even considered swimming across. The hotels on Isla Grande charge about fifty dollars a night, and most of their clients were the wealthy from Panama City. We decided we would return to the motorhome to sleep and not to take our overnight stuff with us. There was a little skiff waiting to take us

across the water and it seemed quite normal to the operator and us when Brindle jumped aboard after us. Dogs are everywhere and hardly noticed.

We walked through the middle of town on the narrow sand footpath between the houses and past the open-air church. This was the main drag! In five minutes we arrived on a small beach on the west-end of the island.

Here was the Hotel Isla Grande, with facilities to provide food service, rental beach chairs, and shade umbrellas for the weekend crowd. This was Tuesday and the place was completely deserted.

We dropped our things on the sand in the shade of a tree and asked Brindle to watch them. The swimming and snorkeling was wonderful. The water felt like warm silk. There were a few reefs with colorful little fish but we saw more beer cans than anything else, which was sad. I was floating about looking for interesting things among the seaweed when I suddenly felt a powerful movement of water beside me. Shark? Alarmed I looked up and there was Brindle. She had swum fifty yards out to see us. She was meant to be watching our things on the beach, but we had been in the water a while so she must have either become envious or worried. I swam back to the beach with her, adrenaline still in my

LEFT: The old customs house as seen from the fort in Portobelo
RIGHT: Kuna molas for sale in Portobelo.

bloodstream. John wallowed a little longer.

It was time for a late lunch, but we failed to find anyone to serve us in the Hotel. During busy times they charged day visitors an admission to use their pool and other facilities, only there was no one on the gate. In fact, we couldn't find any hotel staff at all.

We walked back along the narrow beach and indulged in a good meal and a bottle of beer at a little restaurant overlooking the dock. Good fresh fish again.

We had read about the Banana Village Resort, a glamorous hotel on the other side of the island where we were sure we could get a piña colada. It was a pleasant stroll along the waterfront. Sometimes the path was paved with rocks and sometimes there were bars between the water and us. There were many attractive bars open to the sun, and the breezes, but they were all closed to business. We were beginning to obsess about piña coladas.

ABOVE: Isla Grande
LEFT: Our camouflaged dog guarding our things on the beach at Isla Grande
RIGHT: Brindle leading the way down the main drag around Isla Grande

The narrow beach became rock and coral as we approached the east-end of the island, which was washed by the stronger Caribbean currents. We came to a small artists' colony where they were making a variety of figurines and jewelry. I resisted and we strolled on. Eventually, we came to another charming, but closed, bar at Moon Cabins. This was a lovely spot overlooking the water with a big bamboo bar. There was no one around and of course, no drinks. Nevertheless we made ourselves at home. I washed out a glass that had been left out and the three of us had a drink of water in the shade of their cabana. Then an employee approached and told us the only place that would serve piña coladas on a Tuesday, was the Banana Village Resort. He told us that it was on the other side of the island and pointed to the rise behind us.

Up and over the island we went, past expensive weekend homes and the houses of year-round residents with chickens and vegetable plots. We took particular care with Brindle near chickens because her desire to play and chase can alarm them! As the path descended the north-side of the island it became very overgrown before reaching the water and opening out to the little home of a fishing family.

"Excuse me," I said as we approached the house. A man glanced up and then went back to mending his fishing net, ignoring us. A young boy stood staring at us.

"Excuse me." John addressed the boy this time. "We are looking for the Banana Village Resort. Do you know where it is?"

The boy nodded but didn't say a word.

"Could you tell us where it is?"

The boy nodded again and pointed to a narrow path parallel to the rocks along the shore. We had received several such directions from much more communicative people than the boy, and had landed up lost. It was hot and time for a rest. We had been walking around and across the island for almost an hour.

"Could you take us there?" John suggested.

At this the boy's eyes seemed to open a little wider. Perhaps he smelled gringo money. He glanced at his dad who didn't look up. "OK," he said, and beckoned for us to follow him down the only path along the water's edge.

It was no more than five minutes down a deeply shaded dirt path (where we could not have gone astray if we had tried) that we came to a sign announcing the hotel. We had almost been there. The boy had obviously been taught not to go on hotel property, so we thanked him and gave him his tip.

The Banana Village is a romantic retreat, albeit on the expensive side. The only guests we saw there was a gentleman with an attractive, very much younger lady. We got our piña coladas and sat in the shade of the palms. Some magnificent exotic parrots screeched at Brindle from the safety of their enclosure. I took a dip in their seawater pool and let the sun dry me in the lush tropical gardens. Rested, we made inquiries about how to get back to the mainland. They arranged for a private boat that left directly from their dock. It was a very short ride around the western point of the island were we had been swimming earlier, then across the water to the mainland. We had completely circumnavigated the island. We learned there was a short cut directly across the island to Banana Village from the center of town, but we never saw it.

We would have had our piña coladas earlier but we would have missed most of the island. We can honestly say that we thoroughly explored Isla Grande! This was the furthest point of our journey.

We contemplated staying where we were parked, but decided instead to return to Playa Langosta for the night. We were only about 20 miles away.

The English-speaking manager we had met in the morning was still there. He was a young man who had won a scholarship for a total immersion English language course at Indiana University in Bloomington, where our daughter went to school. He was progressive thinking, and determined to make a success of this little resort and then move on to bigger and better things. He had been out in the bay collecting cans and other litter from the bottom, and now he was assisting his staff to thatch the *bohíos*. The sand on the beach was scrupulously clean and raked.

He described the enormous *langosta* one of his workers had caught the day before, and proudly showed me the knife he had made himself, from blade to handle.

Day 72
Wednesday, March 26, Turning Northward and Visiting El Valle de Antón

We had been to our furthest point from home and now we had to turn the corner and head back towards home. There is no road to South America. The Pan-American Highway turns to gravel in Chepo, about forty miles from the Bridge of the Americas, and then stops altogether 130 miles further on at Yaviza. From there, to continue, you would have to hike or take a canoe through virgin jungle. If you want to take a vehicle to South America you have to ship it from a major port farther north. Add to the lack of road and the unwelcoming nature of the land, there is an unsavory population, particularly in the north of Colombia. We were quite happy to turn around, although we were sad at the thought that we were heading toward the end of our trip.

To get home we had to drive South! We drove back across the isthmus to Panama City. It was our fourth crossing. There had been very little opportunity to purchase locally made craft items except for the *molas,* so I wanted to revisit the souvenir store where we had stopped on our first day in Panama. They had a good selection of items made in various parts of the country and I could have spent all day there. If you are in the area, it is worth the finding this souvenir shop. It is behind the YMCA building and Balboa is small enough that most people know it. The building is opposite a dramatic modern statue of people who look like they are balancing on a beam. The main figure is supposed to be the wife of the previous mayor.

The souvenir barn contains a cluster of independent stalls with plenty of interesting items for sale. There were masses of *molas* of every shape, color and price. There were T-shirts, hats, beach towels, pots, purses, and also woodcarvings, the national Spanish style women's dress called a *pollera,* and so many other things. I was looking for a mask made by the Embera Indians of the almost impenetrable Darien Province. The Indians are known for their baskets and bowls made from reeds and palm fibers, which they dye, with natural extracts. They also make masks using the same techniques. Selling these items to tourists is an attempt to make the tribes independent

and lessen their need to destroy the rainforest for a livelihood.

Our friends, Bert Shelton Sr. and Jr., arrived and disturbed my reverie as I browsed the vast array of crafts. They wanted to show us some Panamanian countryside before we headed home. A good friend of theirs lives in the mountain town of El Valle, a few hours west of Panama City, along our route home. They were going to escort us there for a visit. Bert senior climbed up into the motorhome with John, grinning all the while, and Bert Jr. drove me in his car. First we had to cross the Canal again, and now I could take a picture of the motorhome crossing the great Bridge of the Americas.

We continued on the Pan-American Highway for about an hour, which at this point was a wide four-lane highway.

"We've got to stop at the cheese factory," Bert announced. "We used to get cheese here all the time, when I was a kid. It is a local specialty." And he pulled in where a couple of shops were set back from the road. We bought a bunch of cheese and bread. We had to go back for more bread before we had even reached the car. John and I must have been craving starch, as we ripped the small cheese-covered loaf to pieces in front of the

RIGHT: Crossing the Bridge of the Americas over the Panama Canal

Sheltons, offering them some but devouring most of it in great chunks. It was fabulous.

We left the motorhome at the beach where we had camped a week earlier and backtracked a little to the turnoff just before San Carlos, and headed towards El Valle. This was another winding road following the cattle trails up into the hills.

El Valle de Antón is in a valley of an extinct volcano. It is blessed with lush vegetation, hot springs, and a very pleasant climate. Because of this, many Panamanians have weekend homes, and gardens that overflow into the streets. It is also home to the golden frogs and square trees, which are unique to the area and "internationally renowned," perhaps to an exclusive audience. We had never heard of them, and we saw neither tree nor frog.

We visited an American friend of Bert's who had retired after 40 years with the Canal administration. He lives in a pleasant house, surrounded by a colorful tropical garden. It was an enjoyable afternoon of socializing. We felt more like we were in Rancho Santa Fe, California than in Panama. Bert's friend had satellite TV and could watch U.S. television programs. We visited the local country club which could rival most of the upscale clubs in the States. When America turned the management of the Canal over to the Panamanians in 1999, many of the workers and executives of the Canal Authority chose to retire to places like this.

When we told Bert's friends that we were returning to camp at Playa Santa Clara, they assumed that we were staying at a place called XS Memories, an actual RV park a few miles from our beach site. They knew the American owners, and

went there often for dinner. We had just discovered the only RV park in Panama. When the caravan folks had told us to stay in Playa Santa Clara, they meant XS Memories.

We headed back to Santa Clara to check this place out. It is truly an Americanized RV park complete with satellite TV, English language games and books, and a very social atmosphere with hosts Dennis and Sheila. We had a nice meal and conversation, and then we headed across the highway to our campsite on the beach; there we said our farewells to the Sheltons. We were happy to be in this idyllic location, on the Pacific Ocean, where the waves could lull us to sleep again.

Day 73
Thursday, March 27, Crossing Panama Again

The beach was deserted at sunrise. Brindle raced flat out, nose and ears streamlined, down the beach towards a bird that lazily took off and circled slowly over the water and back to the sand. Brindle turned and cantered back, ears flopping and tongue lolling, until she found something interesting to sniff.

We took advantage of the facilities by emptying our tanks, and filling up with water. We left Playa Santa Clara at the civilized hour of 9:30 a.m. and began to retrace our path half-way back across Panama. We were at the southernmost latitude of our trip now, about 8° north of the equator (about 550 miles). Our furthest point, Isla Grande, was actually about 140 miles farther north. There is only one east-west road across Panama. We headed west on the dual carriageway and couldn't keep up with the 100 km speed limit.

LEFT: El Valle de Antón, Panama

Our return plan was to cross Panama once more taking the road from Chiriquí to Chiriquí Grande on the Caribbean. From there we would either take a ferry to Bocas del Toro, or drive on a new highway to Almirante. We intended to cross back into Costa Rica at the little used Guabito/Sixaola crossing on the Caribbean. Our friend Catherine, from Panama City, assured us that the highway was fine.

There wasn't much traffic so it was west at Mach speed. We saw several speed traps. The highway limit is 100 km/hr (60 mph), but the road passes through towns all the time. There are little signs that limit you to 50 km/hr or even less. Sometimes there are towns and no signs. We noted four cops on the watch in the first 150 miles.

All of a sudden, in the middle of nowhere, there was a traffic jam. John happened to be behind the wheel so I walked to the head of the line to see what was happening. (John could drive now. John's secretary had Express Mailed his new Texas license to the Shelton's address.) There hadn't been an accident, as we had originally thought, but a blockage by taxi drivers. They were protesting the government's proposal to issue more taxi drivers licenses. This would presumably mean less work for each of them.

"You're going to be here for a while," I was told by a local I passed sitting in his car. There was nothing we could do about it, if they block the Pan-American Highway we would just have to wait. There was no other road. I reported back to John and settled down for a long wait. John took the dog for a walk and I broke out one of our mangos, and was caught with juice on my chin when engines started revving up and we were all on our way. It had only been a twenty-minute stop after all. The taxi drivers had made their point.

After the town of Aguadulce, we lost the divided highway and the road reverted to the familiar two-lane black top. There were tall stands of a variety of mahoganies imported from Africa, as it grows faster than the native kind. It is an attractive tree with a mottled trunk of grays and greens.

As we traveled west, we saw less of the clusters of banana trees that announce that there are people living nearby. About 204 miles west of the capital we approached the town of Tolé, where we had stayed before. We started watching out for stalls by the roadside selling bead necklaces. This is the only place we had seen them for sale except for a few in the souvenir barn in Panama. The indigenous people live in small clusters and, if you pass them by, you can miss their specialty. We stopped and bought more of the smaller necklaces. The large ones that are about four inches deep are a bit much to wear back home.

The first real rain we had to drive through on the entire trip then greeted us. It rained steadily all afternoon. It cooled us down even though we were still just as sticky. It was sort of nice for a change. After a while we had had enough,

but it continued to rain. People continued to go about their business in the downpour as though nothing had changed. We did note one man had put a big plastic sheet over his horse, but I believe it was to protect the elaborate saddle rather than the animal. Suddenly, the sun came out and many of the women were carrying umbrellas as sunshades.

At Chiriquí, just east of David, we took the road north and for the fifth time were crossing the Isthmus of Panama. It might be the dry season, but as we climbed it became very wet, green cattle country. The rain stayed with us until we found a place to stop for the night. The road was narrow and constantly wound around bends as we climbed into the hills. It had a good surface but there really weren't any places to pull off.

We had read in *Lonely Planet* about a place called Finca La Suiza, which sounded like a delightful place to camp on this highway, but when we found the turnoff, it was padlocked shut and deserted. There didn't seem to be any way to enter. We continued over the continental divide and came to a house with a wide area in front, which looked like a place where they erect stalls and sell merchandise during busy days. We went up to the house and asked if we could park there for the night, and they were obliging. The home had a big sign with the name *Vista Hermosa,* or beautiful view.

The Pacific Ocean was out there somewhere, but the rain and clouds kept

LEFT: Evening at Vista Hermosa, near the Panamanian Continental Divide
TOP RIGHT: Sunrise on the Continental Divide, Vista Hermosa, Panama
RIGHT: A gully in the Panamanian mountains

it from our view. We should have expected rain and clouds in a rainforest. After dark, the clouds lifted a bit and we could see the lights of the popular tourist town of Boquete, and another town way in the distance. Boquete was a town John wanted to visit, as he heard it was very pretty. Admiral Byrd, after his visit to the South Pole, and Charles Lindbergh after his Atlantic flight, both lived there for a while. We had bypassed it on our south-bound journey because of the Canal transit schedule, and now there it was, only eight kilometers away down the mountain. Our hosts were not too clear about the dirt road that cut across the hillside, or its condition. If locals didn't know, who would? They said the road was below Mary's restaurant. This was one of the places we had been looking for as a possible camping spot, but hadn't been able to find it. We would have to visit Boquete on our next trip to Panama.

We slept well in the cool mountain air listening to the rain on the roof.

Day 74
Friday, March 28, Returning to Costa Rica

This morning we woke up to clear skies and a truly *Vista Hermosa*. It was so very different from what we had seen the night before. We were right on the top of the Continental Divide and, had there been no haze in the distance, we could have seen the ocean.

I saw some locals walk down a path on the other side of the road, and the

dog and I decided to follow. The path was a walk through a natural garden filled with flowers and ferns, moss covered fallen logs and boulders. The little gullies were filled with pink impatiens, orange lilies, ferns and rich foliage and looked as though they were carefully tended gardens instead of ditches filled with weeds.

The road surface was really good, even though there was a double yellow line the entire way. There was little traffic, and we were happy at 30-35 mph. We just winced and pulled to the right as banana trucks sped past on the corners. There were a number of Chiquita Banana eighteen-wheelers coming in the opposite direction. I call this the Banana Road. There must be some reason that the best road in the country goes from the banana-growing region to the port. The drivers would often wave in a friendly way, as would many people along the roadside.

This was the best jungle road we had driven on. Although it was one continuous S-bend, the surface was good and the views spectacular. The scenery was really lovely and lush in all directions with enormous trees and sweeping views of valleys. In the middle of all this was Lake Fortuna with a huge dam and hydroelectric power generation. We did find some interesting discrepancies in the map we were using, but that might be due to the new roads that were opened in 2000. There were numerous waterfalls splashing down this side of the mountains.

Once we were over the divide we noticed some of the vegetation change and the homes were definitely different. Now the houses were on stilts and clustered in more distinct villages.

John pointed out the Trans-Panamanian Pipeline that followed the road. The 81-mile pipeline consists of large diameter pipe spanning many canyons and ravines on its way from Puerto Armuelles on the Pacific coast of Panama, to Chiriquí Grande on the Atlantic side. This pipeline was built in 1982 to carry Alaskan crude to the U.S. East Coast. This was an economical alternative to the Canal when Alaskan oil production was at its peak, but it was closed in 1996, when Alaskan oil production went into decline, and the decision was made to export Alaskan crude to Pacific Rim countries. All Alaskan production is now going to California and other Pacific ports. The pipeline capacity is 860,000 barrels per day, and may be reactivated for Ecuadorian crude. Currently, about 625,000 barrels per day of crude oil and petroleum products transit the Canal.

We don't make it a habit of picking up hitchhikers, but we did pull over when a family flagged us down. There was a sense of urgency in the way they were waving, not the usual casual hitchhikers' gesture. There were two women, a toddler and an old man. The women looked like they had put on their best church clothes. They were *indígenas,* of Indian origin. Once we stopped, the faces of the women indicated they had a real problem. The young woman could hardly pull herself up into the bus. We thought that they all were coming, but the old man stayed behind with the toddler, who began bawling like crazy when his mother left him. The young girl had deep set, brown eyes and she was wearing a freshly pressed white dress with blue print flowers. She was in a great deal of discomfort and sat on the sofa. In no time she lay back and her mother helped her to lift her legs up. I offered her water but she declined, clutching her stomach.

"El hospital. El hospital en Rambula." The mother gestured for John to drive on. She was wearing a frilly blouse over a neat skirt. She sat at the dinette splitting her attention between her daughter on the sofa and the road ahead. I couldn't understand her Spanish directions but the road only went one way. We were now an ambulance.

When the mother calmed down, comfortable that we were going to take them to the hospital, she spoke more slowly and carefully for us. As we began to communicate better she explained that this was her daughter and that she had two sons in addition. When she asked about our family I pointed to the pictures of our girls on the wall. She counted off the names of five pueblos we were to go through before we would reach Rambula. Some of the *pueblos* she mentioned were so small we didn't realize we had passed through them. There was just a hut or two near the road.

She sat forward and said "Rambula. Es Rambula," waving her hand for us to keep going as though flipping flies out of the way. She directed us to a small hospital and darted out of the motor-

home calling to the staff, who produced a wheelchair. Her daughter carefully clambered down and sat in it with a sigh of relief. She couldn't have had a much more comfortable ambulance. I hope she is all right. As the attendant wheeled her to the hospital the mother turned back to pay us for the ride, which of course we didn't accept.

We had set our sights on exploring Bocas del Toro, if we could get over there easily. Bocas del Toro is the capital of the state. It's a small village on the Island of Colón out in the Caribbean. There are beaches all around the island, good snorkeling, and good restaurants. There used to be a ferry from Chiriquí Grande to Bocas, which then continued on to Almirante. We had read the Plaxton's account of the ferry ride from Chiriquí Grande to Bocas in their motorhome, which sounded wonderful. A new road now connects Chiriquí Grande with Almirante, making the ferry redundant. We set out to explore Chiriquí Grande and to find out if the ferry still ran; then we would decide what to do. As was so often the case on this trip our plans were flexible and rarely extended for more than a day.

We drove into Chiriquí Grande and right up to the old ferry terminal. We

LEFT: Lake Fortuna, Panama
RIGHT: Chiriquí Grande, Panama

found out as soon as we parked that the local customs officer had little to do. He was quickly at our door asking for vehicle papers. Our papers were all correct and he politely answered our questions. The ferry indeed didn't run from Chiriquí Grande anymore.

The residents in the area were a very mixed group including *indígenas* in traditional clothes, dark skinned, and blond haired people, Caribbean blacks and Rastafarians. It was a good melting pot. There was little activity here other than a few shops.

We backtracked to the Almirante turnoff and took the new road to the north through some lovely green pasture, with cattle grazing under palms, and vast trees that might have once been king of the jungle. We would often see children waiting at a bus stop, always in uniform even though sometimes with bare feet. We also spotted uniforms hanging on the clothesline outside thatched huts.

The road went inland against the foothills. There was a wide savanna between the coast and us. A few times we were tempted to take a turnoff down a dirt road that looked like it might lead to a secluded beach on the coast, but we were in a mood to press on. We were still not sure if, or how, we might get to Bocas del Toro.

It was lunchtime. and we found a restaurant about 11 miles south of Almirante. Restaurante y Bar Onelys; it had a large grassy parking area and a spectacular view of the archipelago. The manager, Pedro, made us quite welcome. He was interested in our motorhome and how he might accommodate motorhome camping at his facility. He said he sees about three to five motorhomes per month going by. They don't all stop. We told him if he put in a dump station with a septic tank, the motorhomes would definitely come. As it was, he welcomes campers and has water and electricity available. We had a good lunch together with some local road workers.

Almirante was a bustling and somewhat intimidating experience. From the moment we arrived over-helpful salesmen and boys trying to arrange transportation for us to Bocas del Toro besieged us. At the outskirts of town a boy grabbed onto the doorjamb and was prepared to ride on the running board all the way to the docks. Brindle helped discourage him and eventually we managed to shake him. Then halfway through town, a man on a bicycle intercepted us. I gathered there weren't too many motorhomes around. We had the look of tourists, and that meant business to the locals. He was insistent on leading us to the ferry terminal in the hope of selling us a ticket and perhaps more.

We had missed the ferry for that day. It leaves from Almirante at 9:00 a.m. on Wednesdays, Fridays, Saturdays, and Sundays. It returns at 5:00 p.m. on the same days. We could take the motorhome on the ferry and camp at Bocas del Toro. This option appealed to John at first, then we found out it cost about $50 to take a vehicle this size each way, versus $1.50 for passenger service. Our options were to find a place to park for the night and take the ferry in the morning, leave the vehicle and take a water taxi to Bocas today, or keep going toward Costa Rica. A two-hour boat ride with the dog in that heat wasn't very appealing. Our friends, William and Niny, had previously brought their "tank" from the Belén Trailer Park in San José, Costa Rica, here for a visit. They parked it at the fire station and took the passenger ferry to Bocas del Toro. They described Bocas del Toro as a party town for the young and those into SCUBA diving. Our daughter had also visited a year earlier, and only gave it a lukewarm review.

There was another factor in our decision. Once we turned the corner at Isla Grande, our attitude about this trip changed. We began to think about getting home. It wasn't a strong pull. All along we had planned on spending *Semana Santa* in Antigua, Guatemala. That was still 18 days away, but we had an underlying urge to keep moving.

It was 1:30 p.m. and we still had time to make Costa Rica, so we left Almirante behind.

Suddenly we hit the banana plantations. Even the towns were called Finca 4, Finca 32 and Finca 42. These rather industrial names were for commercial farms that have grown into communities. There was row upon row of banana trees held up by tethers and separated by irrigation ditches. Each cluster of bunches was in a blue plastic bag so they would ripen evenly and not be blemished by insects that would be unsightly for the export market. We passed some packing plants where the four-foot clusters of banana bunches were maturing. Bunches, which were in exactly the right condition, were being boxed in the containers that we recognize in the supermarket. They would be transported in trucks that keep them cool so they

LEFT: The new road between Chiriquí Grande and Almirante showing Bocas del Toro Archipelago
TOP RIGHT: Most of the river crossings were via railway bridges. This one was just outside Changuinola, Panama
RIGHT: Banana train by the road from Changuinola to Guabito, Panama

would not mature before they reached their market.

Bunches of green bananas had fallen off trucks and lay in the road. Many were squashed by successive trucks. I hated to see the waste so we stopped and collected some to ripen in our motorhome.

Now we came to the first of the three railway bridges. These had been built in the early 1900s by the United Fruit Company for the *fincas* to get their bananas to the packing-houses. Now the bridges served as road, railway and foot bridges for everyone. The bridges were modified to accommodate cars by throwing down planks on either side of the rails. The sleepers support the planks. It is apparently a common practice on these bridges to have to move the planks as you progress. In this case all planks seemed to be in place and in good condition.

There was no clear way to know who has the right of way. Imagine meeting an eighteen-wheel semi-trailer in the middle of this. There was not any kind of railing and many of the planks laid along side of the tracks are not fastened down. It made for an interesting experience and I discovered how long I could hold my breath!

In the town of Changuinola we once again became slightly lost. This is the commercial center of this district, but poorly signposted. They don't get many visitors. This necessitated stopping every so often and asking for directions to the border. Usually it was *directo,* but on one occasion we had strayed off the path into a military barracks. We had read that the Panamanian army was disbanded after the Noriega capture in 1979, but this place did look like military. Anyway the helpful guard showed us the way. We turned around and found the right road.

The approach to the border is on a dirt road. We found, on many occasions, that the worst roads in a country would be the ones closest to a border. I guess there is no interest in encouraging commerce or travel between the countries. In this case, however, there was a lot of commerce. The banana plantations continued on the Costa Rican side of the border and we passed several more packinghouses.

We made it to Guabito, which is the Panamanian side of the crossing, at about three in the afternoon. We thought we would have enough time to go through the Panamanian *aduana.* Costa Rican

LEFT: Above is the railway track to the border crossing at Guabito, Panama.

ABOVE: Up on the railroad tracks for the crossing from Panama to Costa Rica at Guabito, Panama, looking south

time is an hour earlier, which would give us an additional hour to clear there.

However, there were no signs to the border. We got completely lost and must have asked a dozen people. We went in circles under this narrow dilapidated bridge looking for the bridge over the River to Sixaola, in Costa Rica.

Eventually, John understood that he was to drive up onto the dusty railway embankment, straddle the tracks over the little bridge, and then onto the big bridge that crossed the river.

I walked up the steps where pedestrians descended and could see the bridge we wanted. I signaled to John to go ahead. A few minutes later he came into view on the railway tracks up on the embankment.

I turned around and took a picture looking north.

Just before the railway bridge that connects the two countries there were a couple of blue and white sheds. These

housed the Panamanian border control. John took the passports and the vehicle documents and I took the dog file. I was glad that I had insisted the clerk stamp the entry into the country, as this official really wanted to see the record of her admission. He put his stamp on the side of the page and wrote something indecipherable next to it. He then said "Perfecto," and handed everything back to me. I met John coming out of immigration with our passports and we went to customs with the car papers. The whole process of leaving Panama had taken twenty minutes and cost us nothing. Then a pickup truck approached over the bridge from Costa Rica. There was clearly only room for one vehicle, but there was no one to say who had the right of way. We had the bigger vehicle, and a semi trailer had appeared behind us. The Toyota therefore had to get out of the way. It proved to be a difficult maneuver for him to get off the tracks, and down onto the sidewalk and almost into the customs buildings so that John and the eighteen-wheeler could pull past. He then had to remount the tracks in reverse. We were then free to cross into Costa Rica.

The bridge had obviously been repaired in the past six months.

ABOVE: Looking north toward the border crossing in Guabito. The pedestrian has just crossed the dilapidated bridge we had just driven under. The blue customs building and the sixty- year-old steel truss river bridge are visible beyond.
RIGHT: Looking down through the bridge at the muddy Sixaola River, between Panama and Costa Rica.

However, I could still see the brown water flowing below the rusty supports that held up the old railway ties. Some of the ties had weeds growing out of them. The planks on either side of the tracks were, by and large, in good condition and mostly nailed down although very uneven. Frequently as I trod on one end of a plank the other end would come up. There were plenty of places for me to trip as I tried to get ahead of John to take a good picture.

Our friend, Catherine Woodward, the Smithsonian student we had met when we crossed into Panama on the Pan-American Highway to the south, comes through this border frequently. She crosses this way on her field trips to study the flora of the tropical cloud forests of Costa Rica. She told us that the last time she had made this crossing the bridge was in such bad repair that she had to pay boys to carry the planks

for her to drive on. As she progressed they picked up the plank behind her and carried it in front and so on, on each side of the track. Catherine also told us to say hi to Omar, the Costa Rican border agent she had come to know.

We arrived safely on the other side, and stopped on the tracks. There was nowhere to go until we had cleared into the country. We completed the immigration forms and had our passports stamped. John went to the next room with the motorhome papers. I took the dog papers and disturbed the agricultural officer who was reading his newspaper. He looked at the sheaf of papers and dismissed me. Once again I had to insist that he stamp them showing that we had visited *cuarentena* and that Brindle had entered the country

---

ABOVE: Driving over the Panama/Costa Rica Bridge.
RIGHT: The line of three trucks behind us waiting to enter Costa Rica

legally. I was in and out and he was back reading his newspaper paper in about three minutes: No charge.

John was not having such an easy time with the vehicle papers. First the official, who was Catherine's friend Omar, needed a copy of the papers we had been given on our original entry into Costa Rica. We had surrendered these to the officials on our departure from Costa Rica at Paso Canoas a few weeks earlier. When we told them we would be returning, their only comment at the time was *"no problema."* At this point we discovered how efficient the Costa Rican system could be. Omar was able with a phone call to retrieve a copy of our previous paperwork in a matter of minutes via fax!

Unfortunately, getting the information faxed didn't speed things up. Omar had to enter all the data manually again to give us new permission. He was using a very advanced computer program that had pull-down menus for all the entries. This created problems when he came to our vehicle, because the menus didn't have things like "Coachmen Class C Motorhome." He wanted to know if it was a Ford, Chevrolet, Toyota, etc. John was helping him find the right entries. He had a particularly hard time entering my nationality. I am British, or is it English? His menu did not have "británico" (British), inglés (English) or "gran britania" (Great Britain). After about 10 minutes, John came up with the right answer: "reino unido" (United Kingdom). I guess Omar doesn't see many British subjects pass by here in RVs.

Next time we make this trip we will make copies of all the documents we get at each border crossing. This is another reason to carry a scanner and printer along with the laptop. For one reason, you'd have a copy if you lost the original.

Secondly, you could show it at the next crossing, so the official would know what had been done before and how to fill in the blanks. This was particularly true of the dog's papers. On the other hand, if you are not in a hurry most crossings don't take more than two to three hours in any case.

Meanwhile the line was growing behind us. Not that we were keeping anyone waiting, everyone was going through the same kind of paperwork. Semis spend hours at these borders having their cargoes, or at least manifests, checked. By the time Omar finished our paperwork there were three semi drivers sitting in the room patiently waiting. Their big trucks were parked behind us on the bridge. The driver I was chatting with said he was carrying paper. While this was going on, pedestrians were wandering back and forth across the bridge, squeezing past the eighteen-wheelers and us.

No one tried to enter the bridge in the opposite direction. Don't ask me

how we were so lucky as to land at the front of the line, but we did. I asked the truck driver how he knows when to cross and if there is any kind of control.

"No," he said, "I just look to see if it is clear."

At last we were free to move forward and roll off the tracks, down the embankment and into the town of Sixaola, on the Costa Rican side, past the line of cars, pickups, eighteen wheelers and buses waiting to go into Panama. We had cleared in about one hour, and had not needed to pay anything to anyone. Of course, if we had missed the opportunity to be first over the bridge, we might have been waiting there until morning.

As I walked ahead of the motorhome into Costa Rica, I looked back and noticed two signs.

One said *Peligro,* Danger. The other said, *Puente en mal Estado,* meaning the bridge is in bad condition. I'm glad we didn't see these before we crossed!

ABOVE: Coming off the tracks in Sixaola, Costa Rica.

CHAPTER 8

Four Countries

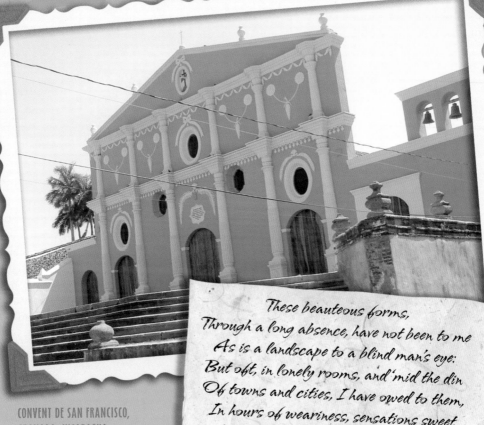

These beauteous forms,
Through a long absence, have not been to me
As is a landscape to a blind man's eye:
But oft, in lonely rooms, and 'mid the din
Of towns and cities, I have owed to them,
In hours of weariness, sensations sweet

TINTERN ABBEY
William Wordsworth

CONVENT DE SAN FRANCISCO,
GRANADA, NICARAGUA

HE ROAD FROM SIXAOLA TO Bribri in Costa Rica was true to the rule that the worst roads in any country were those closest to the border. Our Dutch friends in Belén had warned us about this road. It is a dirt road, 15-20 mph maximum, and incredibly, there are still speed bumps. Here in Costa Rica they're called *los tumulos*, which literally means "burial mound," or *los badenes*. The speed bumps were almost impossible to see on the dirt road at dusk. When we hit one, cups, glasses, bowls, and food items would fly all over the motorhome. On one occasion we succeeded in breaking another tumbler and a cup. Brindle went crazy whenever things went flying, acting like we were under attack.

This was still banana country. Many huge stake trucks passed us carrying bananas to the packinghouses. They apparently had problems with the speed bumps also, as we found many bunches of green bananas along the road. We collected some, but they were still green and inedible three weeks later.

Bribri is the name of an indigenous Indian tribe, and you can visit some of their native villages out of Puerto Viejo. The road from Bribri to Puerto Viejo was, thankfully, paved and in decent shape. We kept thinking we were through with rough dirt roads, but there were always more ahead. This road was a pleasant change.

We made it into Puerto Viejo just as it was getting dark. After a few trips up and down the main drag, we parked next to a pleasant restaurant, the Salsa Brava. They served a good piña colada and dinner. A few feet in front of us, the Caribbean was gently rolling over coral ledges onto a sand beach.

Puerto Viejo is a lively tourist town selling sarongs and colorful seed necklaces. Most of the signs were in English, advertising jungle tours, internet cafes, and vegetarian meals. We saw more gringo tourists here than we had anywhere so far on the entire trip, except perhaps in Monteverde. There was plenty happening in town. A discotheque was generating lots of noise a hundred yards down the road.

It had been a long day. The cool mountain lodge of Vista Hermosa seemed a world apart from this hot steamy tropical beach. We had been through jungle passes in the mountains,

served as an ambulance, visited a derelict and forgotten coastal town, seen spectacular views of the Bocas del Toro archipelago, been intimidated away from a Garífuna village, passed through lush banana country, succeeded in making a unique border crossing, and found where the gringo tourists hung out in Costa Rica. We went to bed. No one disturbed us.

Day 75
Saturday, March 29, Puerto Viejo

The town Puerto Viejo was set up for tourists from the U.S. There were gringos everywhere, and the stalls full of beach towels, beads and sarongs had English-speakers to sell the souvenirs. There were also masses of little hotels and restaurants. They seemed to be mostly houses that had been expanded in one way or another to accommodate the visitors. The beach was lovely, and in spite of our proximity to the road we decided to stay where we were at least for the morning.

We took a few steps across the short sand beach into the water in front of the motorhome and snorkeled for ages. There was nothing very dramatic to see, but it was pleasant in the water. The dog swam out to us and stood on a nearby ledge of coral until we drifted away. She swam up to check us out again, and then found another place to sit or stand. I was worried that she would cut her feet on the coral, but she didn't. She just wanted to be out there with us, and seemed to enjoy the water as much as we did. The water was blue and clear and very pretty.

This was obviously a very popular place for both the young and old from North America, but we had come south to enjoy the company of the locals. Pretty though it was, we decided to move on.

We drove a few miles north towards Cahuita (pronounced cah-wheeta) to visit the National Park. The park comprised a small peninsula, and was reported to have great beaches and snorkeling, as well as places to camp. We were reminded that no dogs are allowed in the Costa Rican National Parks, so we had to find ourselves another place to overnight. This was only the second time we could blame Brindle for stopping us from doing what we wanted to do. On both occasions it was Costa Rican Parks, and I don't hold their policy against them.

Cahuita was a much more laid back town with none of the tourist hubbub of Puerto Viejo. We drove around town to an out of the way street with no traffic and stopped. There were just a few trees between us and the coral filled water. I got out my beach chair and laptop, and John went for a bike ride.

John had such fun that after lunch we both went for a long bike ride. The dog darted ahead, smelled something of interest that would entertain her until we were almost out of sight, and then dart to catch up and repeat the exercise. We rode around town and then continued along the gray dirt coastal lane passing numerous weekend homes. Some were two-story concrete block buildings, others were hardly standing clapboard shacks. They all had a magnificent view of the crystal water.

Along the way we met a man with half a dozen green coconuts for sale. I was thirsty, and I enjoy the milk, so we paused. He hacked the top off with his machete and handed it to me. A green coconut with a two or three inch thick husk is not the easiest thing to drink from. It ran all over my face and down my chin but, as it is not sugary, I was not left sticky. However, I made a note to add a straw to our all-purpose backpack.

The vendor was an interesting man. Tall and lean, he showed a great set of white teeth with his frequent smiles. He was Garífuna, from Bluefields on the Caribbean coast of Nicaragua's Mosquitia region. Aiming to better himself, he had headed to the tourist areas of Costa Rica. We thought that was a good plan because, like most Garífuna, he spoke both English and Spanish fluently. He

LEFT: Coral reefs twenty feet in front of the motorhome, in the center of Puerto Viejo.
RIGHT: Cahuita, Costa Rica

had taken a boat up the bay from Bluefields to the mouth of the Escondido River, and then upstream for about ten miles to Rama. There was a major road to Managua from there. We had not known there was a land route out to the Caribbean coast. It is now on our list of must-do things for our next trip.

We finished our coconut drinks, thanked him, and continued our ride beside the fine black-sand beach. Families were frolicking in the surf and squealing in the waves. There were quite a few places we could have pulled the motorhome off the road and parked next to the beach. If we had been staying longer we would have moved here. Next to a restaurant and bar there was a plot of land where we were told other motorhomers had parked. It would have been ideal, and the bar next door made good piña coladas! They were a good deal tastier than my straight coconut milk.

We cycled back to the motorhome and arrived just before the rains came again.

Day 76
Sunday, March 30, Puerto Limón and Guayabo

It rained heavily during the night, and the pounding on the roof was accompanied by thunder and lightning. We woke up in the morning and looked up to a brilliant sky and warm sun. We looked down to see that we were standing in six inches of water. Fortunately, the ground beneath us was firm and the water warm. We waded around for our morning check of everything. Unfortunately, the darn dog was wet when we set off, in spite of a good toweling down. She loved the water. Whenever she was hot she found a puddle or beach, and just lay down in the water, or the mud, as though it were the most natural thing in the world.

Today was John's birthday, so I reverently took the last piece of frozen prime rib out of the freezer to thaw in the fridge. This one eight-ounce piece was more beef than we had eaten between us in ages.

Continuing our trek homeward the next place we were to visit was Puerto Limón. I had wanted to go there on a trip to Costa Rica eight years earlier, but we had been told it was unsafe. There were no such warnings now. Driving past the airport there was a good view of the harbor and the three cruise ships in port. We were in the center of town with curbside parking in no time.

Christopher Columbus had paused at an island off this coast on his fourth voyage, an event that is celebrated enthusiastically every October. Other voyagers now stop there. Puerto Limón is Costa Rica's only Caribbean port, and therefore has become a routine stop for cruise ships plying the coast. This was Sunday, so most of the shops were closed, in spite of the hundreds of passengers from the ships trying to spend their money. Puerto Limón, a thriving port city of 76,000 thousand people, is not a good example of the country that portrays an image based on ecotourism.

The park was interesting. It must have been very old, judging by the size of the palm trees and it had a comfortable used feel about it. We didn't spot the sloths that are said to reside there, but it was welcoming and friendly, and we enjoyed our stroll through to the waterfront. Returning to the town center we walked the four blocks of the pedestrian way and headed to the mercado for our necessities.

On the coast north of Limón, is Tortuguero National Park that can only be reached by plane or boat. We had taken a boat there a few years earlier. The journey itself was interesting and so was the cluster of homes called the town of Tortuguero. It is an attractive place and well worth the trip, especially if you are interested in turtles and other wildlife. When we were there before, we saw more monkeys and macaws on the boat ride through the canals than we did anywhere else in Costa Rica.

LEFT: Black sand beach at the north end of Cahuita, Costa Rica
ABOVE: Parque Vargas, in the port city of Puerto Limón, Costa Rica
RIGHT: I enclose this picture of the horse on the truck not because it is unusual. To the contrary, it is the kind of thing you might come across anywhere in Central America.

Leaving Limón, we were again in the center of banana growing country, and all we could see for mile upon mile was bananas. The twelve-foot trees are staked and trimmed carefully, and the fruit protected in blue plastic bags. Even here, in this wet country, there is a need for irrigation, and channels have been dug throughout the fields, and pipes laid to carry the water. Although damage done by residual fertilizer is unseen, care is now taken not to let old plastic bags spoil the environment. The banana industry does provide employment for the locals.

The Dutch travelers we had met at the San José campsite, William and Niny,

recommended that we visit the Guayabo National Archaeological Monument. This was off the southern route back to the capital near the town of Turrialba. Once off the main road we were traveling on a narrow, dirt road that wound up the side of the extinct Volcán Turrialba. It took us 45 minutes to go 11, but it was a pleasant drive. A light rain kept the dust down.

We came to the park, which had facilities on either side of the road but no real parking lot. To the right was the archaeological site and to the left were restrooms, a small museum, and a pleasant fenced in picnic area. We pulled over and made inquiries. The attendant said that we were welcome to stay the night where we were, so we leveled the motorhome and made ourselves at home. We only heard two vehicles going slowly down the road that evening. The hooves of a horse awakened us as its rider passed by in the morning before the first bus. Traffic was no problem here.

There was no literature in English, but the attendant produced a trail map and guide pamphlet in Spanish. He was very

ABOVE: A banana plantation in Costa Rica. The fruit is protected with plastic bags.
LEFT: 3,000 year old graves in Guayabo, Costa Rica
TOP RIGHT: Guayabo, Costa Rica
RIGHT: Aqueduct in Guayabo National Monument

enthusiastic and really wanted us to go into the park before he closed it at 4:00 p.m. It was raining quite hard but he assured us that it would also be raining in the morning. It was a treat to be cool, and there was not another person in sight.

This was the most attractive and interesting ruin site we had seen. Even though many people have not heard of Guayabo, it is considered by some to be the most important archaeological site in Costa Rica. Only ten percent has been excavated. There were markers, and the pamphlet told us what was of interest at each point. There were a couple of carved stones depicting a jaguar and a crocodile near the entrance, and just beyond there was a gravesite. These were stone-lined sepulchers softened by the passage of time, moss, and pretty impatiens flowers. It was amazing to think that they had been made three thousand years ago, and were still in such good condition.

I was to be even more surprised when we came out of the trees to see the aqueducts and waterways which had been built to catch and preserve the

limited rainwater. There were no springs in the area.

The whole place was like a garden, with flowers, lawns, stone paths and waterfalls. It was the ruins of a town that had been occupied between 1000 B.C. and 1400 A.D. It was like the "follies" that wealthy English noblemen built to entertain their friends. Perhaps it was the rain that made me think about England. So many of the ruined cities we had visited were stark and barren and hot. This was friendly and inviting, with dense leafy jungle wrapped around the neatly

cobbled constructions, with lawns softening the edges.

It was a special tranquil place where the excavations had only just begun. We lingered, absorbing the charm, but were driven out by the rain. Drenched to the skin, we returned to the motor-home for dry clothes.

I needed to cook John his birthday treat of chocolate chip cookies. This necessitated cranking up the oven for the first time. We were very hungry by the time I was done cooking and had sung "Happy Birthday". We were also craving sugar treats and ate most of the cookies while they were still hot. After that we had no desire for the prime rib. I made a salad and saved the precious meat.

Day 77
Monday, March 31, Belén and the Big Red Truck

It was a clear bright morning with none of the rain the caretaker had gloomily predicted. We seriously considered re-entering the park before the attendant arrived; it had been so appealing the night before. The serenity and temptation were broken when the first minibus arrived, oozing tourists.

Now that the sun was out we could enjoy the spectacular views back to Highway 10. This highway is the less traveled route between San José and the Caribbean coast. It was a pleasant drive

with considerably fewer large trucks than we had been experiencing.

Down off the slopes of the volcano we returned to sugarcane growing country. It was beautiful until we came to the fields they were burning. They burn the cane to remove the excess leaves before it is cut. It is then transported in open cage trucks to the mills, and often the first signs that you are in sugar cane country is the spilt cane littering the sides of the road.

TOP LEFT: These circular mounds were the foundations for important buildings.
LEFT: The road into the town of Guayabo that was built 3,000 years ago
ABOVE: Driving south on the slopes of Volcán Turrialba, Costa Rica

As we climbed again we returned to the altitude where coffee grows. We passed through manicured hillsides with trimmed coffee bushes and their high shade trees looming above.

At three in the afternoon we were back in the Belén Trailer Park. An amazing group had overtaken it. The trailer park was full of tents and our favorite site was not available. A truck with two-dozen rock climbers was pausing there during a trip around the world. The vehicle was about the ugliest thing I had ever seen. It was like an enormous red tank, with a rock-climbing wall on the back and coach seats inside. The tour participants of various nationalities would join this adventure-in-progress as it traveled around the world. They drove through each country looking for mountains or cliffs worth climbing. Each member took turns purchasing the food and cooking for three days, while others made sure there was enough firewood for cooking and took on other responsibilities. They all sleep in their own tents.

The driver of the truck, Fiona, was a professional intercontinental driver who works for a company that puts together exotic adventure caravans in the most remote spots on earth like Tibet, Kenya and India. Fiona has crossed Asia twice. She was hired to drive this truck around the world for three years with the rock-climbers on board. They started in London, made their way across Europe to Istanbul, then to Cairo, Nairobi and Cape Town in ten months. They had the Big Red Truck (BiRT) shipped to Ushuaia, Argentina (Tierra del Fuego) where they proceeded to Santiago, Chile La Paz, Bolivia Central America and then

eventually to Anchorage, Alaska. From there they ship the truck to Sydney, Australia and head back to London by way of Bangkok, Xian (China), Delhi and Istanbul. They were less than halfway when we met them. Fiona seemed an unlikely driver of the Scania 112M truck (it is not to be mistaken for a bus, even though it has 29 coach-style seats). This friendly and vivacious British girl was neither a linguist nor a mechanic, but she could navigate through any country in the world with a vehicle that dwarfed our little motorhome.

This adventurous group opened our eyes to the potential for safe adventure. People had told us our trip was going too far away from civilization. Heck, these people were crossing the Sahara Desert and the Himalayas on the same trip. If the reader wants to sample some far out overland adventures of this

---

TOP RIGHT: Sugar cane country, west of San José
RIGHT: Costa Rican coffee groves with their tall shade trees.

sort, Fiona gave us these web sites as a reference: www.dragonman.co.uk, www.exodus.co.uk, www.culturevultureonline.com.

We had prime rib for dinner. We had become so unaccustomed to any fat in meat that the eight-ounce slab we shared was really rich for us. Boy it was a good!

Day 78
Tuesday, April 1, To Liberia

We made a late departure from the RV park in San Antonio de Belén, as we thought it might be our last opportunity to clean up for a while. We had full hook-ups and, importantly, we could get rid of the dirty water.

Laura, the manager of the trailer park, permitted us to do internet flash sessions from our laptop. This enabled us to send off reports and catch up on our email. It was so very convenient and much nicer than having to find and sit in an internet café working on their ancient unreliable computers. The internet cafes seldom have coffee, and are often just a bank of rather antiquated computers with dubious connections.

When the last of the wash had dried, we topped off our water tank, dumped

our wastewater, said goodbye to our various fellow travelers, and left at 11:30 a.m. We stopped at the supermarket and also filled up our propane tank on the way out. We retraced our steps north through scenery that was nice but not exceptional. We could happily wave to the cops at the speed traps, as there was no way we could exceed the 80 kpm speed limit (50 mph) on the bumpy roads.

We were heading for Liberia for the night. Liberia is the jumping off point for those who are heading for the beaches on the Guanacaste coast. It was full of gringos. We had heard that the Hotel Guanacaste permits motorhomes to stay overnight and we wanted to check it out. It turned out to be an unattractive small gravel parking lot opposite a brewery with heavy trucks coming and going. Although the hotel looked nice enough, it was not the kind of campsite we preferred.

Circumnavigating the town square we made our way back to the Pan-American Highway. Directly across the road stood the nice Hotel Aservadeno, with restaurant and soccer field next to a very large field with several shade trees. Perfect! It was close enough to town that we could walk to the action and far enough away that we could leave the dog untethered.

Unfortunately, they wanted to charge U.S.$16 even though they had no services, which was a little steep for us considering there were hotels in town charging half of this for a room. We had gotten used to camping for nothing. It was an easy decision to drive the additional five kilometers north and return to the quiet El Delfin Trailer Park where we had stayed on our southward journey.

When we pulled in to the deserted parking area, I started looking around for the best shade tree. It was then that I noticed that one of the horses was in trouble. Two of the animals were tethered together and one had his leg over the rope between their halters. I couldn't imagine why they would be left to roam a pasture with a rope tying their halters together in the first place. While their heads were down grazing, one had stepped over the rope when it was on the ground. Now, when either animal raised its head, his leg was forced up off the ground. If they became frightened and ran they could be seriously hurt. Although they seemed tame and friendly and I was experienced with horses, I did not want to handle animals I didn't know without permission. I got out of the motorhome and approached some men, leaving John to find a place to park for the night.

"*Hay una problema con el caballero,*" I said. The literal translation meant that there was a problem with the cowboy. OK, so my Spanish isn't quite there yet.

The men naturally looked perplexed.

I pointed and tried to rephrase it and said, "*Los caballeros. Hay una problema con el cordo,*" I was still saying cowboy instead of the horse, but my mention of the rope had clarified it a little.

They smiled and one said, "*El caballo! Ah!*" The horse! He said something to his friends and walked over with me towards the animals.

Talking more slowly to me, he explained that one of the horses would leave the ungated field and wander down the road. The other horse was well behaved and always stayed, so he tied them together. We walked together to the animals and he made the tether between them shorter so they were less likely to step over it. There was very little good grass for the horses, and they were constantly on the move searching for nourishment from the dry grass. Now they had to move in tandem, but they didn't seem to mind, and the man handled them with care and respect.

The wind had been blowing hard all day, which had caused mangos to be knocked off the trees. I collected some enormous windfalls that the horses hadn't found. They never did ripen properly, so I suppose they have to be cared for better than I could in our bumpy motorhome.

I learned later that really green mangos never ripen, but not knowing that at the time, they sat for ages in a bowl with the very green bananas we had picked up off the road in Costa Rica. I threw them all out eventually when the mold set in as we approached Belize!

We had traveled a hundred and thirty-seven miles, and were in striking distance of the border. That was quite a good day for us.

Day 79
Wednesday, April 2, Return to Lake Nicaragua

We took advantage of the fresh water and the availability of a septic tank at the El Delfin campsite, even though we had done all this yesterday. We never knew when we would have our next opportunity.

We were out of El Delfin in good time, and in little over an hour we were at the border with Nicaragua.

The first sign that we had reached the border was the line of trucks. There must have been fifty or sixty of them, and they weren't pulled over to the side, just stopped in the right lane of the two-lane road. There were also a number of them parked on the left just barely off the road. After waiting a little, we decided to follow the cars down the other lane on the wrong side of the yellow line, squeezing between the behemoths without damaging our protruding side view mirrors. As we got to the head of the line there was a boy of about nine or ten waving frantically, directing us into a driveway. Sure enough, we recognized it as the place we processed the car papers when entering the country. We pulled into the drive just enough to get off the road and parked.

"I am a guide. We will help you." I blinked and the boy had miraculously become two. "Come with us." They had very faded jeans and very old t-shirts with holes worn in them from being scrubbed clean. They had fetching grins, and looked as though they had cut each other's hair. They were very anxious to help and led us on foot down the drive towards the *aduana* building, looking back all the time to make sure we were following.

When they were about twenty feet away from the building they held back and pointed. "You go in there." Louis, the leader, pointed to a door. He was carefully eyeing one of the uniformed *federales* as though he expected to be yelled at and sent running at any moment.

I turned to Louis and said, "Gracias," in order to show the *federale* that he was assisting us, but the kids stayed at a respectful distance. We were processed through Costa Rica customs quickly and returned outside.

Louis and friend were waiting for us. "Give me your passport." I am reluctant to part with my passport to anyone, let alone a couple of scruffy boys. Then I recognized the crumpled pieces of paper he was waving about as battered blank forms we would need to complete for immigration. They were trying to be helpful and earn their tips. We handed over a passport to each boy who proceeded to fill out the short form, leaning against the front of the motorhome.

However, Luis entered my nationality as "Europe" which is the topmost word on my passport, and my profession, "Tourist." Our other helper had managed to copy John's name incorrectly. Hey, they were young and at least they could read and write enough to fill out a form. No matter, we made the corrections and let them direct us to the "Leaving Costa Rica" line where we handed in our amended forms.

"You go there now," Louis pointed. With a boy on each running board and hanging onto the doors we moved slowly forward to the next parking place. We went through the Costa Rican formalities in twenty minutes. If we had driven to the right of the *Aduana* building, right up to immigration, it might have been even quicker. We hadn't really needed the boys, but it was worth the two bucks each. And besides they were learning a trade.

The new guide to assist us entering Nicaragua definitely earned his five bucks. Pablo Gonzalez was personable and efficient, and I would recommend asking for him to anyone following our path. He was dressed well in pressed khaki slacks and a white knit shirt, which contrasted with his jet-black hair. In Nicaragua, a guide needs a license to assist travelers, and his name was entered on at least two of our forms. He considered himself a professional and behaved like one. In all we made stops at twenty (new and repeated) doors, windows and locations to enter the country. I will detail it because I want to share the experience, and provide a taste of Latin American bureaucracy at its finest.

1. Immigration. While waiting in line at this first window we were approached by a belt vendor. He was a big robust man with armsful of embossed leather belts of various lengths and in shades of browns and black. John purchased a new short belt, to fit his diminished girth. We reached the low window with a little slit and passed our passports under it. Struggling to hear and understand through the glass, John was informed that as I am British, I needed a photocopy of my passport cover page and the page with the Costa Rican exit stamp

on it. We paid $7 for John's entry papers into Nicaragua and received his receipts. They required payment in U.S. dollars.

2. We walked over to the duty-free shop, where they had a copy machine, and made the copies of my passport and a few extra ones that we knew we would need at other border crossings. Pablo advised us of other copies we would need here, so we made them all at the same time.

Walking across the vast parking lot we heard a shout of recognition and there was Juan, the guide we had employed on our southbound journey a month earlier, waving at us. He came over and politely wished us a pleasant crossing once he saw that Pablo had us in tow.

3. We returned to immigration where my passport was stamped, and paid the additional U.S. $7 for my entry. I received a receipt for $5 for my tourist permit and another for $2 for something else incomprehensible. The official, made these out by hand in duplicate with carbon paper. That was immigration.

4. Aduana. Pablo led us to where the customs inspector was sitting at a high desk outside in the shade. He asked what we were driving and filled out a little form with the make and number of the motorhome.

5. We took this form to the customs' window of the same building where we had just been. A lady typed a bunch of stuff onto a form and produced our official vehicle permit.

6. Pablo then took us through a door next to the lady's window. Inside the cool building we went to the customs' office. Here we were offered chairs, and

Pablo stood in the doorway behind us, as the paperwork was reviewed, initialed, and stamped by a boss. We know he was a boss because the friendly belt salesman was there and the official had just bought a belt with "Big Boss" stamped along it. When the official directed his attention to the paperwork, Pablo came over to be ready to answer questions. The Boss didn't have a pen so he reached up and took Pablo's pen from his pocket. He initialed and stamped the forms, and put the pen in his own pocket. Pablo didn't say anything.

7. We went back to the customs inspector's desk outside. There was now a busload of people opening their suitcases and displaying the contents of black plastic trash bags full of possessions, for inspection. Pablo cut to the front of the line, interrupting the officer mid-client, and handed the official our papers. At this point we thought that this inspector was meant to check that our documents corresponded to the vehicle. However, there were all these bus passengers lined up in front of him so he took Pablo's word for it when he pointed to where the motorhome was parked out of sight behind the coach. We later noticed that the VIN (Vehicle Identification Number) on the form was missing a digit and hoped that this would not cause us grief when we left the country. We had read where you should always make sure the VIN number was correct on your vehicle permit.

8. We then headed for the bank and made a deposit in payment for the vehicle permit and received our receipt.

9. Then it was back to the customs' office, but this time to see the man in the desk next to "The Boss." He was having a problem with a truck driver, which caused a wait before he approved our form as being paid.

10. In spite of the fact that the vehicle certificate was written in triplicate with carbon paper floating about, we had to return to the duty-free shop for an additional photocopy.

11. Then we had to purchase insurance. This is something that we didn't have to do when entering the country the first time, but it was explained that we had to get it when entering from Costa Rica. It was $10 and we hadn't a clue what the coverage was for.

12. We returned to the outside customs' inspection desk for the third time. This time we saw a different person who was in police uniform. Pablo explained that his job was to inspect the contents of our vehicle for contraband. He didn't move from his stool behind the desk, but he put a nice stamp on the certificate.

13. Pablo then led us to a window with *Policía* painted over it, where an officer put another stamp on the certificate.

14. We then needed a copy of this highly stamped certificate so we returned to the duty-free shop for the third time. This copy was for customs. John decided that this might be an opportunity to make a stop at the motorhome to get some of the pens he had brought from home. He gave a bunch of them to Pablo to hand out to the officials who were pen-less, and smooth the path for other travelers. We had now finished with the requirements for the vehicle and us; we had been there two hours.

We just had to get the dog into the country now.

15. We took the five-minute walk to the cuarentena office where agricultural inspections were conducted. I had met the same man on my way out of Nicaragua, but now we were entering his domain. He needed us to deposit about five dollars in the bank and bring him the receipt. He did not need to see if the two-year old brindle dog in our motorhome matched the certificate. The bank was a hot walk back toward the customs and immigration office.

16. John went to the bank with Pablo while I chatted to the inspector and kept an eye on the dog's papers. We could replace our passports if they went missing but I don't know how we could replace the dog's USDA certificate. I didn't want them out of my sight.

17. Ten minutes later, after walking across the compound and past more than 100 tractor-trailers and eighteen-wheelers waiting in limbo to get into the country, John and Pablo returned and handed the receipt for 75 *córdobas* ($5.10) to the official.

18. We thought we were done. We returned to the bus, paid Pablo for his services and drove off.

19. There was a booth in the middle of the road with two trucks facing us filling the left side so we logically kept to the right expecting the barricade arm to rise so we could leave the area. Wrong! We had to wait for the trucks to come forward and maneuver past them to approach the booth on the "wrong" side of the road. Here, some of the papers we

had worked so hard to get were taken from us. Now we were out, but not through.

20. We were about to drive through when a man from the municipality came up and requested one dollar per person. I didn't think he was legitimate, so I asked for a receipt. He dashed away to a building fifty yards away and returned a moment later with a receipt that was for our donation towards municipal health projects!

21. Two miles down the road we encountered a man in white overalls, tanks on his back and wearing a gas mask. He flagged us down and walked around the vehicle spraying the wheels and gestured for us to follow the truck in front. We did this and drove off. Then John saw a woman come out of a kiosk waving at us. He waved back and I continued slowly down the bumpy road behind the truck. A minute or two later there was a man on a bicycle frantically peddling beside the motorhome and gesticulating for us to stop. I pulled over and he explained that we owed three dollars for the fumigation.

All in all, it had taken us two hours and thirty minutes of activity to enter Nicaragua. If there had been as much time spent waiting in lines as we had experienced at other crossings, it would have taken all day. It was just a ludicrous, disorganized lack of any system, staffed, for the most part, with pleasant people. It cost us three dollars to leave Costa Rica and fifty dollars and four ballpoint pens to enter Nicaragua. When we entered Nicaragua from Honduras on March 5th, it had cost us thirty-five dollars and six ballpoint-pens! It seems

Nicaragua is short on ballpoint pens, so we suggest travelers bring a supply with them. You also need U.S. dollars for some of the payments as well as the local *córdobas* for others. Sometimes you pay directly to an official, but other times you are required to make a deposit in a bank. The officials were not always flexible, so it was important to have both currencies or yet another trip to the bank would have been required. We would still be there if it hadn't been for Pablo. These guides are invaluable and well worth the dollars and pens they earn. Don't try this crossing without one.

We stopped for a quick lunch in the same place we had used before on our southward journey. The same man from the restaurant made the long walk over to us and invited us to visit his facility to see the exotic animals and enjoy a meal. We declined because we needed to get to San Jorge to arrange for the ferry to Ometepe Island. This time there was an ox-cart driver there as well. As I approached with my camera his dog appeared to keep me away.

Ometepe is the largest island on a lake anywhere in the tropics. The island was created by two volcanic eruptions: the two volcanic cones make a figure-eight-shaped island with a narrow isthmus. One of the volcanoes is still active and forms a perfect cone, usually sporting a cap of cloud. Combined they make Ometepe the largest fresh-water island in the world.

There is no bank on Ometepe, so before heading for the lake we drove into the lively and thriving town of Rivas to get some local currency. There was even a Tropigas propane distributor across from the Shell gas station at the main intersection with the highway. It was a fun place and I could have spent more time there but we wanted to catch the 2:30 p.m. car ferry. The next one at 5:30 p.m. would get us there in the dark.

We arrived at the pier late, after two o'clock, and parked the bus where we could see the gate for the pier. Gray and white clouds were scudding across the sky, being blown by a brisk wind, but it was still warm. We couldn't seem to get an answer as to whether or not we could get on the ferry. The guard (or was he the ticket taker?) was evasive and we never really found out. He stood at a twelve-foot iron gate painted burgundy that controlled access to the pier. It would have been an easy access for the motorhome, and trucks in line gave us encouragement that we would at least fit on board if there were space available. The guard said he would try to get us on, but there was a problem docking the boat or something. There was another comprehension problem and the man was very vague. John stayed there so he could act if anything changed.

I walked the dog. Returned. No change. I went into the Ometepe Tours

LEFT: A typical oxen cart in Nicaragua, near a camping place two miles north of the Costa Rican border.
TOP RIGHT: Pigs and horses on the shore of Lake Nicaragua
RIGHT: Washing clothes in Lake Nicaragua

office next to the beach where they had been so helpful before, and asked about the ferries. This time the owner was not there and his assistant was not interested in anything other than her boyfriend who was milling about. She told me to get my ticket at the green building. The green building was a little booth, empty and padlocked behind a white wrought iron fence. That was not an option. We should have made reservations. I went back to report to John and see if he had any news. By now John was on a first name basis with the guard, Alex, and he introduced us. It was now three o'clock and nothing had moved.

There was a long line of taxis and two-wheeled horse buggies waiting to take passengers to their homes in Rivas, and a scattering of ice-cream and other vendors waiting for hungry, disembarking customers. No one seemed to know what had happened to the ferry.

I took Brindle on a longer walk around to the left of the buildings and

the pier, and was greeted by a wandering horse and some pigs rooting in the sand. Two women and a man were standing in the water with tables set up loaded with heavy pumice stones and clothes. They were doing the washing, dipping the clothes in the lake or scooping water up onto their stone scrubbing boards. They slapped the clothes down as hard as they could as though they were beating the dirt out. I suppose a little sand in the water and a lot of elbow grease with volcanic pumice will go a long way to clean

clothes. It is no wonder that their clothes are all in tatters. All the while, the wind-whipped waves were breaking around their legs.

As I walked towards the water and looked over to the pier I realized what the problem was with the ferry. The high winds had blown it onto the sand and it was grounded.

There was a man standing in the water pushing, but I don't think he was having much effect. He was standing pushing against the car ferry with all his weight as though he could move the giant boat back out to deeper waters. A 30-40 knot wind was keeping the ferry hard to the shore. It reminded me of the "Candid Camera" skit where someone was asked to hold up a wall and was then deserted. This man was attempting the impossible.

I went back to fetch John to have a look. I couldn't see us boarding any time soon.

As we watched, a man jumped off the back of the boat and swam with a line to a little launch. In the distance I could see a little green boat approaching and in time the swimmer took another line over to it. Now there was a line between the little launch and the stuck ferry and another one from the launch to the little green boat. Eventually, via a swimmer, they transferred a line directly between the larger of the two vessels. The little green boat, try though it would, could not pull the ferry off the sand. Even though the man in the water was still pushing, honest! We learned the next day that the little green boat lost a propeller during this exercise. The boys of the town were back in the water the next morning searching for it.

At this point one of the passengers had had enough and jumped overboard with his belongings. He landed in waist high water and waded ashore. Another and then another passenger followed suit.

We were standing next to some dugout rowboats. John remarked, "some enterprising person should take one of these over." Just then two youths came running up yelling and laughing. One had shorts and a ragged T-shirt and the other wore long pants and was bare chested. They tossed their sandals high up the beach and started pushing the boat into the water.

John then commented, "they don't have any oars!" but as soon as the words were out of his mouth we realized that they didn't need oars. The water was only a couple of feet deep and they pushed the boat right up to the ferry a hundred yards out. There they helped their customers climb down the four feet and into the wooden boat.

At this stage the little green boat was still trying to pull the ferry off the sand.

Young men who usually acted as porters on the dock appeared and ran leaping over the waves whooping. One did a back flip to match his friend's summersault in the shallow water. They were

going to carry people and their goods across the water. The passengers lined the side of the ferry on all the decks and were spilling over the lowest gunwale. The captain realized that he was losing his passengers and decided to make it easier for them by lowering the vehicle ramp at the back.

The dozen or so taxis that had been waiting up on the pier near our motorhome, realizing that their rides were not coming in at the usual place, also came down onto the sand.

Then along came the ice-cream vendor and the ladies selling homemade cookies looking for customers. We bought some cookies, but they were not very good and the last of them went to the birds swooping overhead. There were a variety of dogs milling about besides Brindle, along with children playing in the sand. There was a healthy crowd of spectators laughing and enjoying the show and horses and pigs were still browsing on the fringes. The men and women who were washing clothes continued to slap the garments on the rocks with one eye on the entertainment.

Between the ice-cream vendor and the water was a sign painted with a skull and cross bones that warned of deep

LEFT: Passengers began to climb off the grounded Ometepe ferry
ABOVE: Porters carrying the passengers' belongings ashore
RIGHT: Ometepe ferry off-loading carnival

water and dredging equipment. There was not enough of either!

The atmosphere was like a carnival, with everyone laughing and joking and chatting. Twice one of the young men fell while carrying a passenger on his shoulders. A great cheer went up each time with the numerous spectators roaring with laughter and clapping, so the dunked client could hardly get upset. Even though the sky was dark and the day blustery and gray, it was warm. The water, made choppy by the wind, was also warm and shallow so even the non-swimmers had nothing to fear.

A herd of cattle was ushered to the water nearby for a drink.

Eventually it looked like everyone who didn't own a vehicle on the ferry had come ashore one way or another. We could see that we were not going to get to the island that night, so we returned to our motorhome and moved her to a quiet place on the other side of the pier near the water. We parked about twenty feet from the lapping water, near a new

palapa (thatched roof built for shade) that the city had just erected. They were readying the beach for the *Semana Santa* tourists.

Day 80
Thursday, April 3, Ometepe Island

After witnessing the grounding of the ferry we decided not to attempt taking the motorhome across to the island. We set our sights on the ten o'clock passenger boat across Lake Nicaragua to Isla de Ometepe. The name in the local Nahuatl language means "between two hills", which was suitable. We needed somewhere safe to park the motorhome and drove to the pier, but were not able to park in the barn with other vehicles as we had hoped. They didn't think we could negotiate it. We knew we could have, and it would have meant that the motorhome would have been in the

---

ABOVE: Horses and cattle drinking from Lake Nicaragua
RIGHT: Loading eggs onto the Karen Marie for the trip to Ometepe Island.

shade. However, we were quite happy to have it locked up on the pier behind a secure gate with Alex on guard. I parked it so far forward that the bicycles were touching the wall, which would have made them even harder to remove had someone cut the cables. The charge for the one night and two days parking was twenty *córdobas*, or about one dollar twenty cents.

We packed our backpacks and wandered down the pier to the dock. We were going on the Karen Marie, a little passenger boat that was being loaded with supplies for the island. There was a mattress, a refrigerator that two men carried on their heads and loaded almost unaided, and many, many eggs.

We climbed down onto the deck and called for the dog to follow. She hesitated before jumping the gap between the floating dock and the moving boat. Another passenger gave her a nudge with his foot, and she was on. OK, so he booted her on, but she didn't look back. I wanted her to maintain a low profile and made her sit at my feet between the bench seats. This was fine until we started to move and three inches of water sloshed across the deck. She crossed to the Ometepe Island nervously on my lap. No one gave her a second glance.

The wind was still up and it was quite a choppy crossing. It took over an hour

and the three of us were grateful when we drew into the lee of the island where the waves were less pronounced. We docked at Moyogalpa, and had to disembark from the top deck, up a flight of plank steps. Brindle followed with hardly a pause and leaped ashore. We walked the one block to the Hotel Ometepe to rent a four-wheel drive Jeep. It was white and stripped bare of everything but the essentials: fuel and temperature gauges, and an odometer that was stuck. It had seen better days. I could only just turn the crank to open the windows.

We set off north through town to find the one road around the island. The town of Moyogalpa is probably twenty blocks wide but there are no signs. When we found the road that led round the island, it was not surfaced and no attempt had been made to grade it since the rains. We were very glad we had not brought the motorhome. There were several forks in the road and an acute shortage of signs. When a one-lane dirt track forks into two one-lane tracks it is hard to know which one is the main road. We felt as though we were driving down a riverbed. At this point, we stopped at a little *refresquería* for directions and a cold drink. It was very hot. The shopkeeper confirmed that we were going the wrong way, but that we were near a pretty bay and should continue on to see it before we returned. We enjoyed our drinks, and then noticed that we had a flat tire. Now this really wasn't fair! We had had enough of our own on the motorhome without a rental car letting us down.

John set to work and the merchant stepped up to help him. As they worked, a herd of cattle passed on their way to the lake for a drink. Then a herd of horses passed in the other direction.

More animals and their keepers wandered up and down the riverbed road. I sat in the shade in front of the little shop and took photographs. They ran out of Coke after the first round so we progressed to whatever they had on hand. I don't think they have many customers dropping in for a drink.

John thanked the man (financially), and we bumped our way to the bay. The shopkeeper was right: it was pretty. It was also interesting. Livestock wander about nibbling on tufts of dried grass; they came in herds for a drink, with a herdsman either on foot, horseback, or a bicycle.

There was no sand; the shore was made up of boulders of pumice and lava

rock. In places the rocks had been piled up to form tables with larger flat rocks placed around the top. These were wash tables and some were being used. The clothes were placed on the flat rocks and scrubbed with a piece of pumice. I didn't see any detergent being used.

The island was very dry and hot. We were melting. Although we made many wrong choices as to which track to follow, we couldn't really get lost since the road was always somewhere between the volcano and the water.

We paused for a late lunch in a small cafe in the village of Altagracia. The outdoor john, with its double seats, was interesting. We wondered if you were meant to sit holding hands.

We made inquiries about the Museo de Ometepe, which was advertised in *Lonely Planet,* and were directed to another little house where a young girl, Sola, waited for visitors. She was a pretty young lady with wavy black hair that would be the envy of any beauty queen.

TOP LEFT: John supervising the changing of the tire. Ometepe, Nicaragua
LEFT: A washing table on Ometepe, made from volcanic rock
ABOVE: Altagracia, Ometepe Island

She welcomed us with an attractive smile and invited us to take a personal tour of the two-room museum. We planted Brindle in the shade and told her to stay, and paid our admission. I have a feeling that the guide would just as happily have included the dog. Sola touched two wires together where the light switch used to be. The lights disturbed the bats and they swooped through the room to find a dark corner. Sola spoke clear Spanish, and went slowly so we could learn about her island. Back in the lobby we were greeted by Brindle who had snuck indoors. There were carved gourds for sale in the lobby. The gourds could be seen growing wild around the island but they are not edible. When dry they become hard and the Indians make them into water containers, using a bit of corncob as a cork. Sola explained that there was an Indian lady in the village who braided the carrying straps and carved and scraped the patterns into the gourds, creating cream colored designs in the mottled green-brown skin. I paid one dollar for one with intricate designs. They must have taken her hours to make.

Continuing around the island it was a relief when we came to one of the hotels of the northeastern shore that was mentioned in *Lonely Planet.* If we had had the strength to read the next paragraph, we would have known that the second hotel next door was the better one.

We had a swim off the white sand beach, cooled off, and relaxed. We had earned it. Dinner was at the neighboring hotel, Hotel Villa Paraíso, where we preferred the ambience.

TOP RIGHT: The beach at the Finca Santa Domingo Hotel, Ometepe Island, Nicaragua
RIGHT: White-throated magpie jays were everywhere. They are considered a rarity in other parts of Central America

We walked along the beach in front of our hotel under a sliver of a moon and a blanket of stars. We slept well in the sparse room with a polished tile floor and two small beds. Brindle slept on the floor between us. The hotel staff was completely unconcerned about the dog.

Day 81
Friday, April 4, Back to the Mainland

In the morning, after breakfast at the neighboring hotel, we continued around the island keeping the lake on our left. The dirt road improved slightly, but it would have been grim in the motorhome. It was bad enough in a little junky

Jeep without springs or air-conditioning. We cut across the isthmus between the two volcanoes, as we had been told that the coastal road around Volcán Maderas was bad. We could not imagine it!

Exploring further along the south coast of Ometepe we made a little foray and found the coastal camping spot of *El Tesoro del Pirata,* or Pirate's Treasure. This required a sharp lookout for a sign to the turnoff from the main road. Once there, we found a fence and locked gate, and two very large German Shepherd dogs guarding an attractive area under some large trees. There was a *champa* bar/ restaurant (thatched hut) across the field. The owner was there waving to us and signaling that we were to open the gate and come in. There was no one else around.

The owner quickly stilled the dogs, which turned out to be friendly, but we kept Brindle in the Jeep just in case the shepherds became overly protective. We opened the gate and drove into the deep shade under great old ceiba and mango trees. We had found a really nice place to camp on the island.

Carlos, the owner of this place, welcomed us. We were probably the first visitors in over a week. Carlos claimed the bay was a favorite stopping place for pirates after they raided Granada, and that there was still treasure in the water. The San Juan River is navigable into Lake Nicaragua from San Juan del Norte on the Caribbean coast, and the lake provided refuge to pirates and other sailors from storms.

It was early yet so we didn't have an excuse to buy a meal, but we had a couple of sodas as we talked with Carlos, who was energetic in his welcome.

The mangos that filled the trees and littered the ground had attracted howler monkeys. There was a troop of at least a dozen clambering about overhead. There was a grand old male and a couple with babies on their backs. I watched them for ages. Of all the places we visited, this was the best place to watch wild monkeys. Later we came closer to them at the Baboon Sanctuary in Belize, but they were a little too tame.

John took his GPS reading and we moved on. If anyone makes it to Ometepe in an RV, or is even just looking for a campsite for a tent, El Tesoro del Pirata would be a good destination. The owner has actually added some motel units to make the place more accommodating. The hotel area on the isthmus is also delightful. The southern road from Moyogalpa to El Tesoro del Pirata and on to the isthmus would have been passable in an RV. I would not try it in the rainy season, however.

Concepción the 5,000-foot active volcano, was always in sight, sometimes with a cap of clouds floating like a halo or with her summit completely hidden. Once, when I looked over, the clouds were rolling down her sides like a veil. She is a popular place to hike, but in the heat I preferred to admire her from a distance. Perhaps it would be more comfortable higher up in the clouds, but getting there would have just about killed me. It was stinking hot.

LEFT: El Tesoro del Pirata, Ometepe
ABOVE: There were dozens of howler monkeys at El Tesoro del Pirata, Ometepe
RIGHT: Volcán Concepción is always in sight on Ometepe Island

Concepción Volcano last erupted just fifty years ago.

We made numerous side trips looking for places that sounded interesting but just could not find them. There were no signs and few people to ask. We felt that to see the island properly you really needed a guide, or plenty of time to explore. There is a lake within the island and a variety of ancient petroglyphs and carved stone statues, and we missed them all.

There was a ferry waiting at the pier in Moyogalpa, but we had to wait for it to be unloaded before passengers were allowed on. The pier was much higher and I was worried about Brindle boarding. She didn't even pause, but leapt down onto the boat after us and down the steep planked steps onto the main deck.

The wind had died down, which made the trip back much more pleasant. On the mainland there were ladies selling mango, which apparently prevents seasickness. I would have appreciated one or two the day before. We returned to find all sorts of local weekend vacationers enjoying the beach at San Jorge. It was good to see the place being used.

The motorhome was just as we had left it. We cranked up the air-conditioning and relaxed. Our friend at Ometepe

Tours had told us about a dumpsite or *Basurea*. We followed his directions and all we found was a series of outhouses next to a field on a dirt road about 200 yards from the beach. The outhouses would have worked had they been at a lower elevation than the motorhome, but they were elevated from the road, impossible to feed with a gravity system. We went on.

We needed to get some fresh produce so we visited the bustling town of Rivas again, which I really enjoyed.

Granada was one of the cities we had hoped to visit from the beginning, and it lay just fifty miles away. After living in Texas, the places in Central America seemed so close together, but of course the driving conditions were not quite the same. We had left the pier in San Jorge at midday. It was four in the afternoon by the time we found a place to park in Granada. Yes, we did get lost. We had been following the signs for *Centro Turístico* and found the street market instead.

In the end we found the *Centro Turístico*, or Tourist Center, which is a large park that stretched for over a mile

along the beach. It was a grand recreational area designed for Nicaraguans. There were children's play areas, a musical amphitheater, food stalls, and restaurants and more than one discothèque. With our navigational skills we had come through the back entrance where there wasn't a ticket taker to charge us admission, but we didn't work that out until the next morning. We drove across the park and then turned right, drove over a mile, and stopped under a shade tree across the road from the lake. There was a wide grass verge on our side and another one on the other side of the road with plenty of good shade trees before the wide sand beach. This was probably where the caravans of motorhomes made their overnight camp. The caravan operators hire special *vigilantes,* and without that measure of security we felt that we were in too lonely a spot. It was attractive though. Once again, we witnessed herds of livestock being brought to the lake for a drink even though we thought we were in the middle of the city.

We returned to the more active center of the park and were invited to park across the road from one of the discos,

where their *vigilante* would watch out for us. Thinking there might be a little too much entertainment there, we drove further on and found the park police who would perform the same service for a small contribution. John wound up having a long conversation with one of them later. This fellow had a very official big flashlight but no batteries. John gave him a set. It was a good location with a pleasant view of the lake and just enough families around that we felt secure but were not disturbed.

Day 82
Saturday, April 5, Granada and León

Once again John needed to add air to a troublesome tire. We are so glad that we brought the compressor with us. It has had a workout. So had John, changing all those wheels, so it was not surprising he

LEFT: Mango sellers in San Jorge and the beach where we camped in the background
ABOVE: A street market in Granada

was vigilant about checking the pressure each morning.

The *Centro Turístico* was being well used when I took the dog for a run soon after seven in the morning. Children were swimming in their underwear, and adults were frolicking in the water fully clothed. They didn't seem to own swim suits. Footprints in the sand were those of people of all ages, some in shoes, some not, along with footprints of cattle and horses. Here, right in the middle of one of the largest cities of Nicaragua, there is livestock wandering wherever there is fodder and water.

Driving through Granada along the waterfront, we came across a statue of Chamorro, an ex-president. It was unusual not because of the gray stone or concrete it was made from, but because his shirt was freshly painted white and his tie black. Pedro Joaquín Chamorro was the popular newspaper owner/editor who openly opposed Somoza. His assassination was the catalyst that united

bread sticks. It was like having jam on miniature hot-dog buns. Traveling is one endless surprise after another!

The buildings around us were freshly painted every color imaginable in soft muted tones, almost as if they were faded. The horse-drawn carriages, that brought locals home with their shopping, added to the charm. The streets were wide and easy to navigate, and it felt like a real city, going about its business but rich in old charm.

We visited the Convent de San Francisco, a sixteenth century landmark. The American, William Walker, used this convent as his headquarters when he took the city with his army of 56 men in 1855. He was later elected

the moderate factions who eventually joined with the Sandinistas who, with U.S. aid, forced Somoza to resign. It was interesting to see a statue maintained in this way.

We realized why everyone said we must visit Granada when we reached the main square downtown. It had the pleasant feeling of a large European piazza with open-air coffee shops. We took advantage of one of these and just sat in a sidewalk café enjoying the ambiance of the area. Brindle relaxed under the table. John saw French Toast on the menu and ordered some for breakfast. Our idea of French Toast is bread, dipped in egg batter and fried in a pan. Instead he got three little

president and declared English the official language. Had he not tried to take all of Central America, he might have changed world history. As it was, we couldn't even find his ignominious grave in Trujillo, Honduras. On his retreat from Granada, Walker razed the city, but this building has been restored to the gentle tranquility of a convent. The

TOP LEFT: Granada, Nicaragua
LEFT: Convento de San Francisco, Granada
ABOVE: Interior courtyard of the Convento de San Francisco, Granada

rooms now house an interesting art exhibit and some pre-Columbian zoomorphic stone statues.

We returned to the central park and sampled the famous fruit drink served from the corner kiosks, then wandered back to the motorhome. We had forgotten to lock it. It was still there and all was intact.

As we drove out of town, we noticed that the houses were painted in the same soft colorful hues. Terracotta tile was the only medium we saw used for the roofs. Some of them fluctuated where the beams had sagged. The town seemed real and not dolled up for the tourists. We liked Granada.

We drove on to Masaya, a center for artisans. So far I had seen few handmade items in Nicaragua. The only part of the *Mercado Viejo* (Old Market) in Masaya

still standing was the external wall, which provided great charm and character. Although it was a good market for tourists, there wasn't much that was actually made in Nicaragua. Most of the items for sale had been imported from other Central American countries and from as far away as Peru.

ABOVE: Parque Colón, Granada
RIGHT: The colorful streets of Granada

Wood furniture was made locally, and the only items we found small enough to transport home were a couple of folding stools. The shopkeeper thought we had overpaid, which in fact we hadn't, and tried to return some of our money. Among smiles and laughter we befriended another honest person. We had our lunch there and chatted with some other North Americans and local business people. It seemed to be the social place to lunch for those who could afford it.

There is no way around Managua, and getting through it was not fun. We must have asked a dozen people for directions. There were absolutely no signs for León until we came to a T-junction in the road on the outskirts of town. Here there were two signs to León pointing in opposing directions; one was the old road and the other the new road. Because of the traffic lane we were in, we were swept down the new road. No more signs. After a while we recognized the road we were on as the one through

Managua towards Estelí to the east. There was the supermarket we had shopped at when we had passed through Managua a month before. We stopped at another gas station, and were directed back to another turnoff. Once again we got lost and asked again at a gas station. The gas station attendant was most helpful and pointed us in the direction of the new road, but a taxi driver listening in insisted that the new road was closed by a landslide and we had better take the old road. We turned around and headed back to the old road, this time without further incident.

The old road from Managua to León was the worst "paved" road we had driven on. There were so many potholes it was hard to decide where in the road to drive. Fortunately, there was so little traffic we had the choice of the entire roadway. Then it went from potholed blacktop to no blacktop in places. There were stretches of blacktop, just long enough

ABOVE: The Mercado Viejo in Masaya.

for you to let out a sigh of relief and begin to accelerate before you came to a four-inch drop back onto the gravel. These stretches would range from a few feet to a couple of hundred yards. This was no fun. Now we realized why there was so little traffic. In spite of the landslide, the new road would have been a better choice.

It might not have been so bad if the scenery had been interesting, but this was dry, parched land. The only greenery was little trees with large spikes, which prevented the cattle from eating them. It was flat for miles in all directions with very few inhabitants or points of interest. At last we joined the new road, and we could let out a long sigh of relief as we joined the host of trucks, eighteen-wheelers, and buses into León on smooth pavement. We could not figure out where all the traffic had come from if the road was supposed to be closed.

We got lost again in León. Then when we eventually found the parking lot mentioned in the tour books as an overnight parking lot, the caretaker turned us away not wanting a motorhome. He did direct us to an alternative, however. We once again got lost, but a friendly man on a bicycle offered to lead the way. We followed him to the walled-in parking lot at the Salmán Market. The bicyclist smiled and waved as he sped away before we could give him a tip.

We had become accustomed to paying for any favor, which seemed the American way. Actually, except in the big cities and tourist areas, I don't think people expected a tip. They were just naturally friendly and welcomed the opportunity to meet a foreigner.

The parking lot at the Salmán Market is a great place to stay right in the middle of town. Unfortunately, we had just done a big shop and now had to stretch our imaginations as to what else we could buy. We felt it was important to be seen going shopping and also to appease our ethics. John understood the parking *vigilante* to say the charge for the night would be ten dollars. When John tried to give him the equivalent in *córdobas* the attendant gave us a strange look. He meant ten *córdobas*, or about seventy cents. Later he provided us with an electric power extension and showed us the water tap.

Armed with the name of a good restaurant, we walked the half dozen blocks between the colorfully painted buildings of León to the cathedral and the main plaza. It was delightful. The town was full of people enjoying the Saturday night air and each other's company. There was an obelisk in the center of a fountain guarded by four enormous lions. People were sitting on the ledge, and children were clambering on the lions and calling to their parents to "look at me". We had read that on Saturday evenings people dance to impromptu musical combos in the central park, but we just saw happy locals strolling about.

As we sat and had dinner al fresco, we became fascinated by the local etiquette. Many people had bicycles and there were usually two people on each. It seems that the owner of the bike gets to either sit on the crossbar or stand on the back wheel hubs, and becomes the passenger. The non-owner gets to do the peddling. Of course this does not hold true if a man invites a lady to ride his bike, and we witnessed some gracefully romantic dismounts. Everyone wheeled their bikes across the plaza, and I saw no signs that said they were not permitted to ride. All the while there were people strolling, children playing, sweethearts holding hands, and cyclists riding up and down the road.

We walked back to our little home past a wild disco and a busy internet cafe. León was a city of ancient buildings that were being used by modern people. It was lived-in and friendly, and filled with charm and pleasant people.

Day 83
Sunday, April 6, Leaving Nicaragua and Meeting the Pinto Family

Church bells awakened me soon after five in the morning. John happily slept through them, but he didn't sleep through the seven o'clock siren. We hoped that it was just a test, or perhaps a city-wide wakeup-call.

The cathedral in León is known for the splendid view from the top so we walked back to the center of town in the hope that, although it was Sunday, we might be able to make the climb. The friendly friar in his white ankle-length hassock politely denied us access as services were in progress.

León was the capital of Nicaragua for over three hundred years and has the character to show for it. The cathedral is the largest in Central America, and took over a hundred years to build. There is a depth of history here that is not evident in most of Central America.

León, and the rich colonial city of Granada, represent important contrasting historical landmarks in Nicaragua. They both retain their European charm and the character that differentiated them in the early 19th century. Both cities are worth a visit.

On the way back to the motorhome we did our shopping at Salman's grocery, then John went to work filling our water tanks. One of the hoses we have collapses flat for easier storage. The pressure was so low that it could not even inflate the hose! This was another case where we should have filled our water tanks the night before, when the pressure was up. We headed for the border with our water tank empty.

Although the streets were well marked, which is unusual for that part of the world, some of them didn't seem to go anywhere or ended abruptly at a canyon. There was also a one-way system that was not always in our favor. Again everyone was very helpful, always telling us *"derecho"* (straight ahead), occasionally with a wave of the hand in one or other

direction first. In fact one man said *"dere-cho"* before we even told him where we were going. Helpfully he pointed straight ahead. He was right!

The road to Chinandega was fine and we were entertained by a volcano off to our right, which was putting on a dramatic display with plumes of smoke or steam belching into the sky. In an hour we paused to swap drivers. From there on the road was dreadful. Once upon a time it might have been good, but now it was so full of potholes that John wove continuously back and forth over the road to find a passable stretch. In some cases he left the road altogether for the more level dirt. The only nice bits were where the Japanese government had contributed and built some bridges in the reconstruction after Hurricane Mitch in 1998. Mitch dumped vast quantities of water causing mudslides

---

LEFT: The road north of Chinandega, Nicaragua.
ABOVE: Pump station where we filled up with water, between Chinandega, Nicaragua and the Honduras border

that literally washed away two complete villages and buried thousands of residents.

We took a picture that shows two vehicles that had chosen our side as the best, whereas John was driving off the road on the dirt to avoid the holes where he was. All the drivers were very courteous and always returned to their side in plenty of time and usually waved, acknowledging mutual suffering.

An hour later, and about fifteen miles from the border, John found a wide place and pulled off so we could change drivers again and let the dog go for a run. While waiting for the dog, a man came out of what looked like a pumping station whose access drive we had pulled into. There were a couple of bright blue concrete block huts, surrounded by a formidable, new, chain link fence with three or four strands of barbed wire around the top. The operator was curious about us. We chatted with him and discovered that he was in control of all the water for the area. We only needed a little! *"No problema."* He opened the double chain link gate and in a few minutes the thirsty bus was drinking up the mountain water from a direct connection at the pumping station. I gave him cold lemonade and John gave him a couple of dollars and we were all happy. Alfredo worked twenty-four hour shifts: one day on and one off. He was a nice man who lamented he could not afford to send any of his five sons to university. He himself had gone to technical school. He was bored with his job and enjoyed our interruption. He seemed to get a great kick out of being shown around inside the motorhome. I would not hesitate to stop at a one of these pumping stations again if we needed water.

Refreshed and tanked up, we returned to the terrible road. The stress of the constant bumping and the swerving from one side to the other was very tiring. It was a genuine white-knuckle ride. It was just after noon and, with breaks and changing drivers each hour, we hoped we could make it to the Honduras border in time to get across. We were told that it closed at five, and it usually takes at least a couple of hours to get through.

The scenery was not very interesting either, just a few concrete block houses, but nothing I could recognize as a village. Some houses had tin or tile roofs, but most were thatched with the palms almost touching the ground. In the settlements there was not so much as a blade of dry grass. Dust devils swirled and there were hundreds of dusty cattle and horses foraging.

Being Sunday afternoon there were some interesting activities going on. We saw a large gathering watching baseball being played in smart, colorful uniforms on the basic clay field. We had noticed in Nicaragua, and in Panama, the local sport was more likely to be baseball than

soccer. Cockfighting was also popular and we passed three arenas in full swing. In the little town of Chinandega, there was a big sign boasting that they had Pan-America's prize winning fighting cock.

At last, we came to the border with Honduras. No problems crossing here: just lack of staff and efficient equipment. Fortunately, there were very few private vehicles. One lady was typing a truck manifest with about six sheets of carbon paper on an ancient Imperial typewriter. This was the kind of typewriter they made in the 1940s and they sell in antique shops. Long mechanical fingers tapped onto black and red ribbon. I hate to think what would happen if she made a mistake. As it was, the thickness of the papers was causing them to rip. We traipsed from one little window to another, past the first and on to another and then to the bank to make a deposit and then outside to have the vehicle inspected. We were told that the crossing didn't close at five, just the bank. If you cannot make the bank deposit you can not cross the border with a vehicle!

We pulled into a parking space on the Honduran side next to a car with California plates. It had been there quite a while. All the wheels were on their rims. It just sat there rusting, taking up a parking place. It looked like the owners had locked it a couple of years ago and never made it through the *aduana*. We looked at each other wondering whether it was left there as a warning. I always feel vulnerable crossing the borders. This made me extra uneasy, but our concern was unwarranted here.

The dog was no problem. The inspector did ask to see her. This was the first

RIGHT: Making balloon animals for the Pinto family of San Jerónimo, Honduras

time anyone other than our vet at home had actually linked this dog with the stack of papers. Before I could open the motorhome and bring her out to meet him he slapped his hand on the window. She barked and snarled and pressed her nose on the glass. He moved his hand and put it back on the glass again. Brindle leaped at it with teeth clacking on glass. He laughed and stepped back. *"Está sano,"* he said, declaring she was healthy.

We then returned to his cool office where he provided a cold drink of water and pleasant conversation as he filled out the forms and relieved us of eight dollars. This was the same amount we had paid to bring Brindle into Honduras before. Later, while waiting for some other formality John was handling, I took Brindle out of the bus for a walk and introduced her again to the nice inspector on a more even footing. The friendly man seemed pleased that he had

admitted such a nice (healthy) little dog into his country.

It took us a total of two hours to get through the border and onto a decent road. There were several works projects with credit given to various national Red Cross Societies and the European Community. They were probably post-Mitch reconstructions.

It was more difficult to find a parking place for the night in a big city than it was in a pueblo. With this in mind we took a turn off the main road and followed a sign for Namasigue, which was not on our maps. This was about 15 miles south of Choluteca, the main city in these parts. We came to a fork in the road, both dirt, and branched left to a place called San Jerónimo. Soon it felt like we were in the middle of nowhere. We had seen a *pulpería,* or little shop, where the road widened and we turned around heading for it. We could just pull off the road and still open the door

against the barbed wire fence. We walked up the concrete path and asked if we could stay the night where we were.

The proprietor, Alba, was alone with her young daughter. Great conversations ensued in rapid Spanish, all to the affirmative, but they thought we should drive up their steep path and park on their property. It didn't look like we would fit, so we told them we were just fine and settled down to enjoy some orange juice, which was the only drink they had for sale. Several children appeared from nowhere so I produced my balloons and began twisting them into animals for the children. Soon, Alba's mother and father, her sister, Alma, and another load of kids appeared. When we arrived there were two people in the shop. Now we counted about twenty-five.

At our request the family posed for a photo. We ran out of the allotted supply of balloons, by which time my fingers were numb from tying knots. I hope they did a good business at the little shop.

By the end of the evening the grandmother was wearing one of my balloon hats. Everyone was having a great time.

I went back to the motorhome to avoid requests for more balloons and to start on supper. When John returned he reported that Alba's husband, Renaldo, insisted that we would be much safer if we pulled up onto their property. We might have made it up their steep concrete drive, but we didn't want to be right in front of their shop. In their effort to help us, they had found another way for us to get up there. Alba's husband had pulled up fence posts so that we could pass at the far end of the yard. Although it was already dark we decided to comply. We made it through the fence and up onto the plateau next to the house and under the trees without incident. I believe the safety factor was more a matter of avoiding the children that surrounded us who might have tapped on the motorhome disturbing us. They were shooed away by Alba. The neighborhood kids had only gone onto the property by the shop when I had the balloons out.

Alma wanted to invite us to her home. We were tired and ready for bed, but we agreed to come over the next morning at eight. This sounded great. It is a thrill for me to visit people in their homes and to experience how they live. She also invited us to have breakfast, but I declined. The family didn't have much and I definitely didn't want her to go to that expense and effort.

At last, after a long day and a fun evening we could politely excuse ourselves and relax on our own with a cool beer and supper before bed.

LEFT: Grandma and Grandpa Pinto having fun with the balloons.
RIGHT: The Motorhome parked at the Pinto pulpería in San Jerónimo, Honduras

Day 84
Monday, April 7, Making New Friends

The next morning I got up to take Brindle for a walk. I had her on the long expandable leash as there were cats and all sorts of domestic birds about, which I didn't want her to harm. A small flock of guinea fowl chased us. These are rather pretty, round, gray-speckled chicken-like birds that were acting exactly like guard dogs, and creating a terrible din. They went after Brindle en masse. The dog ran! Alma must have been alerted by them as she appeared out of nowhere to ask if we were ready to come to her house for coffee. It was only seven o'clock and John was still recumbent in the bus. I said he was shaving and would be ready in a while. I thought we had agreed upon eight o'clock.

I headed for the road where the dog could run free. Not more than fifty feet away I found a tree with bright red cashew fruit and took a photograph. An old lady, carrying a chicken in the crook of her arm like a baby, was on the other side of the fence. She saw me and picked up a stick and knocked a cashew off her side of the tree. It dropped to the ground and she bent over, still cradling the chicken, picked up the fruit and handed it to me through the branches and over the barbed wire fence. She had been prattling on all the while and I had been making the appropriate grunts, smiles and nods, but I really didn't understand a word. She waved to her husband on the other side of the small paddock and called something to him. He found a larger stick and proceeded to beat a bigger tree, knocking more fruit down for me. I was suddenly worried about what I had agreed to with my nods and grunts, and now I had to stop the process. The cashew fruit is attractive, and I wanted to show folks back home what it looks like, but I didn't need a whole bushel. The man came over and he and his wife passed a handful of the fruit to me. I thanked them sincerely. Everywhere we went people were so nice to us, always doing more than was expected.

The cashew fruit has no seed inside, just the nut hanging off the bottom. When ripe the fruits are shades of red and yellow with skin that will peel off. It is strange to be able to cut through a fruit of that size with no stone or seeds inside. The flesh is a cross between a banana and an avocado, with lots of clear juice that runs freely. Unfortunately, it is just too bitter for my taste. There are many people who don't like the cashew fruit, but it does appeal to others. The trees are frequently planted in the towns as decorative shade trees. The tallest we saw were about twenty feet. Most people in Central America will tell you that the raw nut is poisonous and must be roasted to be edible. However, all my life I have enjoyed what was labeled "raw cashew." It was never put to the test here as the shell is like a rock. Both nut and flesh are reported to be good for your kidneys.

Brindle had another new experience as we returned to the bus: the cats attacked her! There were four of them, all less than a year old, and they went for her. It was a brief scrap and no one was the worse for it. I hope it will put Brindle off chasing other cats if she knows they can be nasty up close. I don't think Brindle enjoyed her encounter with the Pinto family as much as we did.

John was showered and ready, so we scoured the motorhome for our last unopened packets of cookies from home and some other goodies. Alma was waiting for us as we stepped down from the motorhome and walked us under the enormous mango trees to her home. I had watched grandma sweeping away the leaves earlier, clearing the path for us. Alba's daughter was mopping the front porch tiles, and I felt this was all in preparation for our arrival.

We were invited to make ourselves comfortable. I sat in the hammock and John took a chair while dad, grandma, grandpa, and sisters sat around, and we chatted. Alma brought us sweet coffee with a lot of milk. Then, although we had declined breakfast the evening before, it was now served. I was asked to join John at a little table that was the only other furniture on the patio. Breakfast was rice, a small piece of chicken with sautéed onion, tomato and potato on the side, and tortillas, which Alma had made herself earlier that morning. Also, there was a little bottle of orange juice for John and myself, one that she must have bought from Alba's store. I hated for them to have spent real money on us, but all we could do was to

TOP LEFT: Cashew fruit on the tree
LEFT: The bitter cashew fruit with the nut attached
RIGHT: The porch of the Pinto family house

enjoy the meal and express our thanks. It was far more than I usually eat, so I didn't do very well. Grandpa, eating from a bowl in his hands, was the only other person to eat with us. Grandma sat in a chair, and other family members perched on the hammocks or stood around watching and listening.

I asked if I could see inside the home. Alma was happy to show me. The house was new, as the old one had been destroyed by Hurricane Mitch. There were two rooms built from concrete blocks with about 500 square feet in all. The first room had the doorway to the patio and two windows. The room could just fit a double bed and three single beds with woven matting for mattresses. The back room had a doorway and a window into the first room for light, but no windows to the outside. This room had five single beds and one double. There were neat little stacks of clothes on the floor and on the beds, and there was just enough room for a person to squeeze between the beds. Apart from a couple of paper pictures fixed to the concrete block walls there was nothing else. There wasn't room for anything else!

Outside the sleeping quarters, about twenty feet away, was a shelter where the cooking was done, and there was yet another little shelter for the washing. The toilets were further away. There was no running water in the house, but they had a well, and water was available outside in a sink. They had been having trouble with the well since Hurricane Mitch, however.

As always, there were little fires burning trash. We realized that this was not only disposing of trash, but the smoke was keeping the insects away. Unfortunately everything including plastic and Styrofoam goes into the fires. After a while I became accustomed to the smoke and didn't notice it any more.

Grandma and Alma walked me under a row of ancient mango trees to the back of their land. They had twenty acres in all. They had twelve head of cattle as well as two different kinds of sheep; one for wool and the other for meat. At the end of the cool tunnel of trees she showed me a fence that could be removed so we

could pass through to the shade of the mangos if we wanted to stay another night. It would have been a perfect camping place under the high branches. They repeatedly invited us to stay longer, and asked when we were going to return. I hope that someone reading this will go and visit them. You couldn't wish for a more friendly welcome and it really was a good, dry campsite. They were a delightful, warm family.

Walking back to the house, Grandma María unlocked a little shed that was hers and Grandpa's retreat. I was surprised to see a lock on it. Inside, were two guitars leaning against the wall, a table with a couple of plastic flowers, and a pink plaster Buddha (I'm sure the Pintos were Christian) and a very dilapidated deck of cards. They did not sleep there. Perhaps the lock indicated that the local kids could have been a problem had we parked on the street.

We wanted their address so we could mail them copies of photographs we had taken. The only cousin who could write was called to write down the address.

Translated it reads: a quarter of a block south of the hardware store, Libertad, Honduras. It must be the address of a family member as we weren't in Libertad and there was no hardware store nearby.

When we returned home to Texas, we mailed a slew of photographs and things to various people we had met on our trip. Besides sending the Pintos photos of their family, there was a postcard of Texas longhorn cattle for dad, more packets of vegetable seeds, balloons and a couple of decks of cards. We were overjoyed when, a month later, we received a long letter in return, plus

some small mementos. We never knew if the other people we mailed things to ever received them. We also received a Christmas card from the Pintos later.

It was time to make our farewells and move on to the Salvadoran border. Forty miles north we came to another town called San Jerónimo, so we hope people looking for the Pintos don't get confused.

This was mango country. They were growing everywhere and there were buckets and bowls of them at the side of the road. There were also piles of cashew fruit for sale. People were standing by the road holding out bags of fruit, or trying to sell piles of firewood.

Just west of the town of Nacaome, we came to the river of the same name. It was a large river and there was a lot of activity on the shore. There were not only cars at the water's edge, but also little

TOP LEFT: The home of the Pinto family
LEFT: Grandma Pinto, Alma in the foreground, and her daughter outside Grandma's hut.
ABOVE: Approaching the Honduran/Salvadoran border at El Amatillo.

hut-shelters. People were playing in and around the water and it would have made another great place to stop. It was like a makeshift resort.

We passed through countryside with craggy hills, and then came to the infamous border crossing of El Amatillo. This was the border we avoided on the southbound trip by going directly from Guatemala City to Copán. We had heard that it was one of the most expensive borders to cross in Central America. We were sooon to learn why.

As we approached the border there was a line of parked trucks, first on the right and then on both sides of the road. We squeezed between them and had some interesting moments when other vehicles came in the other direction.

We were "attacked" by several young men who wanted to be our "guides." We selected one and drove on with him standing on the running board. We cleared out of Honduras in thirty minutes, which was good, and there were no exit fees. The guide took us to each department showing us where to go

through the formalities. That was the hardest part, finding out where you were meant to go through each process.

We then drove over the bridge and into the Salvadoran chaos. There was one large building on this side of the border that contained all of the necessary offices. Our guide directed us around the building to a small parking spot in front of some shops and cafes across from the border edifice. We noticed an abandoned motorhome very similar to ours with Texas plates. I went over to find that the registration had expired in 1995. The motorhome was stripped to the skin. We wondered what happened. It made us nervous.

We had to do our own immigration, so we stood in line with everyone else to have our passports stamped. Then the guide wanted to run off with the dog's papers. No. I didn't ever let them out of my sight. No problem with *cuarentena* once the official found the Salvadoran ten dollar stamp with an official El Salvador frank had I received at the consulate in Houston. I think we might have had problems here if we had not had the correct documents for the dog.

Now we only needed the papers for the motorhome. The guide took the title and my passport and said he would be back in about an hour. We normally don't like to let these documents out of our sight, but it was terribly hot running around, and we had the air conditioning going in the motorhome. We waited, then took a nap. Two hours later we went looking for the guide. I don't know what we would have done without air-conditioning at this point. By this time we had met a couple of our guide's friends; one of them spoke some English. Whenever we would poke around to find our guide, one of his friends would be there to tell us that it would just take a little longer. All together it took about three-and-a-half-hours before the guide returned with our papers.

At last we were ready to go. We usually tip the guides between two and four dollars. We gave the guide more than usual: about eleven dollars. We were not

ABOVE: This motorhome had been abandoned at the Salvadorian border several years ago. It was had been completely stripped.

returning to Honduras so we emptied our pockets of local currency. He had multiplied into four people, and the one who spoke English said that we had to pay a hundred and fifty dollars. What! He explained this was *mordida* (bribes) that they had to pay to the officials for all the paperwork they had "rushed" through for us! He insisted that money had been paid to the officials on both sides of the border and for the dog. No way! I was there. An argument ensued. In the end, John gave them fifty bucks and they seemed quite happy. In retrospect we both feel that most, if not all, of the money went straight into their pockets. Next time I would tell the one guide in advance, that we will not pay anything without a receipt, and that we will only pay **him** for his services, not his friends. We will also accompany him everywhere, although our nap in the cool bus was very nice. At the time we had the shell of the stripped motorhome fresh in our memories and John, not wanting confrontation, decided to make an offer. Fifty dollars was about the upper limit in fees for any border crossing, so he thought it was a reasonable price to escape from this place.

The El Amatillo border crossing is reputedly the worst, and most expensive in Central America. Our experience bears this out. It was not hard for us to sit for four hours in our air conditioned motorhome, but we were not prepared for the prices the guides tried to get from us.

We drove off to the final border checker who now wanted to see our papers for the bicycles. We have never had any! A conversation followed and this time we were able to pass without too much ado. Phew! Yet one more official check before we were on our way.

We found an agreeable Shell station in the town of San Miguel, an hour from the border. This station happened not to have any gas to sell, but all we wanted was a safe place to park for the night. We handed the *vigilante* a dollar, found an electrical hookup, and enjoyed another episode of M★A★S★H before turning in.

Day 85
Tuesday, April 8, San Salvador

The gas station manager told us that the Pan-American Highway between San Miguel and San Salvador was pothole ridden and slow. On his recommendation we drove towards the coast and took the Littoral Highway west. Just past the small Laguna El Jocotal, where they were selling fish by the road, we noticed numbers of people carrying large jugs and water bottles. It was an area where there was no running water. People were fetching water to their homes. Every few hundred yards there were faucets, and at some there were social gatherings. These would have made useful places for us if we had needed to fill our tanks. It was sad to see how far some people had to carry their water. There were also pickup trucks filling up fifty-five gallon drums.

You never know what to expect on the highway. We were trucking along when we found ourselves entering a town. The road became one-way and more and more vehicles were parked on either side. Then there were market stalls on either side of us. We could have reached out and bought anything you could possibly want from mangos to melons; from fans to footwear; from chairs to chewing gum; from bread to bananas. If there had only been a place to stop. There were busy people going in every direction, idle people in the spaces, and dogs everywhere. All we could do was to crawl forward at the pace of the bus in front, between the stalls and the crush of people. We thought we had made a wrong turn, but there was nothing we could do about it. Then the stalls thinned and the speed picked up. There were a couple of tailors sitting at sewing machines waiting for customers on the sidewalks. The road became more passable, joined the other lane coming from the east and became a recognizable highway again. That was the market town of Usulután, and Tuesday must be market day. Fortunately, John had been driving so I could enjoy the spectacle.

West of Usulután, we came across a *barrio* with new wide dirt streets that were curbed and guttered. All the homes were equally spaced in the little subdivision, but they were self-built from corrugated metal sheets and a mixture of other scraps. This looked like some ugly post–Mitch work. The residents might have been provided the land to replace what they had lost, but not the means to build a proper home.

The countryside became flat rolling farmland with sugar cane and cattle, and always a volcano in close proximity that looked as though it had just burst up out of the landscape.

As we approached San Salvador, the terrain became hilly and tree-covered. Many of the trees were in full bloom. We had friends in the capital whom we had agreed to meet at the Radisson Hotel. We never could find the Radisson, although we enjoyed the drive around various embassies. After a while, I think one of the embassy security guards began to eye us suspiciously as we kept going in circles past him. We finally found a large Marriott hotel and decided to check in and tell our friends where we were. It would be easier for them to

find us than the other way around. The hotel had an enormous covered parking barn with a roof twenty feet above us that let the air circulate. We could park the motorhome in the shade and they would accept the dog in the hotel. The overnight parking cost a dollar, plus tip. We could have stayed in the motorhome and saved the $150 it cost for the room, plus a charge of $20 for the dog. We decided we needed a proper shower and bed for a treat. We luxuriated in long showers with the water running, and watched CNN in an attempt to catch up on the news. We never did catch up on world news as we could only get information on the war on Iraq. We watched the toppling of a statue of Saddam Hussein and I have to admit it was compelling viewing. I'm glad we can't get the news on the road.

Refreshed and dressed in our only smart outfits, we went downstairs to meet our friend. He was chatting with his friend, the president of a major bank in El Salvador, and introduced us. Our friend, Mauricio, was actually the father-in-law of John's work colleague. His daughter worked in Houston as an engineer, and Mauricio ran the largest construction company in El Salvador. We were mixing with very different people those with which we had breakfast the previous morning.

Mauricio's home was glorious. It was single story with a charming garden courtyard with nothing but blooms, grass and greenery. Plants overflowed from the courtyard into the house through open portals making it all one tropical garden. Mauricio served Chivas Regal. The maid brought us a vegetarian meal of traditional foods like tamale, frijoles, queso, yucca and several other items. It was great to have the dishes prepared well and served

ABOVE: Santa Ana

in such an elegant setting. Mauricio frequently eats vegetarian dinners.

It was a relaxing evening with good company. Although they both spoke English we spent the whole evening speaking Spanish, except for the stray English word when our Spanish vocabulary failed us. It was good to know we had progressed that far with our language skills.

Day 86
Wednesday, April 9, Santa Ana

My only regret about staying at the Marriott was that we didn't go downstairs early enough to pig out at their buffet breakfast. We got an extension on the checkout and eventually left at about one in the afternoon feeling relaxed, cool, clean and refreshed.

We were making good time on our return trip. Our plan was to return to Antigua, Guatemala for *Semana Santa*. It was Wednesday, and we planned to be there the following Monday or Tuesday to enjoy the festivities. We found our way out of San Salvador, heading toward the town of Santa Ana but, in order to get to Antigua, we needed to turn west towards

Sonsonate, a few miles out of town. We watched diligently for the signs to this turnoff. After a while we realized we had missed the intersection and made a U-turn on the busy highway. We found a shopping mall where we could ask directions, and also get some badly needed cash from an ATM machine. As we sat in the motorhome contemplating our situation and looking at the map, a severe case of get-home-itis hit us. If we continued on toward Santa Ana, we reasoned that we could enter Guatemala close to the familiar area of Esquipulas and make a direct run to Tikal, Belize, Mexico, and home. Later we would regret not going to Antigua for Easter. But there is something that happens on these trips, regardless of the length, when you cross a psychological bridge and touring is no longer the highest priority. Maybe it was the night in the Marriott and the social evening, or simply missing a turn in the road, but we both decided, then and there, that it was time to head directly home.

Another U-turn and we had cemented our decision. We didn't make it very far that day, all of forty-one miles. We drove through steep little hills and then began looking for a location to park in Santa Ana. It was a lovely town with a large town square with recently restored large old colonial buildings.

A couple of camping places we had heard about didn't pan out and we were getting concerned. One of the places we thought we could camp was at the Turicentro, a nice park with a large parking area. They were closed when we arrived at five-thirty, and although the guard called the management on our behalf, we were turned away. However, he gave us directions to a nearby church with a large parking lot. We found the caretaker of the church who checked with the priest, who said we would be welcome. We thought we were going to park in the front parking lot and made our way carefully under the arched gate in the high wall. The caretaker then beckoned us to follow him to an area around the back where we would be out of the way of the activities. This was a great spot to camp in a large walled yard.

There was a school attached to the church and the children were letting out. They looked neat in their uniforms. While watching the children and following the caretaker, we didn't notice the phone lines drooping overhead until we had pulled them in a great sagging loop almost to the ground. Fortunately,

we had just unraveled the excess that had been coiled on the roof and we had not broken any connections.

The smiling caretaker fetched a ladder and climbed onto the roof as though a motorhome disturbs his routine every day. He said would spend his tip on "dulces y Coca Cola." It was a very embarrassing incident for us. We hid in the bus and had our dinner.

Day 87
Thursday, April 10,
Teaching in School in Santa Ana

We planned on a very early start, and John was up walking the dog out in the street beyond the church grounds before seven. I had had my cup of tea and was waiting for the shower water to heat up when there was a knock on the door. I ignored it. There were kids about and besides I was in my pajamas. There was another, firmer knock. I peeked out, and there were three young ladies in school uniform of about twelve years of age. I had to get them to repeat their question three times, and eventually understood one saying, "We want to know you," in Spanish.

How could anyone resist that? "Momentito", I said and went inside to throw shorts and a T-shirt over my pajamas.

I then opened up the bus and sat on the step and told them who we were and where we were going. I asked them if they wanted a look inside. The three girls had multiplied as children always seem to in this part of the world, and now there must have been twenty standing in a polite circle, hanging on my every broken Spanish sentence. They understood well enough when I told them they could go into the motorhome. I showed them around two at a time. Outside they lined up in pairs holding hands. John returned and now some boys made themselves known. The first three girls, I only remember Francesca by name, now invited us to visit their school.

John was not prepared for this. He had jumped out of bed earlier to walk the dog. He was wearing shorts and a shirt but no underwear. He hadn't even had time to throw water on his face, let alone shave or comb his hair.

They were so sweet. They introduced us to the director and got permission to show us around the whole school. They led me, holding my hands, into every classroom and introduced me to every teacher they could find. The school must have operated double shifts since, when we arrived the previous evening, there were children going home at five o'clock. This seems to be the norm in Latin America to make better use of the facilities.

It was almost exclusively girls that accompanied me, whereas the boys hung around John.

After being shown the library they got special permission to take me to see their old kindergarten teachers. Next

was the cafeteria, which was just a little stall selling chips and the like. The school bell buzzed and I turned to go.

John caught up with me and said that we had been invited to tell the class about our experiences.

We went in and I met *El Profesor*. The children formed two lines outside their classroom; girls on one side, boys the other. As they entered the class, a monitor checked the cleanliness of their hands and made sure that each student had a hankie. The seating arrangement was girl-boy-girl in both directions in a checkerboard pattern. When everyone was assembled they said a prayer, after all this was a Catholic school, and were seated. Professor Jaime introduced us, and as John's Spanish was so much better than mine was, he led the discussion. He gave a brief rundown of where we had been and where we were from. As John finished the

LEFT: Francesca and her friends.
TOP RIGHT: The girls showing me around their school
RIGHT: John in discussion with one of the teachers.

teacher asked if there was a question. A boy stuck his hand up and asked, "Which is your favorite country?"

I was ready for this and responded saying all the countries were favorites with me and listed reasons. I liked Guatemala best because of the weaving, Honduras because of the beaches, Nicaragua because of the colonial cities, and Panama because of the Canal. I concluded by saying that it was the people in El Salvador that made that country my favorite. There were a few more questions and then we took a group picture before excusing ourselves.

I found it interesting in retrospect, that only the boys asked questions. The girls seemed interested, but just didn't put their hands up. It was a boy who was called upon to thank us on behalf of the class. It was, however, girls who had had the courage to knock on our motorhome door in the first place, and I thanked them in front of the class for that. John had done his usual number though, telling them that we had been to El Salvador years earlier, for the wedding of a lady engineer (Mauricio's daughter) who had sisters who were also engineers. If John had his way the whole world would be populated with female engineers.

Once again we had lost our early start, but what an experience! We took plenty of pictures and sent copies to the school after our return to the U.S.

We arrived at the border with Guatemala at the small village of Anguiatú. This little traveled out-of-the-way border was a welcome relief after our experience at El Amatillo. We picked up a guide, cleared the vehicle out of El Salvador and drove over the bridge into Guatemala.

It was here that we cleared out of El Salvador Immigration with a Salvadoran official in the same room as a Guatemalan Immigration officer in Guatemala. They had different little glass windows though, and you had to wait in a line before one and then wait in the adjacent line. It was nice to see them working together.

The dog was easy to get in. The officer just removed the staple from the stack of papers and slipped the two pages I had acquired at the consulate in Houston through his little photocopier. This was interesting on two accounts: first, we didn't have to traipse all over the place to make the copies as we had at the other crossings; second, I am sure that by unstapling the pack of papers, the two affidavits that were attached were now null and void. I think that the last thing of concern around here would be a bunch of staple holes in the corner. On closer examination I saw several staple holes I had not noticed before so it had probably been taken apart numerous times.

The papers for the motorhome took a little longer. They cost $6.50 and that was all. We paid the guide $5 and were away in an easy, no hassle, hour-and-three-quarters. Only three more borders to go.

LEFT: John in front of Prof. Jaime's class at Centro Escolar Madre del Salvador

CHAPTER 9
Wild Fires & Blue Lakes

FIVE BLUES LAKE

The use of traveling is to regulate imagination by reality, and instead of thinking how things may be, to see them as they are.

SAMUEL JOHNSON

OUR GOAL FOR THE NIGHT WAS Rio Dulce. This is where the lake, Lago de Izabal, forms a river that flows north into the Gulf of Honduras. We had plenty of time and the road was good. We could drive at 45 mph. I decided to take a nap and was awakened by John pulling into a gas station with yet another flat tire. At least this time he didn't have to change

the wheels, as they did it for about a dollar. Unfortunately, the old tire was shredded. It was the one that had been giving John such a hard time with its slow leak.

They didn't have the right replacement tire there, so we put the spare on and headed three miles down the road to a major Firestone dealer in Rio Hondo. This is on the main highway

261

across Guatemala from the Pacific to the Atlantic. They did not have the right size tire either. They tried to convince John to use a different size, but he insisted on getting the right one. The Firestone garage manager agreed to order one and have it shipped, but instead of waiting in Rio Hondo, they agreed to have it shipped to Rio Dulce. We had heard horror stories about people waiting months for parts, and Rio Hondo would not be a fun location in which to wait. We had to pre-pay in cash, and they arranged for us to pick it up the next day at the bus station. The tire cost about 20% more than it cost in Panama City. Changing and fixing a tire is cheap, but getting a new one is not.

We had to take a chance, not only of the tire never arriving, but also of driving to Rio Dulce without a spare.

I was driving and noticed packs of trucks coming towards us, and then for a while, nothing, and then another pack. Sure enough, a few miles up the road we came to a halt. A few vehicles at a time were being allowed to pass in each direction. Most of the vehicles on the road were trucks of one kind or another. Eighteen-wheelers made up at least half, and there were large "stake trucks" filled with bananas, pineapples, cattle, and sometimes people. There were pickup trucks, often filled with standing people, with rails designed for passengers to hold onto. A truck seldom passed without someone standing, sitting, or lying on the back. The rest of the vehicles were buses, and a very few private cars. We eventually reached an accident scene, where there was a shredded eighteen-wheeler lying on its side. The traffic speed picked up again.

When we reached the town of Rio Dulce, it was completely dark, but we knew of a place to camp. Fortunately, we had good directions from our friends, Bill and Carol, whom we had met in Atitlán. We went over the long modern bridge to where Bruno's Hotel and Restaurant is located next to the river, under the bridge. We had to do a U-turn, and try to cross under the bridge. The path beside the bridge was lined with carnival stalls in preparation for the mighty Semana Santa celebrations. We were too tall to pass under the bridge, where there was a road, and had to go to where the ground was lower before we could pass beneath and backtrack to Bruno's.

Bruno is a Swiss adventurer who came to visit Rio Dulce and never left. There were others like him around. Although the camp was five minutes from a town with a bank, internet café and whatever else you might need, it was also insulated from the traffic by the bridge. There was a swimming pool, bar, good restaurant, hotel rooms, boat slips, and the wide Rio Dulce. It was almost like a yacht club for international visitors.

We had a good shrimp dinner overlooking the pier where several elegant yachts were moored. We made arrangements with the bartender for a boat ride in the morning to the hot springs up river. It was all very casual, but we were assured that the catamaran would turn up at eight the next morning. It averages 120 inches of rain a year there, and we hoped we would not be stuck on the open deck of a catamaran in the rain all day.

Day 88
Friday, April 11, Rio Dulce and Livingston

There was not a cloud in the sky when we woke up. We had breakfast back in the bar/restaurant enjoying the stunning view across the river. Walking back to the motorhome, we realized that in the dark we had parked under a coconut tree. This

ABOVE: Rio Dulce near Lago de Izabal, Guatemala

is a dangerous thing to do if there are ripe coconuts, but these were very green and we survived without any damage. We told Brindle to look after the bus, picked up our things, and returned to watch for the eight o'clock boat.

We were going to Finca El Paraíso, on Lake Izabal, where there were hot springs and cool waterfalls. It sounded very appealing. Typical of this part of the world, on this day the catamaran was going in the other direction! It was going to Livingston on the coast. There was another couple who had spoken to the owner first, and they had requested a trip to Livingston. It didn't really matter to us where we went. We just wanted to see something of interest since we had a day to enjoy while waiting for our tire to be delivered. Well, we hoped it would be delivered.

We left at 9:15 a.m. and sat under a canopy on the canvas between the twin hulls of a very nice catamaran. There was a gentle breeze. This was the life. Livingston, a Garífuna town on the Gulf

of Honduras, is only accessible by boat. The main attraction of the excursion was the trip there.

The river was as wide as a lake, and might have been called part of Lago de Izabal, which technically began above the bridge. This is Guatemala's largest lake. Just above the bridge are the remains of a Spanish fort that used to protect the villages around the lake from the buccaneers who would sail upstream to wait out the hurricane season. This is an ideal safe haven for seafarers, past and present.

The waters narrowed as the cliffs grew higher. On either side of the deep water, sheer cliffs rose vertically, covered in jungle foliage where they touched the sky. It was very appealing. One cliff must have been three hundred feet high as the river went through the gorge lined with jungle. The rock wall looked like a piece of wedding cake with green icing. It was here that parts of the original Tarzan movies were made.

This is an area known for manatees, but there is hardly a chance to see these great gentle beasts. They can live for up

to 50 years, if left to themselves with enough sea grasses to eat. The water here is as much as 80-feet deep, so these ten foot shy "mermaids" have plenty of space to drop out of sight.

Little, palm-thatched homes perched precariously on stilts, on scraps of flat land between the river and the cliff. The residents fished the rich river from canoes, which were their only means of transport, and ate bananas and coconuts that grew around their houses.

The cliffs grew higher as the river narrowed and we sailed down the canyon. Then suddenly, we turned a corner, and there were no more cliffs and the bay opened out before us. I could imagine how exciting it would have been for the early explorers to sail into this pleasant bay and discover the deep canyon of water that would take them to the safe harbor of Rio Dulce and the lake beyond. Sweet River was an apt name.

When we reached Livingston, we circled around the harbor between expensive yachts and abandoned, smelly vessels taken over by gulls and pelicans. We came to a dock of a hotel where several gringos had moored their yachts for the season. We almost stayed to sample their piña coladas. A skiff came and took us into town.

The town was comprised of two-story clapboard buildings, painted in gay yellows and pinks, with balconies displaying immaculate white wrought iron balustrades. Corrugated iron roofs painted terracotta, blue or white were waiting for the next downpour of rain. Some homes were built of concrete block and were painted crisp white, while others looked liked their thatched roofs were holding them up. The road was concrete and had some serious drainage ditches. Neat, little, white picket fences were alongside the road. There were just enough tourist shops to add a little extra color, with towels and sarongs flapping in the breeze. Banana trees and coconut palms swaying over everything added to the Caribbean feel.

The locals greeted us with smiles as they moved slowly about their business

LEFT: The canyon of Rio Dulce
ABOVE: Villages along Rio Dulce, Guatemala
RIGHT: Livingston, Guatemala

in the tropical sun. They were a very mixed blend. There were Garífuna, gringos, Latinos, and some *indígenas,* women in the traditional *huipiles.* Although some of the *huipiles* were of heavy woven fabric, most here were of the traditional design, but made from light cotton creating a very full, loose and cool top.

Kekchi Maya and Garífuna live side by side, but I'm not sure it is all that comfortable. As we sat on an open balcony enjoying more shrimp cooked in coconut milk, I watched an exchange between a Maya lady and a Garífuna. Three Maya ladies were sitting on the curb a couple of feet from us, selling tortillas that were being kept warm in baskets wrapped in colorful fabric. The Garífuna man approached one of the ladies to make a purchase and was rebuffed. I could not understand the words they spoke but the body language from the Mayans was definitely negative, as she turned her shoulder away from him and addressed her friends.

There are no roads to Livingston, so it had the feel of an island. It was pleasant to wander around without the worry of being hit by a car, although there were a couple that must have been ferried in. Of course there were always bicycles to watch out for, but most people walked about gently, trying not to work up too much of a sweat.

Halfway home, we pulled over to the side of the canyon where the high cliff met the water, for a swim in the *agua caliente.* There were no markers, nothing to distinguish this part of the cliff from any other, unless you were very familiar with the river. The water of the river was pleasantly cool when we jumped in, and our guide's young son joined us. We swam up to the cliff to where some rocks formed a shallow area, and suddenly the water was hot. Very hot! There was the slight smell of sulfur, and a little steam, but there is no way an inexperienced eye could have found the spring.

Like Old Faithful, the heat came in waves. We were happily soaking in the warm water when again it suddenly became very hot, and we had to swish the water about to mix it with the cooler river water.

It was a good excursion and I would recommend it. There were faster boats available that could have done the 23 miles more quickly, but I would not do that if I had to sacrifice our little dip in the hot water spring.

Upon returning to Bruno's, we found Brindle guarding the motorhome, asleep underneath it. We took her for a walk into town to fetch the new tire. It was not at the bus station as had been promised. That meant we would have to wait another day. What a shame, I thought with a smile all over my face! We just hoped that it would arrive eventually. We understood how some travelers could get stuck in a place like this for months and never complain.

Unfortunately, with the carnival stalls and the visiting *Semana Santa* crowds had come some undesirable characters, and Bruno had to put on an extra guard. Nevertheless, while indulging in another seafood dinner, we were interrupted by a lot of scampering about and shouting. Men were running up and down the

dock, and then the two guards jumped in a motorboat and sped away. One guard carried a handgun, and the other wielded an automatic rifle. The thief had stolen a tank of gas from one of the skiffs and was swimming away with it. I was kind of glad they didn't find him or shoot at him in the water with the gasoline. I hate to think of what might have happened.

We finished another good meal at Bruno's restaurant and spent the rest of the evening in interesting conversation, visiting with yachtsmen who were stalled there. One man had sailed in several years earlier and it didn't look like he was planning on moving on. Rio Dulce could do that to a person. He had purchased some real estate in the hills and was planning on developing it into a resort.

Day 89
Saturday, April 12, Rio Dulce to Santa Elena

The town of Rio Dulce was bustling in preparation for Easter and the *Semana Santa* celebrations. The stalls for the festivities lining the roadway created a carnival atmosphere.

First order of the day was to see if the tire we had ordered had arrived. We returned to the bus station, which

LEFT: Hot springs in Rio Dulce
ABOVE: Onions for sale

consisted of a concrete block booth that was taller than it was wide, providing just enough shaded space and authority for the man in charge. The bus parked in front partially blocked traffic on the only road through town. No tire. Then someone asked if we had tried the bicycle shop down the road? No, indeed we had not; we needed a truck tire. He was insistent, and reluctantly we followed

him down the main street a couple of blocks to the bicycle shop. Our tire was waiting for us! That is where the deliveries were sent, but our Spanish had not made sense of what we had been told. We thanked everyone, and were both relieved and disappointed. We now had no excuse to stay.

New tire in place, we were ready to continue on our journey, except that we needed more cash and some groceries. There were about twenty people being kept waiting outside the bank by the *vigilante*. I was invited to enter ahead of the line either because I was the only woman, because I was the only gringo,

or because I was head and shoulders taller than anyone else there. The men who were clutching checks came up to my chin.

With *quetzales* in hand, we returned to the stalls for our shopping. Trucks overflowing with produce were parked along the road.

As always, there were trucks carrying everything from produce to people. The scary thing is the speed at which they drive, and overtake on blind corners. They operate as buses, and are full of men, women and children, often with youngsters sitting up on the rails.

Our fridge and water tank were full and now we needed to put some miles on so we could camp close to Tikal. We went back to the motorhome and drove it carefully under the bridge, between the stalls, under the hanging cables, and up onto the road.

North of Rio Dulce, little hills protruded through flat ranch land, showing white chalky rocks where the grass on the steep slope met the jungle balancing on the top. There were some large trees, with a haze of purple flowers covering them and others with a dusting of deep pink blossoms, and foot-long black seed-pods added an interesting contrast. There was also the occasional young

ABOVE: Truck overflowing with melons and mangos for sale, Rio Dulce
RIGHT: A pickup truck disgorging its passengers. This is a very common means of transportation in Central America. The truck owner charges for the ride.

pine forest. Through it all we were able to keep up a speed of about thirty-five miles and hour.

John and I had driven this road twenty-seven years earlier in a cherry-red VW beetle. It was a one- lane dusty road then, with holes big enough to swallow our rented bug. Palm fronds joined over-head, creating a tunnel of shade through the dense jungle. It went on for hour after hour. It was fascinating, hot and dusty, and took all day. Jungle completely surrounded our entire route

Today we drove the same path, but this time on a good, two-lane road between numerous villages, houses, and ranches that had replaced the jungle. The little rock hillocks that were hidden twenty years before produced an unusual lumpy skyline. Heavy undergrowth bristled from the tops of the outcroppings, creating little islands of jungle in the pasture. It was as though some giant

hand had given the earth a poodle cut. The old growth was keeping the tops of the little hills protected. As we passed, the secondary growth was being burned again, as it struggled to take over the flat-land. There was always smoke in the air. It was a sad change from what we had experienced before, but the locals needed to farm to live and to feed their families.

We paid a quick visit to Finca Ixobel, near Poptún. This is a working farm geared toward ecotourism. There is good space for campers and accommodation of every kind. They had fifty-six guests, more than we have seen anywhere else. It had the feeling of a pleasant jungle-style dude ranch. There were lots of volunteer opportunities. We bought a loaf of freshly

ABOVE: Coming out from under the Rio Dulce Bridge at Bruno's
RIGHT: Hillocks too steep to be used as farmland, north of Rio Dulce

baked bread and moved on to the Cuevas Actun-Can, in Santa Elena. We arrived at the limestone caves just after they closed at five. Carlos, a pleasant young man who had grown up in Los Angeles, welcomed us to park, and even invited us to visit the caves. I would not recommend travelers go out of their way to see the limestone caves, but the dry campsite couldn't have been better.

Day 90
Sunday, April 13, Tikal

We made an early start driving through the bustling market of Santa Elena. Flores looked appealing across the bridge, but we were on our way to Tikal. The drive was through more ranch land where jungle had once been. It was delightfully cool, with no sun for a change, which made the morning pleasant.

We were reminded that it was Palm Sunday when we passed a little parade in a village along the way. There were no more than forty celebrants walking slowly behind the church leader. All were dressed in their best clothes, with crisp white T-shirts and the little girls in pretty skirts and dresses. The children held hands with their parents, grandparents, or, if they couldn't find a free hand, they dragged happily behind, clutching a skirt. Some parishioners held palm fronds, which had been twisted and bent into patterns. Although they walked slowly, it was a happy family event.

This was one of the few areas in Central America where there were not only good roads, but plenty of signs, so the trip to Tikal was easy. We knew that we could not take the dog into the national park, so we had to search around for somewhere to leave the motorhome where it and Brindle would be safe. We couldn't leave her locked inside on the off-chance that the generator that cranked the air-conditioning might stall. The heat was already stifling, so we had to leave her with access to the outside.

At the far, east end of Lago Petén Itzá, is the town of El Remate. It is made up of a collection of houses and businesses along the waterfront. There were some nice places to park out by the lake. We could have camped there and even left the motorhome; however, seeing children selling little wooden carved crocodiles told us something. The lake was known for the secarnivorous reptiles. We preferred returning to the built-up area and risking a break-in to losing the dog to a crocodile. We found a fork in the road, which created a fairly large triangular island, where there were some

good-sized shade trees and a couple of horses grazing.

We took a walk to get a feel for the area, and found a North American who lived across the road. We enjoyed a hearty conversation with him. He was friendly and rotund, and lived with his *Latina* wife in a little cement block home with a panoramic vista across the lake. It might have been the smell of her cooking that led us in their direction in the first place. He said he would have offered to look after Brindle in their fenced yard, only his dog was very territorial. He assured us that the motorhome was OK where we had parked it, and that he would keep an eye on it. We paused on the way back and chatted with a young man who was parking cars for visitors to an upscale restaurant. He also said that it would be fine, and that he would watch the motorhome for us.

My main concern by this time was the gaggle of boys who had found their way into the trees hanging over the motorhome. Not that they would crawl through the doggy door, which they could have assuredly done had Brindle not been around, but that they would drop onto the roof and go right through.

Turning our back on Brindle, who was watching us from the driver's seat, we flagged down a passing tourist bus and for five dollars got a ride into Tikal. Most of the way there was through pastureland , and then, suddenly, at the gate to the park there was jungle, thick dense jungle. Beyond the fence it was like a wall through which someone had cut a path. It gave the feeling that we were entering a vast, dark, secret garden. This was what John and I remembered driving through for a hundred miles,

twenty-seven years earlier. The park was all that was left of the jungle.

The vegetation opened out at the park's headquarters for the parking lots and other tourist facilities. We were dropped off beyond the park's buildings, and right at the path to the ruins. This cut down on the walking distance, but we had bypassed all the information booths. Walking towards the ruins we found ourselves behind two couples with an English-speaking guide. We listened for a while, and then asked if we could join them. They were accommodating and we paid our share. It would have been a great mistake to pass through this vast area without a guide.

Tikal is the granddaddy of all ruins. It is massive and would take at least two days to see it all. If you had a lot of interest, it would take a lot longer.

It was interesting to see the recently excavated homes of the Maya elite. Ordinary citizens' homes, made of cane and palm, would have dissolved back into the jungle centuries ago. The home that is shown here belonged to a priest. It had two bedrooms and a central room. Stairs went out to a platform that faced one of the large courtyards. It was as if a priest could step onto his back porch to address the faithful. Our guide pointed

to rectangular boxes the size of a double bed and said that they were beds but they were also tombs of the residents' forefathers. They would sleep over the deceased. Hearing that brought to mind the gravedigger in the town of Copán Ruinas, who told me how his ancestors would use the sepulchers as beds. It tied together nicely and gave the information a special realism.

There were no cooking or other facilities so perhaps, like the families we had recently visited, the cooking was done away from the living area. I could visualize where palm thatching on the slanting roofs would make the home waterproof and cool.

Our guide showed us the palm leaves most favored by the ancient, and current, Mayan for thatching. He explained

that it is important to the Maya to cut the leaves when there is a full moon, as then they will last on the roof for five years. Otherwise, the roof would have to be re-thatched in half that time. He explained how modern research has shown that there is more sap in the fronds at this time and, therefore, it is stronger. The skeptical engineer I'm married to doubts the theory.

Temple One is the structure most people picture when they think of Tikal. It has a wonderful timeless quality. It is awe-inspiring. There are numerous stelae scattered about the complex, some of which have clear carvings, whereas others are faded and almost smooth.

Once our guide left us to our own devices, we sat and enjoyed the feel of the ancient city. It was easy to imagine throngs of ancient peoples going about their business. It was probably just as hot then too. We were beginning to wilt.

LEFT: Home of a priest in Tikal
ABOVE: Houses of the elite in Tikal

Excavations were being conducted all the time, not just of undisturbed mounds, but also beneath the temples themselves. Temples and stone carvings are being disclosed beneath the visible temples. Because the buried ones have not been subjected to the elements, some are in remarkable condition.

Spring is a season when people all over the world celebrate new life and ask for a good harvest. This is true of the Maya who still come to Tikal to ask favors of the gods. At this time of year, they come in groups to hold ceremonies in the main plaza with traditional offerings of chicken and chocolate. While we were there, there were a lot of indigenous family groups with the women in traditional clothes. It was hard to know if they were enjoying the ruins as tourists like us, or if they were here for a deeper religious purpose.

There were also many Latino families celebrating the holiday there. Judging by the expensive cars in the parking lot, there were wealthy Salvadoran families, parked next to pickup trucks that would probably have been packed with working class locals. It was nice to see so many people enjoying their heritage.

We climbed Temple Four again, as we had twenty-seven years ago. Instead of clambering hand over hand up the loose rock, this time there was a sturdy wooden stairway. This is the only temple, open for the public, where you can climb to the top. The other temples are closed to climbers. There have been too many accidents, some fatal. From the top of Temple Four was the same glorious view we remembered. All we could see for miles in all directions was a green mat of the jungle canopy, with the occasional tree blossoming red. Other temples showed their crowns through the tops of the vegetation. That hadn't changed. This was the setting used in the opening

LEFT: Temple One, Tikal
ABOVE: Two carved stone faces were revealed during excavations beneath a temple. A second, original, flight of steps was also uncovered.

scenes of the movie *Close Encounters of the Third Kind*.

We had not seen or heard any of the howler monkeys or exotic birds that are meant to frequent the area, but we were accompanied by the chirping of frogs.

Another tourist bus took us back to El Remate, where we found the motorhome and the dog just as we had left them. Brindle jumped out to greet us. There was a note tucked under our windshield from a North American with an invitation to camp at his house for the night. Unfortunately, he lived in Santa Elena, about an hour and a half in the wrong direction. The other North American who lived across the way was nowhere to be seen, nor could we find the valet to give him his tip. We reasoned that, if we could drive away without him noticing, he didn't deserve a tip.

ABOVE: The view from Temple 4 with two other temples breaching the jungle in the distance.

We had noted that the closer we were to a border, the worse the road became. This was certainly true as we approached the Belize border. The road east of Tikal was good at first, then it completely fell apart. The last dozen miles took an hour over a grim gravel and dirt road. We were down to 15 mph, which blew our timing and caused us once again to wonder where we were going to camp. You would think that it would be important to give travelers a good impression when entering the country, and pave those thirteen miles.

The crossing into Belize was relatively easy. This was the one country where I had been unable to get anything in writing for the dog, as there was no Belize consulate in Houston. I had phoned the Health Department in Belize, from Houston, and spoken to the man in charge. Dr Gongongore told me about the procedures we needed to go through, all of which had to be completed three days before we entered the country. As this wouldn't be possible I asked what would happen if we just turned up.

"Oooh," he said in his deep rich Caribbean accent. "Then you would have to pay a fine."

"How much would it be, do you think?"

"Oooh. Fifteen, twenty-five dollars, maybe" he informed me.

Armed with that information we approached the border with nothing more than our now highly stamped and franked USDA form and the good doctor's name. That was enough.

The charge for the dog was just five dollars. In addition, we had to pay a dollar toll for the bridge between the countries. An inspector came on board and confiscated our meat and fresh vegetables on entering the country. This was more annoying than anything, as it left us without any supper. He put it all in one of our plastic trash bags, and I have a funny feeling that he had a better dinner than we did. I would actually prefer that he enjoy it, rather than having it go to waste.

Once we crossed the border, the character of the land was amazingly different. This could have been England! The land had been firmly under British influence since the middle of the seventeen hundreds and it showed in the style of the

homes and the fences around the little fields. I immediately felt at home. A hot home I'll admit, but the English atmosphere was dramatic.

There were published campsites in Belize, and we had our sights on Caesar's Palace Guest House in Santa Elena, about thirty minutes from the border. We made it just after sunset. Unfortunately they had guard dogs. Although these pedigree German Shepherds were very nice to us, they had a reputation of not being friendly toward other dogs. Brindle had to spend all the time in the motorhome. The owner shut his dogs up for a while so we could take Brindle for a walk, but that was it. The camp had all the hook-ups we needed, but it was a bit like parking in the back of a lumberyard.

The shop at Caesar's was worth a visit, as it was packed with interesting and high quality imports from all over the world. The proprietors bought wood-carvings in various parts of Africa and then duplicated them on site. We didn't try the restaurant for more than a beer and a chat with a fellow traveler going solo to Panama. I scrounged up enough food for a meal in the motorhome and with the power we were able to watch another episode of M★A★S★H★ before we turned in.

Day 91
Monday, April 14, Belize and the Blue Hole and Fire

Distances are very short in Central America, and that is especially true in Belize where the roads were good. The Hummingbird Highway across Belize was a good, well sign-posted, two-lane country road that meanders between rolling hills. This country was British Honduras forty years ago, and yes, they speak English. This enabled us to relax and chat with the locals more easily. There are *topes* and raised pedestrian crossings, simply called bumps. The signs are enough to get an imaginative man to slow down!

There was a handmade sign outside a farmhouse that advertised: SPECIAL COW FOOT SOUP, which wasn't so appealing.

Another hand painted sign read:

HIGH TAXES

HIGH CRIME

THIS GOVMENT HAFFA GO

We were at the Blue Hole National park before we knew it. This is a deep sinkhole, or *cenote*, formed by a collapsed limestone cave. This is not to be confused with the Blue Hole Natural Monument. The latter is a vast blue hole, 1000 feet across and 400 feet deep, off shore on Lighthouse Reef, which divers can visit.

Over the years this little hole has been softened by time and jungle undergrowth. Belize is riddled with underground rivers, and this is a stream that, because of the cave-in, meets daylight here before it returns underground. A rapid little stream carries water underground again as it leaves the pool, keeping the water fresh and clean.

We clambered down the steep steps into the deep shade where only mottled sun reached the water. It was really blue. Swimming was lovely with all the trees so close around touching overhead. The pool was cool, small, and very deep. It was a little spooky swimming where the water is very clear, but so deep that I had no idea where the bottom was. There might be an ancient monster in this

bottomless hole about to grab my leg! As it was, there were plenty of little fish swimming around my feet. The bottom is actually about 25 feet down. It was a magical place. I could imagine an ogre hiding in the rock crannies, or good fairies living among the ferns and mosses on the cliff edges.

There were some Brits there. John and the husband sat, on a ledge in the water at the far side talking for hours. He was an engineer running a branch of his construction company. The couple now lives in Belize with their son, and they were taking a visiting relative to see the sights.

We could have camped in the parking lot of the park, but we set off to try to find something off the highway. We arrived at nearby Ian Anderson's Caves Branch Jungle Lodge in the middle of the afternoon. It was rather like summer camp, complete with daily activities,

LEFT: These signs warning drivers of speed bumps, are unique to Belize
RIGHT: The Blue Hole National Park, Hummingbird Highway, Belize

buffet, and family style meals. Unfortunately, they also have rather aggressive dogs, so once again Brindle had to stay in the motorhome. Fortunately, there was plenty of shade. The area around Caves Branch used to be a cacao farm, and as we walked Brindle, we could see some of the old cacao trees surviving as the jungle grew back. Purple pods drooped from the branches with their precious beans.

The lodge serves up a rather expensive buffet dinner that didn't appeal to us, so we ate in the motorhome, which

I'm not sure made them happy. They charged for the parking, with no facilities, so we didn't feel we owed them the dinner purchase.

Day 92
Tuesday, April 15, Cave Tubing

The appealing thing about Ian Anderson's Caves Branch Lodge is the variety of tours they offered. We selected an excursion that took us "tubing" through limestone caves. We had gone tubing a few times in Texas. It sounded cool, and anything cool had to be good.

We had been hot for so long. It turned out to be very unusual and interesting, and not at all what we expected.

First, there was a thirty-minute ride, standing on the back of a trailer pulled by a tractor. The trailer was filled with about thirty people and more than thirty inner tubes. These tubes weren't rejects from flat tires, but they were made especially as floats. The tubes had a bulge on one side for better back support. The drive itself was fun, and went through

TOP LEFT: Orchids at Ian Anderson's Caves Branch Jungle Lodge, Belize
LEFT: Tractor pulling us through orange groves in Belize
ABOVE: Adventurers and tubes about to go on the underground river

vast acres of orange groves, filling the canyons between jungle covered limestone cliffs.

The tractor came to a halt where the path between the orange trees dead-ended at a limestone cliff. We all piled out, grabbed a tube, and were divided into small groups.

We carried the tubes to a stream for a safety briefing, and we were each issued a flashlight that strapped onto our head like a miner's lamp. We flopped clumsily into the tubes in the refreshingly cool clear water, and paddled upstream. Paddling upstream was not difficult; it was passing under fallen trees dripping with cobwebs and many-legged critters, and avoiding rocks and tropical undergrowth that was the challenge. It reminded me of a Disney ride, but it was all real!

Once inside the cave, the river became too shallow for the tubes, so we walked a short distance carrying them. There were bats hanging about overhead, and crickets and birds clinging to the walls. As we looked into the water

the red eyes of catfish reflected the light back from our headlamps.

We alternated between walking and tubing, making our way upstream. The stalagmite and stalactite formations were special. There were lime curtains in folds, bulges of sparkling crystals like avalanches of snow, frozen waterfalls of stone, and long tentacles reaching down to touch fingers pointing up. We paddled under and between them, or we walked around them.

Lovely as they were, this tour was not just to see limestone caves. Of particular interest were the Mayan fire sites. These were where ancient Maya religious leaders made offerings to the gods 2,000 years ago. Over 450 ceremonial fireplaces

ABOVE: The Caves Branch River leading to the caves. The cave entrance can be seen at the foot of the cliff wall.
TOP RIGHT: Carrying tubes through the caves
RIGHT: Sparkling formations in the Anderson Caves

have been found in these caves. Many have shards of broken pottery and some have human bones. After the ancient ceremonies, the Maya broke the pots with their offerings to allow the spirits to escape. It seems that the each little fire was used only once or twice. I only noticed evidence of smoke on the ceiling where a fire was on a high ledge.

Our guide explained to us that these were sometimes sacrificial offerings, perhaps of the blood drawn from important people. The Maya believe there are seven steps to the after-life below ground. These caves lead to Xibalba, the underworld where gods live. On the brighter side, the Ceiba tree leads the Mayan spirits to the first of thirteen steps to the heavens above. The dark, vacuous cave dripped spirits and I could feel the gods breathing around us in the rustle of the river. It was mystical to sit in a close circle around the remains of a little fire which had been lit over two thousand years ago. I could imagine the priest and his supplicant, with a small flickering flame in this dank emptiness, paying homage to their gods.

One area was thought to be used for fertility ceremonies. If the woman who had entered the cave asking for children subsequently conceived, her first child would be brought back to the cave and sacrificed to the gods. She could keep the rest of her children. Here, deep in the cave, we saw a god chiseled into the limestone. Close by there was a stalagmite that they think was carved to represent a pregnant woman on one side and a mother with baby on the other. The carving was blurred by the additional accumulation of lime over the centuries and took a little imagination to see.

Current opinion is that the cave was only used on very special occasions. We saw about a dozen sites, many with broken pottery on ledges high above the flood level of the water. Others might have been washed away during floods. The whole place had a special, you could almost say awesome, feeling. Strange limestone formations were all around, and the river was constantly rippling over the smooth stones. It was understandable why the ancient people had held these caves in such esteem.

The mood was broken by our guide asking, "Is anyone hungry?"

LEFT: A two thousand year old Mayan sacrificial fire and shattered pots.
ABOVE: Fertility god. Look for the detail!
RIGHT: The main road ends in Hopkins

The guide spread a white tablecloth in the middle of the cave and began to cover it with quantities of food from her backpack. I was ravenous, as I had been wet and cold for what seemed like hours. The guide insisted that every scrap and crumb be wrapped up in the cloth and carried out with us.

The caves have only recently been discovered, and the only way to enter is with small groups lead by a guide. It was incredible to me that we were clumsily walking around these ancient offering sites.

The only downside of the excursion was that we were sitting and walking around in our wet clothes for four hours in a cool cave. Nevertheless, if you are interested in caves and geology, not to mention archaeology and the ancient Maya, it is a fascinating trip.

We returned to our base early enough to have a quick bite to eat before heading east on the Hummingbird Highway for one last night on the Caribbean. It was four miles, over a dirt road, off the Southern Highway to the town of Hopkins. The road passed through swampland with ditches on either side and over the occasional little bridge, where the swamp became a flowing waterway. The paved road ended at the Caribbean in the town center.

We could have parked right there, fifty feet from the bluest of blue waters, behind the police station. We chose to explore, and turned right, heading south. We drove for a few miles on the dirt road but couldn't find a place to pull off. On either side was a continuous ditch broken only by driveways to private residences. There were a couple of places that looked like hotels, and I'm sure that we would have been able to park on their grounds, but we preferred to get away from tourists. We finally found a place that had recently been cleared for a home site. There didn't seem to be any activity in the neighboring homes.

I was slightly nervous, being out on our own so far from anyone. What if a drunk came and started banging on the motorhome? We maneuvered the

motorhome on the packed sand, and turned her to face out so we could make a hasty retreat without driving across the soft sand that otherwise surrounded us. We still had a great view of the magnificent blue water.

We had to hurry so that John could have his cocktail while watching the sun drop beyond the Caribbean. Conveniently, the holiday home to our right had a long pier built over the water. We took advantage of it to avoid the little sand bugs on the beach, and carried our chairs to the pier's end.

Brindle had been a great dog to have along, but we never claimed that she was the brightest of animals. When she saw us on the pier she swam straight toward us not realizing that it would have been much easier to go along the beach to the pier. The water was lovely and clear, and I looked forward to a swim in the morning. Now I felt a little waterlogged after spending all morning wet.

At eleven thirty that night I woke up to an eerie crackling sound which wasn't the wind or the waves we had been listening to earlier. I thought it was someone walking around the motorhome, and the hairs bristled on the back of my neck. It was worse than that. I looked out of the window and there was a sheet of flames a hundred feet high just on the other side of the dirt road. Flames were licking the sky and ash was wafting around like snow. There was an off-shore wind, and sparks were falling everywhere around us, including on the motorhome and in the brush next to us. The flames were leaping toward us. I went cold with fear.

Our back was to the beach. To the south on either side of the road were trees and scrub. From our earlier explorations we knew the trees went for several miles. We didn't want to get caught on that narrow road, and we didn't know if it even went through. Driving north past the flames was not much of a choice either. We would have had to go too slowly on the pot-holed dirt road very close to the flames. There were some people with garden hoses watering down the palm and scrub growth. We had a brief debate about staying in the clearing. I had visions of John, the dog, and me backing into the water, watching our motorhome burning. We chose to try to outrun the fire by heading south. We pulled out, careful not to get stuck in the soft sand around us. I was so glad we had parked facing the road. We drove south, parallel to the beach, with scrub and water to our left and flaming swamp to our right. We were genuinely afraid.

The two maps we had did not show the same roads, and neither showed that the one we were on ever returned to the main road.

When the flames were no longer visible, we relaxed a bit. The road was a well made, raised dirt road, but the bridges were very narrow, and we don't like driving at night at the best of times. There was a steep drop-off on either side into blackness beyond. We had two choices by then: either keep going, or stop in the middle of the road. There was nowhere to even turn around if we had to.

At last we saw a sign for a Texaco station, and we thought if we followed the signs, they would lead to the main road. Not exactly! The sign directed us onto a smaller dirt road and to a boat dock on a river with no one in sight. It was a dead end. Dry swamp and palm shrubs surrounded us, with a gas tank in the middle. This was not exactly where we wanted to wait out a fire. We turned back to the larger dirt road and followed our compass away from the fire and towards where we calculated the main road would be. We were glad we had

brought the compass, as there was nothing else to guide us. All we could see was the yellow dirt road and the occasional narrow bridge over swampy ditches. Our flashlights illuminated dry brown scrub on either side of the road. Beyond that was an eternity of blackness inhabited only by crocodiles.

We came to an area that had already burned black. We stopped to see if this was where the fire started. It was an old burn and quite cold. Then I saw something incredible. There was one palm tree entwined with dead vines that was covered in little sparks as though it were decorated in holiday lights. There were lots of little sparks of light all up and down the trunk. We drove on. Looking back a minute later there was a hundred-foot Roman candle shooting flames into the night sky. The whole marsh was igniting round us.

We drove on for what seemed forever, until we came to some habitation. We could see houses, and there were green grass verges instead of deep ditches and dry weeds. We came to a soccer field. We could no longer smell the smoke and felt we were far enough away to stay there the night. There was plenty of

LEFT: In a clearing on the Caribbean just south of Hopkins
RIGHT: Just south of Hopkins, Belize

open area around the playing field, which we felt was an adequate fire-break. There was a sense of security having people around.

When our pounding hearts and adrenaline permitted, we returned to bed and tried to sleep. I lay wide-eyed, listening all night long.

Day 93
Wednesday, April 16, Sittee River Village

We woke up to another clear bright day and found ourselves in Sittee River Village. There were brightly painted wooden plank houses with colorful contrasting trim beside the road. The motorhome was parked on the edge of a soccer field under a breadfruit tree, just a hundred yards from the Sittee River. It would have been hard to find a prettier campsite, and we had done it in the middle of the night.

There were no chickens about. This indicated to me that there were crocodiles. Chickens are easy prey for a crocodile

and you don't want to encourage the beasts around your house. We kept a close eye on the dog.

Across the road from where we had parked, was a bright yellow and green house that had a sign promoting boat rides. I went in to inquire about the fire.

"What fire?" was the retort. Apparently the brush is frequently self-igniting and there are swamp fires all the time. Not next to our motorhome!! It was no big deal for them, and they hadn't even heard about the fire that had come so close to us.

This little business was run by a North American lady who had come to Belize as a tourist, fallen in love with both a man and the country, and stayed. Besides selling boat excursions, which her husband operated, she also sold hemp products. She had a variety of products from clothes to makeup, all made from the cannabis plant. She told me that it is legal to grow it in Belize, but she didn't offer me a smoke!

We wanted to see for ourselves what damage the fire had caused, so we retraced our steps to Hopkins. There was no sign of the fire. The high brush where the men had been hosing in the middle of the night ran along a ditch. There must have been enough water in the ditch to keep the brush there thoroughly saturated. It acted as a fire wall. I didn't think the man with the hose could have stopped the fire.

We paused in town and wet our feet in the Caribbean. We would have missed a lot of excitement if we had stayed right there next to the Welfare Center. There was plenty of space to park. I would not have wanted to leave the motorhome unattended because of all the children about, but it would have been a fine place for the night.

The white-sand beach stretched in either direction and children played in the water. During our drives back and forth, we had passed some high-end resorts hidden behind the tropical growth. If we wanted a real get-away, we would seriously consider returning to Hopkins. Just water and sand.

Heading back to the Southern Highway, we had a new awareness of the dry swampy scrub that extended for miles in either direction.

We retraced our tracks to the Hummingbird Highway. The road was good although the bridges were somewhat narrow. It was an easy, pleasant drive.

Back on the Hummingbird Highway I saw a sign for Five Blues Lake. We liked the sound of that, and without a thought, we turned off the surfaced road. There was a tourist information sign with a

map, and we asked the lady in the house opposite about the lake.

"It's closed," she said. "But don't let that stop you. You go on there. It's nice down there."

She was right. There was a long stretch of bumpy dirt road between sharp hills. Then as the road became less traveled, it became not much more than a wide grass path.

We were encouraged into thinking we were going the right way when we met a van full of local tourists. We kept on going! It would have been hard to turn around. It was six miles in all, but worth it. The path ended in a very nice, deserted park maintained by the local community. There was quite a large covered area for

LEFT: The Sittee River, Belize
TOP RIGHT: The beach at Hopkins, Belize
RIGHT: The Southern Highway, Belize

picnics, which contained a museum display and information on the numerous trails that you could take. There were all sorts of places to park. A log barrier prevented us from driving down the wide, grass avenue leading to the lake. On later examination, we decided that the tourist van had moved the barrier and had driven down to the lake. We could have done the same. It was about a ten-minute walk to a large open area facing the lake where there were plenty of great places to park overnight.

There was a canoe with a sign inviting us to borrow it. If we had paddles we definitely would have. There were plenty of signs and we followed the ones to the swimming area. The lake was another *cenote,* and the varying depths of the water and the light created the different

shades of blue. There were shelves of rocks dropping off to a depth of forty feet. Schools of very hungry fish enjoyed the crumbs of our snack.

Besides the pier the locals had built, there was a high diving board that was too high to tempt either of us. But I would have liked to see someone else use it. I am sure the place is well used on weekends and holidays. It was very well maintained and we were happy to put our entrance fee in the "honor box" back where we had parked.

Cool and relaxed, we headed back through the hills to the Hummingbird

Highway. We were tempted, just out of curiosity, to try one of the rustic bed and breakfast places. I do not know how you would make a reservation.

I wanted to see the capital of Belize, Belmopan, and insisted that we didn't bypass it again. We followed the signs, but couldn't find the city center. Then to our surprise we discovered that we had circumnavigated the entire city, and hadn't known it. Where we had stopped at a bank and bought milk on our way into the country was actually right next to

TOP LEFT: Lush countryside approaching Five Blues Lake
LEFT: The last stretch of road to Five Blues Lake
ABOVE: Sitting on an limestone shelf in Five Blues Lake

the national Assembly Building. This country is so compact, just 174 by 68 miles, with a quarter of a million residents, that it doesn't need great parliamentary buildings.

The only real supermarket we could find in town, Brodies, didn't sell fresh milk. There was surprisingly little for sale. We were grateful that we would be back in Mexico soon to replenish our perishables. They didn't let you bring vegetables and meat into the country, but they didn't have any worthwhile produce for sale either. If we had been staying any length of time in Belize we would have eaten Chinese food, as there were Chinese restaurants everywhere.

Back on the Western Highway, we continued on our northward route and eventually pulled into a restaurant with a large gravel parking lot. This was a place mentioned in one of the guidebooks as a good camping site. The deserted bar

was rich in British airforce memorabilia. The girl behind the bar didn't seem to understand why we would want to camp there, but she took us to the owner's house. The owner conceded that we could park in their lot for a fee, but she couldn't give us any electricity or water. We felt like we were putting them out by being there, so we drove to the place next door that also had an enormous parking lot. Here we were made to feel very welcome and enjoyed dinner with the owner. She didn't charge for parking there overnight.

ABOVE: There was a high diving board over deep water of five Blues Lake
RIGHT: The National Assembly Building, Belmopan, Belize

Day 94
Thursday, April 17,
The Baboon Sanctuary in Bermudian Landing

We made a good start in the morning and were turning off the highway onto the dirt road for the Baboon Sanctuary before eight thirty. The turn-off is just south of Big Boom Bridge. I love the names around here. There were some pleasant places to park under the trees at the riverside next to the Olde River Tavern, just before the town of Barrel Boom. It would have been tempting to stop for a beer had it been later in the day.

The names of some of the towns in the conservancy are charming, like Double Head Cabbage.

The first sign we were in baboon country was the rope ladder slung across the road between high trees. The road had been cut through the forest, creating a wide break in the trees. Bridges had been constructed overhead so that the primates would not be forced to go down to the ground to get to the river for water.

We went to the park headquarters and met with a gentleman who introduced himself as Fallet Young; he made us feel very welcome. It turns out that Fallet was one of the original organizers of the baboon project. He was adamant that our motorhome would be safe wherever we parked, and we should just look for shade. Our friends, Carol and Bill, told us of an incident that illustrated Fallet's determination that visitors and their belongings remain safe. They had their battery charger stolen from their rig while parked at the park headquarters. Fallet was quite upset and questioned everyone in town until it was returned.

The Community Baboon Sanctuary is an progressive enterprise. The primates aren't really baboons, but a variety of black howler monkey found only in Belize. The neighboring communities have agreed not to burn any more of the forest around their farmland, thus preserving the land of the black howlers.

The locals realize that, if nothing else, there is good money to be made through tourism if they can keep the monkeys around. To get over a hundred and fifty farmers to agree to this voluntary program is an amazing accomplishment. It is now managed by local women, which appealed to my feminine nature.

Fallet recommended that we get a guide for a tour, and later go on a boat ride. We followed his advice and were happy to make a contribution to an organization like this by paying for the services of the locals. We left Brindle with the motorhome so she wouldn't scare the animals. We hadn't gone more than a couple of hundred yards when we came upon a troop of black Howlers. They were clambering around some cashew trees. We went into the shade under the trees where our guide picked a ripe fruit and offered it to a male that was close. The animal climbed down through the branches and took the bright yellow fruit. John was offered the same opportunity and fed one of the monkeys. These animals were obviously used to humans.

There was a young lady watching what was going on and we began a conversation. She was working on her doctorate, studying the monkeys. She was trying to gauge their health, and the best way to do that without the traumatic experience of capture, was through a stool sample. She was waiting for the

opportunity. We learned that the animals would not normally come to the ground, but a couple had scampered across the path, illustrating how their behavior has been modified by the presence of humans. Of course our feeding them was a clear example of this.

We walked further through the undergrowth and our guide picked more ripe cashews. I thought it was to tempt other baboons to approach us, but he ate them all himself. At one point we heard someone calling. It turned out to

LEFT: A sign for a baboon bridge to the river. It is a rope ladder that is strung high over the road, so the animals can cross without descending.
TOP RIGHT: Some of the communities that have combined to create the Community Baboon Sanctuary
RIGHT: In Belize they call the native black howler monkeys "baboons". This one is enjoying a cashew fruit.

be Fallet. He had come after us on a bicycle because we hadn't prepaid for the canoe ride; he needed the cash to get the tour confirmed. It was amusing to see him pedaling off down a jungle path on his bicycle.

We did see another troop of monkeys but they were high in the trees where they were meant to be. Wandering along the river, we learned a little more about the plants and the 200 species of critter that live in the area.

Leonard, our canoe guide, was waiting when we returned to the park head-quarters. He led us down to the Belize River. If you have seen this river in Belize City, where it doubles as a sewer, you would not believe how pretty it is upstream. It is a big wide river, deep in places, that meanders all over the place, always inviting a swim.

Leonard entertained us with stories, information on the area, and songs, as he

paddled us along. In shallow areas we would hop out of the canoe. The swim-ming was glorious for the four of us. The guide insisted that the local crocodiles don't bite!

Any bottled color my hair once showed was almost grown out after three months. My now gray hair was far too long and out of control. Leonard said his cousin could braid it in corn-rows for me. As soon as we returned to the motorhome he took me to her house. Leonard's cousin, Sarah, was lounging in the front yard, happy to see a customer. I've never had my hair done in these tight little plaits before, and it was quite painful. Sarah had only done half when I felt the cool air on my head. What a difference it made. I was so much cooler that I didn't care what I looked like. When I looked at myself

---

ABOVE: Canoeing on the Belize River.

later I was quite pleased; I actually liked the look. Unfortunately, it only lasted a week because my hair wasn't long enough and it just didn't hold. It was worth it though. Her work had cost $5, a small fraction of what it would have cost in Houston. Besides, we wanted to contribute what we could to the community.

We headed back down the dirt road to the Northern Highway and up to the border town of Corozal. In Corozal, we headed for the only campsite in town, and were looking forward to filling up with water and emptying our tanks. When we pulled in, three large dogs lunged at the motorhome in such an aggressive manner we didn't think any of us could get out. Brindle would certainly not be welcome. The whole place had the appearance of a used car dump with scrap metal and broken cars lying all over the place. We didn't even stop, but drove right through and out the other side.

Almost opposite, on the Caribbean side of the road, was a park with a grass lawn and the waves breaking behind a low wall. We drove onto the grass and made ourselves at home. Once again we had an expansive water view from our window; this time it was the sweeping Bay of Corozal.

Day 95
Friday, April 18, Back to North America

This was Good Friday, and there was no telling what the traffic would be like at the border crossing. *Semana Santa* is the biggest holiday travel time when most of Central America goes visiting. We had no choice but to either sit where we were, and wait it out, or get into line and wait. We might as well wait in line. Hoping to beat some of the crowds, we left camp early and were at the Belize

crossing before seven thirty. We needn't have hurried. The border was deserted.

Apart from the money-changers, we were the only people not in uniform in this new building. We cleared immigration and then went to clear the motorhome at customs. As frequently happens, they put an entry stamp in one of our passports and if we left the country without the vehicle we would have to pay duty on it.

A coach load of European tourists arrived but we were ahead of them.

We had crossed this same border twenty-seven years earlier. At that time the customs building was literally a wooden shack. I don't know how many generations of customs buildings followed, but this one was really lovely. Even the detention cell looked attractive.

Between the two countries there is a very large duty-free zone, used mostly I believe by Mexicans wanting electronics and the like. It was closed for *Semana Santa*. We almost damaged the motorhome on a wild speed bump on the approach to the bridge. Too late we remembered one of the four other motorhomers we met telling us how they broke their suspension on this bridge bump. Fortunately we were OK.

We already had the correct sticker on our windshield from our southern pass through Mexico and all our paperwork was still in good order. We only had to show it to the authorities and the vehicle was in. Then it was simple to fill out the form and get our passports stamped. We decided not to mention the dog and see what happened. Nothing happened. Several different officials saw her but no one said anything. I wouldn't cross into Mexico without the USDA papers, but they didn't seem to care about the dog on either of our entries.

As so frequently happens there was yet another authority to appease before we could drive off. Leaving the *aduana* area, men in army fatigues flagged us down and told us they needed to look inside the motorhome. They leaned in the two front windows, and a handsome young soldier put his hand out to Brindle and asked if she was friendly. I said "un poco bravo," and she snarled appropriately, baring her teeth. The soldier and his friend satisfied themselves with walking around the exterior of the vehicle and looking in the windows. They waved us on and we left. Thanks Brindle.

We drove away into Mexico thirty-five minutes after we had arrived at the border. That must be a record: half an hour to do a border crossing. We didn't want to drive without insurance in Mexico, and tried to buy it, but all the offices were closed. That was the only down side of crossing on Good Friday.

Back on the main road we passed under a sign that read:

MEXICO

NORTH AMERICA.

HAVE A SAFE TRIP / FELIZ VIAJE

I thought that was very nice of them. Two miles farther up the road we came to the place where they spray the vehicle for bugs. There is always one more border crossing formality than you expect.

We had avoided buying any gasoline in Belize where it was $3.60 a gallon, and now we needed a fill-up. We were told that there were no gas stations on the road west, so we went out of our way and drove into the town of Chetumal. Actually there were plenty of gas stations on the road to Villahermosa.

The scenery west was dull, to say the least. In past years it had been a long straight road through dense jungle. Now it was a long straight road through scrub that didn't seem to be used for anything. Some was pastureland and there were acres that were recently burned for future use. Then we came into sugarcane country. The land was flat with rippling hills. When we went over a rise you could see the road for ten miles in front and in the rear vision mirror you could see back another ten miles. We'd then come to a bend and there would be another straight stretch ahead. This went on for a hundred miles or more.

We saw the tall pink trees that our guide, Leonard, in Belize had called mayflower. An elderly gentleman, to whom we gave a lift, called them *San Diego*. None of the local buses were running during the holiday so we gave a few people rides.

The yellow trees were lovely and they were everywhere, lots of them. There would be a dozen in a pasture with a herd of cattle lying among the fallen blossoms. These trees had no leaves at that time of year, so the dark branches sweeping upwards and out were silhouetted against the sky, and showed black against the blossoms. The flowers were trumpet shaped and hung by fistfuls at the ends of the twigs. They had a wonderful airy feel to them while scattering various shades of pink blossoms across the pastures and the road.

There were a few little clusters of Mayan homes with their thick, palm-thatched roofs, supported by cane walls with plenty of ventilation to let the air through. These homes were interspersed with tin huts of the same design with corrugated roofs. Some were of rough hewn-wood planks with corrugated roofs. I thought the ancient design would have been cooler.

About three hours out of Villahermosa, we hit an area of heavy smoke. It didn't affect the driving but cut the visibility down so the hills and the trees were obscured. This smoke stayed with us into the city and through the night.

Brindle was off her food, and, although she was behaving normally, we were becoming concerned about her. We began to watch her more closely.

Our campsite was the unappealing parking lot of the Carrefour Super Store in Villahermosa. We went into the supermarket to restock the perishables, but they didn't sell fresh milk.

Fortunately, once we are inside our little home with the blinds closed, it doesn't matter where we are.

Day 96
Saturday, April 19, Putting on Miles on the Mexican Toll Roads

We could still smell the smoke in the air when we woke up. The exit from Villahermosa was down an attractive tree-lined boulevard with little stalls along the way, mostly selling bananas and plantains, varying in size from ones that looked like chubby little fingers to twelve inch giants. All were in various shades of green and yellow.

Banana fields began to replace the barren pastureland, and the ranchland became much greener. There were also those lovely pink San Diego trees coloring the landscape. The haze of smoke again obscured the view of the distant hills.

We decided to splurge and take the toll road to Veracruz. Not only was the route shorter, but smoother, by passing as it did the (interesting) towns with their painful speed bumps and potholes. On the toll road we kept up a steady 55-60 mph and had a much more relaxing trip.

It wasn't an easy decision as the tolls are exorbitant. All together this short cut cost us $59.50 in tolls, but we calculated that it saved us a whole day. Today we drove 402 miles.

After the toll road we headed back to the Emerald Coast, where we knew there were plenty of campsites. We just hoped they would not be full on this holiday week. Turning a corner, and coming over a hill, we suddenly were faced with the ocean and a long white beach. We had reached the Emerald Coast! As we approached the town of Casitas, the traffic picked up just as suddenly. The town had its seaside decorations up with strings of T-shirts, colorful inflated floating devices, beach towels and cooler boxes for sale. Little *comedores* with new sunshades were selling refreshments, and chicken was being barbequed on fifty-five gallon drums.

The traffic became heavy, all of it going north into Casitas. *Semana Santa* holiday-makers were returning from the beach and heading to town for the evening. Everyone from all walks of life seemed to be taking time off, and the schools were having their spring break. Every car was packed to the gills with passengers, luggage, chairs, and beach equipment. There were little VW bugs with six people stuffed inside and a load of luggage on top. There were stake trucks and cattle trucks filled with fifteen or twenty happy holiday-makers, standing with bundles of luggage or beach gear. There were people wrapped in towels and others in new Easter finery. It was a long slow string of stop and go traffic, traveling at about ten miles an hour. We were happy to go slowly because we were looking for a campsite. We were occasionally nudged off the road onto the shoulder so an impatient driver could get one vehicle ahead. It was mostly friendly and slow, and everyone was happy and relaxed.

We found a trailer park, and it was absolutely chock-a-block full. When we came south three months earlier, we were excited when we saw one RV anywhere along the Emerald Coast. Now this campsite was full of tents, and there were three RVs from the U.S. We decided to go in and check on the situation in general. It was six o'clock and we needed somewhere to park soon, after our long day. The sun was low in the sky.

John had hardly walked twenty feet down the drive, when he was met by the manager, who welcomed John and showed him a space between two tents. It all looked like chaos. There were tents and tables, children, and inflatable beach toys; clotheslines of towels and swimsuits overflowed everywhere. But everything

was actually within designated spaces. Many had electric hook-ups, as we noticed later when the lights and TVs went on.

We parked so the motorhome was not directly under any of the hundreds of coconut palms and walked to the beach. A few hardy families were having their last dip as twilight fell and mothers folded towels in the wind, sand flying as they did. There was a bar next to a swimming pool full of kids. We tested the quality of their piña coladas. We sat by the swimming pool watching the activity, as it grew dark.

There was no sunset as the smoke haze completely obscured the sky. We could not see the full moon, nor the stars. The dog coughed and sneezed every time she stepped outside, and my eyes itched. We grew accustomed to the smell of smoke. It was cool and clear when we were on the Emerald Coast

three months earlier, before the dry season burning set in. The rainy season should start soon and, if nothing else, it will put out the fires and clean the air.

It was hot and muggy, so we set the table up outside to cook. Being only a few feet from the other tents, conversations soon began with passing adults and children. Many people settled down to sleep outside on air mattresses, to take advantage of any little passing breeze. All manner of blankets and tarps were strung up for shade and privacy, but most people had decent tents and camping equipment. John pointed out that many of the cars had come all the way from Mexico City for the holiday.

The dog was lethargic and stayed very close to us. Then she threw up. We were getting worried. She had survived three months in the mountains, jungles and beaches of Central America, but she seemed to be having problems dealing with the trappings of civilization.

Our fellow campers had had a lot of sun and water time and were tired. A sun-baked quiet settled over the camp quite early.

Day 97
Sunday, April 20,
Last day in Mexico and a Sick Dog.

We woke up to the unusual feeling of people close around us. They moved about quietly breaking camp and packing up. When I went out to take pictures, the crowd of cars and tents had thinned out measurably and the multitude of flapping towels had been taken down.

We decided to forgo a walk along the beach in the hope that the air would improve further north. The air seemed

LEFT: Neptuno Campsite on the Emerald Coast, Mexico. This is as busy as it gets for Samana Santa

worse this morning. We wanted to get as far north through Mexico as we could.

The dog was not well. We thought we could be home in a couple of days and hoped we could take her to her own vet. She was completely off her food and lethargic. She had thrown up the night before, and now had diarrhea. She was climbing up on our laps, a sure sign that she was unhappy. She had done this when she first rode in the motorhome and was unsure about the rattling. Once she was comfortable she was all over the place, if not sitting up on her blanket on the couch. Now she was climbing on our laps again as though trying to tell us that something was wrong. It added urgency to our travel.

Today we decided to count the *topes, vibradores,* or speed bumps, whatever you want to call them. Sometimes they came in groups, and most of the time they were sign-posted, but sometimes they were not. Sometimes they trick you and say there is one and there isn't. Sometimes there is an unpainted one right out of the blue with no sign at all. One like that caused me to break a cup this day, on the bypass around Tampico. It opened the cutlery drawer on the uplift, and at the same time it threw a plastic bottle out of the sink, which landed in the cutlery drawer before it closed again. We came across other dangerous unmarked *topes* in Cerro Azul. You can drive over the little ones at about ten miles per hour. The big ones you have to stop at and climb over. Frequently, another vehicle takes advantage of you at a *tope,* and whips past. *Topes* are usually in the towns and villages, just when there are a lot of other things to look at. Anyway these *topes* are nasty things. Today we went over 291 in 107 miles. That is almost two a mile.

And this is the main coastal road. You can see that they tend to get annoying.

Apart from the *topes,* the road was good, with most of the traffic coming against us filled to overflowing with holiday-makers. I've never seen so many VW bugs. We counted seven people in one with Mexico City plates and argued over whether there was an eighth person. That is a long way to travel in a bug with that many people.

Farmers in traditional dress were working the fields, or walking beside donkeys laden with bundles of grass. The men wore pajama-like pantaloons, full white blouses and Stetson-style straw hats and they carried the ever-present machete. The locals seemed incongruous with the carloads of holiday-makers with beach toys and towels in the open backs of pickup trucks. VW beetles came flying toward us, with bundles wrapped on top as high again as the car, their strings flying and fabric flapping.

A dozen people could be seen standing in the backs of stake trucks, hanging on and laughing and having a great time. Then there were pickup trucks with built-in metal bars to hold onto, sometimes with covers to shade the people sitting in the back. Whole families would be crowded in. I could see them eating watermelon or oranges as they overtook us. Children, parents, and grandparents were having a party in the back of the truck. These were not unusual sightings, but quite the norm. Well, the seven or eight in the VW Beetle was a bit unusual.

ABOVE: Revelers cooling off on Easter Sunday. Notice the haze of smoke.

Citrus groves gave way to fields with various crops, and then there was not much besides pastureland. When we had been driving south, with clear skies and the excitement of our adventure ahead of us, the scenery had not been very interesting. Now it was downright dull. Well, when seen through clear eyes you could say it was pleasant cattle country. The smoke was ubiquitous. You could see it all the time on the horizon, and then when you stepped out of the vehicle, the smell hit you. The flat range-land disappeared into the smoldering air.

This was Easter Sunday and, although we didn't see any religious celebrations, we did see people enjoying themselves. At a wide, sandy river there were tents on both sides providing cool spots to buy beer and food. There were cars parked close to the water on the hard-packed gravel and sand. Hundreds of people were in the water and playing on the beaches wandering in and out of the water fully clothed. They didn't seem to notice the omnipresent smoke in what otherwise would have been a bright sunny day.

We followed the bypass around Tampico, taking the shortest route back to Matamoros and Brownsville. We turned off Hwy 80 as it headed east, and took Hwy 180 directly north. From our southward journey we knew that there were no official campsites on this road, so we began looking for somewhere to stop. It was half past six when we saw a little *comedor,* or food stand, in front of a house within a large fenced dirt area. We pulled up and John, in his most polite Spanish, asked if we could stay next to the food stand for the night. We were immediately invited to come inside the fence and they moved barrels and things to make it easier for us.

The extended family lived in two houses and had numerous children. Of course the children were curious about us, so I got the balloons out and made a balloon sculpture for each child. Then, realizing that this was going to be our last night in Mexico, we pulled out all the other gifts we had brought. The school-aged children all received pens and we gave our last soccer ball to the eldest boy. Unfortunately, he immediately broke the little pump we had brought to go with it, but his dad assured us that they could blow it up at the school. School was out for the Easter break so he would have to wait to use his new soccer ball. We went to the *comedor* for our dinner, and they cooked us what I think was the only thing on the menu: tasty little burritos served with soft drinks. We ate several and probably made pigs of ourselves. It was an enjoyable way to thank them for letting us park on their property.

Day 98
Monday, April 21, Back to the USA

We awoke to continued smoke haze and a sick dog. She had not eaten overnight. I couldn't tell if she had drunk any water. We were only a day out of the U.S., but we needed to stop at the first vet we could find. We said good-bye to our new friends, and set off early into the smoky haze, with the dog curled up on my lap.

We didn't think any vet's office would be open before nine, and we didn't want to stop in a small village. We needed a vet familiar with small animals, not just cows and horses.

Soto La Marina was the first town of any size that we came to, and we immediately started looking for *veterinario* signs. We saw one and crossed over the road. I went in but it appeared that they were just selling saddles and horse tack. I explained that I had a sick dog and needed help. I was told I needed *un medico,* which I thought sounded more like a doctor, but I was assured that it was a *medico* that we needed and I was given explicit directions.

We backtracked and went down a short alley. There were no signs but we went to the open door. It was the back of another feed and tack shop. We told them our problem and a man immediately followed us out and into the motorhome, insisting that the dog should stay where she was. He listened to John describe her symptoms and said that she had an infection. He didn't touch her beyond a casual stroke. He then went to the pharmacy for medication and returned a few minutes later. We were to give her a shot once a day and pills twice a day. He also gave us a tube of something like molasses that he said was a general vitamin boost. He gave her the first shot and left us with a spare syringe and a couple of extra needles. Neither of us had ever given an injection before.

Brindle threw up again. She couldn't keep anything down, not even water. All we could think of was to get home to our vet as fast as we could. To get her this far, and to lose her at the very end of the trip would be terrible.

There were giant yucca plants along the way that looked like the Joshua trees from California. Along the side of the road, there were shrubs that we had not noticed coming south, but now that there had been rain they were covered in pretty white flowers with five petals. The cattle didn't eat them, or perhaps they were more interested in the emerging grass. As we progressed north we came to the yucca and sage that we are familiar with in Texas.

It was the middle of evening rush-hour by the time we reached the border town of Matamoros. There were no signposts when we needed them, and we went in circles before we found the border crossing. We did the exit paperwork for Mexico in the same room where we had been processed into the country three months earlier. The challenge was getting an official to come to the vehicle to remove the sticker.

We were already in line to the U.S. before I remembered the syringes. All I could do was to hope that would believe us that they were for the dog, and wouldn't think we were a couple of junkies.

The line was short, and in no time the immigration officer was asking, "What is your citizenship?"

"American" John said. I passed him my green card, which classes me as a resident alien. He looked at the card and passed it back.

"Do you have any fruits or vegetables?"

I leaned across John and started to list the vegetables in the fridge, "Two carrots, three onions…" He stopped me with a dismissive wave and directed us on to the secondary inspection area.

We expected this. Now we would see what kind of inspection the United States would give us. The motorhome was about as dirty as it could be. It was covered in caked dust and mud from eight different countries. John had worked hard on perfecting our long list of items we were bringing back with us, and had it available on his Palm Pilot. There were a variety of crafts, which I wasn't worried about, but I didn't want to lose the cans of beer that we had collected for our daughter. We had a couple from each country and some, like the one from Belize with the dude in dreadlocks on the label, were colorful and fun.

Then there was the dog. I just hoped all her papers were in order and that there wasn't some quarantine that we didn't know about. She didn't look sick to the casual eye but she was, and would not pass a veterinarian's inspection.

We were directed to a very large shed that was open at each end. The next uniformed agent asked John for his passport and told him to park behind the van ahead. He told me to get out and to wait in the corner where there were some plastic chairs.

"What about the dog?" I asked.

"Take any cats and dogs you have and go over there with them." I don't know why I brought her up but I suppose it was because I didn't want a customs officer to meet her head-on when he opened the door. Clutching Brindle's file of papers in one hand and her leash in the other, I left John to drive off into the shade of the great barn. A minute later he joined me and we waited, the sick dog lying miserably at our feet.

We became aware of a strange mechanical noise, and then saw a ten-foot arm gliding vertically along a track beside the vehicles. We decided that it was x-raying or scanning in some way.

The officer came towards us, returned John's passport and told him to drive on. We climbed back in and proceeded. I was still clutching the dog's papers, looking for the next official stop. The road opened up and looked like the freeway. It was a freeway.

"Is that it?" said an amazed John. "It can't be."

"There must be a stop further along to check inside the bus, check over the dog's papers or at least spray us with

noxious insecticide." Nothing. We were bewildered by the lack of formalities.

"There's a McDonalds. We **must** be through!"

We kept driving. We were half way through Brownsville before we were convinced that we weren't going to be pulled over by just one more uniformed officer.

No one had even asked us about the dog. Don't take this as the norm, as we have heard horror stories about people without proof of rabies shots trying to return to the U.S. Perhaps with the heightened security they had more to worry about than a dog.

We stopped for gas and a milkshake. Ahhhh, a real milkshake at last.

As night fell we relaxed, confident that there were no more unexpected *topes* to slow us down. We set the cruise control at 55 and headed home.

Day 99
Tuesday, April 22, Home!

We had been driving for 15 hours and home was still two hours away. It was midnight. Neither of us felt tired. We let the speed creep up closer to the less fuel-efficient sixty miles an hour. The eighteen wheelers we were driving alongside looked exactly like the ones we had been driving with for the past three months. Were they the same vehicles?

The midnight sky was clear and we were both surprisingly wide-awake. There was no question of stopping. It was easy driving and we covered six hundred and twenty-seven miles that day.

"John." I said. "Where do you want to go next?"

"Um" I heard him grunt in the dark as he drove. "There are a lot of places we missed. I think I'd like to go back to Central America."

We pulled into our drive in Houston at two in the morning of April 22nd. We had been on the road 99 days and driven 8,398 miles visiting eight countries. It had been utterly wonderful.

So was my own bed!

I let the water run while I brushed my teeth.

I took a long shower.

I sat on the bed.

I lay on the bed and could stretch my arm up without touching the ceiling.

I lay on the soft inner-sprung mattress spread-eagle, like I was making a snow angel until John joined me.

We slept very well.

What a trip!

Postscript

At eight in the morning I was at our vet's office with Brindle. A full examination, a string of tests and $200 later, the vet came to the same conclusion the Mexican vet had reached for 150 pesos. She had an infection. The medication was better though. We had been giving her a sulfur-based medication which, although good at fighting the infection, tended to make dogs vomit. I'll vouch for that! After a string of pills for six days and expensive dog food, she was back to her full frisky self.

APPENDIX 1
Useful Information

THE FOLLOWING INFORMATION IS PROVIDED TO AID FELLOW TRAVELERS. Prices, border crossing procedures and other conditions are subject to change. We will update information on our web site, as it is obtained www.brindlepress.com.

FACTS AND FIGURES

Trip length: 99 days
Average time to cross border: About 2 hrs.
Maximum time to cross border: About 5 hrs.
(Honduras to El Salvador)
Minimum time to cross border: About 45 min.
(Belize to Mexico, and Mexico to USA)

Total Distance Driven: 8398 miles
Gasoline Used: 845.9 Gallons
(Avg. 9.9 miles/gallon)
Cost of Gas Purchased: $1782
(Avg. $2.17/gallon, or $.24 per mile)

Per Gallon Price:	
Mexico	$2.25
Guatemala	$2.31
Honduras	$2.29
El Salvador	$1.95
Nicaragua	$2.24
Panama	$2.18
Belize	$3.60
U.S.	$1.40

EXPENSES

The following is a breakdown of our expenses on the trip which John recorded faithfully on his Palm Pilot. We haven't included the initial "investment" in the motorhome or the minor repairs after we returned.

Type Expense	Comment	U.S.$
Gas	793 gallons	$1,782.00
Communications	Email, phone card, fax, satellite & cell phone	893.00
Lodging	Camping, parking charges & two hotel nights	771.00
Excursions	Admissions, tour guides, tours, boat rides	763.00
Food	Includes groceries and snacks	656.00
Souvenirs	Mostly Guatemala	635.00
Tolls	Road and bridge tolls, *mordida*	530.00
Eating out		532.00
Border Crossing Fees	Average $30 per border, fourteen crossings	423.00
Supplies	Includes two new tires	294.00
Pre-Trip: Visa and Dog Fees	Visa for U.S. citizen required in Panama and El Salvador, and all the dog papers. See "Dog" section for details	290.00
Language School	14 days Harriet + 10 days John. Includes all meals & accommodation	234.00
Cleaning & Repairs	Includes bike repair in Antigua, & all the flats	181.00
Taxis	Includes a ride from the Atlantic to the Pacific Ocean!	160.00
Medical (inc. dog)	Doctors & vet. charges and medications	87.00
Car Rental	2 days Jeep on Ometepe Island, Nicaragua	71.00
Incidentals	Such as laundry, copies, haircuts, car wash	65.00
Propane	Used for cooking, refrigerator	43.00
Bus fare		6.00
Postage		4.00
GRAND TOTAL		**$8,420.00**

BORDER CROSSINGS

Border crossing fees averaged $30 including tips to the border guides, and varied widely as shown in the following table. Two borders were free. These were the little used, off the beaten track borders.

Border Location	Cost
U.S. – Mexico (Brownsville)	$57.00
Mexico – Guatemala (La Mesilla)	17.82
Guatemala – Honduras (El Florido)	13.10
Honduras – Nicaragua (Las Manos)	0.00
Nicaragua – Costa Rica (Peñas Blancas)	37.71
Costa Rica – Panama (Paso Canoas)	22.75
Panama – Costa Rica (Guabito)	0.00
Costa Rica – Nicaragua (Peñas Blancas)	81.44
Nicaragua – Honduras (Guasaule)	52.32
Honduras – El Salvador (El Amatillo)	61.00
El Salvador – Guatemala (Anguiatú)	7.32
Guatemala – Belize (Melchor de Mencos)	10.00
Guatemala – Mexico (Corozal)	22.50
Mexico - U.S. (Matamoros)	40.00
Total	**$422.96**

VALUABLES AND SECURITY

We never had problems with thieves, vandals or the like. No one tried to break in nor was anything stolen from us or the motorhome. We were careful to find secure places to park or camp, we didn't drive or wander around at night and we avoided urban areas throughout the trip. We never parked overnight in a city other than next to the Balboa Yacht Club in Panama City, and at the Marriot Hotel in San Salvador. The dog was a good deterrent.

We took sensible precautions and always greeted people as friends. We were rewarded with overwhelming friendliness and honesty.

Valuables

Neither of us wore jewelry so we didn't present the opportunity to have it snatched. But there was no way we could blend in with the locals; we drove a motorhome and both of us are six feet tall. Valuables like computers, the satellite phone and other electronics were kept out of sight. If someone wanted to break into the vehicle there wasn't a lock in the world that would keep them out, and once inside, a lock would have attracted attention to where valuables were hidden.

Pickpockets and thieves are reported to frequent the more populated markets. John found a kid tugging on his backpack at San Francisco El Alto, Guatemala (day 18) but otherwise we had no problems. Common sense should be used in protecting wallets and other valuables in these public places. Keep valuables in your front pockets.

We had two bikes that were always securely locked on the front of our RV. Everywhere we went people wanted to buy the bikes, but they never tampered with them. We put the bike seats inside the motorhome. We had friends camping in El Salvador who left their bikes unlocked for a short time while they ran an errand. The bikes disappeared. We had other friends who left their passports and wallets exposed in the back of their car while they swam at a beach in Costa Rica. They were stolen. Another friend had his wallet stolen at knifepoint in broad daylight in Guatemala City. Poverty breeds theft. We used common sense and avoided situations which would be tempting. We minimized time in major tourist destinations, avoided large cities, kept everything of value hidden and/or locked at all times, and never carried large amounts of money or irreplaceable valuables.

We made it a rule that we each carried a full set of keys. There was a spare set inside the motorhome and a set hidden on the outside.

A scanner, colored printer and laminating paper to duplicate documents would have been useful. Whenever we flashed a colored copy of something, it was immediately assumed to be the original. In hindsight, if John had had a color copy of his driver's license, it would have made his life much easier.

We had copies of the vehicle title and our passports hidden in a safe place as well as the copies we had to hand out at every border. We also left a set of copies home with family just in case the entire bus went missing and we needed new passports.

Cash

We started out with about $1200 in various sized bills hidden about the motorhome. Some were hidden in a hollowed out book and more was put in an empty frozen orange juice container in the freezer. More cash was in an oatmeal carton with a false lid and oats on top. We also had ready cash in a peanut tub along with spare credit cards. If anyone nasty broke in or demanded cash from us we hoped that any one of the containers would appease them. Likewise, we tried to carry spare pocket cash we could offer to a bandit if we were approached away from the motorhome. It never happened.

We drew money from ATMs in the local currency, where and when needed. U.S. dollars were required at several of the border crossings. On many occasions we had to buy gas with cash. This is true throughout Mexico. If we had insufficient local currency, U.S. dollars were usually accepted even though the exchange rate was not good. Money changers hover at all the borders and their rates are not bad.

Credit Cards

Credit cards were hidden around the motorhome and we each carried one. We had credit cards and ATM cards in three different accounts, some in my name and some in John's. We would recommend taking at least two independent credit and ATM cards so that if one is lost or stolen, and you have to cancel the account, you have another account upon which to draw. This was useful when John lost his wallet (see Day 37) as we could still use one card to make purchases and get cash out with another. You might want to alert your credit card company where you will be traveling, to prevent them from blocking their use.

Driving

Driving was mainly on two-lane roads without shoulders! Bus and truck drivers overtake aggressively and you have to stay alert. Driving after dark is very dangerous because of vehicles without lights, livestock, pedestrians and potholes, to mention a few of the obstacles. There was not much traffic on the dirt roads so we could go at our own pace, which was sometimes about ten miles an hour. A flashing left turn signal on a highway seemed to indicate that the driver in front thinks it safe for you to overtake. It is always best to be cautious and not to hurry.

Insurance

Most of the time, except in Costa Rica and in Mexico, we were self-insured. We bought insurance in Guatemala, but it was only for up to $6,000 in "civil damages" and it cost us $100 for a month. After we returned we learned that Sanborn's in Brownsville might have been able to insure us for the entire trip. They accept applications for motorhomes and insurance is subject to approval. There is a charge for the application and you need a good record to qualify. Contact Mary Staves at Sanborn's Brownsville office. Telephone (956) 546-6644, or (800) 258-1658

Kirkbride/Regan bought full coverage insurance through AIG. They don't like to insure vehicles that are worth more than $50K but they insured theirs for $120K with a little pushing. It was expensive...about $8K for 6 months.

Mordida (Bribes)

Police in most countries were courteous and helpful. Fees at borders were generally accompanied by a receipt and were not outrageous. We have read stories about people being detained at borders while their RV or camper was emptied to check its contents. This did not happen to us. We had one uncomfortable experience at the El Amatillo border between Honduras and El Salvador which is a notorious rip-off place (see Day 84). You will find young guides at most border crossings that are anxious to lead you through. We found them most helpful and they were happy to accept a $4 tip for their services.

We were stopped in Veracruz for an illegal lane change. The cop let us go with $100 in his pocket. In retrospect, this was too much and we should have negotiated. (I was furious that John was so generous). Veracruz is notorious for this kind of problem with RVs. Following the bypass routes given in Churchs' book (see Bibliography) is good insurance. When the police in Nicaragua caught John driving without a license, we had the choice of returning to Managua 3-4 hours back to pay a $2 fine, or complying with the police request for $40. Harriet was stopped for driving with the bicycles tied to the front of the motorhome and she just refused to concede that this was illegal and in the end the police let us go. It seems to be a matter of who you are and who you are up against. A couple of motorhomers we met said that they just pretended not to understand anything and were allowed by the frustrated police to continue.

Locking Gas Cap

We had a locking gas cap. This prevented any distracted gas attendant from filling up our motorhome with the wrong kind of fuel. We also heard that less scrupulous attendants sometimes don't wipe the previous sale off the register before they start filling your vehicle. A lock gives you time to check the gas price and the zeroing of the pump before fueling starts. And, of course, it deters theft.

Overnight stops

All of our camping places and others recommended to us are included in the "Camping Places" section of this book. There are only a handful of trailer parks in Central America, so most nights were spent "boondocking", or parking without services.

Our goal was to arrive at a destination a couple of hours before sunset to allow the scouting out of possible camping sites. With one exception, we always asked a local about the safety of a place before boondocking. Many of the places we parked had a security guard, locally called a *vigilante,* working for the management. We made a point of introducing ourselves and tipping him. We slept in the vehicle every night except during our Guatemala home stay, and two nights in hotels.

Good candidates for overnight stays include: tourist attractions (e.g. ruins), balnearios (bathing resorts), beach parking areas, next to shops with the owner's permission, ranches and farms, public parks, city squares, fire stations and most importantly gas stations. The major gas stations (especially PEMEX in Mexico; Texaco and Shell in Central America) have large parking areas and operate like truck stops in the U.S. There is usually a guard who is happy to watch out for you for $1-2. Trucks may be parked alongside for the night. Sometimes there is power and water and even a shower available. It is a good idea to fill up with gas at a station, or eat at a restaurant, before asking if you can spend the night in their parking lot. If in doubt about a safe place to stay, you can ask at a local police station.

Often we would stop at a commercial establishment, however humble, and make some purchases. If the storekeeper seemed pleasant, and they always did, we would ask if it would be all right for us to stay nearby. Without exception they said yes, and usually went out of their way to make us more comfortable. Meeting the locals in this way was one of the pleasures of our trip. The only occasion we were declined was at the Butterfly Farm in Monteverde, Costa Rica, where the North American owner cited insurance reasons.

On three occasions we stayed at schools. The headmasters welcomed us and the kids were happy to talk to us "gringos." They were curious about the RV and our lives. We always made a hit with our balloon animals. We also had brand new soccer balls and ball point pens to hand out.

HEALTH

Consult your doctor before going to determine if you need any shots, and to stock up on medications, both prescription and over the counter. Although we did not suffer any intestinal problems, it was comforting to know that we had some powerful anti-diarrheal medicine that our doctor prescribed before we left. We also had a dose of antibiotics (Cipro) which proved useful.

John gets the credit for our lack of intestinal problems because of the care he took with the water purification (see below under "Motorhome and Systems"). We drank bottled water, but cooked and made hot drinks with the water straight from the tank. We also cleaned our teeth with tank water.

We did try to take our vitamins every day, but because of concerns over dengue fever we didn't take our usual 81 grams of aspirin. We understand the first signs of dengue fever usually come with a headache and the worse thing you can do for dengue is to thin the blood with aspirin.

We did find a couple of ticks on us that we thought had dropped out of trees.

Our worst problem was boils. We had never had them before and hope never to again. They were very painful. These "furuncles" are caused by bacteria that erupt initially at an ingrown hair or where skin is sweaty. We got them on our rear ends. John was prescribed ibuprofen and antibiotics and told to apply warm compresses. His visit to the clinic in Copán, Honduras cost the equivalent of $12.50 including antibiotics, and the ibuprofen was $2.90. I was duly sympathetic. About a week later I developed one that demanded much more sympathy! The doctor I went to lanced it and removed as much matter as she could with me writhing and gritting my teeth. There was no painkiller. When I stood up it immediately felt better and after a night on antibiotics I was myself again. The infection had been affecting my whole body and previously all I had wanted to do was lie down and die. My doctor in Estelí, Nicaragua cost $14.27 and medication was $6.67. We both had subsequent smaller boils but we kept them under control with hot compresses, ibuprofen as an anti-inflammatory, and antibiotics (Cipro). All were available over the counter at a fraction of the U.S. cost. The extreme hygiene measures we needed to take were not easy in a motorhome. It took about six weeks to completely get rid of the boils.

John found his clinic because it was listed on the tourist map for Copán. Mine was found on the main road where he saw the sign for a pharmacy *(farmacia)*, which also turned out to be a doctor's office. We were both quite happy with the service, hygiene, and the setup of our clinics, not to mention the price.

The importance of a good first aid kit was clear. We couldn't replace the gauze we used to cover the boils so used feminine pads cut to size. We were glad we brought plenty of antiseptic ointment. It would have been useful to have *Mayo Clinic's Medical Reference, Family Health Book* that we had left at home.

THE MOTORHOME AND SYSTEMS

Preparations

We had bought the motorhome second hand at a dealership six months earlier. It was our first and we had never driven one until we left the parking lot on the test drive! We wanted the smallest vehicle we could get and seriously considered a class B minivan. The down side of these is that as they are about twice the price of the class C, and have very skimpy wash and lavatory facilities, and almost no storage space.

We settled for a twenty two foot 1997 Coachmen Class C model. It had a 6.3L, V10 Ford engine that let us overtake going up the steepest grades.

We stuck to roads that a truck or bus had been on before us and we reasoned that if they could make it, so could we. The height (11.5-ft) was a challenge and we did snag some overhead lines when we were off the main roads. Others have made a similar trip in everything from a 38 foot Class A behemoth to a Volkswagen Beetle.

One of the features that sold us on this model motorhome was the large dining table. It could seat four and that was important since we were to be able to set up the computer and eat in comfort. We put a Central American map on it, under plastic, which we referred to all the time. The table could let down into a small double bed, as could the couch. The rig could sleep six, just.

The storage space was quite adequate. I cut boxes to size in the food cabinets so that the bottles and cans would not slip about and fall over. Driving on rocky roads and going over speed bumps all the time is different than driving on U.S. freeways. Very different. I had shoe boxes for various items and stackable plastic boxes that were invaluable for things like medical supplies, electrical equipment and the like. We stored fabric souvenirs and rugs under the mattress.

We took the RV to a mechanic and had him check it out. The belts and hoses were in good shape. We bought a new house battery and serviced the generator. We took small spare parts like belts and a good tool kit. If anything went wrong with the truck itself, local mechanics were more than qualified to fix it.

The tires looked good enough to get us there and back. Big mistake! We had six flat tires. In the future we will get all new tires! There are places everywhere to fix flats (look for the ubiquitous *"pinchazo"* signs). Two tires completely blew out and had to be replaced. One tire was punctured and two valves failed. Each repair cost a couple of dollars. The sixth flat tire was on a rental Jeep! A truck tire air compressor was essential. We topped up the tires many mornings. If you need to buy a replacement tire, try to do it in Panama City for price and availability. Otherwise, tires of the right size were only available in the capital cities. One time we found a Firestone dealer in Rio Hondo, Guatemala that ordered the correct tire from Guatemala City and had it delivered to our next stop, Rio Dulce, by bus. We had to pay in full upfront, but the tire arrived in two days.

We didn't get any of the interior motorhome systems like the fridge, air-conditioning, and heater checked. We just ran out of time before we left, besides those other excuses for not getting things done. Apart from the fridge locking up on us once and needing a defrost, we had no trouble with anything. This was a good thing as I don't think the locals would have been able to fix the complex propane-electric refrigerator.

There was a four-burner cook top and a gas oven. Because of the heat we only used the oven once. If I had the choice again I'd get a motorhome with a door at the back next to the kitchen for better ventilation. The twelve-inch fan was of little help. We had an adapter rigged to the propane tank so we could use a portable gas camp-stove for outdoor cooking.

Power

The microwave needed the generator or good city power to operate. We found the TV and VCR could operate on our 150 watt inverter. We bought a 500 watt inverter that never seemed to work properly. An inverter is invaluable for watching late night movies without the noise of a generator, but be sure not to drain your battery. Before using the inverter without the alternator or generator running, check the reserve capacity of your battery. This is the time, in minutes, that the fully charged battery can operate at 25 amps without an alternator. A typical car battery has a **reserve capacity** of around 100 minutes. Marine/RV batteries have reserve ratings of 120-400. A 150 watt inverter draws about 12.5 amps and would drain a battery with a reserve capacity of 100 in about 200 minutes. A movie could last this long! If you plan on using an inverter with the alternator off it would be best to invest in a battery with a high reserve rating. If the inverter is designed to use the cigarette lighter, adapt it to run off the house battery for more reserve.

We needed to crank up the generator if we wanted to air-condition the RV unless we had a good landline. The quality of land power varied considerably. Often, the voltage drop in our 15 amp extension cord was sufficient to prevent the microwave and/or air conditioning from working properly. We would recommend taking as a minimum a 100 ft. extension cord with a wire size of AWG 14 or larger, and a shorter extension cord for convenience. Electricity is 110 volt service throughout Mexico and Central America. However, many places have only the small two-slot outlets. Bring a two prong adaptor and have a ground wire with alligator clip attached to the adapter to close the circuit to ground on a pipe. Also buy a polarity tester and be prepared to reverse the adaptor if necessary.

Communications

Our primary communication was by email. We composed epistles on our laptop and pasted these into emails that we sent from internet cafes. These cafes are plentiful in the tourist locations and in major cities, albeit somewhat slow. We did not find any broadband locations. Telephone service is available in towns, but often not convenient. We used an Iridium satellite phone for calls. It was a good backup, but reception was not often clear and it was expensive ($1.50 per minute). Our Triband cell phone worked in El Salvador, Panama City and major cities in Mexico. You can rent cell phones that work in each country. This would be a good option if you're staying in one country for a while.

New technology is constantly becoming available and affordable. A group we know that toured Central America in 2004, used a DirecWay satellite dish. With a reasonably large dish (.74 meter), they are able to have broadband internet access and low cost phone service as far south as El Salvador and Honduras. Service below about 14 degrees latitude is not reliable at this time.

For low-tech communications we used a Grundig shortwave radio and were able to listen to BBC World Service most evenings. Frequencies can be found at: http://www.bbc.co.uk/worldservice/schedules/internet/800/radio_frequencies_caribbean.shtml

You need an outside antenna for best reception. A wire wrapped around the receiver's telescoping antenna extending outside is sufficient.

Water and Sanitation

Our fresh water tank holds 42 gallons. Although we ran short on occasions we never ran out. We used a Hydro Life® filter when filling the tank. This filter is supposed to remove most of the pathogens. We also super-chlorinated the water in the tank with a bleach solution in some areas such as Lake Atitlán where we heard there might be a problem. Bleach is available in most grocery stores and markets, and the proportions of bleach to water for super-chlorination are written on the bottles. Be sure to buy pure bleach without perfumes and additives. Although these steps should purify the water in the tank, we restricted ourselves to drinking bottled water (and beer and soda). Individual water bottles were sometimes hard to find so we refilled ours from the five liter containers that were readily available. We cooked with tap water and used it for coffee and tea.

We had a full shower and flush lavatory. Treated sewage was dumped at stations at trailer parks or into toilets when available. We only needed to perform five wayside dumps. They were done well away from populated or traveled areas, or water. We used Enviro-Chem® (containing Exosite), a product that breaks down the "bad" organisms in the sewage tank. It is diluted with grey water as it is dumped. Formaldehyde principally masks odor and slows or stops decomposition, so we didn't use that. Chlorine products such as Javex kill all bacteria including pathogens, but in so doing arrest decomposition, so we didn't want to use that either. Our expert in the field advised us that mixing the wastes that were treated with Exosite results in residue which is similar to animal wastes in a pasture and it will decompose naturally. It will decompose more rapidly in warm climates and without risk to human health if spread in dry areas away from streams or other waterways. We carried two fifteen-foot sewer hoses.

Propane

Propane will last a long time under normal circumstances but, if it is warm, the refrigerator can use it fairly quickly. Our refrigerator operated on 110 volt AC if we had power, or propane, otherwise. Propane (LPG) is readily available in most countries. Propane is sold in most villages in bottles, but for filling the tank in the RV you need to find a larger distributor. Here are a few locations we identified:

Mexico: We received propane from a truck at the Hotel Bonampak Trailer Park in San Cristóbal de las Casas, Chiapas. We saw a propane distributor at km marker 43, southeast of Villahermosa on highway 181.

Guatemala: There was a distributor on the road between Quetzaltenago (Xela) and Cuatro Caminos. Propane is readily available in this country.

Honduras: We filled at a Tropigas distributor in La Ceiba, on the highway across from the entrance to the airport (N 15° 45.738' W 86° 48.774'). We saw a second distributor four miles east of La Ceiba. Other distributors are in San Pedro Sula and Tegucigalpa.

Nicaragua: We saw a Tropigas distributor five miles southwest of Granada on the road to Nandaime, and on the Pan-American highway in Rivas, opposite the Shell gas station.

Costa Rica: There is a Tropigas distributor in San José (N 9° 56.970' W 84° 8.598'), two miles east of Sabana Park on the road to the suburb of Pava.

Panama: There is a Panagas distributor on the Pan-American highway, 39 miles from the Costa Rican border and nine miles east of David. We also saw Panagas and Tropigas distributors 25 miles south of Santiago.

Belize: Butane is used in Belize instead of propane. Butane won't vaporize if the temperature is below freezing, so don't use this if you expect to return to a cold climate with butane left in your tank. Butane was for sale two miles north of Orange Walk, milepost 57, on the Northern Highway.

DOG

We had lengthy debates as to whether or not we should take the dog with us. Besides the inconvenience there was the real possibility that something could go wrong and that we might lose her. We would take sensible precautions, but we were not going to keep her chained up or locked in the motorhome all the time either. We had been told that you could-n't take a dog into Guatemala, Panama and perhaps other countries. It would have been sad to have to turn around because of the dog. Also there would be places we would not be able to visit if we had her with us.

ABOVE: Brindle in alert mode in her favorite place in the motorhome

Brindle is a fixed bitch *(perra con operación)* of very mixed lineage. We found her at the Humane Society. She is three years old, medium sized, and weights about forty-five pounds. She is big enough to keep a stranger at bay while not too large for the confines of a small motorhome.

Getting the official paperwork needed for her to enter all seven countries and return to the U.S. was an interesting challenge. First I needed our veterinarian to check the dog, update her rabies and other shots and complete the official USDA form entitled *United States Interstate and International Certificate of Health Examination for Small Animals* (APHIS Form 7001). He charged $72 for this service. Then I needed an officer of the USDA to verify it. This could have been done by mail but we were lucky that there was a representative of the USDA in Houston. He charged $32 to authorize the form. If there isn't an office at your nearest international airport, call USDA in your state capital for local information.

I took the verified form to the consulates of each country we were to visit, for their approval. This was also a good opportunity to gather travel information and to confirm what was needed for us and the RV. By the time we left on the trip we had visited each consulate as many as four times. Some consulates needed to keep the papers for a few days.

The staff of some consulates said that the certificate would be invalid if it was over three days old. When I pointed out that we were driving, not flying, to their country, they shrugged and it didn't seem to matter any more. It was important to tell them that we were only passing through their country *(tránsisto)*, and not importing the animal.

We had to get the papers notarized twice. The first was for Honduras and the second was to satisfy the Nicaraguan consul. Nicaragua also required a letter from the State of Texas certifying that the notary was really a notary in the state. This second notary, knowing the game a little better, wrote her affidavit in Spanish which each agriculture border agent *(cuarentena)* read with interest.

The pages were later unstapled more than once by various border agents to run it through their copier machines, so when you think about it the whole thing was no longer legally notarized. However, it was exactly what we needed at each border.

Carrying plenty of cash in mixed denominations was important as the consulates did not have change. The consulates here in Houston required $10 to $25 for their endorsements, except for Honduras, that charged $80. The Honduran border agents later told us that we didn't need the $80 consulate stamp.

At the Mexican border the agents were not interested in the dog and didn't look at her documents. The documents were useful, if not essential, at all of the other border crossings. Only twice did an inspector ask to look at the dog, and one was satisfied peering through the window. Neither actually touched her. Everyone was friendly and we were often invited into an air-conditioned office and offered cool water while forms were examined and stamped. The *cuarentena* agents seemed bored, and happy for the novel diversion. In Honduras a child had recently been killed by a fighting dog, so if Brindle had been a pit bull there might have been a problem getting her into the country.

There is no Belizean consulate in Houston, so when we entered Belize we just showed the papers we had. We paid five dollars and received smiles, another stamp on the USDA form, and were through in five minutes.

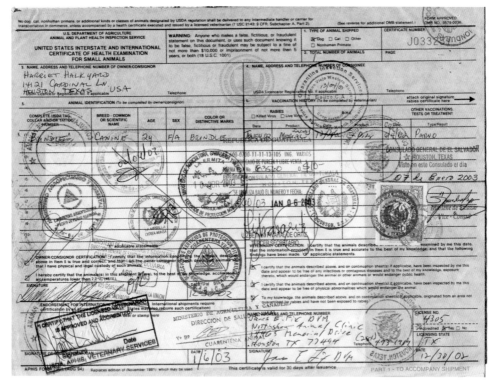

I believe, in most cases, all we needed at the border crossings was the USDA form, and to pay the border fees which ran from zero to twenty dollars. We always made a point of getting a receipt. If you do not get a country's endorsement beforehand in the U.S. and want to play it safe, you could visit the consulate of an upcoming country in the capital city of the previous country. There might be a need to visit a vet there as well. We never needed to do this.

At the borders of each country we were issued a *permiso* document to allow transit of the dog. In the future I would make a copy of this paper in order to simplify the procedure on the northbound entry into the country. Several of the agents had never filled out this paperwork before, and didn't even know what form to use. I made sure to have her exit noted on our USDA form on our way out of each country.

Rules change and the border officials have tremendous power so there are no assurances that the procedures we encountered will be the same next year

ABOVE: Top page of the USDA form after thirteen border crossings
RIGHT: Brindle on the battlements of the Spanish Fortress at Portobelo, Panama

or next week. However, all the agents seemed to want to help and only in Honduras were we given any limitations. There we had to be through the country in 14 days, but that limit could be extended if we stopped at the cuarentena office at an international airport.

We expected a hassle returning to the U.S., but the customs agents at Brownsville did not check Brindle or any of her papers. On previous visits with a dog to Mexico, we required proof of current rabies vaccination to return to the U.S.

Getting Brindle through the borders was just another bureaucratic stop that took from ten to sixty minutes, and sometimes an additional charge. Her papers now have more stamps than our passports. There are forty-five various stamps on all sides of each page including the carbons, five seals or stamps affixed to them and twenty-five signatures or initials that I can make out.

The major brands of dog food were available in the larger supermarkets, and there were pet stores in the major cities.

We found that most Central Americans were very wary of dogs. A sign reading *Perra Brava* (Dangerous Female Dog) was enough to keep everyone away. She also shortened police inspections. Once the dog started growling, armed *federales,* with formidable machine guns, no longer wanted to inspect the interior of the RV.

There were only a couple of times when we could not do as we planned because we had a pet with us. Costa Rica will not permit animals in their national parks, so we had to hunt a little harder for camping places, and we could not take her to Tikal, in Guatemala. We put her up in a vet's overnight when we worked as line handlers on a yacht transiting the Panama Canal.

Brindle is on a regular regimen of Sentinal® for heartworm and fleas and we never found a tick on her, even though we found them on ourselves. Next time I would ask my vet, in advance, for a supply of medication for a stomach infection and would keep a closer watch to see if she was off her food. She picked up a stomach infection towards the end of the trip which would have been hard to prevent, but would have been easy to remedy.

ABOVE: Brindle enjoying a canoe ride down the Belize River

When we were parked we opened an interior and exterior door to one of the storage lockers and this became the dog's passageway. Yes, a small person could have wriggled through it. However, knowing the general fear of dogs we did not feel that a local would risk finding himself in that vulnerable position facing an unfriendly Brindle. We took a calculated risk when we were comfortable with our location as regards the security of our equipment and the safety of the dog. It paid off.

All in all, we were very glad that we had taken Brindle with us. She made us laugh with her antics and she quickly learned that to stay with us she would have to jump into canoes and climb stepladders. She swam in both oceans and every river she found. She learned that pigs don't like to romp and that sheep will head-butt when disturbed. She also provided valuable protection. Judging by the way she races towards the motorhome at every opportunity, she can't wait for another trip.

LANGUAGE AND LANGUAGE SCHOOLS

English is rarely spoken in Central America except in the tourist areas. Belize is the main exception where English is the standard language. English is also spoken in the Garífuna villages dotted along the Caribbean coast. In some of the remote Indian villages from Panama to Guatemala neither English nor Spanish is spoken well. We are not fluent in Spanish, but from a combination of living near the Mexican border for many years, some high school Spanish (in John's case), many vacations in Latin America and a few weeks of "total immersion", we managed to communicate just fine. Being able to meet and communicate with the locals made the trip immeasurably more enjoyable and less stressful. We know others who have made a similar journey with far less conversational skills in Spanish, and they enjoyed themselves also. If you are planning an extensive trip through Latin America and have no Spanish skills, we recommend that you consider flying down to Costa Rica or Guatemala for 3-4 weeks of "total immersion" first.

Below are some of the Spanish language schools that we know of, and about which we have heard good reports. We have experienced "total immersion" training in both Costa Rica and Guatemala. Both have their advantages and disadvantages. Costa Rica has a well-developed ecotourism industry, but there is little indigenous culture. You will find it more comfortable and familiar, but more expensive and less of a "total immersion". Guatemala is rich in the Mayan culture, but the tourism industry is less developed.

Quetzaltenango, Guatemala, has few gringo tourists and very little English is spoken, which presents a good total immersion environment. The schools are in the quaint old section but there is also a modern area with malls and McDonalds a bus ride away. Nora and Rolando Herrera at the Guatemalensis Spanish School (gssxela@infovia.com.gt, +502-765-1384) were most helpful and promptly found us a family that would take us and the dog. They knew a secure place we could park our motorhome. The tuition for a single was $170 per person per week but as a couple we doubled up and the cost came down to $120 each. This included five hours of one-on-one instruction, lodging and three meals a day with our family. Guatemalensis used *Primer Libro, Spanish First Year* (by Robert J. Nassi and Bernardo Bernstein, Amsco School Publications, Inc) as their workbook. They made photocopies of various pages for me, but I wished I'd brought the book sitting on my shelf at home.

Antigua, Guatemala, is noted for its culture and total immersion Spanish schools. Our friends there recommended the Christian Spanish Academy (www.learncsa.com). It runs $195 per week for five hours of private instruction per day, and a home stay with a local family, including three meals per day. Antigua is charming and clean, and in the middle of very interesting places to see. Most of the people you will meet in town speak some English which may, or may not, be a good thing if you want total immersion.

Panajachel on Lake Atitlán, also in Guatemala, is beautifully situated and has numerous schools but we don't have first hand information about them. The location is hard to beat though. Regan/Kirkbride recommended *Jardín de las Americas.*

As a family we had done some total immersion in Costa Rica a couple of times on previous trips at **Centro Panamericano de Idiomas** (www.cpi-edu.com, anajarro@racsa.co.cr, phone 506-265-6866, fax 506-265-6213). It provides four hours of instruction a day with a maximum of four students per class for $340 a week. Five hours of daily instruction costs $420. This was about the norm for Costa Rica. CPI provide written materials and airport transfers. The branch in Monteverde is in some of the most fascinating tropical jungle in Central America. It also has campuses in Heredia, near San José, and Playa Flamingo, on the Guanacaste coast. Our daughter spent nine weeks at these venues and managed to receive U.S. university credits.

There are hundreds of other schools, and many in the same cities we have mentioned. Be sure to ask how many people will be in the class with you, and how many meals are included, as it does vary from school to school. Of course the prices we quoted may have changed as well.

You should also be aware that the Spanish spoken in Central America is not Castillian, or European Spanish. Spanish here is as different as English in the U.S. is from that of Great Britain. For example, when conjugating verbs they don't teach the second person, familiar plural in Central America. There are also discernible differences in the Spanish spoken in the Central American countries. When selecting where to do your Spanish immersion, you might want to consider where you are going to use it.

The experience you have will very much depend on the individual teacher and the family you live with. If you are not happy with either, immediately contact the school administration and request a change.

Take your own notebooks, pens and dictionaries. We also recommend *501 Spanish Verbs* by Christopher Kendris, published by Barrons as an invaluable resource.

We found each time we have gone it has been an educational experience in understanding the culture of another land as well as helping us learn the language. You can't beat the price for an all-inclusive vacation.

WHAT TO TAKE

I could find just about all the groceries I wanted in the *supermercados* throughout Central America. Belize was the least well-equipped country, even in the capital. Peanut butter was available but pricey (what we brought made a great gift for ex-patriates). We couldn't find our favorite salad dressing and what was available was expensive.

The meat in Central America was extremely lean and therefore tough. We were grateful for each piece of meat we took with us. Meat was available but I found it hard to buy a cut from an animal carcass hanging up in an open air market. I gave up on beef and went for the pork in the supermarkets and chicken in the *mercado*. We also ate a lot of eggs.

Apples were often available in the *mercado* and looked great and often had the same stickers we have grown used to. However, none that we bought were worth eating. It must be a lack of care in shipping.

Fresh milk was not always easy to buy so we kept some ultra-pasteurized box milk on hand. It lasts months without refrigeration.

I should have taken more paper towels as the locally-made ones were expensive and not very good, and of course the special, soluble toilet paper used in the motorhome was unavailable. We took loads.

We were glad we had the small crock-pot and the George Foreman grill. I could cook in the crock-pot as we traveled and dinner was ready when we arrived. It was invaluable for that tough meat, and it didn't add much to the heat of the motorhome. (Don't forget you'll need an inverter and a long extension cord.) The grill cooked quickly and produced little ambient heat. Next time we go we will take a bread machine as we couldn't find good bread south of Mexico.

Take a spirit level and install it inside near the driver's door so you can check it quickly when parking. Take 100 feet of hose for filling the water tank, and 100 feet of AWG 14 or larger electrical cord for power.

Cotton bath towels take time to dry. Washing wasn't always a problem but getting the things dry was a challenge. It is not always appropriate to hang out your washing and we didn't stay in one spot for very long.

The stick-on hooks we had installed dripped off in the heat and humidity, so we resorted to screw-in hooks.

We hardly used the bicycles and I would not take them again if I intended to keep moving as we did on this trip. However, next time we would like to go more slowly and spend more time in some areas and then they would be most useful.

We took heaps of books, books on tape, CDs and videos but hardly used any. We thought we would listen to books on tape and CDs while we were driving, but there was too much of interest outside the windows. We didn't get past the first chapter of *Murder on the Orient Express*. We watched just two video movies but we did enjoy the boxed set of M★A★S★H★. We were not usually up for a long movie, but a lighthearted half-hour was great. Twenty-four episodes lasted the whole trip. A medical reference book or CD would have been useful.

We brought seed packets to give away and they were a hit. We always carried them in our pockets, and could give them to just about anyone. Some were flowers but most were vegetables.

Soccer balls were good give-aways for families, schools and the like. Postcards and other pictures of home, and calendars with pictures are all very welcome handouts.

Check the weather for the time of year and the altitude you will be experiencing. We were surprised at how cold it was in the mountains.

Long sleeved shirts are useful to protect from insects and the sun.

If you are taking a digital camera and laptop computer, include a CD burner or external hard drive for backup. Take digital pictures at the highest resolution. We regretted not doing this.

Further information on what to take may be found above under "The Motorhome and Systems".

APPENDIX 2
Camping Places

T HE FOLLOWING LISTS CAMPING PLACES WE USED DURING THE TRIP AND others recommended by other travelers. Very few of these places are certified "campsites." Although we found each place safe, and for the most part enjoyable, we cannot guarantee that they will even be available when you arrive. One of the pleasures of the trip was finding new locations, and we would certainly like to hear about new campsites that readers find. Send updates to updates@brindlepress.com. We will post updates on our web site at www.brindlepress.com.

Most campsites are boondock parking places, which means there are no services. We have indicated services, if any, as Ⓦ Ⓔ Ⓓ (Water/Electricity/Dump).

Refer to the maps at the beginning of each country for reference to the day we arrived at a new camp. If we stayed in the same camping place for more than one day, only the first day we stayed there is indicated for reference. The extremely rough roads, where the average speed was 10-15 miles per hour, are indicated as dashed lines on the maps. Costs are in U.S. dollar equivalents. Our thanks to Bill Cone, Carol Kulish, Kathe Kirkbride and Colleen Regan for providing data on additional camping places.

U.S.A

Day 1 Raymondville, Texas. Wal-Mart Parking Lot. Hwy 77 Freeway off ramp. $0.

Mexico (Day 2 - 10, 95 - 97)

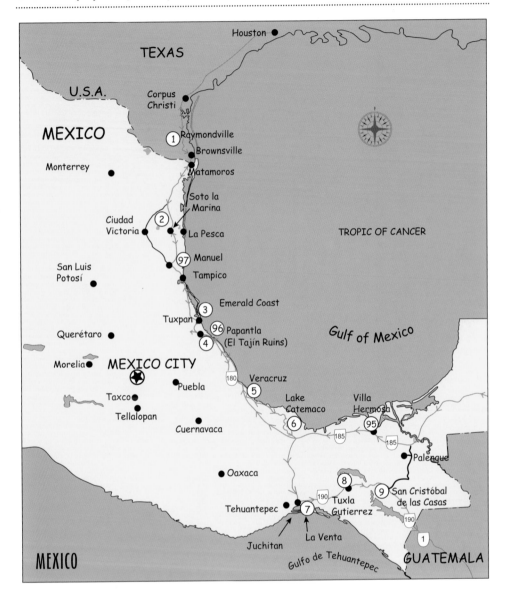

HOUSTON

TEXAS

U.S.A.

MEXICO

Monterrey

Corpus Christi

① Raymondville

Brownsville

Matamoros

Soto la Marina

Ciudad Victoria ② La Pesca

San Luis Potosí

⑨⑦ Manuel

Tampico

TROPIC OF CANCER

Emerald Coast

③ Tuxpan

⑨⑥ Papantla (El Tajín Ruins)

④

Querétaro

Morelia

MEXICO CITY

Puebla

Gulf of Mexico

Taxco

Tellalopan

Cuernavaca

180 Veracruz

⑤

Lake Catemaco

⑥

Villa Hermosa

⑨⑤

185

185

Palenque

Oaxaca

⑧

190 Tuxla Gutierrez

⑨ San Cristóbal de las Casas

190

Tehuantepec ⑦

Juchitan

La Venta

MEXICO

Gulfo de Tehuantepec

GUATEMALA

1

Day 2 North of Soto La Marina, Tamaulipas. Cafeteria Ojo de Agua. (N24:13.218 W98:12.504) $0. Route 180 between Km markers 201 and 202. 144 miles south of Matamoros (about 3 1/2 hours). **Comments:** Barren highway with not many stops. The owner of this store allowed us to park behind the restaurant. **Other Sites:** There is a trailer park at **La Pesca**. Adventuretours stops at La Gata Camp in **Soto La Marina** (Starcher). See day 97.

Day 3 Tuxpán, Hidalgo. On the beach (La Playa). $0. Take Route 180 into Tuxpán, and follow signs for La Playa. **Comments:** We bypassed Tampico and tried to reach Poza Rica. Look for a small stand selling refreshments, with a packed sand drive beyond it passing between houses to the beach parking lot.

Day 4 Monte Gordo, Emerald Coast, Hidalgo. Trailer Park Quinta Alicia. Ⓦ Ⓔ Ⓓ $10. Route 180 between Poza Rica and Nautla; Km marker 84, just north of Monte Gordo. **Comments:** A fine place with full hookups. We had it to ourselves. A large caravan was staying up the road at Hotel Playa Paraíso campsite. **Other Sites:** There are numerous campsites all along this beach. (See Day 96)

Day 96 (return) Monte Gorda, Emerald Coast, Hidalgo. Trailer Park Neptuno (N22:48.856 W98:17.896). Ⓦ Ⓔ Ⓓ $13. Six miles north of Nautla near km 81 marker. On Route 180. **Comments:** Swimming pool **Other Sites:** Numerous trailer parks along this beachfront road

Day 5 Veracruz, Veracruz. Balneario Mocambo. Ⓦ Ⓔ Ⓓ $15. South of city center on Boca del Rio, behind the Hotel & Balneario Mocambo. **Comments:** Extra charge for electric hookups. **Other Site near Veracruz** (Courtesy Carol Kulish) **Playa Chachalacas, Veracruz.** $0. North of Veracruz about 30 miles where Route 180 joins Route 140. Follow signs to Playa Chachalacas and watch for signs to the Playa, about 5 more miles. This is close to

the Zempoala archeological site. See http://www.playachachalacas.com/ **Comments:** No services. Busy place until dark, lots of stands and boat rides available. Watch for soft sand.

Day 6 Lake Catemaco, Veracruz. Trailer Park La Ceiba. Ⓦ Ⓔ Ⓓ $15. Take main Catemaco entrance off Route 180 next to Pemex station. Turn right just before arch. 0.5 mile down hill turn left on the malecón (jetty). The trailer park is on your left in 0.1 miles.

Day 7 La Venta, Oaxaca. Refresquería Lolita. $0. There is a turn south to La Venta off Highway 190, about 12-15 miles east of the intersection with the cross isthmus road, 185, at La Ventosa. The store of Sra. Dolores Giren Carrasca is on the right just before the town square. **Comments:** See write-up for our nice experience here.

Day 8 Ocozocoautla, Chiapas. Hogar Infantil. Ⓦ Ⓔ $0 (donations to U.S. address encouraged). From the west, turn off towards town at the beginning of the bypass. Pass a cemetery and at 0.5 miles turn left just before the bus terminal. Go 0.4 miles and look for the Hogar on the right. **Comments:**

Electricity had reverse polarity. **Other Sites:** The entrance to **Sumidero National Park,** 14 miles (23 km) north of Tuxtla Gutierrez.

Day 9 San Cristóbal de Las Casas, Chiapas. Hotel Bonampak Trailer Park. Ⓦ Ⓔ Ⓓ $16. From the west, avoid the Periférico and continue into town. The hotel is just beyond Pemex #0349 on your right. **Comments:** Plenty of interesting sights in the area. **Other Sites Near San Cristóbal** (Courtesy Carol Kulish) **Tziscao.** Lagunas De Montebella National Park. About 35 miles east of Mexico 190 between Guatemala border and San Cristóbal in Chiapas (turnoff at La Trinitaria). Take first left in town, down a hill and then left along the lake to the end. Ⓔ $4. **Comments:** Watch for overhead cables. Power and showers at the restaurant. **San Cristóbal de Las Casas, Chiapas.** (N16:44 W92:39) "…camped in a grassy area near the edge of town at the local sports complex. Colleen found the man who is in charge of the security here and got permission for us to stay for three nights." (Kirkbride/Regan)

Day 95 Villahermosa, Tabasco. Carrefour Parking Lot (Supermarket) (N17:59.376 W92:59.376). $0. From the west take the first off ramp when crossing the river into town, marked Teapa 195, turn left and pass under the highway. From the east, you will pass a WALMART on your right (another possible camping spot), exit 180 to the feeder road, this is the main boulevard, Ave. Adolfo Ruiz Cortines. Continue on feeder road and you will find Carrefour on your right next to a large cinema complex and near a Sam's Club. **Other Sites: Rancho Hermanos Graham,** 80 miles east, and Campgrounds at **Palenque,** 70 miles southeast.

Day 97 Manuel (Tampico), Tamaulipas. Comedor La Canchita. (N22:48.856 W98:17.896). $0. Hwy 180, 6 miles north of Manuel, between km marker 9 and 10. East side of the road. **Comments:** Friendly family running this *comedor,* let us park on their fenced property.

Other Sites in Mexico (Courtesy of Kathe Kirkbride and Colleen Regan): **Las Cabras, Sinaloa.** "We boondocked in the village of Las Cabras, 50K from the carretera on the road to El Fuerte from El Carrizo. The *comisario,* Rogelio Guerrero, would like other RVers to know that they are also welcome to camp here for 25 pesos per night. I wrote out the words he will put on a sign on the road…it should say "Las Cabras…RV dry camping…25 Pesos". It is a very nice wide area with easy access for any kind of a rig with a large thorny tree near the highway. The money derived from this venture will go to the local primary school. Las Cabras is located at 14 Kilometers from El Fuerte and 50K from El Carrizo on the road from El Carrizo." **Puerto Vallarta, Jalisco.** "…we found a great boondocking spot on a cliff overlooking the ocean near **Punta Mita** several kilometers north of Pto Vallarta. We had originally thought to approach from the road that goes through **Sayulita,** but that turned out to be an interesting side jaunt through a very small town square with lots of onlookers as we extricated ourselves. The map showed a heavy red line for both approaches to Punta Mita and so we chose the shortest route. We ended up about five miles west of the main highway on the south road that angles out to Punta Mita. It was an overlook point that allowed you to see from one end of **Bahia Banderas** to the other so at night we looked south to the lights of Pto Vallarta." **Punta Perula, Jalisco.** (N19:35 W105:7). "…we found a beach access road used by the local fishermen to get to the beach with their boats. It was right alongside the Punta Perula RV Park, where one of our members decided to go for the full hookups for the night." **Cuyutlán, Jalisco.** "a large parking lot (N18:55 W104:4) that was right on the beach near an area that we suspect fills up on the weekends and holidays with hundreds of Mexican families who head for the beaches just like we do…" **Maruata, Michoacan.** (N18:16 W103:20) "at the end of an abandoned airstrip in front of a military outpost at the east end of town." **Playa Linda, Guerrero** (N17:41 W 101:39). "…a free camping spot just down the street from Club Med **Ixtapa.** It is a large, sandy, peninsular area with ocean on a couple of sides and a lagoon with beautiful egrets just behind where we camped." **Acapulco, Guerrero.** Diamante RV Park (N16:47, W99:48). **Pinotepa, Oaxaca.** (N16:20 W98:4) "…abandoned airstrip next to a soccer field." **Puerto Escondido, Oaxaca.** (N15:51 W97:3). "…incredible boondock spot. We strung ourselves out along a sandy road that paralleled the main street right next to the beach. As we parked, two men from a nearby hotel arrived to tell us that we couldn't park there as it was parking for their guests. The cook in the restaurant on the beach told us that it was really to keep us from blocking the view of their guests and that it was a public street and it was fine to stay there. We found a policeman who told us that it was fine and we stayed for two nights." **Zipolite Beach,** 43 miles east of **Pto. Escondido, Oaxaca.** (N15:40 W96:31). "…a dirt lot owned by the church…negotiated a rate of 300 pesos for all the rigs for two nights. That works out to $2.50/night/rig." **Tapanatepec, Oaxaca.** (N16:22 W94:11). "…a parking spot between a construction site and the public market." **Chetumal, Quintana Roo.** (N18:39 W88:25) RV park called Cenote Azul, across the street from the *cenote* near Chetumal.

Guatemala (Days 11-36, and Days 87-89)

Day 11 Huehuetenango. Hotel Los Cuchumatanes. (N15:18.561 W91:27.667). Ⓦ Ⓔ $5. Ask taxi driver to guide you upon approaching town! Sector Brasilia, Zona 7, Huehuetenango, Apartado Postal No. 46 Phone: +502-764-1951 Fax. +502-764-2816. **Other Sites:** Ruinas Zaculeu (or "further on the same road at the riverside"). The ruins are west of town (N15: 20.023 W91:29.529) and worth a visit. Approach is difficult from town because of the narrow streets. A better access to the Ruins with an RV is as follows: The Ruins are 17.2 miles off the highway. Turn west off Pan-American Highway at yellow, *zona militar* (N15:18.397 W91:31.621), pass big military base on left. This turnoff is 3 miles west of the main turnoff for Huehuetenango (N15:17.000 W91:29.474). At the Metro gas station (N15:19.294 W91:29.717), go Northwest between soccer fields on dirt road. Take two left forks. At main blacktop road turn left about 0.4 miles to the ruins.

Day 12 Quetzaltenango (Locally called Xela). *Servicio Mecánico Industrial.* $33/mo parking **Comments:** This is where we stored our rig while living with the dePalma family. Guatemalensis Spanish School can set you up, see Language Schools section. The owner of the machine shop where we parked is Dona Mariana, +502-761-2807. **Other Sites:** Hiperpaiz, Avenida Las Americas, Zona 3, allows parking in their lot.

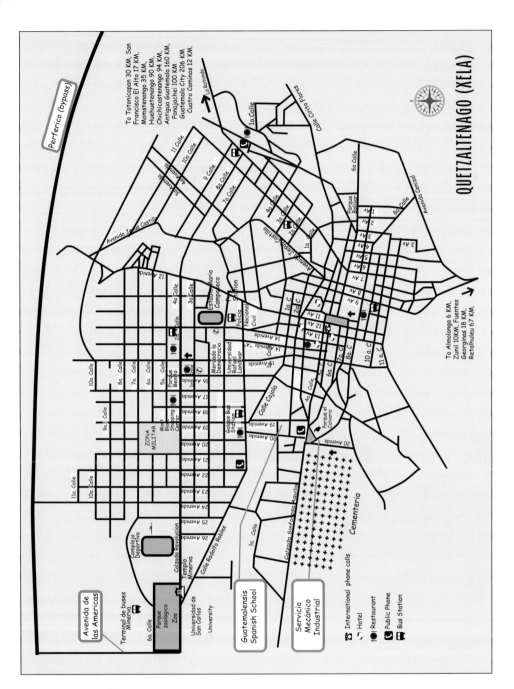

QUETZALTENAGO (XELA)

Perférico (bypass)

To Totonicapan 30 KM, San Francisco El Alto 17 KM, Momstenango 35 KM, Huehuetenango 90 KM, Chichicastenango 94 KM, Antigua Guatemala 160 KM, Guatemala City 206 KM, Panajachel 100 KM, Cuatro Caminos 12 KM

To Almolonga 6 KM, Zunil 10KM, Fuentes Georginas 18 KM, Retalhuleu 67 KM.

Avenida de las Américas

Terminal de buses Minerva

Parque zoológico Zoo

Universidad de San Carlos
University

Guatemalensis Spanish School

Servicio Mecánico Industrial

Complejo Deportivo

Templo Minerva

Cementerio

Parque Benito

Parque el Calvario

Parque Bolivar

Mercado la Democracia
Universidad Rafael Landivar

Estadio Mario Camposeco

Policía Nacional Civil

ZONA MILLITAR

Mont Blanco Shopping Center

Galgos Bus Station

La Rotonda

Calle Curto Flores

Avenida Central

Avenida Jesús Castillo

Avenida Lesús Castillo

Calle Cajola

Calzada Revolucion

Calle Rodolfo Robles

Calzada Sinforosa Aquilar

🖥 International phone calls
🛏 Hotel
🍽 Restaurant
📞 Public Phone
⛽ Bus Station

Day 19 Chichicastenango. Shell Gasolinera. Ⓦ Ⓔ Ⓓ $4. Take highway from Los Encuentros to Chichi. Turn right on 7th Ave. Shell Gas station is between 6th and 7th street, next to Hotel Santo Tomás.

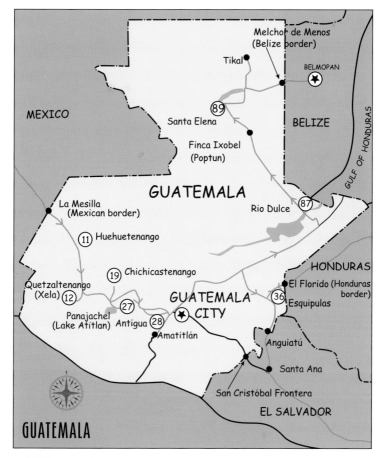

GUATEMALA

Day 27 Panajachel, Lake Atitlán. Hotel Visión Azul. (N14:44.936 W91:9.866). Ⓦ Ⓔ $6. Turn off the Interamerican Highway towards Sololá west of Los Encuentros. Pass through Sololá. Turnoff to Visión Azul is just before the town of Panajachel, but the turn is too sharp for a motorhome. Continue into town and turnaround at the bottom of the hill. **Comments:** There is electricity and water available in the bar next to the swimming pool. Bring a long extension cord and hose. This was our favorite location. www.latinlatitudes.com gives a different view. **Other Sites: Panajachel.** Hotel Tzanjuyu has space for parking many RVs. Ⓦ Ⓓ

Day 28 Antigua Guatemala. Private home. We found Antigua difficult to navigate. Ask a taxi or a local guide to lead you to your destination. **Comments:** This town is not friendly to large vehicles. To visit Antigua you might consider parking your motorhome at Hotel Vision Azul at Lake Atitlán, and either rent a car or take a bus. There are plenty of good hotels and restaurants in Antigua. **Other Sites, Antigua Guatemala:** The Kirkbride party stayed at a regional park called Florencia, just outside the village of **Santa Lucia Milpas Altas** (N14:34 W 90:41). Hotel Jorge, 4a. Avenida Sur, Calle del Conquistador No. 13, Tel/Fax: 832-3132) (Plaxton). Plaxtons also stayed at the Hotel Santa Lucia. Hotel La Real Plaza, 9a Calle, Pte #40,

Tel 832-2239, email <u>operasa@itelgua.com</u>. Experimental Botanical Garden "Valhalla". Email <u>exvalhalla@yahoo.com</u> and their website is www.exvalhalla.org. El Rosario at 5a. Avenida Sur final No. 36. and Hotel Antigua at 8a Calle Pte 1. It is possible to get to both of these places without going through the main town and they are near each other. Call these places in Antigua before you go, and you might have to rent a room. **Other Sites: Southern Guatemala.** The "best campground" in Central America is Turicentro Automariscos (Plaxton). This is South of Guatemala on the road towards Escuintla between **Amatitlán** and **Palín** at km marker 33.5. Telephone +502-330479.

Day 36 Esquipulas. Pollos Camperos Restaurant. $2 tip to guard. Take the left fork at the approach into the town. Follow signs to Pollo Campero, next to Basílica. We parked right next to the restaurant with permission from the guard. **Comments:** There are two huge grass parking lots near the restaurant for pilgrims that flock on special days. Adventure Caravans uses these lots when they come through. There is a small charge.

Day 87 Rio Dulce. Bruno's Hotel and Restaurant. (N15:39.573 W89:00.122). Ⓦ Ⓔ $6.50. Brunos is under the north end of the bridge over the river. There is a small slip road on the east side of the bridge where the north end of the bridge joins the town. Northbound, make a U-turn immediately over the bridge onto the slip road. About 50 yds. down you can pass under the bridge to reach a gated entrance for

Bruno's. The clearance at this signposted underpass is too low for most RVs! Instead, continue about 300 yards towards the water where the bridge is higher off the ground, and backtrack. **Comments:** Bruno's is a hangout for the yachting crowd. For more on Rio Dulce see <u>http://www.mayaparadise.com/index.htm</u> **Other Sites:** Planeta Rio (previously Hotel Ensenada) on the south side of the river (N15:31 W 88:59). Finca Ixobel in **Poptún** is a remarkable eco-tourism resort that allows camping. It's about 3 hrs north of Rio Dulce and 1-1/2 hours south of **Santa Elena.** The resort is 2 km off the main road. Turnoff near Km 376 marker (N16:18.558 W89:24.868). Cost about $3 per person. Buffet dinner for $4.50 and many tours offered.

Day 89 Santa Elena, Cuevas Actun Can. (N16:54.206 W89:53.704). Ⓦ $6.50. From the south go to Santa Elena. Pass the Tikal turnoff, and airport, and keep right at the Texaco station where the road becomes one way (this is *la calle*). At the causeway to Flores, turn left on 6a Ave and take it about 3/4 mile past the market and microwave towers to the end. Turn left about .2 miles, turn right at the electricity generating plant and go another 0.6 miles to the site. **Comments:** The caves are a tour opportunity. They close at 5:00PM but you can park overnight. Carlos, the manager, is from California and speaks English. Bring a flashlight. Tikal is a 1-1/2 hour drive from here. **Other Sites in Peten:** (Courtesy Carol Kulish): **Tikal Ruins.** On right just after Visitors Center. $7.00 **Comments:** Large grassy field with thatched roof, cement floor *palapas*. Unisex bathroom and showers. Very quiet at night. Easy walk to

tour the ruins and visit the museums. There is one small store and several restaurants. No pets.
Yaxja. This is 33 miles west of Melchor de Mencos, on the Belize/Guatelamala border, then about 7 miles north on a passable dirt ,track during the dry season. Do not go in the rainy season. $5. **Comments:** Large grassy field on Laguna Yaxja with toilets and *palapa* with pit fireplaces. Restoration of the ruins is in progress. When the road is improved, it will rival its neighbor Tikal.

Honduras (Days 37 - 50, 86)

Day 37 Copán Ruinas. Doña Belia's. $0. From the SW corner of the Parque Central head three blocks west (watch for low overhead cables in town), turn right (north), go to the end of the block and turn left. This is the road out of town. Wind to your left on this road and you will see the large dirt area between cemetery and Doña Belia's house. Coming from Guatemala, the main road cuts off from the highway about 5

miles from the border, but there is no sign. Look for a nicely paved and curbed road going to the left as you head away from the border. If you come in on this road from the border you go right by the cemetery before you enter town. **Other Sites:** Romilio Daniel Sandoval owns Hotel and Restaurante Katu Sukchij and balneario about 9miles west of the **El Florido** border on the Guatemala side, east of **Jocotán, Guatemala,** at the Rio Grande river crossing at a place called Puente Jupilingo, km 204 marker. +502-946-5205 (Spanish only). **Gracias, Lempira** (N14:35 W88:35)…behind the DIPPSA gas station". **Lago de Yojoa** (N14:56 W88:00). Finca las Glorias, a resort and conference center on the lake. We camped for free on the soccer field." Between **Jesus de Otoro** and **Comayagua** (N14:27 W87:38). Tracasa truck stop. (Kirkbride/Regan).

Day 38 Copán Ruinas. Texaco Gasolinera (N14:50 W89:09). Ⓦ Ⓔ $3. Take road to archaeological site, this is right next to the site entrance. **Comments:** Electricity available between the coke machines in front. They had water but no pressure in the morning. Top off when you can. **Other Sites:** We observed a nice Balneario in **Santa Rita,** 6 miles east of Copán ruins, 1 km west of Shell gas.

Day 40 Tela. Honduras Beach Plantation, Tela Beach Club (N15:47.379 W87:30.770). Ⓦ Ⓔ $11.50. This is actually in **San Juan,** about 5 miles west of Tela. Take 9a Calle southwest until it turns left. Follow the dirt road straight on for a few hundred yards, turn right and follow the signs to "Tela Beach Club", about 3 miles of dirt road through the village of San Juan. **Comments:** The "Plantation" is a private land development. They have eight cabanas for rent

about 400 yards off the beach where we parked. Electricity available at an outside plug of the closest cabana, and we used an irrigation tap for a water hookup. Management said they would rig up a dump to their septic tank with advance notice. This is a good self contained resort with a nice beach, pool, bar and restaurant. Warning: watch for soft sand. Garífuna tours (www.garifuna-tours.com) has an office in town on 9a Calle NE near the south corner of the plaza. The Mango Café is the tour meeting area and also an interesting internet café. Other Sites There is a Tourist Police office with secure concrete parking lot at the foot of 4a Ave NE next to the beach. They are very helpful and you can camp for $1.75 per night. There is an electrical outlet in the bathroom, and water. **Other Sites: Tela** (N15:44 W87:27) "Lancetilla Botanical Gardens…and enjoyed the area." (Kirkbride/Regan).

Day 43 Corozal (La Ceiba). Hotel Brisas del Mar (N15:47.237 W86:40.890). Ⓦ $3. Corozal is about 15 km east of La Ceiba on the coast road towards Saba and Trujillo. To reach Brisas del Mar, go about 0.2 miles east of the main Corozal turnoff. Turn north at the small white sign for the hotel, and follow the dirt road across railroad tracks to the beach. **Comments:** We met Francisco Vivas runs La Ceiba Eco-tours in this area. AP 70, La Ceiba, Honduras, Ph. +504 443-4207. **Other Sites: La Ceiba.** (N15:46 W86:52) "We had heard about an RV park run by a Canadian and found it just east of La Ceiba. It was a very tight squeeze getting down the little dirt lane, and our CB antenna was a casualty of the tree limbs." (Kirkbride/Regan)

Day 45 Trujillo. Christopher Columbus Hotel. (N15:55.592 W85:56.385). Ⓦ Ⓔ Ⓓ $0. Turn north from main road to airstrip, about 1/2 mile east of town. Cross airstrip to large hotel next to beach. **Comments:** We took advantage of their electricity, water and sewer, and earned our keep by eating in their restaurant and enjoying their Piña Coladas. This is a beautiful spot for a hotel stay too. **Other Sites: Trujillo** (N15:54 W85:59) "Campamento, an RV park with cabanas and a restaurant right on the beach west of town about 5 miles. We stayed five nights there and enjoyed getting to know Trujillo and swimming at the beach in front of where we were parked. The owners, Orleis and Arturo Ramos, were very friendly and welcoming." (Kirkbride/Regan). Thor Janson recommends a restaurant/campsite that is about half-way between Trujillo and **Puerto Castilla** on the road around the bay. As we left **Saba** going east we noted The Executive Hotel that had a pool and a walled in lawn with easy access. It would have been suitable for camping. There is also an enormous gravel lot, big enough for twenty motorhomes, opposite the Texaco station in the town of **Saba.**

Day 48 La Union. Muralla National Park. (N15:5.837 W86:44.314). $11 for the tour, for the two of us. Turn west off main (dirt) road into La Union and continue through town. There is a river to ford which may flood in rainy season. At a T-junction a sign directs you 8.4 miles (14 km) to the National Park. The park headquarters is about a mile past the sign announcing entrance to the park.

Day 49 Valle de Angeles (Tegucigalpa). Parque Turístico. (N14:8.412 W87:2.400). Ⓦ $3. Proceed 1.2 miles west of Valle de Angeles, on south side of road to Tegucigalpa. **Comments:** This is a large public park with swimming pool and ball courts designed to handle day trippers from the capital. Plenty of space for caravans! **Other Sites:** Caravans stay in **Valle de Angeles** near a "wood factory" and the pavilion of arts and crafts has a large parking lot. (Plaxton)

Day 50 Danlí. Esso Gasolinera. (N14:1.497 W86:35.085). $1.20. This is on the west end of town on road from Tegucigalpa (CA6). **Comments:** *Vigilante* on duty all night. Pay money directly to him. **Other Sites:** Texaco in town. Also there is a soccer field close to downtown we were told could be used.

Day 83 San Jerónimo, near Choluteca. Pinto family farm and refresquería. (N13:11.173 W87:8.267). $0. This is off main road between Choluteca and the border at **Guasaule** (not the Pan-American which goes to El Espino). Between Km 15 & 16, turn north on dirt road next to "Pepsi Emanuel" store. Go about 1 km to end of dirt road and turn right. The Pinto shop and farm is a few hundred yards on your right. **Comments:** One of our best experiences meeting the local people. See text.

Nicaragua (Day 51-51, 80 - 82)

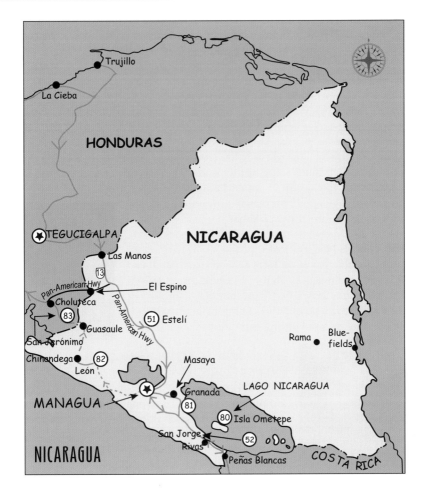

Day 51 Estelí. Colegio Adventista Maranatha (N13:4.211 W86:20.933). Ⓦ Ⓔ $0. This is south of town, about 1/4 mile south of the intersection of the Pan-American Highway and Calle Principal. Turn west just north of restaurant Mirador, with viewing tower. Colegio is about 100m off highway. **Comments:** Administrator Ronaldo gave us permission to stay. Caretaker Alberto is on duty all night. **Other Sites: Ocotal** (N13:06 W86:21). Gas station. **Estelí.** Fire department "where we were made very welcome". **Sébaco** (N12:51 W86:06). "Just off the main highway in front of a large vegetable warehouse…We paid the night watchman 100 *córdobas* for watching our rigs." (Kirkbride/Regan)

Day 52 San Jorge, on Lake Nicaragua near Rivas. In a small parking lot next to restaurant. (N11:27.554 W85:47.468). $0. Go east from Rivas to San Jorge. Turn left at the main square of San Jorge and right toward beach (La Playa) after a few blocks. **Comments:** Park on hard packed sand beach or next to restaurant. A caravan comes here once a year. Ometepe Tours is to the right of the ferry entrance. (Sr. Cipriano Quiroga +505 453-4779) **Other Sites:** There is a tourist restaurant and small zoo about 2 miles north of the **Peñas Blanca** border crossing. It has a very large flat area perfect for parking. The restaurant has showers and water available, probably power also if you park next to the restaurant. Also, 35 miles south of **Rivas** there appears to be camping opportunities at Cabana Castilas and Hotel Colinas del Norte.

Day 80 Sto. Domingo, Ometepe Island, Lake Nicaragua. Finca Sto. Domingo. (N11:30.737 W85:33.277) Hotel. $20. We parked our RV in the secure parking at the dock in San Jorge and took a passenger boat to Moyogalpa, Ometepe. **Comments:** You could bring a small RV on the ferry that runs from San Jorge. It would be an adventure and not worth it unless you planned to spend several days on the island. Reservations recommended, 278-8190. The road around the south side of the island from Moyogalpa around Concepción is rough but OK. The road north between Moyogalpa and San Marcos is terrible and not recommended. The Isthmus road is OK as far as Belgue. Hotel rooms are cheap at Sto. Domingo beach. Hotel Villa Paradaiso next door is recommended. **Other Sites:** "El Tesoro del Pirata" is on the South Side of Concepcion. Inquiries may be made at Hotel El Pirata in **Moyogalpa** (tel 459-4262). There is a bar/restaurant, a few new cabanas, restrooms and open air showers. Water & power is available. El Tesoro is reached by taking the road around Concepcion south from Moyogalpa about 12 miles. There is a turnoff signposted just beyond marker Km 11, which goes to the beach (right turn). The campground is a kilometer or so down this road on the right (N11:29.359 W85:37.088). Camping fees for a motorhome would be less than $2. They also rent tents and have the cabanas for about $4.

Day 81 Granada. Centro Turístico. (N11:55.264 W85:56.356). $4 plus tips to two *vigilantes.* From Parque Colón, take Calle La Calzada east to lake front and turn south. Entrance to Centro is directly in front. About 1/2 mile down row of bars and restaurants is a small place to park on the east (left). **Comments:** We were expecting a lot of activity but Friday night was quiet. **Other Sites: Managua.** The Plaxtons parked their RV at the Managua Camino Real while they took a flight to the

Corn Islands. The hotel is located at 9.5 km Carretera Norte, 1.5 km south of the airport. **Masaya.** "We are camped in front of the police station along the malecón overlooking Laguna de Masaya." (Kirkbride/Regan)

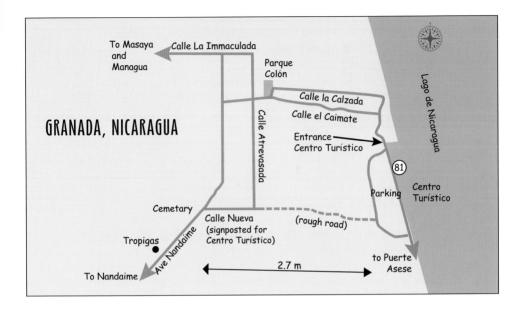

Day 82 León. Parking Lot, Salman Market. (N12:26.20 W86:52.96) Ⓦ Ⓔ $2. From Parque Central, take 1a Av north three blocks, turn east (left) 3a Calle NE for three blocks, turn south (left) on 4a Av NO. Parking lot is on east side (left) in 2nd full block between 2a and 1a Calle. **Comments:** Electricity went off in the morning when they turned off the lights. Water pressure is bad in the morning. Note: Road from Chinandega to Honduras border is terrible. It took us nearly 5 hours to get from León to Guasaules. **Other Sites:** A few miles west of **Nacoame,** about 18 miles east of **El Amatillo,** there is a shallow river with a wide hard packed gravel approach that would have made a great camp, or at least cool lunch stop.

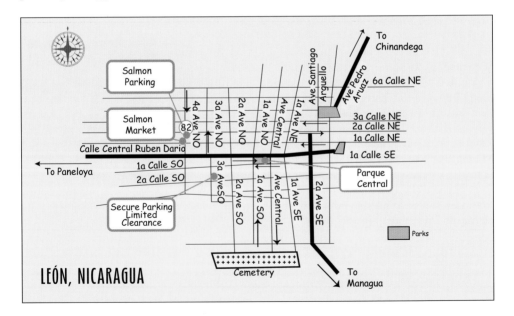

Costa Rica (Day 53-63, 74-76)

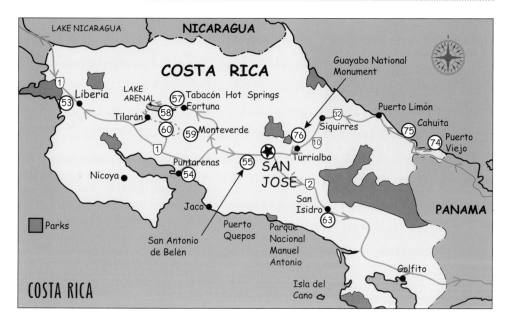

Day 53 5 km N of Liberia. Delfin Trailer Park. (N10:39.441 W85:28.156) Ⓦ Ⓔ Ⓓ. $4 + $2 for the swimming pool. Look on the west side of Interamerican Highway, 3 miles north of Liberia. **Comments:** It is a large field with a long white fence and a small sign next to the entrance. The place is a decommissioned trailer park but there is a welcoming caretaker, and central water, electricity, dump and shade. **Other Sites: Parque National Santa Rosa,** 22 m north of Liberia, has camping by the park headquarters (4 miles from the highway). Pets are not allowed. There are also campsites on the northwest coast that we didn't visit. "Brasilito" near **Flamingo Beach** and North of Flamingo, Playa Potrero reportedly have camping. Lonely Planet lists campsites near **Playa Tamarindo.** Hotel Capazuri, 1.2 miles north of **Cañas,** has places suitable for camping (phone +506-669-6280, fax +506-669-6080, Email capazuri@racsa.co.cr). A Shell gasoline station 2 miles north of the route 18 turnoff from the Interamerican Highway, about 11 miles south of Cañas, has a huge parking area. **Las Juntas.** "…a jumping off point for Monteverde. We found a place to park the rigs at the Balneario Cayuco where we were assured that they would be fine while we went off to other areas. We tipped the manager $16 U.S. when we got back for all six rigs for 3 nights in his parking lot." (Kirkbride/Regan)

Day 54 Puntarenas. Paseo de Los Turistas. (N9:58.469 W84:50.647). $0. Take main road (Rt. 17/ ave Central) westward from the Interamerican Highway to the end of the peninsula. Turn left onto Paseo de Los Turistas. Park anywhere along the beach. **Comments:** Puntarenas is active on weekends, quieter camping is found toward the west end of

the beach. **Other Sites on the Central Pacific Coast of Costa Rica:** There is camping at **Playa Herradura north of Jacó.** Caravans have used the Marriott in Jacó. Parque Manuel Antonio near **Quepos** has unconfirmed camping. RV parks can be found on the **Nicoya Peninsula** at **Tambor** and **Cabuya.** "You can park near Playa Bejuco, between **Jacó** and **Quepos**". (Plaxton). Caravans we met drove from Palmar Norte to Quepos along the coast. Some were spooked by the narrow railroad bridges they had to cross.

Day 55 San Antonio de Belén, San José. Belén Trailer Park, P.O. Box 143-4005, Belén, Heredia, Costa Rica. Phone 239-0421, Email: lasutter@racsa.co.cr (N9:58.801 W84:10.727) Ⓦ Ⓔ Ⓓ $12. Exit Pan-American Highway just east of the 12k marker. Turn south toward San Antonio. After 0.4 miles, turn right at flashing yellow light (beginning of one way). Take first left 0.1m, then 0.5m on left immediately past gas station is the small, poorly signposted entrance to the trailer park. If you miss it go forward about three blocks, turn left one block and return on the parallel street where there is another entrance past a tall concrete wall. **Comments:** The owner, Laurie, is a transplanted Californian. This is a good place to stop and regroup after boondocking. Caravans stop here and do their Costa Rican tours by bus. Laundry and hot showers are available.

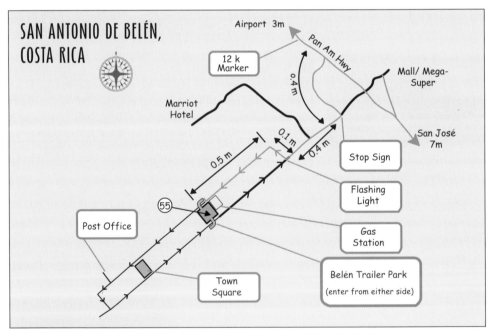

SAN ANTONIO DE BELÉN, COSTA RICA

Airport 3m
Pan Am Hwy
12 k Marker
Mall/ Mega-Super
Marriot Hotel
0.4 m
0.1 m
0.5 m
0.4 m
San José 7m
Stop Sign
Flashing Light
⑤⑤
Gas Station
Post Office
Belén Trailer Park
(enter from either side)
Town Square

Day 57 Near Fortuna. Tabacón Hot Springs. (N10:29.245 W84:43.380). $0. About 6 miles west of La Fortuna. **Comments:** This is across the road from hot springs and restaurant. **Other Sites:** Other RVers told us you could camp on the grass next to Cabinas Sissy at the west end of **Fortuna.** There is also campground across from the

Arenal National Park entrance (N10:27.691 W84:44.404). In **La Fortuna** "we camped right next to the bullring on a large gravel area in front of Hotel Dorothy (N10:28 W84:39) for free." (Kirkbride/Regan).

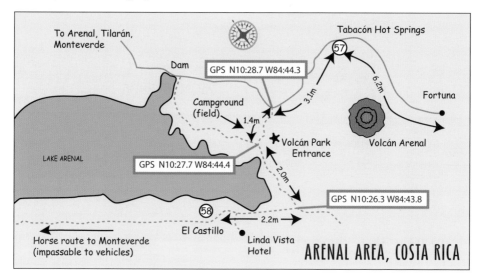

To Arenal, Tilarán, Monteverde

Tabacón Hot Springs

Dam

GPS N10:28.7 W84:44.3

57

6.2m

Fortuna

Campground (field)

1.4m

3.1m

Volcán Park Entrance

Volcán Arenal

LAKE ARENAL

GPS N10:27.7 W84:44.4

2.0m

GPS N10:26.3 W84:43.8

58

2.2m

El Castillo

Horse route to Monteverde (impassable to vehicles)

Linda Vista Hotel

ARENAL AREA, COSTA RICA

Day 58 El Castillo (Arenal Volcano). El Castillo. (N10:25.969 W84:45.001). $0. This is north of Tabacón. Turn toward Volcán Natl Park on dirt road. 1.4 miles to Park Entrance, pass entrance and turn left toward "Linda Vista" hotel. Two miles on dirt road, turn right just past "Linda Vista" to pueblo of El Castillo. Next to soccer field. **Comments:** Beautiful view of the volcano across the lake. Horses are available to ride to Monteverde.

Day 59 Monteverde. Ecological Reserve. $0 Follow signs to reserve from Sta. Elena, through Monteverde to the end of the road. **Comments:** We received permission to camp in the lower parking that is usually closed at night. We had to promise to keep Brindle in the RV. The road to Monteverde may be impassable in the wet season. Approaching from Tilarán is better than directly from the Pan-American Highway.

Day 60 Sta. Elena/ Monteverde. Orquídeas Bar and Hotel. (N10:18.777 W84:49.650). $0 The bar is 1/2km out of Sta. Elena on the San José road, on the left next to toll booth. **Comments:** The owners, Danilo and Nadia Zamora, lived in the States and speak English. They are very friendly and helpful. Excellent view and wildlife.

MONTEVERDE

Tilarán 26m
(2 hrs)

Sta Elena Reserve
3.2 m from Sta Elena

Soccer
Field

Sta Elena Center

0.3 m

60

22.6m
to Pan
American Hwy
towards
San José
(2.5 hrs)

Las
Orquideas

Butterfly
Farm

Cheese
Factory

Monteverde
Ecological
Reserve
(3.8m from
Sta Elena)

59

MONTEVERDE AREA, COSTA RICA

To San Luis
Waterfalls

Day 63 San Isidro de El General. Shell Gasolinera. (N9:20.459 W83:40.374) $0 This is at the southern edge of town on the Pan-American Highway. **Comments:** Restaurant next door cooks traditional Costa Rican food. **Other Sites:** Gas stations at the north end of town were hosting many 18-wheelers. North of San Isidro is a beautiful mountainous area in the **Rio Macho Forest Reserve.** There were several camping areas advertised off the main road that we didn't explore. 60 miles south of San Isidro we found a nice pull off next to the Grande de Terraba river just east of **Palmar Norte** (N8:57.896, W83:17.209). 3 miles south of Palmar Norte there was a huge 24 hour gas station with plenty of camping room. The road to Golfito is 26 km. Seven km before you reach **Golfito** there is camping at La Perruja Lodge (Box). The beaches and National Parks in the area may provide camping venues.

Day 74 Puerto Viejo. Salsa Brava Restaurant (N9:39.532 W82:45.082) $0. This is in the center of town, two doors south from the discothèque! Public parking is next to restaurant on the beach. **Comments:** A more tranquil campsite might be at north end of beach, about a mile from town. **Other Sites:** You can camp by the beach in **Manzanillo** (Kirkbride/Regan).

Day 75 Cahuita Village. Under tree by beach. (N9:44.231 W82:50.337) $0. Turn off the highway to Cahuita. Turn right in town, left just before the National Park entrance. Shady spot at end of street offers welcome coolness. **Comments:** There is additional camping along black beach about one mile north, and you might be able to camp in the National Park without a pet.

Day 76 Guayabo. National Monument (N9:58.244 W83:41.363) $0. Take road to Guayabo monument from **Turrialba**. The turn is signposted near the west end of town. 11 miles on poor road takes about 45 minutes. **Comments:** Archeological site is well worth visiting. We parked on wide flat spot on road directly in front of entrance. No traffic at night. **Other Sites: Guapiles.** "we stayed at the PoliDeportivo about 2 miles north of the highway on the road to **Cariari** near the swimming pools (N10:14 W83:47). It was an incredibly wonderful facility and a secure place to leave the rigs [while we went to Tortuguero]. As always the group left a tip for the watchman." "…It was a beautiful mountainous drive through Turrialba to **Orosi** where we spent the night in the center of town next to the soccer field in front of the church (N9:48 W83:51 Elevation 3490)." (Kirkbride/Regan)

Panama (Days 64 - 73)

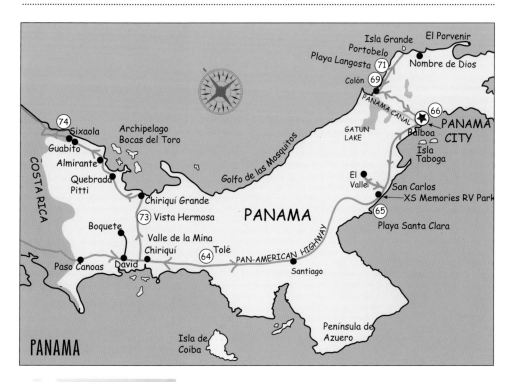

Day 64 Tolé. Public commons. (N8:14.048 W81:40.387) $0. Turn east off highway 58 miles south of David. **Comments:** Plenty of room for caravans. There is a fixture near the east end of the commons where you might get electricity and water by asking.

Day 65 Playa Santa Clara. Beach next to Restaurante Y Balneario Playa Santa Clara. (N8:22.478 W8:06.402) (Turnoff is N8:23.253 W80:6.600) Ⓦ Ⓔ Ⓓ $3 per person. The turnoff for Playa Santa Clara is 4.2 miles east of Rio Hato between Km markers 113 and 114. This is about 3 miles east of the Santa Clara airport runway, which crosses the Pan-American Highway. The turnoff is marked by an overhead footbridge. The beach is 1.8 miles south at the end of the road. **Comments:** This is a beautiful beach with cabanas. One power outlet is available at a cabana near the defunct pizza stand. There is a latrine at the far end of parking area we used to dump our tanks. Water to fill tank is available outside a nicer restroom and shower closer to the entrance. We visited mid-week and had the place to ourselves. **Other Sites:** Panama's only true RV park with full hookups is just across the highway from the **Playa Santa Clara** exit. Turn north off the Pan-American Highway at this exit, and 100 yards down the road is XS Memories (www.xsmemories.com, 507-993-3096). Americans Dennis and Sheila run this secure, friendly, place, and arrange Kayak expeditions. Caravans stay put here and visit Panama by coach. The food is excellent.

Day 66 Balboa, Panama City. Country Inn, Balboa Yacht Club. (N8:56.486 W79:33.310). Ⓦ $0. Cross Puente de las Americas eastbound and take 1st exit to Balboa. Turn left at bottom of exit on Calle Amador (leading to causeway). Take the first right. **Comments:** Balboa Yacht Club used to allow camping but since the clubhouse burned down there doesn't seem to be a yacht club parking lot. The guard would not let us overnight in the enormous lot. You might have better

luck. The hotel manager next door condescended to letting us stay in the hotel parking lot. **Other Sites:** We heard that the Hotel Plaza Paitilla, **Punta Paitilla,** offered parking to Caravans for the price of a room night. Locals suggested the parking lots of the Horoko Golf Course on the West Bank, and the Summit Golf Course on the road north towards Gamboa, as well as the Police Academy grounds. Another idea is to ask Kunkel-Weise, an engineering firm in the Rodman compound. This is where a caravan stayed (Starcher). This area is reached from the west side of the Bridge of the Americas. Take a road northbound from **Lacona,** about 1.2 miles west of the bridge.

Day 69 Near Playa Maria Chiquita, Portobelo. Bar y Restaurante Las Palmeras. (N9:27.329 W79:44.330) EL148 Ⓦ Ⓔ $5 dry. $8 w/elect. Take the trans-isthmus road from Panama to **Colón.** Turn off towards Portobelo just north of **Sabanita.** This Restaurante is 2 miles north/east of Playa Maria Chiquita, or about 9 miles from the turnoff at Sabanita. **Comments:** This is right on the beach. The Caribbean is cooler and more pleasant than Pacific Beaches. The owners changed price on us when we decided to stay a second day.

Day 71 Playa Langosta. Playa Langosta (Bar, Restaurant). (N9:28.223 W79:43.444). Ⓦ Ⓔ $10. This is 10 m east of Sabinita, a couple of miles past Las Palmeras. **Comments:** Contrasted to the black sand at Maria Chiquita and Las Palmeras, this is a wide white-sand beach. The helpful English speaking manager, Omar Vega, said power is available in the restaurant, but it is a

long way from the beach parking. There is good snorkeling and lobsters were being caught while we were there. **Other Sites:** We took a day trip through Portobelo and on to **Isla Grande,** or more correctly, **La Guaira,** which is the mainland jumping off point to Isla Grande. You can park your RV and take a boat to Isla Grande where there are numerous hotels. Or you can spend the night in your RV on the mainland. The Bananas Village Resort (<u>www.bananasresort.com</u>) is the classiest place on the island.

Day 73 Chiriquí Department. "Vista Hermosa". (N8:40.450 W82:13.308) $0 This is near the continental divide, on the road between **Chiriquí** and **Chiriquí Grande.** It is 27 miles north of the turnoff from the Pan-American Highway, 1 mile N of a toll plaza. **Comments:** "Vista Hermosa" is on a sign next to a residence where there is a place to pull off the road. This was a cool respite from the coastal heat. **Other Sites:** Between **Chiriquí**

Grande and **Almirante.** There is a place by the river between km markers 20 and 21 that looks like a nice boondock. The Restaurante Onelys, just east of km 50 (village of Quebrada Pitti), (N9:11.589 W82:20.308), 18 km south of **Almirante.** The manager, Pedro, welcomes tourists. There is a large grass space to park and *palapas.* Water and electricity is available. There is a terrific view of the archipelago. This is a tranquil venue compared to Almirante itself where we would not recommend camping. If you take the boat from **Almirante** to **Bocas del Toro,** you can park your RV at the fire station in Almirante.

El Salvador (Day 84-86)

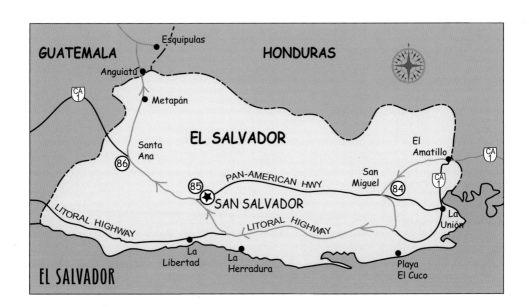

Day 84 San Miguel. Shell Gasolinera. (N13:30.462 W88:9.185) Ⓦ Ⓔ Ⓓ $0 (tip for guard suggested). On CA7 from **El Amatillo** (not the Pan-American Highway). This is a better road from the border. The gas station is on the east side of town, between km 140 and 141, on the south side of the road, Ruta Militar. **Comments:** The station has electric hookups in the back where you park. Water is available near the lube station. There is a concrete sewer cover in the back which can be slid to the side for dumping. The owner said we could also dump into the toilets. Showers are available. **Other Sites:** We were told that the Metrocenter in **San Miguel** would make a suitable campsite.

Day 85 San Salvador. Hotel Marriott Parking Lot (ex Hotel Presidente). (N13:41.535 W89:14.417) Ⓦ $1+tips. Turn north on Ave. Revolucion off the Pan-American Highway just after the turnoff to Autopista Sur (coming from the south/west). Continue straight at the roundabout (traffic circle) for Blvd del Hipodromo. Covered parking is opposite hotel. **Comments:** We stayed in the hotel but the parking attendant said that we could stay in the vehicle. There might be electricity if you ask.

Day 86 Santa Ana. Centro Escolar Madre del Salvador. (N13:59.373 W89:32.834) Ⓦ $2 Contribution. 23 Ave Sur between 7th and 5th Calle Oriente, near the Turicentro Sihuatehuacan. From Parque Libertad, in the center of town, take Libertad Oriente eastward. Turn right on 23rd Ave Sur (this is two blocks west of the turicentro, look for telephone kiosk on the southeast corner). Go three blocks.

Church and school are on the left where the road splits into two one-way streets. **Other Sites:** The Turicentro might let you stay if you arrive before closing. Hotel y Restaurante Montevista, 6 miles south of Frontera **Anguita,** north of Metepan. (N14:21.933 W89:26.960) has a big lot.

Other Sites in El Salvador courtesy of Kathe Kirkbride and Colleen Regan. **San Miguel** "…at another Shell Gas Station (N13:29 W88:28) for $2/night." **Playa El Espino** on the Pacific Coast: "…we were shown a place to park under a palapa for $5 for the day. This fee also included chairs and a hammock hanging under another palapa right on the beach." **Santiago de Maria** on either side of the Parque Central (N 13:29 W 88:28 Elev 2181'). **San Vicente** at a Puma Gas Station on CA-1 (N13:41 W88:46) "…where they had a large area where we could park and gave us permission to stay the night. It was big enough that a largish caravan could fit; they were very welcoming of us and had a security guard 24 hours a day." **La Libertad.** "…found an absolutely delightful place to camp at a private recreation center called Rio Mar (N13:29 W89:17 E 46') just east of town less than 2 miles. It has two swimming pools, a restaurant, lots of palapas, difficult access to a rugged beach, and beautiful palm and almond treed grounds. We are being charged $5/night per rig and think it is a bargain. Talking them into allowing us to stay after they close at 5:00 pm was another fine example of persuasive communication as they were definitely not open to the idea when Colleen and I first approached them. After 5:00 we have the place to ourselves." **Playa Costa del Sol,** 30 miles east of La Libertad, Hotel Tesoro Beach "…lends itself to large RV caravans with tall rigs. Colleen talked to the receptionist there who said that RVs could stay there and use the resort; …the cost would be $15/day/rig. The beach is beautiful, clean, and has good boogie boarding."

Belize (Day 90-94)

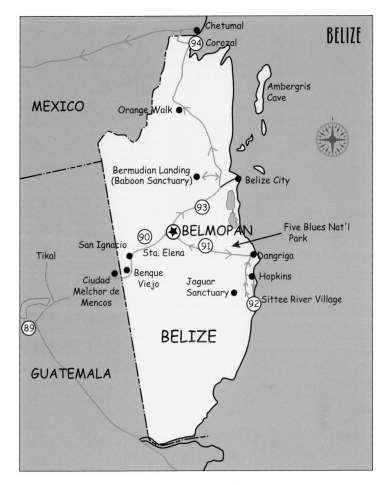

Day 90 Santa Elena. Caesars Place Guest House. (N17:12.261 W88:57.169) Ⓦ Ⓔ Ⓓ $5 for water and sewage, $3.75 pp camping. This is 6 miles east of the center of Santa Elena, near milepost 60 on the north side of road. Look for the signs for the Guest House and Gift Shop. **Comments:** It is not dog friendly because of local guard dogs. There is a very good gift shop here. **Other Sites: Santa Elena.** "...the Inglewood RV Park on the western edge of town (N 17:08 W 89:05) ...is owned by Greg Carrillo who lived for 30 years in Southern California and has now retired to his home country. The park is the nicest one we have stayed in our entire trip so far. He charges $7.50/night with electricity extra if you need it." (Kirkbride/Regan).

Day 91 Hummingbird Highway. Ian Anderson's Caves Branch Adventure Company & Jungle Lodge. (N17:10.043 W88:41.012). Ⓦ $2.50 pp The turnoff is near milepost 33 on the Hummingbird Highway, almost across from the Blue Hole swimming area. Tel +501-822-2800, fax 888-265-4579 (US), www.cavesbranch.com. **Comments:** This is an all inclusive eco-tourism resort, but there are no special areas for RVs. Parking is available near the main building. Water hookups are along the dirt road. You need to stay here to participate in their tours, which are among the best in Belize. Dogs are accepted but they have territorial dogs on premises. **Other Sites:** Blue Hole National Park allows overnight parking at the Visitors' Center for $2.50. They can also arrange a guide for cave tubing. Five Blue Lake National Park, closer to **Dangriga** at milepost 22, offers an off the beaten track boondocking opportunity near lake. The unmanned Visitors' Center is 4.5 miles off the highway on a dirt track. $4. **Dangriga** "...we found two places to stay and part of the group stayed at a town park ...and the rest of us stayed in a grassy area near a bar called the Malibu Beach Club by the Pelican Bay Resort (N16:59, W88:14). Both spots were free, grassy and right on the beach." (Kirkbride/Regan)

Day 92 Sittee River Village. Public park next to soccer field. (N16:49.611 W88:18.072) $0. From southern highway take Sittee Road east for five miles to Sittee River Village. The Sittee Road turnoff is about 3 miles south of the Hopkins turnoff. To get there from Hopkins, take Sittee Road turnoff 1.7 miles south of the Hopkins Road intersection with the main street. **Other Sites:** Several sites appeared

interesting along the beach in Hopkins and South of town. Best site in town appears to be at the foot of Hopkins Road from the Southern Highway (next to pier and police station). South of Hopkins check out the "Beaches and Dreams" hotel about 0.4m south of the Sittee River Rd turnoff. On Sittee Road, next to river instead of ocean, Toucan Sittee have space for camping.

Day 93 Belmopan, Western Hwy. Amigos Restaurant (N17:19.141 W88:34.234) $0. This is between mile markers 31-32 on the Western Highway. **Comments:** The friendly owner, Sue Bufford, says she can make a dump available through her septic cleanout valve, and can provide water. Electricity is expensive in Belize and she wasn't sure how to work out the reimbursement.

Day 94 Corozal. Public Park (N18:23.090 W88:23.605) $0. Follow the main road through Corozal town. Where it runs along the ocean is a public small park that is available for parking on the grass. **Other Sites:** Caribbean Village trailer park is almost across the street from this location, a block south of the Hotel Maya. Lagoon Campground, 1 1/2 miles from the border at mile marker 91, looks attractive and is reported to be one of the nicest campgrounds in Belize.

Other Sites in Belize Courtesy of Carol Kulish: **Bermudian Landing.** Community Baboon Sanctuary. Ⓔ $2.50 per person. At west end of town on left. Information Center for Sanctuary is well marked. **Comments:** The $5 entry fee into the Sanctuary includes a guided walk. There are pit toilets, a thatched roof palapa with cement floor, and a nice inexpensive restaurant next door. **Maya Centre.** Cockscomb Basin Wildlife Sanctuary (Jaguar Reserve) $2.50 per person East of Maya Centre about 6 miles on a good dirt track **Comments:** Parking is in Sanctuary's grass parking lot. Toilets are the only amenity. The $5 park fee allows endless hiking in the jungle. Best short hike is to the outlook for a view of Victoria Peak. Tubing and night hikes can be arranged. Good wildlife spotting. **Gales Point** $7 Large, sloped, grassy area on left hand side heading north about 1/4 mile before resort, at end of spit. Park, and someone (possibly James) will show up to collect. **Comments:** Many men in the town make and play beautiful wooden drums. If it is not your favorite instrument, you may not sleep well. **Placencia.** Harrys Cozy Cabanas. $10 Ask at Information Center. Turn right after soccer field, about a block before main road into town hits wharf. Take a right in one block, then a left at next block. Follow this road straight about 1/2 to 3/4 mile. Go straight past next right, and watch for a small sign on the left. **Comments:** Room for a couple of small rigs. Outside cold shower is only amenity. Beach is as close as you dare drive your rig. Watch your head on the Tree of Knowledge. This huge tree provided nice shade and is the local social center. **Punta Gorda.** TCs By the Sea B & B Hotel. Ⓦ Ⓔ $7.50 w/o power. Driving south towards town, it is about 1/4 mile after road hits the waterfront on the right hand side. About a mile north of Punta Gorda. **Comments:** Excellent restaurant. Bathrooms, with shower (extra charge). (Courtesy Kirkbride/Regan) **Orange Walk.** "…parked on the soccer field right in the center of town where we all had fun talking and playing with the kids… We were glad when we moved down to the edge of the New River at the Lamanai Riverside Restaurant and Retreat (N 18:05 W 88:33) which we found when we took the boat trip. What an incredible spot to camp for the four rigs that moved there from the town square…"

BIBLIOGRAPHY

Primary References We Used

1. Church, Mike and Terri, *Traveler's Guide to Mexican Camping,* Second Edition, Rolling Homes Press, (www.rollinghomes.com). This is an essential reference for RVing in Mexico and also for general information on preparations, border crossing, etc.
2. *Central America on a Shoestring,* 4th Edition, Lonely Planet Publications, Victoria, Australia. This was our primary reference. Guidebooks for individual countries would be prefered if you are spending much time in any one country.
3. *Belize,* Lonely Planet Publications, 1st Edition, Victoria, Australia
4. Box, Ben, *Mexico & Central America Handbook,* Footprint Handbooks, Bath, England
5. Plaxton, John & Liz, *Mexico and Central America by Campervan,* ITMB Publishing, Ltd., Vancouver, Canada, 1998. This describes a trip similar to ours only for 270 days instead of ninety-nine!

Other Guidebooks

Moon Handbooks, Published by Avalon Travel Publishing (www.travelmatters.com), are recommended. In addition to several selections on Mexico, they have guidebooks on Belize, Guatemala, Honduras, Nicaragua and Costa Rica.

A recommended reference for El Salvador is *On Your Own in El Salvador*, published by On Your Own Publications, P.O. box 5411, Charlottesville, VA 22905 USA (or order by e-mail jjb9e@uva.pcmail.virginia.edu).

Recommended Reading

Startcher, Ron "Panama or Bust". *Trailer Life Magazine*. Nov. 2003 and Jan. 2004 (2 parts)

Mahler, Richard, and James D. Gollin, *Guatemala: Adventures in Nature* (1st Ed)

Janson, Thor, *Maya Nature: An introduction to the ecosystems, plants and animals of the Mayan World*, Vista Publications, Guatemala, 2001 (vhbookshop@intelnet.net.gt)

Janson, Thor, *Mundo Maya*, Editorial Artemis Edinter, Guatemala, 1997 (artemisedint@gold.guate.net)

Janson, Thor, *Quetzal*, Editorial Artemis Edinter, Guatemala, 1997 (artemisedint@gold.guate.net)

Janson, Thor, *In the Land of Green Lightning: The World of the Maya*, interspace Navigation and Exploration

Janson, Thor, *Belize: Land of the Free by the Carib Sea*, Bowen & Bowen, Ltd., 2000

Maps

Best maps are the ITMB Travel Maps for each country: International Travel Maps, 530 West Broadway, Vancouver, B.C., Canada V5Z 1E9, www.itmb.com. Also, pick up country maps and tourist information at consulates whenever you can.

RV Caravans: Guided RV Trips

Adventure Caravans, (800) 872-7897, www.adventurecaravans.com

Adventuretours RV Tours, (800) 455-8687, www.adventuretrek.com

Alaska RV Caravans, (800) 842-7764, www.rvalaskatours.com

Baja Adventures RV Tours, (800) 383-6787, www.bajawinters.com

Copper Canyon RV Tours, (800) 206-8132, www.coppercanyon.com.mx

Creative World travel, (800) 732-8337, www.creativeworldtravel.com

Fantasy RV Vacations, (800) 952-8496, www.fantasytours.com

Good Sam Club Caraventures, (800) 664-9145, www.goodsamclub.com

Overseas Motorhome Tours, (800) 322-2127, www.omtinc.com

Tracks To Adventure, (800) 351-6053, www.trackstoadventure.com

Web Sites

Links to useful web sites can be found on our web site: www.BrindlePress.com.

INDEX

ORDER FORM   Give the gift of *99 Days to Panama* to your friends and fellow RVers

On-line Orders: www.BrindlePress.com

Telephone Orders: Call (858) 748-8861

❏ Yes, I want _____ copies of *99 Days to Panama* for $24.95 each.

❏ Yes, I am interested in having John and Harriet Halkyard speak or give a seminar to my company, association, school or organization.

Name: _____

Address: _____

City: _____ State: _____ Zip: _____

Telephone: _____

E-mail Address: _____

Include $5.00 S&H to addresses within the U.S. $8.00 to Canada and Mexico.
Other international destinations $10.00. S&H is FREE for additional books to the same address.

Payment: My check or money order for $_____ is enclosed.

Mail to: Brindle Press, 14121 Cardinal Lane, Houston TX 77079

Payment must accompany orders. Please allow 3 weeks for delivery.

For credit card orders go to www.BrindlePress.com
For further information e-mail Info@BrindlePress.com